FLORIDA

Publisher:	Aileen Lau
Editorial Manager:	Bina Maniar
Editors:	Bina Maniar
	Emma Tan
	Aileen Lau
Design/DTP:	Sares Kanapathy
Illustrations:	Eric Yeo
Cover Artwork:	Susan Harmer
Maps:	Rebecca Fong

Published in the United States by
PRENTICE HALL GENERAL REFERENCE
15 Columbus Circle
New York, New York, 10023

ISBN 0-671-87912-X

Titles in the series:
Alaska - American Southwest - Australia - Bali - California - Canada - Caribbean - China - England - Florida - France - Germany - Greece - Hawaii - India - Indonesia - Italy - Ireland - Japan - Kenya - Malaysia - Mexico - Nepal - New England - New York - Pacific Northwest USA - Singapore - Spain - Thailand - Turkey - Vietnam

USA MAINLAND SPECIAL SALES
Bulk purchases (10+copies) of the Travel Bugs series are available at special discounts for corporate use. The publishers can produce custom publications for corporate clients to be used as premiums or for sales promotion. Copies can be produced with custom cover imprints. For more information write to Special Sales, Prentice Hall Travel, Paramount Communications Building, 15th floor, 15 Columbus Circle, New York, NY 10023.

Printed in Singapore

FLORIDA

Text by Sharon Lloyd Spence

With contributions by:
Morten Strange

Editors:
Bina Maniar
Emma Tan
Aileen Lau

Prentice Hall Travel

New York   London   Toronto   Sydney   Tokyo   Singapore

C O N T E N T S

INTRODUCTION

The Sunshine State 1
An introduction to a land of pure escapism, with beaches, magic mountains, laid back ease and much, much more...

HISTORY, GOVERNMENT & ECONOMY

Indian Iron – History 13
Geological Beginnings - Signs of Humanity - The Fountain of Youth - Land of Riches - Colonial Bloodshed - Spain & England - Florida's Americanization 1800-1865 - Indian vs White Man - Statehood & Another War - Post-War Changes - World War II Boost - Present & Future - Walt Disney World & EPCOT Center
    Indian Aborigines 18
    Florida's Slaves: One Man's Empire
    26
    Famous Personalities 29

Historic Rule – Government 31
Modern Government - Governor Chiles
    Tallahassee's State Capitol Buildings:
    Old & New 34

From Commercial Coast To Citrus Fruit – Economy 39
Modern Economy - A Major Launch - Communications & Information - High Tech Health - Agribusiness - Television - Sports - Finance - Retail Industry - International Markets - Bright Economic Future
    Tampa Cigars: The Birth of Ybor City
    44

Aviation: From Airplanes To Space Shuttles 46

PHYSICAL PROFILE

Geographic Beginnings – Geography & Climate 51
Modern Geography - Wetlands - Inland Waters - Weather
    Hurricanes: A Nightmare Come True
    56

A Paradise of Plants & Wildlife – Flora & Fauna 59
Habitats - National & State Forests - National Preserves & Parks - Fauna - Birds - From Pelicans to Herons - Owls & Ospreys
    Birding in Florida 62
    Alligator Farms 70
    Cattle Country 72

A Natural Heritage — State Parks & State Historic Centers 75
Northwest Florida - Central Panhandle - North Central Florida - Northeast Florida - West Florida - Central Florida - Southwest Florida - South Florida - Coral Parks

MEET THE PEOPLE

Mankind's Medley – People 91
Cubans - African Americans - Native Americans - Jews - Gold Coasters, Conchs, Crackers & Yankees - Scots & Greeks - Retirees
    Floridians You Should Know 94

Sunshine Serenity – Religion 105
Variety of Religion - Catholicism - Cuba-

C O N T E N T S

American's Faith - Judaism - Holocaust Memorial - Church of Scientology - Engram Eliminator - Greek Orthodox Church - Feast of Saint Nicholas - Universalist Church - Community of Mennonites - African American Churches - Baptist & Methodist Preachers - Church of Jesus Christ of Latter-day Saints
Early Spanish Missionaries 108

Celebrate Good Times – Festivals .....
.... 113
Year Round celebrations from January to December
February is Tampa's Month of Fun
.... 122
Miami's Latin Quarter: Calle Ocho
.... 127

Catch The Craze – Arts & Culture ....
.... 135
Northeast - Northwest - Central Florida - Central East - Central West - South West Art - South East Art - Patrons & Creators

FOLLOW THAT BUG

Fun Furore – Central Florida 153
Winter Haven - Lake Wales - Lakeland - Mulberry - Baseball City - Kissimmee - Saint Cloud - Evening Entertainment - Orlando - Winter Park - Ocala - Horse Country - Golf - Jungles, Jeeps & Wildlife
Silver Springs 160
Universal Studios 164
The Incredible World of Disney .....
.... 168

Palm Trees, Pelicans & Peace – Southwest Florida 173
Naples - Fort Myers - North on Cypress Parkway - Scintillating Sanibel - On The Gulf Side - Captivating Captiva - Of Sailing & The South Seas
The Conservancy: Walk On The Wild Side 176
Thomas Edison: The Man & His Mansion 178

History & Fun On The Gulf of Mexico – Saint Petersburg & Tampa 183
Tampa - Touring Tampa - Manatee Mania - Theater & The Performing Arts - A Big Future!
Tarpon Springs: Sea Sponges, Parks & Miracles 188
Wonderful World of Reptiles, Science & Dolphins 191
Cedar Key 194

Creativity & Artistic Inspiration – Sarasota 199
Touring Sarasota - Medieval Times - Flair For Drama - Music, Film & Circuses - Sarasota's Barrier Islands - Shopping - Sports - Scuba Diving
Insider's Guide to Sarasota's Beaches
.... 202
Solving Marine Mysteries 205

Miami Beach & Businessmen – Southern Florida 211
City Tour - Downtown Miami - Key Biscayne - Coconut Grove - Coral Gables - Calle Ochoa - Domino Park - Back To Bayside - Other Miami Attractions - Southern Miami - Sports With a View - Other Sports - Miami

C O N T E N T S

Nightlife - Another Brief Look
  Miami Beach: Pretty Buildings, Pretty
    People 214
  The Holocaust Memorial 221
  Latin American Connnection .. 226

Venice of America – Fort Lauderdale
.... 231
*Water Tour By Taxi - Ships: Cruising &
Fishing - Ships: Underwater Wrecks - Land
Sports - Shopping - Beaches*
  Butterfly World 235

Glamour & Charity – Palm Beach ...
.... 239
Touring Palm Beach - Sports Galore - Museums & Galleries - Complex Culture - The Arts
  Worth Avenue 242
  Henry Flagler: The Man Who
    Dreamed of Florida 244

Space & Speed – East Coast 251
*Daytona Beach - Mother Nature - Space
Coast - Titusville - Cocoa & Cocoa Beach -
Port Canaveral Cruise Line - Portside Fun -
Melbourne - A Real Dragon? - Sebastian
Inlet State Recreation Area - Fresh Eel*
  Merritt Island: Wildlife Refuge . 254
  Kennedy Space Center 256
  Daytona Raceway 260

Historic Saint Augustine – Saint Augustine 267
*Through The Centuries - Touring Saint
Augustine - Attractions & Sights - The "Oldest" Wooden Schoolhouse - The Lightner
Museum - East At The Bridge - Sports &
Recreation - Saint John's County - Festivals*

Saint Augustine's Lightner Museum
.... 270
Saint Augustine Gives New Meaning to "Old" 273

Florida's First Coast – Jacksonville ...
.... 277
*Touring - Culture - Tour Assistance - Great
Getaway - Accomodation*
  Jacksonville Beaches 280
  Jacksonville Zoo 283

Sunshine Stroll – North Florida .. 287
*Panama City Beach - Fishing - Diving - Shell
Island Getaway - Family Fun - Pensacola -
Beaches - Touring Pensacola - Parks &
Views*
  Saint Andrews State Recreation Area
.... 290
  Those Funny, Friendly Shorebirds ..
.... 292
  Historical Pensacola 294

Capital City – Tallahassee 299
*City Touring - Country Touring - Recreation
& Mother Nature - Special Events*
  Tallahassee Museum of History &
    Natural Science 302
  Museum of Florida History 304

Vast Glittering Openness – Everglades
.... 311
*Poetic Landscape - Exploring The Everglades
- Other Visitor Centers - Safety Notes -
Outside the Park - Big Cypress National
Preserve*
  Wildlife In Danger 314
  Touring The Everglades By Boat ....
.... 316

C O N T E N T S

Changes In Latitudes, Changes In Attitudes – Florida Keys 323
Island Variety - Key West - Touring Key West - Key West Sights - Creativity At Work & Play - Special Events - Sports
    Fishing For Big Ones 326
    Hemingway Country 332
    Diving Floridas' Keys 336

WHAT TO DO

The Sporting Life – Sports & Recreation 341
Air Boating Everglades - Baseball - Biking - Canoeing - Car Racing - Fishing - Golf - Greyhound Racing - Horse Racing - Sailing/ Boating - Charters - Snorkeling/Diving - Soccer - Swimming/Beaches - Tennis
    Sport of Kings: Treasure Hunting ...
    349
    Sporting With Dolphins 356

Absorbing Entertainment– Entertainment 361
Daytona Beach - Fort Lauderdale - Keys - Lakeland/Winter Haven Area - Miami Area - Orlando/Kissimmee Area - Palm Beach County - Panama City - Sarasota - Tallahassee - Tampa - Clearwater
    Miami Arena 363
    Meet You On The Water 368

Shop Till You Drop – Shopping .. 373
Fort Lauderdale - Jacksonville - The Keys - Miami - Naples - Orlando/Kissimmee - Palm Beach - Pensacola - Saint Petersburg - Sarasota - Tampa

From Sizzling Steaks To Saucy Seafood – Cuisine 383
Sophie Kay's Top of Daytona - The Dock At Crayton Cove - JD's Southern Oaks - Park Plaza Gardens - Mykonos - Five Star - Fiddlestix - Cafe L'Europe - Bern's Steak House - Raintree Restaurant
    Citrus World 386
    Up From The Deep: Florida's Fresh Seafood 389

EASY REFERENCE

Travel Tips 395
Supplement essential for travel planning
Directory 408
Useful listings
Photo Credits 436
Index 437

MAPS

Florida 150
Central Florida 154
Tampa & Saint Petersburg 184
Miami & Vicinity 212
Fort Lauderdale 232
Palm Beach 240
Cape Canaveral 257
Old St Augustine 268
Jacksonville 278
Tallahassee 300
The Everglades 312
Florida Keys 324

you want or

A sign for everything

need to know. Read on for more.

Out of the blue –

bodies.

sun, sea, surf and sunseeking

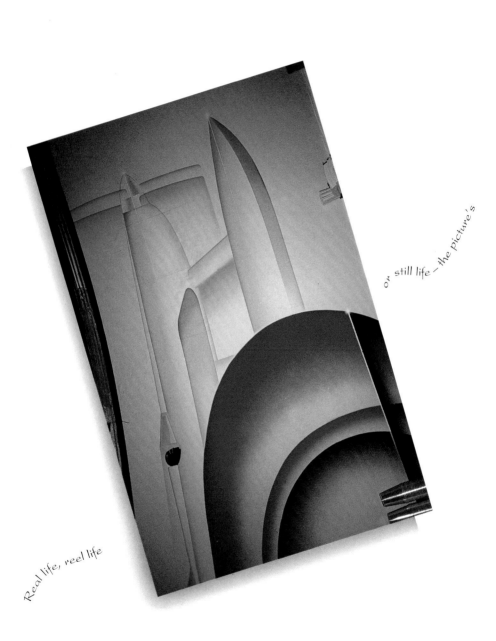

or still life – the picture's

Real life, reel life

wacky and truly

Weird,

wonderful –

So fortunate traveler, you have decided to embark on a journey to Florida. Perhaps you have an itinerary already in mind: a few days at amusement parks, a few hours relaxing on the beach, an occasional appreciative glance at palm trees silhouetted against a glowing sunset, perhaps a lucky encounter with an alligator, a tarpon or a dolphin.

Before you even pack your suitcase, leave that premeditated itinerary at home! Resist your driving need to schedule every waking hour. What you are about to experience, what we at Trav Bug call "The Real Florida", is impossible to imagine, much less schedule. There is much more for you to experience than just those cliched television commercial versions of sun, sea, and sand.

Leave your watch and appointment book at home. No

Leave your worries behind and hang loose on the pristine white beaches. You'll never know what you may catch!

You're never too young to fish and make friends.

need for suits, ties or frilly dresses. Just pack some cotton shorts and shirts, a swimsuit, comfortable walking shoes, sunblock, sunglasses, and your favorite snapshot camera.

And most important of all, bring with you an open mind, a sense of wonder, curiosity, and lots of energy. Be ready to rise with the sun, and bid goodnight to the full moon set among a velvet sea of stars. If you are willing to allow yourself to follow your heart and your map, Florida will unveil her marvels, madness and magic with such intensity that you will return home wondering how soon you might visit again.

By now, you are probably wondering from this introductory fanfare, what is this place that Ponce de Leon of Spain christened "Pascua Florida", in honor of the Easter Feast of Flowers, in April 1513?

Feast For The Senses

Perhaps he emphasized the word "Feast", for Florida is truly a feast for all the senses, as you will soon discover. Merely driving along the eastern Atlantic Ocean or western Gulf of Mexico coast, stopping to dance with the birds and the breezes is a sensual treat in itself.

What's In Store

What does Florida have in store for you? Well, if you begin your trip in the north-

Florida — home to some of the top
100 golf courses around.

east corner of the state there's
Jacksonville's wide uncrowded beaches,
where tots, teens, and grandmothers
ride their bikes along the ocean shore
and dogs play in the frontyards of gracious two-story oceanfront homes. The
city just east is one of America's fastest
growing business centers, with gleaming mirrored offices, a bustling international shipping port along the Saint
John's River, manicured golf courses,
beautiful neighborhoods filled with
museums, outdoor cafés, elegant antique stores and bookshops.

But just a few minutes north from
some of America's top insurance, financial and transportation companies, you
can venture into the wilds of an "African veldt", to chat with wildebeest, kudu,

elan and a fierce red legged masai ostrich. At Jacksonville's Zoo, a top team
of scientists and animal lovers insure
the survival of endangered species by
breeding jaguars, toucans, tortoises, and
in the near future, elephants too!. Now
thats certainly a city with its heart and
head in the right place!

Heading south on Florida's beautiful shoreline A1A highway, you will
drive past the million dollar mansions
of Ponte Vedra Beach, where just the
oceanfront lots cost $1,000,000 upwards.

Soon you will arrive in historic Saint
Augustine where Pedro Menendez de
Aviles of Spain arrived in 1565 to establish what became the oldest permanent
European settlement in North America.

Pastures, ponies and prettiness
in Ocala.

Life's a beach!!

Today, you can still explore the Oldest House, Oldest Wooden Schoolhouse, Oldest Store and the 1756 stone fortress, the Castillo de San Marcos.

Daytona Beach

At Daytona Beach you can see miles of white condominiums dotting the beach, funky surf shops like **A Kick in the Pants**, and family motels like **The Dolphin Beach Club** and **Mermaid Beach Hotel**. After school, kids race for the beach on bikes, balancing handlebars in one hand and rainbow colored surf boards in the other. Nearby, jazzy sports cars race around Daytona's world famous track at 150 miles per hour.

Palm Beach

Heading into Palm Beach, you will see luxury ocean yachts, palatial estates with separate entrances for "owners" and "servants", and Henry Flagler's exquisite Breakers Hotel.

Continue south on the A1A to Fort Lauderdale, where the palm tree-lined beach is situated so close to the highway's edge that you can reach out of your car and touch it. Welcome to the international party of bikinied teens, honeymooners, families, hippies and tourists from all over North and South America, Europe and Asia. How about trying out for the Miss Bikini Contest, or stopping in for a beer at a country and

The art deco area of Miami Beach is well worth a day's wander.

western or biker bar? If that is too much for you, head over to an air-conditioned luxury shopping mall to trade in your flipflops for five star fashion at Saks Fifth Avenue. And just a few miles away from the bronzed beach bodies are clouds of delicate wings at Butterfly World, where you can walk among Mother Nature's other beauties.

Miami Beach

Continuing along the A1A toward Miami, you will definitely get a kick out of the Florida-style humor displayed on some of the highway billboards. One advertisement for a car says, "Have you hugged your road today?" Another advertisement for a ready made Tombstone® pizza, that offers a choice of toppings, asks, "What do you want on your tombstone?" Have a few Florida-style laughs.

Then Miami Beach appears, all rainbow neon, and curvaceous, flirtatious art deco architectural wonders. Buildings so beautiful you nearly miss noticing the Very Beautiful People sipping champagne in cafes out front. But soon the obsessive people watching will capture your attention: bronzed ponytailed weight lifters whiz by on skateboards, as long-legged blondes in shimmering white tank suits strut their stuff.

A lithe redhead in a leopard catsuit carefully studies the outdoor café menu, as a dragon-tattooed beach bum carefully studies her in great detail.

Between the buildings and the bodies you will never be bored in Miami Beach!

Florida Keys

On to Florida's Keys, taking the A1A south to Route 1. Soon you will find yourself diving among schools of pink and turquoise parrotfish, fishing off gleaming white ocean cruisers, buying fresh seafood from the back of a truck called "Prince of Shrimp", laughing and swimming with dolphins at The Dolphin Research Center. Maybe you will be able to experience a Keys-style rainstorm: pelting blinding rain that lasts for just 90 seconds, then bursts again into blinding sunlight.

If you are lucky you might catch sight of the tiny endangered Key Deer, just a few feet tall, and you are sure to see flocks of egrets, herons, seagulls, and brown pelicans wading along the seashore for snacks.

Key West

On to the Keys' Southernmost Point, Key West, where Bed and Breakfasts have names like **The Mermaid and the Alligator,** where Hemingway drank and fished and penned *A Farewell to Arms*, where international music star Jimmy Buffet first crooned "Wasting Away In Margaritaville", where Mel Fisher dis-

plays his cache of treasures from the sunken Spanish galleon **Atocha**, and where writers and artists come to work, dream and give thanks that they live here in this heaven on earth.

When you have had your fill of margaritas and fresh seafood, take Route 1 back north to Miami, and head west

The unique "Gingerbread House" in Miami Beach.

on Route 41 – the Tamiami Trail. This is Miccosukee Indian country, and the stores here offer plenty of interesting souvenirs, supplies, alligator wrestling and unusual conversation.

The Everglades

Continuing west on the Tamiami Trail takes you into the heart of The

Smog and smoke on Tampa's industrial skyline.

Everglades, the legendary "River of Grass", sacred home to snakes, manatees, dolphins, alligators, raccoons, fish and hundreds of different bird species. Few experiences rival the exhilaration of an airboat ride across this magic mysterious swamp and every boat captain has a rip-roaring, spine-tingling, back country tale.

Naples

Continuing westwards on the Tamiami Trail takes you into Naples, where a billboard says it all: "Golf Course by Arnold Palmer, Lifestyle by Mother Nature!" As manicured and lovely as any five star golf course, Naples is a sophis-

ticated town of glorious white oceanfront condominiums, elegant Spanish style homes and shopping malls, dockside seafood restaurants, performing arts centers, a wildlife conservancy, an antique car museum, and (really), a museum of teddy bears as well as many golf courses too! Add on dozens of pristine public beaches, a historic fishing pier and retired corporate CEO's who happily drive you in golfcarts through dense mangroves to the sea, and you may find it impossible to leave this beautiful and hospitable Florida town.

(Many tourists refuse: they visit once, and then move here immediately after. Locals will confess "I came here on vacation and never left.")

If you can manage to tear yourself

away, head north on Route 41 to Fort Myers, where Thomas Edison and Henry Ford had their fabulous summer homes, and spend a few days on Sanibel/Captiva Islands with millions of seashells and thousands of birds. Clearwater Beach has beautiful sunrises and sunsets, and the **Marine Research Center** is home to a dolphin that paints t-shirts!

Sarasota

Continue north to Sarasota, Florida's Cultural Mecca, where you will be enthralled with the Ringling's incredible Museum of Art, a first class ballet company, theater, opera, music, five-star shopping, beautiful beaches and The Pelican Man – a bird lover who has rescued thousands of injured pelicans.

Saint Petersburg

But do not head home yet: Florida has more to share, if you have not run out of time, money and curiosity. Route 41 north beckons you to the magnificent Route 19 Skyway – a sleek bridge that arches up up up into blue skies and white clouds, and then glides gracefully into Saint Petersburg.

Saint Petersburg harbours million dollar yachts, Salvador Dali's million dollar art collection and beaches with million dollar panoramas. At **Great Explorations Museum**, the kids will love the science, creativity and slither-

ing reptiles altogether in one location.

Tampa

Neighbor city Tampa welcomes you with guided walks through historic Ybor City where Cubans created the famous Tampa cigar. Or head over to the Zoo and see those sweet, endangered "sea mermaids" – manatees underwater. Try some Spanish *paella vallenciana* and applaud passionate flamenco dancers at **Columbia Restaurant**, tour Henry Plant's incredible Tampa Bay Hotel, (now **Tampa University**) or hang out with gorillas and gazelles at Busch Gardens.

Central Florida

Heading into Central Florida, it is time to switch gears completely. Pull on your cowboy boots, western hat and drive east into Lakeland. Soon you will find yourself cruising past fields of grazing cattle, fruit and vegetable farms, roadside stands selling fresh peanuts ("Boiled, Roasted, Fried!") and signs that tout "Master Beef Bulls for Sale".

Keep heading east toward that sweet smell of manure and wet grass till you hit **Winter Haven**, where smoked barbecue restaurants are tucked in between world-class golf resorts. Here, are some of the most beautiful gardens on earth: fanciful flowers at **Cypress Gardens**, exotic greenery and carillon concerts at

Fast Facts

Area: 58,664 square miles.
Population: 13,003,363 (1990 census)
Capital: Tallahassee.
Government: Congress- 2 US senators and 19 US representatives.
State Legislature: 40 senators and 120 representatives.
Religion: Protestant, Roman Catholic, Jewish, Evangelical, Greek Orthodox and Mennonite.
People: Caucasian, Hispanic, Black, American Indian, Eskimo, Aleut, Asians and Pacific Islanders.
Economy: Main industries: tourism, agriculture, real estate, banking, electronics, printing and publishing, food processing, phosphate mining, logging and wood products, and the manufacture of transportation equipment, clothing and chemicals.
Language: English
Main Industry: Tourism
State Flower: Orange Blossom
State Bird: Mockingbird
State Song: "Old Folks at Home" ("S'wanee River"). Words and music by Stephen Foster.

Highest Point: 345 feet in Walton County.
Interesting Sights:
Tampa – Lowry Park Zoo and Ybor City
Titusville– John F Kennedy Space Center
Winter Haven –Bok Tower Gardens and Cypress Gardens
Southwestern Florida – Everglades National Park
Kissimmee – Gatorland
Near Key Largo – John Pennekamp Coral Reef State Park
Saint Augustine–The Breakers Hotel, Palm Beach; Lightner Museum
Sarasota – Ringling Museum of Art
Saint Petersburg – Salvador Dali Museum
Orlando – Universal Studios and Walt Disney World
Miami Beach – Art Deco District
Ocala – Silver Springs
Jacksonville – Jacksonville Zoo
Daytona–The Daytona International Speedway
Everglades–Everglades National Park, Everglades
Naples – The Conservancy
Tallahassee – Tallahassee Museum of History and Natural Science

Bok Tower Gardens. Winter Haven is the Waterski Capital of the World, where trophy-winning water athletes somersault over each other on glassy lakes and you can watch the Kansas City Royals work during spring training over at **Baseball City Stadium**.

Kissimmee

Head into Kissimmee on 192 east where thousands of discount outlet shops lure you with tee-shirts, sportswear, household goods and electronics. Fat Boys serves up delicious barbecue chicken and suddenly you are in Orlando, swirling into some of the world's biggest most

incredible theme parks. From Walt Disney World's Mickey Mouse, EPCOT's international pavilions and futuristic exhibits, **Disney/MGM Studios and Universal Studios,** Florida's tribute to television and Hollywood movies, this is the Florida that many kids and parents travel here for. These amusement parks give new meaning to the word "stimulation": you may need a vacation from your vacation here!

North on Route 75 things calm down considerably in charming Ocala, home to thoroughbred race horse champions, antique shops, magnificent Victorian "Bed and Breakfast" guest homes and Silver Springs, where riverboat captains recite poetry as glassbottom boats glide over crystal clear springs some 80 feet below.

Cedar Keys

From here you might head west to Cedar Key for some relaxing fishing, or drive along the beautiful panhandle coastline to see Panama City's sugar white sandy beaches in front of the **U Turn Sunburn Saloon** or trek further west into Pensacola and visit the National Museum of Naval Aviation and The Gulf Islands National Seashore.

Tallahassee

Whatever you do, try not to miss Tallahassee, with her dense evergreen forests, cooler climate and hilly oak tree canopied country roads that wind past graceful southern mansions. Florida's history comes alive throughout this charming city, from The **Museum of Florida History**, to a walk through historic homes. Kids will love the **Tallahassee Museum of History and Natural Science**, a fantastic outdoor museum of historic homes and churches, and natural habitats where panthers, bobcats and black bears roam freely. Downtown, the stately capitol buildings preside, the 1845 domed original, and the 1977 modern 22 floor high rise.

Tallahassee is a delightful mixture of serious government administrators, and happy-go-lucky "good ole boys n'

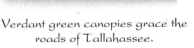

Verdant green canopies grace the roads of Tallahassee.

girls". By day you can observe law makers at work, and at night you can down freshly shucked oysters and beer with laidback locals at **Posey's Oyster Bar**, "Home of the Topless Oyster".

On Your Way

And so, from this brief driving tour of Florida, we hope you are convinced that there is a lot more than just sun, sea, sand and theme parks. As long as you are curious, have an open mind, and a loose schedule, you can point your car in almost any direction, and discover intriguing, exciting, unforgettable Florida.

Turn the page, we have lots to share...

F lorida's emergence from the ocean as a finger shaped peninsula of streams and springs, rivers and lakes, lagoons and swamps covering 4, 298 square miles of tropical landscape, takes us back in time hundreds of millions of years.

Geological Beginnings

■ ■ ■ ■ ■ ■

The clothes and houses of Floridians from Prevost's Histoire Generale Des Vayages, Paris, 1750.

South Florida began life as an arc of volcanic mountains which were buried 13,000 feet beneath the sea. Limestone sediment caused by erosion of the mountains was deposited on the underwater plain, whose weight made the land sink even further. Over a period of one hundred million years, thousands of feet of limestone, composed mostly of the skeletons of microscopic sea animals were formed. Centuries later, fine sand and then clay washed down from the northern mountains, all of which settled over Florida's plateau. The limestone

History

13

Montes Apalatci, in qu
Apalatci

Inhac

Oustaca

Onatheaqua

Potanou

FLORIDA PRO
AB INDIGENIS DICTA IAQVAZA

Ehian

Anouala

Vitta.

Eloquale
Aquouana
Cadica
Mocoso

Patchua
Edelano
Chilili
Calanay
Mayarca

Enca
Ec

Onach

Mathiaca

Hic deferibit
Fluminilis Vamatz
Simus Mogoti.

Mawra.

Marracou
Stane
coun

Lacus
quæ dulc

Sorroch

Adeo magnus est hic lacus
ut ex una ripa conspici altera
non possit. Distat a Charles
fort 380 leucis.

F. Florum

F. Guate

F. Medina

F. Selchepum

Portus Ioannis
Matilalais

Pramadbonsum.

Mexicani Sinus pars

Sinus Ioan
nis Ponce

E Canoes

F Pacis

Aquatio

CALOS

Calos

Oathkaqua

Mocossou

Lacus &
Insula Sarrope

Laguna

Bimini

Insula dicta
Testudines

Scopuli dicti
Martyres

lar di nes

I. Floride

Lucay

Ha

Hauana

chama

Cufns. S
Antonij

Xagua

Guanagnarico

Cuba insula.

Caucher

Insula
Pinorum

Iardines scopuli, na
uigantibus formidabil

S.
Trinitatis

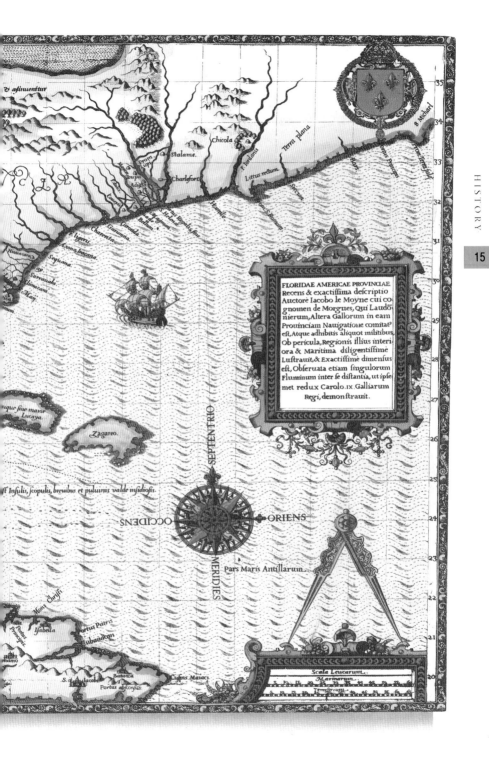

asinuuntur

Chicola

Terra plana

8 Michael

Stalame.

F. Iordani

Littus redum.

Prom Gupl.

Charlefort

Adusta

Promo

Seine

Charentie

R. Ipens.

Sequana

Sarratacht

Maiq

que siue maior
Lucaya.

Zagareo.

f Insulis, scopulis, breuibus et puluinis valde insidiosis.

FLORIDAE AMERICAE PROVINCIAE.
Recens & exactissima descriptio
Auctore Iacobo le Moyne cui co-
gnomen de Morgues, Qui Laudo-
nierum, Altera Gallorum in eam
Prouinciam Nauigatione comitat'
est, Atque adhibitis aliquot militibus,
Ob pericula, Regionis illius interi-
ora & Maritima diligentissimè
Lustrauit, & Exactissimè dimensus
est, Obseruata etiam singulorum
Fluminum inter se distantia, ut ipse-
met redux Carolo.ix.Galliarum
Regi, demonstrauit.

SEPTENTRIO

OCCIDENS — ORIENS

MERIDIES

Mons Chrsti

Pars Maris Antillarum.

Isabella

Portus Patris

Portus
Principis

Albandam

no
ohano

S.o Iacobo

Batiuca

Portus absconsus

Cusps Maiaci

Scala Leucarum.
M.Larinarum.
Terrestrium.

8 escudo

Pieces of the Eight from the McLarty Museum in Sebastian Inlet.

layers arched and parts of Florida rose 150 feet above sea level. Wind and waves along the Atlantic and Gulf coasts extended Florida's peninsula towards coral reefs that slowly emerged, forming marshes and lagoons. This time period is known as the Late Tertiary period.

During the Pleistocene era, an ice sheet covered much of Canada and the northern United States. At this period of development, Florida became cool and rainy. Because so much of the earth's water supply was stored in these ice glaciers, the world's sea level was lowered, leaving much of the continental shelf exposed – Florida was once twice the size it is today.

Herbivorous animals seeking to escape the great ice sheet trudged southward seeking greener pastures in warmer territories. Three-toed horses, giant pigs, rhinoceroses, camels, mammoths, huge sloths, armadillos and peccaries roamed the state.

Soon after, those docile vegetarians became meals themselves for carnivorous beasts of prey: sabre-toothed tigers, four-tusked mastodons, wolves, and lions, who devoured these leaf eaters. It was a scenario of the survival of the fittest, eat or be eaten! Today, their roars and screams are only memories, as archeologists unearth their bones that have been buried in beds of shifting sand over millions of years.

During the Pleistocene and Holocene periods, the northern ice sheet melted and reformed. The sea level rose and fell like an amusement park roller coaster, carving bluffs and terraces into the land resulting in a drier climate, and the winds scattered sand dunes onto the newly formed terraces.

Today, Florida's landscape is still sculpted by rain, rivers, waves and wind. Underground water continuously dissolves the limestone, forming caves and sinkholes and the state metamorphose to change geographically, as the east coast builds up, and the west coast gradually sinks.

Signs Of Humanity

Florida's first human inhabitants arrived c.8,000 BC. There are few clues to the history and lifestyle of these early Floridians except for the tools and other household artifacts unearthed by modern archaeologists. Written records about life in Florida began with the arrival of the Spanish explorer and adventurer Juan Ponce de Leon in 1513.

The Fountain of Youth

Juan Ponce de Leon, who was the Spanish Governor of Puerto Rico, was enthralled by tales he heard from the Puerto Rican Indians. They told of a land called Bimini to the northwest, where land was abundant with reserves of gold, and a magical fountain overflowed with water that restored youth to the aged and health to the infirm.

Although drawings of the time reveal Ponce de Leon as a robust fifty, the adventurous and capitalistic entrepreneur was eager to see these miracles for himself. So on March 5, 1512, he set sail with **The Santa Maria de la Consolacion**, and **The Santiago**. After three weeks of journeying through the Bahamas, he sighted Florida's coast just north of present day Saint Augustine and on April 2, he landed to claim the country in the name of King Ferdinand V of Spain. He never found Bimini, but was delighted with the tropical paradise he did discover.

As Ponce and his crew had just celebrated "Pascua Florida", the Feast of Flowers (Easter) aboard ship before sighting land, so when he arrived in Florida, he prayed, "Thanks be to Thee, O Lord, Who hast permitted me to see something new". Then he christened the land in honor of the holiday season –"La Florida". The name stuck.

Although he sailed down the east coast around the Keys, and back up the west coast to Pensacola during a six months search, Ponce de Leon never found gold nor the fountain of youth he had originally left home for, but he returned in 1521 with two shiploads of colonists, horses, cattle, farm tools and seeds to settle on the land he would now govern, according to King Ferdinand's promise.

However, Ponce de Leon and his settlers never found peace in paradise either. Florida's powerful Indian natives resented their intrusion and aggressively

Indian Aborigines

In 1983 archaeologists discovered exciting evidence that humans lived in Florida some 8,000 years ago. In a peat bog near Titusville, in a site called Windover, they unearthed more than 120 human skulls. Preserved by the bog, the remains were wrapped in cloth. Amazingly, the prehistoric brain tissues were in good enough condition for scientists to conduct intensive tests. Many of the skeletons showed broken bones, bone infections and hip joints imbedded with spear points. Archaeologists believe that these Indians may have migrated from Central and South America, due to their similarities to Indians from those regions.

Wherever their origins, they brought their hunting skills with them. Successfully using these skills to live off Florida's boar, possum, bobcat, dear, woolly bison, quail, marsh hens, ducks and geese. Digs have revealed fluted stones, called Suwanee points, which might have been lashed to long sticks, in the construction of spears called atlatl. The oldest points have been found 60 feet below ground, outside Warm Springs in Venice.

Pottery shards dating back 3,000 to 4,000 years indicate that Florida's Indians traded with Indians in Alabama and Georgia, (the pottery remains unearthed were made of materials not found in Florida).These early residents were seafood lovers. Mounds of discarded shells have been found throughout the state, giving rise to theories that they probably ate clams, oysters and conchs, then used these same shells as cooking vessels, or as tools to build dugout canoes.

Around the year 2000, the Indians began to combine tribal basket weaving with red clay to create pottery. The earliest pieces were mostly simple boxes or bowls, decorated in a checkerboard pattern. Over the centuries, as patterns became more complex, linguists thought that the designs may have resembled a language closely related to the South American Indians, but this has never been proven. By AD 850, pottery techniques had become much more artistic and skillful, and the Indians were making beautiful fire-tempered works of art that can now be enjoyed in museums throughout Florida.

Around 1000 BC, archaeologists believe that

the Indians began to plant land and cultivate crops, as evidenced by irrigation ditches and garden plots laid on dikes above the wet savanna. They also think that the Indians roasted their vegetables, because mound excavations from the time have revealed burned lime, which was common in those days when cooking corn. Archaeologists estimate that by the time white explorers arrived in Florida, there were at least six basic Indian groups, numbering between 16,000 to 34,000 people.

The Timucuans, the largest group, wandered throughout the north central region which is now known as Cape Canaveral, Ocala, Gainesville, and Jacksonville. Explorers wrote that physically they were strong, tall and handsome. The Spanish made their lives miserable, using the Indians as cargo bearers, which they considered beneath their dignity and outlawing their religion, sports and dancing.

The Tocobaga, may have been a branch of the

A 100 year old print taken from A New and Complete Collection of Voyages and Travels, published in London, 1778.

Timucua, and lived in the area ranging from Tarpon Springs south of Sarasota.

The Apalachee, lived in the same region as modern Tallahassee. These natives were prosperous copperminers, although the Spanish explorers Narvaez and De Soto were attracted to their villages by rumors of gold. In 1647, the Apalachee warred against the Spanish intruders, killing three friars and the Spanish governor's lieutenant and his family, while defending their property.

The Tequesta lived in the region where Pompano Beach and Cape Sable are today. They were also hostile to white intruders, and fiercely defended their territories. Indians from this region probably made dugout canoe trips to Cuba, and lived on fruit, nuts, manatees and sea turtles.

The Calusa lived in the area of Tampa Bay south

of the Lake Okechobee area. Archaeologists believe they were not an agricultural tribe and that they mostly survived on fish and shellfish. They also travelled to Cuba.

The Ais lived along coastal areas of the Indian River, Cape Canaveral and Saint Lucie River. According to legend, they captured Quaker Jonathan Dickinson when his ship was wrecked off Hobe Sound in East Florida, but released the family who later escaped to Saint Augustine.

Although Florida's early Indian tribes were talented artists, engineers, hunters and farmers, they were for the most part abused by the Spanish British and French settlers who took their land and changed their rituals and traditions. Less than three centuries after Ponce de Leon's arrival in Florida in 1513, not one of these Indian tribes survived.

History in ancient tombstones seen in a Protestant cemetery in Saint Augustine.

defended their homeland, attacking the Spaniards with stones and arrows. Finally, illness and wounds from Indian battles forced Ponce de Leon and his entire colony to flee for Cuba after just five months, where he soon died, his original quest being in vain.

But other Spanish adventurers had heard of "La Florida" and were eager to colonize it, despite legendary stories of battles with native Indians. In 1539, Hernando de Soto landed somewhere between Fort Meyers and Tampa. He traveled north, discovered the Mississippi, and the inevitable fights fighting with Indian tribes, which eventually caused his demise.

During his travels, de Soto met Juan Ortiz, a Spanish soldier who accompa-

nied an earlier explorer named Panfilo de Narvaez into the Panhandle area. Ortiz' reports of his experience with the Indians was very detailed, and has given historians most of what is known about these early Florida natives.

Although the persistent Spanish explorers found neither gold nor the legendary fountain of youth, their tales of adventure and discovery soon found their way to Europe. During this time, Spain's conquests in Central and South America were enriching her treasury with gold, silver and precious jewels as fleets of treasure laden Spanish vessels, called Plate Fleets, sailed from Mexico and along the Caribbean coast, following the Gulf Stream along Florida's southern and eastern coasts. This often proved disastrous, as they sailed directly into waiting pirate ships, or were smashed to pieces on coastal reefs by hurricanes. In fact, a hurricane storm wrecked an entire settlement on Pensacola Bay, which had been established in 1559 by Spanish explorer Tristan de Luna, for only two years.

Land of Riches

Florida's reputation as a land of riches rapidly increased, attracting other nations who wanted their slice of the pie. The French dispatched the Protestant Jean Ribault to establish a colony for religious freedom in 1562. Two years later, fellow Frenchman Rene de Goulaine de Laudonniere succeeded in establishing Fort Caroline at the mouth of the Saint Johns River, which is near present day Jacksonville.

The Spanish were furious at this French intrusion, and so King Philip promptly commanded Pedro Menendez de Aviles, Captain-General of the armed fleet, to destroy the French colony. In August 1565, Menendez arrived at a harbor he called San Augustin, and the following month he established the first permanent European settlement in what is now the United States.

Colonial Bloodshed

It was a violent era of bloodshed, as Menendez and his troops massacred the French, renaming Fort Caroline, San Mateo and converted it into a Spanish outpost. Spanish missionaries, Jesuit and Franciscan friars, then set about converting the Indians to Christianity, in a vain bid to try to save their "heathen souls", amidst the murders committed by their Spanish leaders in God's name!

Meanwhile in Europe, the French made plans to avenge the loss of Fort Caroline. Dominique de Gourgues launched an expedition, capturing San Meteo, and hanging the defeated Spanish. Triumphant, he returned to France.

England, meanwhile, was eager to make her own conquests. In 1586, the English captain Sir Francis Drake sacked and burned Saint Augustine. But, this did little to diminish Spanish control of Florida, as more and more forts and missions were built throughout the state and up into southern Virginia. This prompted the English to colonize further northwards up the east coast in Jamestown and Plymouth. They wanted more and more New World resources for themselves and gradually pushed the northern border of Spanish Florida southward to its present border.

The English also colonized South Carolina. In 1701, the Carolinians and their Indian allies laid siege to Spanish Florida, capturing the town of Saint Augustine, although they were later unsuccessful and had to withdraw. Two years later, they destroyed the missions in the interior between Pensacola and Saint Augustine, killing and enslaving many Indians.

The towering Confederate Statue sited at Lee Square.

The French also continued their harassment of the Spanish, with their capture of Pensacola in 1719. But, the English threat soon united Spain and France, and the colony was given back to the Spanish. The French returned to their settlements along the Gulf Coast, west of Pensacola.

Spain & England

However, Spanish dominance in Florida began to weaken. In 1740, British General James Oglethorpe seized outlying Spanish forts and bombarded Fort Castillo de San Marcos in Saint Augustine for almost a month of bloodshed until he unsuccessfully withdrew. The English persevered, using other strategies. During the Seven Years' War, 1756-1763, England captured Havana, Cuba from the Spanish. To get it back, Spain relinquished Florida, evacuating the state and leaving it virtually empty.

England split Florida into two parts: East Florida, with its capital at Saint Augustine, and West Florida, with its capital at Pensacola. They offered export subsidies and land grants to attract new settlers, and mapped out most of the inhabited areas of the state. They developed peaceful relationships with the Creek Indian tribes (changing their name to Seminole Indians), who had moved into Florida from Alabama and Georgia. Plantations of indigo, rice and citrus sprang up, worked by slaves brought to Florida from Africa and The West Indies.

But, British domination did not last long. In 1783, Spain avenged her loss of Florida by capturing the British colony of Bahamas. To regain the islands, England returned Florida to Spain. Once again, the tables were turned as the Spanish flag flew over Florida for the second time.

Florida's Americanization 1800-1865

Spain's second attempt to develop Florida was a failure from the start. British plantation owners left, and Spanish and American colonists poured in.

An Indian heritage – a Seminole Indian along the Tamiami Trail.

Florida Territory. By 1824, Florida's capital was established in Tallahassee, where immigrants from Georgia, Virginia and North Carolina began their new lives as Americans. By 1830, Florida's population had grown from 15,000 to 34,000.

Indian vs White Man

Hostilities between whites and Indians increased as more settlers moved in. A government movement was started to send the Indians to reservations west of the Mississippi.

In 1832, after a delegation of chiefs inspected the land they were to relocate to, they refused to sign a treaty committing them to move. Their resistance was lead by a young warrior named Osceola, the stepson of a white trader named William Powell, and the son of an Indian woman from the Red Stick tribe (a branch of the Creek). His grandfather was a Scot.

Although Osceola was not a chief and had no voice on the councils of his tribe, his natural talent for leadership asserted itself, soon earning him the ear and respect of his chiefs.

When the Seminoles refused to leave their homes, the white settlers tried to move the Indians by force, even seizing Osceola's wife Che-cho-ter as a fugitive slave. The Second Seminole War, lasted seven years (1835-42) and took a terrible toll on both Indian and white lives. Indian war parties attacked Fort King near Ocala, and ambushed two compa-

Many were plantation slaves trying to escape from cruel masters. Instead of becoming more Spanish, Florida became more American, although most of the territory still belonged to the original Indian inhabitants.

In 1818, Florida's provisional governor, Andrew Jackson decided to remove the Seminole Indians to the central part of the peninsula, causing the First Seminole War.

In 1819, Spain and the United States began negotiations to transfer the Spanish colony to the United States of America. Two years later, the Stars and Stripes became the fourth national flag to fly over Florida and Andrew Jackson was installed as the first Governor of

Seminole Indian handicrafts as displayed in the Everglades.

nies of US troops near Bushnell, in a battle which is now called The Dade Massacre.

Refusing to surrender, Osceola and his warriors sent a message to the US troops warning "Your men will fight and so will ours, till the last drop of Seminole blood has moistened the dust of hunting ground."

In the end there was terrible loss for both sides. The US Government spent $40,000,000 on the war, and lost 2,500 soldiers. Osceola, who had trustingly entered the American camp under a flag of truce, was captured, imprisoned and died in a military jail and 3,824 Seminole Indians and blacks were sent to Arkansas. Only 300 remained in Florida, some on reservations, others

escaping to the wilds of The Everglades.

Statehood & Another War

With the war over, Florida concentrated on preparing for statehood. Evidence of economic progress was everywhere: steamboats chugged up and down the Apalachicola and Saint Johns' Rivers; cotton and tobacco plantations spread for miles in every direction, and the Tallahassee to Saint Marks and Saint Joseph-Lake Wimico Railroads were completed.

In 1845, Florida became the 27th member of the United States, and William D Moseley was elected Governor. Five years later, the population had grown to 87,445, including 39,000 slaves and 1,000 free blacks. In 1855, the General Assembly passed the first Internal Improvement Act, which used swamp and other land ceded to the state by the federal government to stimulate an intrastate system of canals and railroads.

Despite a period of peace and prosperity, the issue of slavery began to dominate Florida's affairs. Most voters did not object to slavery and were angered about the growing feeling against what they felt was a normal part of life. Southerners moved into the Democratic camp, leaving the strength of the newly organized Republican party to the northern states. With the election of the Republican Abraham Lincoln as President in 1860, the Florida Legislature rushed into a constitutional convention, appropriating US$100,000 for state troops. In 1861, Florida withdrew from the Union, and the War Between the States began.

During the next four years, Florida furnished 15,000 troops for the Confederate Army, a Florida militia, plus salt, beef, bacon and cotton. During the final months of the war, home guards saved Tallahassee from capture by turning back invading Union forces at the Battle of Natural Bridge. Tallahassee was the only Confederate capital east of the Mississippi River to escape occupation.

As the war came to a close, Federal troops entered Tallahassee on May 10, 1865. Ten days later, the American flag flew over the Florida Capitol once again. A Florida constitutional convention convened on Oct. 25, 1865, annulling the Ordinance of Secession. Slavery was finally abolished. However, freedom was still severely restricted, as the right to vote was granted only to "free white male persons of 21 years or more, but none others."

Post-War Changes

After the war, the lives and fortunes of Floridians significantly changed. African Americans who were slaves earlier were now free, and they were paid to raise and pick cotton. But, many slaves were eager to get away from the plantations that had owned them, so, most of the land began to be cultivated by African American and white tenant farmers and sharecroppers.

The last years of the century brought intensive development throughout Florida. Saint Augustine was a peaceful fishing village that began to attract tourists. Key West, the largest city with 18,000 people, was a prosperous naval base, and the center of the sponge and cigar industries. Jacksonville owed its prosperity to lumber resources and naval ports. Pensacola was an important Gulf port and Tampa took off when cigar manufacturers moved from Key West to Ybor City.

Plantations in the north and west produced cotton, corn, and tobacco, orange groves in the northeastern area increased in commercial importance and, vast phosphate deposits were discovered in the center of the State and construction of railroads and tourist hotels in the 1880's by Henry M Flagler and HB Plant drew thousands of tourists eager to see Florida's glorious east and west coasts.

The citrus industry began spreading throughout the state, but cold freezes in 1894-95 ruined most of the groves, forcing many North Floridan growers to turn to other less weathercontrolled industries. However, farmers who survived began to develop new and improved strains of citrus that were hardier and bloomed later in the season, enabling Florida to become the nation's top citrus producer.

Although WWI put a hold on much of Florida's commercial business, the tourist trade prospered, as folks up north

Florida's Slaves: One Man's Empire

Black families were brought as slaves to Florida by Spaniards as far back as 1565. One of the foremost slave traders in the South was a shrewd Mississippi businessman who arrived in Florida in 1803, swearing allegiance to the King of Spain and holding some 67,000 pesos in gold and slaves. It was on Fort George Island, at the mouth of the Saint Johns River near Jacksonville that wealthy, educated Zephaniah Kingsley set up his slave empire–Kingsley Plantation.

Kingsley Plantation became a well known "training facility" for many other slaves that came from Africa and the Caribbean, where they learned techniques for planting and harvesting the highly lucrative Sea Island cotton, sugarcane, oranges, rice, and vegetables.

Kingsley saw slavery as a means whereby black men could rise above their station, eventually buying themselves out of bondage. His plantation operated on the "Task" system, whereby each slave was obligated to perform his specific daily task, and then was free to farm, hunt or fish and sell the fruits of his labor back to the plantation.

This system motivated the slaves to complete their daily tasks efficiently, so they could get on with their own entrepreneurial projects, also enabling them to earn money for themselves and for their families.

Of course, the labors of his slaves mostly benefitted Kingsley, making him an even richer man, but plantation records show that he gave his slaves Christmas week off and gifts of new clothes, clay pipes, molasses and ham.

In Defence of Slavery?

In 1829, Kingsley published a pamphlet titled, "In Defense of Slavery" in which he defended "the peculiar institution", but also applauded African virtues, noting that blacks were "no different than any other man except being bereft of those skills necessary to better his lot in the New World."

Kingsley felt strongly that "a patriarchal feeling of affection is due to every slave from his owner..." and felt that family members should never be separated from each other.

Much later in his life, Kingsley admitted to a London newspaper correspondent that "the colored race were superior to us, physically and morally... being more docile and affectionate, more faithful in their attachments and less prone to mischief than the white race.

If it were not so, they could not have been

came south seeking a new type of gold–sunshine and youth, not from a mythical fountain, but from her beautiful beaches and lush tropical jungles.

After the War, rumors of real estate deals brought thousands of speculators, who came to buy land, and resell it at huge profits, making some risktakers overnight millionaires. Between 1920 and 1925, the population increased four times faster than any other state! A popular movie starring the zany Marx Brothers was "Coconuts", Hollywood's spoof on the con men and their victims

during this temporary real estate boom.

In the spring of 1926, the bubble burst, with banks failing and millionaires turning into paupers overnight. That same year a fall hurricane killed hundreds of Floridians, and left thousands homeless. Two years later another hurricane hit, leaving even worse devastation in its path.

As if all this tragedy was not bad enough, the stock market crashed in 1929, plunging the US into the Great Depression. More bad news came when the Mediterranean fruit fly invaded

kept in slavery." The stunned newspaper reporter responded, "It is a shameful and shocking thought that we should keep them in slavery by their very virtues." To which Kingsley replied, "It is so, ma'am, but like many other shameful things, it is true."

Kingsley's Guilt

Fortunately, Kingsley's guilt lasted until his death, when his will instructed that his entire estate go to his nephews, his African wife, Anna Madgigne Jai Kingsley, (whom he had originally purchased at the age of eight as a slave for his mother!), their children and his two mistresses, whom he referred to as his "other wives," and all their children.

Today, you can visit Florida's oldest slave plantation house on the bank of Saint Johns River, and walk through Kingsley's home, stable, and the skeletal remains of the slave quarters. Guided tours are conducted at 9:30am, 11:00am, 1:30pm and 3:00pm from Thursday through Monday.

Write or telephone Kingsley Plantation State Historic Site, PO Box 321, Fort George, Florida 32226. Tel: (904) 251 3122.

Florida, destroying 60 per cent of the citrus groves. Trying valiantly to recover from these years of crisis, Florida entrepreneurs turned to the development of tangible resources, such as paper mills, cooperative farms, port improvements and commercial real estate.

WWII Boost

During WW II (1941-1945), Florida became a training center for troops, sailors and airmen from the US forces and her allies at Camp Blanding and Camp Gordon Johnston. Tourist hotels and restaurants in Miami Beach, Daytona Beach and Saint Petersburg were turned into manufacturing centers where vessels and tools were forged.

Highway and airport construction were accelerated, so by the war's end, Florida had an up-to-date transportation network, ready for use by local citizens and the endless stream of tourists, which by 1973 had grown to 25.5 million per year.

Present & Future

Since the war, Florida's development has continued to progress well beyond tourism, cattle, citrus and phosphate. New industries have created opportunities in commercial space exploration, biomedical and biotechnology industries, electronics, plastics, public utilities, forest products, construction, printing and publishing, television and movie production, real estate, international banking and international trade.

The postwar era has brought desegregation and steady population growth. Florida is now the fourth most populous state in the nation, with a 1990 census population of almost 13 million residents. The state has witnessed a massive migration of Cubans (fleeing the Castro regime), who have made a tremendous impact on the growth of Florida's social, political, economic and cultural life.

Other trends have contributed to the growing wealth and success of

Florida's State bird – the mockingbird.

Florida: major American corporations have relocated to the state in ever increasing numbers, the completion of the interstate highway system throughout the state, the construction of major international airports, an expansion of the state's universities and community colleges (whose advanced research and development departments contribute knowledge and employees to the state's business sector), the proliferation of high technology and historic accomplishments by the NASA space program.

Walt Disney World & EPCOT Center

With the opening of Walt Disney World in 1971, at an estimated cost of $500 million, and the subsequent opening of EPCOT center (Experimental Prototype Community of Tomorrow), tourism has thrived as never before. These two sites annually attract more visitors from across the country and around the world than Florida has residents.

When Universal Studios Florida, and Disney-MGM Studios opened for film production in 1988, Florida established itself as a major player in the movie and television production industry, which contributed more than $185 million to the state's economy in the first year alone.

Florida's cities have become locations where families can have an excellent quality of life, working in jobs they

Famous Personalities

We could publish an entire book just on all the talented artists, entrepreneurs, and captains of industry who have contributed to Florida's success, but here are just a few:

Henry Morrison Flagler (1830-1913). Flagler came to Florida in the 1880's and saw the potential for opening the state to tourism. He created the Florida East Coast Railway, and built a number of luxury hotels, which opened up Florida's east coast, in turn attracting wealthy travelers from the world over.

Lue Gim Gong (1858-1925). Gong was a horticulturist who experimented with different types of citrus fruit, producing a strain of orange that ripened late in the season after the winter frosts. This enabled citrus growers to expand the fruit growing season and enable them to market the fruit later in the year.

Mary Mcleod Bethune (1875-1955). Bethune was an African American educator who devoted her life to the improvement of educational opportunities for African Americans. She was founder and president of Bethune-Cookman College in Daytona Beach, and was appointed to various governmental posts by Presidents Coolidge, Hoover, Roosevelt and Truman. She founded the National Council of Negro Women.

Marjorie Kinnan Rawlings (1896-1953). Rawlings was a novelist who wrote about the people and nature of backwood Florida. Living in Cross Creek, she wrote *The Yearling*, which won the 1939 Pulitzer Prize for fiction. She also wrote *South Moon Under, Golden Apples, When the Whippoorwill,* and *Cross Creek* which was made into a feature film.

Ernest Hemingway (1899-1961). This Nobel Laureate for literature moved to Key West in 1928, and lived there at period intervals until 1940, writing many of his famous works, including *A Farewell to Arms, For Whom the Bell Tolls* and *The Snows of Kilimanjaro*. He also won a Pulitzer Prize for his novel, "The Old Man and the Sea."

James Weldon Johnson (1871-1938). Johnson, born in Jacksonville, was a consul to Venezuela and Nicaragua, a novelist, author, editor and poet. His book *God's Trombones: Seven Negro Sermons in Verse* (1927), was adapted for the stage. He was also executive secretary for The National Association for the Advancement of Colored People (NAACP), and a professor at Fisk University.

Marjory Stoneman Douglas (1890-). Douglas is a journalist, author, environmental activist and founder of Friends of the Everglades, a non-profit lobby organization created to protect the Everglades. She is author of the renowned book, *The Everglades: River of Grass*, which warns of the fragility of one of America's most important ecosystems.

Zora Neale Hurston (1901-1960). A novelist, folklorist, and anthropologist who won Guggenheim and Rosenwald fellowships for her stories of Florida's rural people. Her prominent works include *Mules and Men, Dust Tracks in the Road* and *Their Eyes Were Watching God*.

George Firestone (1931-). Before being elected Secretary of State in 1978, Firestone served in Florida's House of Representatives and the Senate. Under his jurisdiction as Chief Cultural Officer of Florida, support for the arts increased.

Ray Charles (1930-). A living musical legend, called the "genius of soul", Charles began his musical career at age five at the St. Augustine School for the Deaf and Blind. Known throughout the world for hits like "Georgia On My Mind" and "Hit the Road Jack", Charles is the recipient of 11 Grammy awards for his songs and albums.

Robert Raushenberg (1925-). This influential modern artist from Captiva has his paintings exhibited in the collections of major museums throughout the world. He has both founded and funded organizations to help other artists, such as the Rauschenberg Overseas Cultural Exchange, founded in 1983.

enjoy, living in harmony with nature and wildlife. Florida's people–a population representing every culture and country on earth- have much to be proud of from the past, and even more to look forward to in the future. And tourism will continue to play a vital part in that future.

Floridian government dates back to its earliest inhabitants – the Indians. French explorer Jean Ribault and his mapmaker Jacques le Moyne maintained meticulous journals about their observations of Indian governmental styles in the mid–1500s, describing in great detail the Indian method of government: "The chief and his nobles are accustomed during certain days of the year to meet early every morning for this express purpose in a public place, in which a long bench is constructed having at the middle of it a projecting part laid with nine round trunks of trees, for the chief's seat.

He sits by himself on this, for distinction's sake; and here the rest come to salute him, one at a time, the oldest first, by lifting both hands twice to the height of his head saying 'ha, ha, ya, ha, ha.' The rest answer, 'ha, ha.' Each, as he completes his salutation, takes his seat on the bench. If any question of importance is to be discussed, the chief calls upon his priests, and upon the elders,

Your favorite man – Uncle Sam.

Government

The Florida state seal.

one a time to deliver their opinions. They decide upon nothing until they have held a number of councils over it, and they deliberate very sagely before deciding."

As the Spanish colonized Florida in the 1600s, they governed by the dictates of the King of Spain and from their flourishing base in Havana.

Under British rule in 1763, Floridians were loyal to England, even though the rest of the United States turned their backs on King George III in a revolution on July 4, 1776. By 1783, England gave

rial Governor, William P DuVal and a 13 member legislature. In 1823, Tallahassee was selected as the site of the new capital because of its ideal location between Pensacola and Saint Augustine, and in 1824, the first Legislature met in a log cabin near the site of the present Capitol Building.

By 1845, Florida became a new state, part of The United States of America, under Governor William D Moseley, who presided over a population of 66,500.

Following the election of President Lincoln in 1860, the Florida Legislature met to enact a constitutional convention, appropriating US$100,000 for state troops to protect the state's interest in slavery which caused the state to secede in 1861. It was not until the War Between the States ended in 1865 that Florida abolished slavery. In 1868 a new state constitution was drafted and accepted by the United States government, finally granting freedom to the African Americans, and a free school system for all Floridians.

And at the 1885 Constitutional Convention, cabinet posts, supreme court seats and most county offices were made elective.

Modern Government

Florida's state constitution is basically the same governmental system found at the United States' national level and in all 50 states. The powers of government are divided into three separate

Florida back to Spain in exchange for the Bahamas and Gibraltar. By 1821, Spain had accepted an offer from the United States to cancel US$5 million in debts to Washington, in exchange for the ownership of Florida.

By 1822, the American President Monroe signed a Congressional Act that provided Florida with her first Territo-

Tallahassee's State Capitol Buildings: Old and New

When, by treaty with Spain, Florida became a territory of the United States in 1821, it was still mostly an unsettled wilderness. The British had divided the land into two separate political regions during their rule in 1763-1783 and legislators had to travel back and forth between Saint Augustine and Pensacola.

Finally in 1823, a half-way point between the cities was chosen as Florida's new Capital: Tallahassee. Legislators could now settle into one legislative home, which was just a simple log building. By 1824, they moved into a modest two-story masonry structure.

On June 25, 1845, cannons roared a 28 gun salute, as Florida became a state, William D Moseley became its first elected governor and a new brick capitol building stood proudly completed. By the 1891, the half-century old building was in need of repair and so it was repainted, installed with running water, and a small cupola was added to the top, from which visitors could enjoy "a magnificent view." Boldly striped exterior awnings were also added to shade the offices from Florida's intense sunshine.

In 1900, the state legislature appropriated US$75,000 for the renovation and expansion of their statehouse, selecting Frank Pierce Milburn, a prominent southern architect, to accomplish the task. He added "a beautiful and graceful" dome, that rose 136 feet above the ground, and a colorful art glass "subdome", which enabled light to stream into the rotunda. Milburn also added pressed metal reliefs incorporating details from the State Seal.

Henry J Klutho became the architect of the 1923 capitol addition, doubling the usable space in the building while retaining its classic lines. Most Floridians are familiar with the silver exterior dome, frosted glass skylight above the rotunda, double curved staircase and marble wainscoting that still exists today.

In 1936 and 1947, north and south wings were added for the House of Representatives and the Senate.

The restoration of The Old Capitol took place from 1978-1982 under the creative guidance of Shepard Associates Architects & Planners, who restored the Governor's Suite, Supreme Court, House of Representative and Senate chambers, rotunda, and halls back to their 1902-style beauty. There are several rooms featuring photo exhibits on Florida's symbols and political history.

You can take the free 45-minute guided tour of The Old Capitol on Saturdays at 11:00 am, or wander around freely throughout the building from Monday to Friday from 9:00am-4:30pm, Saturdays 10:00am-4:30pm, and Sundays/Public Holidays from 12:00-4:00pm. The Old Capitol is on the corner of S Monroe Street and

and relatively independent branches: executive, legislative, and judicial.

Executive Branch: Administration and enforcement of the state's laws is the charge of this branch. Florida's constitution is slightly different from executive branches of other states in that it calls for a cabinet composed of a secretary of state, an attorney general, a comptroller, a treasurer, a commissioner of agriculture, and a commissioner of education. These are in addition to the Governor and Lieutenant–Governor.

This means that cabinet officers enjoy equal powers as the governor, and may outvote him on various issues. The only time the governor can not be outvoted is in the granting of pardons.

The governor and cabinet members are elected in even numbered years between national presidential elections for a term of four years. A Governor may serve two terms in succession, and cabinet officers may be re-elected for any number of years.

The state Capitol Building in Tallahassee.

exhibits an interesting display of plaques on Florida's religious history. Be sure to stop by the Florida Department of Commerce Welcome Center at the back of the lobby. Tel: (904) 488 6167.

On the 5th floor, you can sit and watch the House and Senate in session from February to April. The House chambers boasts state-of-the-art electronic amendment television monitors and interactive television screens for voting. Visitors can watch from behind sound proofed glass windows.

The 22nd floor offers a pretty panoramic view of Tallahassee's downtown and surrounding neighborhoods, which are mostly tucked among dense green forests.

The observation deck is popular with university students who like to study by the windows, and local politicos networking at receptions. There is also an Artists Hall of Fame which salutes well known Floridians like Ernest Hemingway, Tennessee Williams, Robert Rauschenberg and Ray Charles.

Take the free 45-minute guided tour which departs every hour from Monday to Friday 0900-1100 hours and from 1300-1600 hours; Saturday, Sunday and Public Holidays 1100-1500 hours.

It is located on Duval Street. Tel: (904) 488 6167 for more information.

Apalachee Parkway. Tel: 487 1902.

Just outside the Apalachee exit is the 22-story New Capitol building, built in 1977 of Italian marble by architect E D Stone at a cost of $43 million. In the lobby is a tiny peaceful nondenominational chapel for meditation, that

Legislative Branch: The Florida Legislature consists of the State Senate, and the House of Representatives. Legislation on any topic may be introduced into either house. The Legislature meets every year for 60 days beginning in February. The Governor may call special 20 day sessions, if needed.

The senate and house have a great deal of influence over the lives of Floridians, by enacting state laws, and laws that affect specific cities, counties or regions and is considered to be the most powerful of the three branches of state government because they control not only the affairs of cities and counties, but because they control the appointments of the governor, as well as exercise investigative and budgetary control over all phases of state government and state agencies.

The senate has 40 members, each elected to a 4-year term. Half the senate is elected every two years, so there will be staggered terms. Each senator represents an area of about 300,000 citizens.

A historical flashback – a park history interpretation of the Castillo de San Marcos in Saint Augustine.

The house has 120 members, but all are elected every two years during general elections held in even numbered years. Like the senate, house representatives are based on population, so there is one senator for each 100,000 residents.

Judicial Branch: This branch of state government consists of courts with differing levels of authority. Judicial power is vested in a Supreme Court, District Courts of Appeal, circuit courts and county courts. The Supreme Court is the highest of state courts, consisting of 7 members, each elected for a 6-year term. The members select one of their group to be chief justice for a 2-year period. There must be 5 justices to constitute a quorum, but 4 members must agree on any issue before a decision is made. This court makes rulings on death penalty cases, civil cases, treaties, or provisions relating to revenue and bonds.

Florida is divided into 5 appellate districts, each with a court of appeals. These courts have 7 judges elected for 6 year staggered terms. Four judges may constitute a quorum, but a majority agreement among all court members is required before a decision is made.

The state's highest trial court is the circuit court. It also exercises the most general jurisdiction. There are 20 judicial circuits, and judges are elected to serve 6 year terms. Circuit courts rule over civil actions involving amounts of over US$2500, settlements of estates, juveniles, tax assessments, titles, boundaries and felonies.

At least one county court judge is appointed for each county, and he/she serves a 4-year term. This court has jurisdiction over misdemeanor cases that the circuit court does not have authority to try, violations of municipal ordinances and civil actions involving amounts of under US$2500.

Change in some Florida laws have directly affected young citizens, such as the 1973 lowering of the legal age from 21 to 18. Today, 18 year olds can work as policemen, firemen, city bus drivers, and become notary publics. They can also gamble, purchase a shotgun or rifle, enter into contracts, obtain credit, buy cars and get married (with their parents approval). Florida's government maintains that for young citizens, the family is still the primary governing body.

Governor Chiles

Florida is now governed by Lawton Chiles, who was elected the 41st Governor in a landslide victory in 1990 with a campaign theme of "This Time the People Win". Governor and First Lady Rhea Chiles celebrated their election with a free inaugural ceremony which was open to the public. Staying in touch with the people of Florida goes back to Governor Chile's former days as a U.S. Senator. In 1970 he earned the nickname "Walkin' Lawton" when he and Mrs. Chiles embarked upon a 1,003 mile walk from North Florida to the Keys to "hear first-hand the needs, ideas and dreams of my fellow Floridians."

Governor Chiles chairs the National Commission to Prevent Infant Mortality, a Congressional committee he helped found while serving in the Senate, and is a member of the Democratic Leadership Council.

First Lady Rhea Chiles is a computer expert and the creator of Florida House–a way station and retreat for Floridians visiting Tallahassee. The Chiles have been married for over 40 years, and have four children and eight grandchildren.

I t is absolutely amazing what can develop when two brilliant businessmen act on the same good idea.

Florida's phenomenal achievement in becoming the nation's leading state for tourism began with the entrepreneurial vision of two forward thinking men: Henry Morrison Flagler and Henry Plant. These savvy barons opened Florida up to the entire United States, building railroads to transport eager tourists south and luxurious hotels to pamper them upon arrival.

Florida's tangiest crop – the orange.

In 1884, Plant's Atlantic Coastline Railroad linked Richmond, Virginia with Tampa, and at the end of the line visitors with healthy bank accounts were welcomed to a world of luxury at the lavish Tampa Bay Hotel.

In 1885, Flagler's Florida East Coast Railroad chugged tourists down the east coast, making stops at his hotels in Saint Augustine, Daytona and

Down in the dockyards in Florida's shipbuilding industry.

Palm Beach, where the famous Breakers Hotel rose into the azure sky. A high priced playground for the rich, Palm Beach soon attracted American millionaires like the Rockefellers, Vanderbilts, Kennedys, as well as the *nouveau riche* who hoped to go there to meet them.

By 1912, Flagler's railroad stretched all the way south to Key West taking tourists to glorious fishing and sailing vacations in The Keys.

News of Florida fun quickly flew northward, and it was not too long before the rest of the country started making reservations for their slice of paradise. Northerners by the thousands began pouring in, in such large numbers that they were nicknamed "Tin Can Tourists" because they camped out in tent cities and ate food from tin cans. Many of them fell in love with Florida's climate and lifestyle, returned home to pack up their families and friends, and then came back to become permanent citizens. This population explosion set off a frenzy of real estate deals, where some became millionaires overnight. Between 1920 and 1940, Florida's population doubled to nearly two million, with 2.5 million tourists coming and going each year. However when The Depression and several major hurricanes hit in 1926, development was brought to a temporary standstill.

But after WWII the tourist industry was resurrected and Miami became a special favorite of sun seekers. Between 1945 and 1954, more hotel rooms were

Shrimpboats out on the open seas shrimping for those tasty crustaceans.

built in greater Miami than in the rest of the states combined! In 1959, Florida inaugurated the first domestic airline passenger service in the US, making Miami just a short hop away from New York by air.

Florida brought dreams to reality for many Americans. The Sunshine State symbolized the Perfect Vacation, the Perfect Escape, the Perfect Retirement spot and ultimately the Perfect Place to enjoy work and play.

Modern Economy

Tourism has continued to flourish, becoming Florida's premier industry, with over 40 million visitors flocking to the state every year. One of the most successful tour attractions in the state, indeed the world, is Walt Disney World in Orlando, a vast complex of theme parks and resorts that have helped make Florida a prime destination for national and international visitors.

Florida's growing economy consists of :
• community, social & personal services;
• wholesale and retail trade;
• finance, insurance, and real estate;
• government;
• manufacturing;
• transportation, communications and utilities;
• construction;
• agriculture;
• mining.

Cigar manufacturing in Ybor city.

Amongst the 50 states, Florida has the sixth largest prime working age population (people between the ages of 18 and 44). In fact, between 1980 and 1990, Florida added more than 3.5 million people belonging to that category to the state's population which now numbers 13.4 million people. With the second fastest growing work force in the nation, Florida is hardly the retirement state that some misinformed people think it is!

For the last two decades, Florida has been riding high on the wave of expansion spurred by a broad range of high-technology industries, including communication, information, biotechnology and defense. Florida now ranks sixth in the nation in terms of high-tech em-

ployment and first in the Southeastern part of the country. She ranks seventh in the United States in the number of manufacturing plants, which produce a wide range of products from electronic components to golf clubs and from sportswear to luxury yachts.

Florida is a national leader in many technological industries, such as: electromedical equipment, guided missiles and space vehicles, ophthalmic goods, radio and television communications equipment, aircraft engines and parts, space propulsion units and parts, printed circuit boards, optical instruments and lenses, computer processing and data processing services.

Growth in international trade, business, health care, retail sales and financial services, has broadened the state's economy, adding to the strength of its agriculture, tourism, construction and retirement industries. And several other resource-based industries such as lumber, wood products, furniture manufacturing and phosphate mining, add to the state's diverse economic mix.

A Major Launch

With the formation of the Florida Spaceport Authority in 1990, the state took a giant step toward capturing a piece of a projected multibillion dollar industry. Dubbed "Spaceport Florida", the recent state initiative has opened a number of federal launch pads at Cape Canaveral to the private sector. Over the next several years, General Dynamics, Martin Marietta and McDonnell Douglas plan to make over 30 commercial launches.

Discoveries made in space will help ensure American technological competitiveness and Florida's role in high tech advancements for decades to come. For example, the growth of protein crystals in zero-gravity fields has permitted the development of potential medicinal materials. The growth of semiconductor materials in space may lead to the development of high-speed computers at the forefront of technology. Florida's existing technological infrastructure and ideal location will ensure that the state becomes a world center in space-related commerce.

The planet industry at Kennedy Spaceport USA.

Communications & Information

Production of communication equipment, electronic components and computing equipment represents over 58 per cent of Florida's technology-based manufacturing. Industry revenues are expected to reach $30 billion by 1997.

At the University of Florida's High Speed Digital Architecture Laboratory, researchers are developing the software and hardware that will bring the power of supermicroprocessors to desktop computers and workstations.

At the University of South Florida, scientists have discovered a process for growing high quality laser crystal fibers

Tampa Cigars: The Birth of Ybor City

Don Vicente Martinez Ybor, an influential cigar manufacturer and Cuban exile, spent years looking for the right location to build his new cigar factory. By the mid 1800's, labor union disputes made cigar manufacturing in New York and Key West too difficult. Finally, Ybor's friends suggested a sandy palmetto covered frontier: Tampa. Tempted by the warm climate, a new railroad, and a shipping port located close by, Ybor obtained 40 acres from the Tampa Board of Trade and in 1885 set about creating his city .

From the opening of the first factory in 1886 until the 1930's, Ybor City was a flourishing Latin community, where top quality cigars were individually hand-rolled . Ybor City soon earned a reputation as "The Cigar Capital of the World", , and became the largest in the world, employing more than 4,000 Spanish, Cuban, Italian, Jewish, German and Afro-Cuban workers. Cigar manufacturers, which included men, women, and some children, earned US$20 per week for hand-rolling their top quality cigars.

One aspect that contributed to worker's enjoyment and pride in their jobs was the existence of "El Lectore", a narrator who sat on a platform above the workers and read them the day's news. He also read popular literature of the time, taking care to end the day on an exciting chapter, so everyone would return the next day eager to hear the rest of the story. The position of "El Lectore" was so highly regarded that the workers contributed a portion of their own paychecks to his salary, which at $80 per week exceeded their own. It was a very prestigious position for a selected intellectual from the community. Life was good in Ybor city. Shop owners lived above their stores, relaxed after work on their ornate wrought iron balconies, and partied in their clubs, casinos and speakeasies. Each ethnic group had their own newspapers, restaurants, mutual aid societies and hospitals.

Towards the end of the 1800s, Ybor City became a support center for the Cuban Revolution. When war broke out between the United States and Spain in 1898, the Army stationed thousands of men in Ybor City, including Teddy Roosevelt and his Rough Riders. On August 12,

Smoking the product in a cigar factory in Tampa.

1898, Cuba won its independence.

Ybor City and the cigar industry continued to flourish until the introduction of more efficient industrial cigar making machines, which made it possible to make thousands of cigars in the same time that it took to roll 50 by hand. The new popularity of cigarettes and the Depression also contributed to the industry's decline. Factories shut down, unemployment soared and families moved away.

Today Ybor City in Tampa is alive once more, as the renovated cigar factories are becoming shops, restaurants, galleries, boutiques, book stalls, and nightclubs. There are delightful free 1 1/2 hour escorted walking tours throughout the town on Tuesday, Thursday and Saturday at 1:30pm. From June to September tours begin at 11am. Tours start at Ybor Square, at the corner of 8th and 13th Avenue in Ybor City. Call Tel: (813) 248 3712 or (813) 223 1111 for more information.

thinner than a human hair. These fibers will be used for a variety of micro-processing applications. Research at the Center for Research in Electro-optics and Lasers at the University of Central Florida has yielded lasers capable of driving computer chips. Florida also boasts one of the most sophisticated fiber optic tel-ecommunications networks in the world. Digital capability is paving the way for an Integrated Services Digital Network, which will send voice, video and data over the same line.

High Tech Health

Florida's international reputation as an important medical equipment manu-facturer is growing. Devices such as the artificial kidney, hormone-testing equip-ment and cell counters were invented within Florida's medical industry, which today employs over 25,000 and sells over $1 billion annually.

University of Miami

The University of Miami's medical school has committed more than $80 million to a wide range of biotech and medical equipment research, including a proc-ess that uses a gamma camera and computer to locate blood clots. Materi-als research at the University of Florida has yielded Bioglass®, which bonds with human bone. It is being used to make hip and inner-ear replacements.

The magnificent tourist accomodation at the Hyatt Key West Resort – Scuba Dive Class.

High Tech Agribusiness

Food processing is Florida's fourth larg-est manufacturing sector, with over $660 million in annual exports of agricul-tural and food products, such as citrus, sugarcane, nursery and greenhouse plants, and vegetables. Timber, com-mercial fishing and phosphate mining are also important primary industries.

One agricultural discovery will have a particularly far reaching impact. Sci-entists at the University of Florida are working with colleagues in the Soviet Union on the method of extracting pec-tin from sugar beets. This compound will be used to remove high levels of

AVIATION: From Airplanes to Space Shuttles

Florida's year–round mild climate has always been a key element in making the state an ideal spot for training pilots. In 1914, the Pensacola Naval Air Station opened with three instructors, 12 mechanics and nine seaplanes. In 1915, the station scored an important first by launching Lieutenant Commander H D Martin and his aircraft from the deck of the USS North Carolina, by means of a catapult. This led to the development of aircraft carriers which played a major part in WWII.

By July 1917, Pensacola had 45 instructors, 200 student flyers and more than 1,200 mechanics, and when the war ended in 1918, there were more than 400 officers and nearly 6,000 enlisted men at the base. Meanwhile even before the end of the war, aviation pioneers were working at developing the airplane as a means of transporting passengers and mail. The most well known pioneer was Tony Jannus, who started the first scheduled airline service in the United States when he began plying a regular route between Saint Petersburg and Tampa. His first trip was on January 1, 1914, when he flew the mayor of Saint Petersburg AC Pheil to Tampa. Pheil gladly paid US$400 for the honor of being the first passenger.

Soon Jannus was operating two flights every day, a service he continued for 187 days.

By 1927, Pan American Airlines was created, and started making regular flights between Key West and Cuba. Eastern Airlines was born on January 1, 1931, when it established the first regular passenger service between Mi-

ami and New York, using six passenger Kingbirds in its fleet of airplanes. By 1934, Captain Eddie Rickenbacker, who had been America's ace pilot during WWI and was now president of Eastern, bought a group of DC-2 aircraft and began dawn to dusk flights between Miami and New York.

Also in 1934, National Airlines began operating from its home base in Saint Petersburg, delivering mail to Daytona Beach, Tampa, Lakeland, Orlando and Saint Petersburg. National's President Ted Baker added passenger service in 1935, using Stinson aircraft.

Aviation Heroes

One of Florida's most famous flyers was Albert Witten, who was the chief instructor at Pensacola and served in the Navy until 1919. After his Naval discharge, he bought a Bluebird aircraft and returned to Saint Petersburg where he entered commercial aviation. As a top instructor he was able to introduce hundreds of Floridians to flying. He also built his own commercial use aircraft, and christened it *The Falcon*. Unfortunately the aircraft developed a problem during one flight, and Witten and his four passengers were killed in 1923 near Pensacola in a crash. Another of Florida's aviation pioneers was Captain Dale Mabry, who served as a pilot in 1917 during the war, and who served in France as a member of the balloon corps of the American Expeditionary

radioactive metals from survivors of the Chernobyl nuclear disaster.

Television

The arrival of the Disney/MGM Studios and Universal Studios Florida has not only given tourists two new attractions to visit, but has also propelled Florida's

already booming television and feature film industry into the big time.

In 1992 over 50 major productions were filmed in Florida, generating revenues near the $1 billion mark that put Florida firmly in third place behind California and New York. Producers find that Florida's extraordinary climate and variety of locations makes location shooting a breeze, and appreciative of

forces. After the war, he served as commander of the Italian dirigible *Roma*. Shortly after take-off on February 21, 1922, the dirigible struck high tension wires near Langley Field, Virginia, exploded in flames and crashed. Of the 45 men on board, 11 jumped to safety, but Captain Mabry and 33 others died.

Pilots of the Future

Today's pilots have opportunities to "reach for the stars" at US Space Camp at the Astronaut Hall of Fame in Titusville. Young students interested in science, technology and space exploration can experience a five day introduction to shuttle flying, which includes realistic astronaut training, propulsion exercises, a NASA tour and a simulated space shuttle mission.

There are programs in Titusville for children in grades 4 to 7, a parent and child space camp weekend for ages 7 to 11, and adult space academy sessions for anyone 19 and older. At the Astronaut Hall of Fame you can watch these kids go through countdown, launch, orbit and return to earth in front of simulated mission control boards, and later talk to them about their experience. If you would like to sign up your child or yourself, call 1-800-63SPACE or stop by the US Astronaut Hall of Fame, 6225 Vectorspace Boulevard, Titusville, Florida, Tel: (407) 269 6100. The Hall of Fame is open seven days a week, from 9 to 5pm, and is just west of Kennedy Space Center.

the one-third savings they achieve in Florida as opposed to other states.

Sports

Florida's climate and natural resources have also spawned a big league industry in professional sports. Eighteen major league baseball teams come to Florida

for spring training, and two NBA teams and two NFL franchises make their homes in the state.

Among the sports organizations that have headquarters in Florida are the Tennis Professionals Association, the Women's International Tennis Association, the PGA of America, the PGA Tour, the Ladies Professional Golfers Association, and the Tournament Players Club at Sawgrass. Florida has more than 1,000 golf courses, which is one reason it is "Golf Heaven" for so many tourists!

Finance

Florida enjoys an undisputed position as the epi-center of finance and trade with Latin America and the Caribbean. The massive immigration of Cubans after Castro's takeover has given Florida a very highly educated and sophisticated bilingual business community, many of whom work within the financial industry. Florida continues to experience growth, both in numbers of banks and in assets, with many of the world's leading international banks having established offices throughout Florida to service Latin America, Europe and Asia.

Retail Industry

With total retail sales of almost $98 billion, Florida leads all other southeastern states, and ranks fourth nationally in terms of sales volume. Retail sales are expected to reach $135 billion by 1994. Florida is a hot spot for shopping center growth, ranking second in the nation in terms of the number of shopping centers. Currently there are over 2,700 shopping centers for you to choose from! Tourism has created additional demand for hotels, restaurants, gift shops, attractions, recreational facilities and travel services. This in turn develops needs for grocery, hardware, furniture, lawn and garden stores; and personal and professional services in health care, cleaning and laundry, legal services and automotive repair.

International Markets

Florida has become one of America's major overseas shipping points for both sea and air cargo. In 1990, a record $30.6 billion worth of international traded products flowed through the state to and from Canada, Brazil, Colombia, Venezuela and Japan. The 1990 Top Five export commodities were fertilizers, aircraft parts, office machine parts, spacecraft/satellites and passenger vehicles. The top Five 1990 import commodities were passenger vehicles/trucks, shellfish, apparel, shoes and coffee.

The passage of a 1990 International Trade Bill instituted a state level agency chaired by Florida's Governor to develop international business. Florida has many foreign offices worldwide, in locations like Toronto, London, Japan, Brussels, Korea, Germany and Brazil, and,

many foreign owned companies have set up headquarters or regional offices throughout the state.

Bright Economic Future

As a US leader in new business starts, and a population that is growing at the

Following the lay of the land the magnificent Fontainbleau Hotel.

rate of 900 persons per day, Florida's entrepreneurial spirit is at an all time high. The climate, quality of life, and exceptional opportunity for success and growth lends a pioneer feeling.

John Lombardi, the President of the University of Florida in Gainesville, sums it up this way: "Florida is booming, energetic and experimental.

Things have not settled down yet and people do not know quite where the boundaries are. It is exciting, like the opening of the West in California's Gold Rush Days!"

Florida's geography has greatly contributed to her success as America's favorite playground, and they are in fact uniquely intertwined.

Throughout the state's 58,560 square mile peninsula, Florida has no areas that are more than 60 miles from the saltwater. Imagine : You are never more than a short drive away from alabaster sand, crashing waves and the cooling breezes of The Atlantic Ocean or The Gulf of Mexico. That simple geographical feature enables Florida's visitors to have the best of all her worlds: sophisticated cities for shopping, sports and culture, and soothing natural shorelines for relaxing and getting away from it all.

Billions of years ago, Florida was just an arc of steaming volcanic islands. Gradually erosion and deposits of silt and sand clay buried the volcanoes. Geologists boring 13,000 feet into the ground have found evidence of molten rocks that hardened into igneous gran-

Sal tree forest with a lush undergrowth.

51

The Everglades – an ecological haven.

ite rhyolite, forming Florida's solid foundation. They have also discovered bones of bizarre shark–like mammals called zeuglodons, ancient whales, and early relatives of the manatees.

Twenty to thirty million years ago, Florida emerged from the sea, first as a sandy area, before gradually becoming an 18,000 feet repository of thickened limestone. The Ice Age caused the seas to ebb and flow over her shores, until the tides carved out a stepping stone of bluffs and terraces that range from 150 feet above sea level at Lake Okefenokee

so famous. Mineral phosphorus deposited by the waves settled in the sand and clay, giving Florida the rich undercoating which eventually became a fertile bed for the exotic flora and fauna who call her home.

Modern Geography

Today Florida is the United State's 22nd state in terms of size, with the highest point at 345 feet in the northwestern Panhandle region and the lowest at sea level.

The state's land regions are divided into three main areas:

• The Atlantic Coastal Plain, a low level plain ranging in width from 30 to 100 miles, covering the eastern part of the state. Just beyond the mainland, there is a narrow ribbon of sand bars, coral reefs, and barrier islands. Between this ribbon are shallow lakes, lagoons, rivers and bays. This plain includes the Big Cypress Swamp and The Everglades at over 1.5 million acres. Also within the Atlantic Coastal Plain are The Florida Keys, a chain of small islands that curve 150 miles off the southern end of the mainland from Miami.

• The East Gulf Coastal Plain has two sections: the southwestern part of Florida, and the curves around the northern edge of the Gulf of Mexico across the Panhandle to the western border. Here are also long narrow barrier islands and coastal swamps. The Florida Upland separate the two sections of the East Gulf

to barely 10 feet at Silver Bluff.

The Ice Age was followed by hundreds of years of pelting rains which filled the holes left in Florida's brittle limestone crust. Fresh water accumulated in these underground holes. Bursting through the thin surface, it transformed sinkholes into the sparkling clear fresh water springs for which the state is

Coastal Plain from each other, and separate the northern section from the Atlantic Coastal Plain. This region is higher than the others, at about 200 to 300 feet above sea level. There are many lakes, some formed from sinkholes. A sinkhole is formed when a limestone bed near the surface has been dissolved by water. The Upland area features fertile valleys, pine, softwood and hardwood forests, and rolling hills of red clay.

Florida has 1,197 miles of coastline, more than any state except Alaska. The Atlantic coast is 399 miles and the Gulf coast, 798 miles. Some 800 miles of Florida's coastline are beaches, and inland are more than 30,000 lakes, including Lake Okeechobee which at 730 square miles is the fourth largest lake in the United States. Another interesting fact is that 4,424 of Florida's 54,136 square miles are water, which more than adds to the delight of fishing and boating enthusiasts.

Florida has more groundwater than any other state because so much of the state sits on top of groundwater reservoirs called aquifers. Florida has six primary aquifers supplying excellent drinking water throughout the state: The Floridian, Biscayne, Chocoloskee, Hawthorn Formation, Sand Gravel, and Undifferentiated aquifers.

Wetlands

A large area of Florida is covered by

wetlands, which are categorized as cypress ponds, prairies, floodplains, river swamps, hammocks, freshwater marshes, salt marshes and mangrove swamps. There is a delicate ecological balance between the wetlands and the plant and animal life that survive within them. Just to acquaint you with some of the areas you will be seeing, here is a brief explanation of their characteristics:

Hammocks, is an Indian word meaning jungle. You will know it by the thick tangle of vegetation in very fertile soil. Trees growing in hammocks include cypress, live oaks, hickory and magnolia.

Cypress Strands are found in the Fakahatchee Strand and Corkscrew Swamp in South Florida. You will see canopies that soar over 100 feet tall intertwined with vines, ferns and brilliantly hued orchids.

Freshwater Marsh is basically what makes up the state's Everglades. Sometimes the grasses are wet or dry depending on rainfall. Keep a sharp eye out here for alligators and dozens of different species of birds.

Mangrove Swamps feature plants that live in saltwater and serve as breeding places for fish and shellfish. You will see them along the east coast from Saint Augustine southwards, and on the west coast near Cedar Key.

Estuaries are a combination of fresh and saltwater. As the spring water flows toward the Atlantic Ocean or Gulf of Mexico, it gets saltier, forming different habitats for a variety of animal life. Frogs, and water insects prefer freshwater, whereas jellyfish, flounder and barnacles like saltwater. The water in between – half salt and half fresh – is "brackish", and you are likely to spot crabs, turtles and egrets among the tall grasses.

One of Florida's interesting phenomena is her "disappearing lakes". During dry seasons, a lake may shrink down to a pond, mud bed, or completely evaporate! Then the underground spring water will seep through and bubble to the surface, causing the lake to reappear. So if you see a lake one week that is mysteriously gone in the next, you will know that Mother nature is up to her tricks again.

Inland Waters

Stephen Foster's song **Way Down Upon the Swanee River** made this Florida's best known river, but the most historically important one is the Saint Johns', which starts in East Central Florida, flows northward and empties into the Atlantic Ocean near Jacksonville. It was at the mouth of the Saint Johns where Ponce de Leon first landed in 1513 and proclaimed Florida as "feast of the flowers", in the name of the King of Spain. The Frenchman Jean Ribault built his Fort Carolina on the Saint Johns' in 1562. And it was the Saint Johns' area that became Florida's first resort destination in the 1870's and served as a transportation system for steamboats ferrying

Hurricanes: A Nightmare Come True

The damage done to a homestead by Hurrican Andrew, August 1992.

Most storms that enter Florida approach from the south or southwest, entering the Keys, the Miami area, or along the west coast.

Caused by wind rushing toward a low pressure area, hurricanes take on the shape of giant doughnuts, with high winds revolving counterclockwise around a calm center the "eye".

Ranging from 60 to 1,000 miles in diameter, a hurricane is defined by winds of more than 74 miles per hour, accompanied by heavy rains, enormous waves, and dangerously high tides. Outside the eye, winds may reach up to 125-200 miles per hour and blow rain in horizontal sheets.

Once a hurricane is formed, it becomes a nightmare for people and property, as wind, waves, and rain destroy anyone or anything unlucky enough to be caught in its path.

A brief look back at a few of Florida's worst hurricanes:

1896: On September 22, this hurricane entered the west coast fishing village of Cedar Key, claiming more than 100 lives, and leaving behind some $7 million in damage.

1919: Classified as one of the great storms of the century, this hurricane severely damaged Florida's Keys before ending in the Gulf of Mexico.

1926: Striking on September 6, the storm hit Miami, with floodwaters of 10-12 feet and 243 people drowning. Property damage was estimated statewide at between $27-37 million.

1928: This hurricane struck Palm Beach, with gusting winds of 130 miles per hour. Some 1,836 people died.

1935: Called "The Labor Day Hurricane" for striking on August 31, this hurricane was considered the most severe to-date in terms of wind velocity, central pressure and storm tides. The hurricane passed over the Keys, moved up the Gulf to Cedar Key and left 408 people dead.

1960: Striking on August 29, Hurricane Donna had winds of 175 miles per hour and left damages totaling $140 million, including $60 mil-

produce to markets. The Swanee River begins in the Okefenokee Swamp of Georgia, and wends its way through the middle of Florida, finally pouring into the Gulf of Mexico at the town with the same name. There are four state parks near the banks of this river.

Several of Florida's rivers start in

the 730 square mile Lake Okeechobee, which was once a hole in the ocean floor. The lake is the fourth largest in the United States.

Florida has more first-magnitude springs than any other state: 17. This means the spring is discharging 100 cubic feet or more of water every second!

ion to the state's citrus crop. Fifty people died, and 1,144 were injured.

1964: Hurricane Cleo stuck Miami, moved up the east coast into the south Atlantic states, leaving $128 million in damage.

1975: Christened Hurricane Eloise, she hit Florida's panhandle on September 23 with winds of 135 miles per hour, leaving $100 million in damage and 17,000 residents of Panama City and Fort Walton homeless.

1985: Hurricane Elena hit the west coast from Saint Petersburg to Pensacola, forcing the evacuation of 1.2 million people and causing $1 billion in damage.

1992: Hurricane Andrew struck Homestead and Florida City in Dade County on August 24, with winds of 150 miles per hour, leaving 40 people dead, 250,000 homeless and $20 billion in property damage. President Bush declared a national emergency, and authorized 8,500 military troops to aid in the clean-up and establishment of "tent cities", offering shelter, clothing and food for those who lost their homes.

The American Red Cross, United Way, Federal Emergency Management Agency, religious organizations, and thousands of private citizens from all over the United States joined hands in helping to rebuild the lives of Andrew's victims.

The purpose of this list is not to frighten you away from Florida, but to impress upon you that hurricanes are serious and dangerous business. If you hear about hurricane warnings before your trip to Florida, check world weather services reported by radio, televisions and newspapers before leaving your state or country. Do not risk your life by being ill informed.

Weather

Besides geography, climate is one of Florida's most valuable natural resources. Her year-round mild temperatures and almost constant sunshine are a tremendous lure for families weary of the depressing grey skies and mostly indoor living back home. You will discover why Florida is nicknamed "The Sunshine State" ! The Gulf of Mexico and the Atlantic Ocean alternately provide cool breezes in summer and warmer ones in winter. The Gulf Stream flowing near the coast also contributes its share of warm winds.

Florida does have her chilly months though. January can get as low as 41°F at night. January afternoon does not get much higher than 76°F. But June through September are hot and humid, with daytime temperatures soaring to 91°F and nights still warm from 70-80°F. The summer months are also the rainiest, but the thunderstorms can be predictable, occurring at the same time every day. South Florida experiences rain everyday of June and July. The hurricane season is long: June through October, with most of the hurricanes occurring in September or October. As this would definitely put a damper on your plans for a suntan, you should check world weather maps before your arrival as you may have to reschedule your visit. Miami's National Hurricane Center tracks storms by radar and satellites, so in the event of a storm, you will receive up-to-the-minute advisories and evacuation warnings from the local radio and television broadcasts. With the steady track record of *The Saint Petersburg Evening Independent*, it is safe to assume that you will most likely be enjoying Florida's sparkling sunshine, and cloudless sapphire-blue skies.

As Ponce de Leon stepped off his ship in 1513 to a paradise of plants and wildlife, it is all too easy to imagine why he christened Florida the "isle of Flowers".

During the past several centuries botanists have discovered and classified more than 3,000 varieties of flowering plants in Florida, ranging in size from the mighty magnolia to the petite terrestrial orchid.

The gloriously plumaged Colourful Parrot in captivity at Sea World.

Habitats

Florida's vegetation is divided into distinct habitats: flatwoods, scrublands, grassy swamps, savannas, salt marshes, hammocks or hardwood forests and high pinelands. Within these habitats are more varieties of trees than in any other state, such as the oak, pine, palm, mangrove and cypress. Living sometimes to the ripe old age of 6,000 years, the cypress is considered by some scientists to be the oldest living thing on earth!

Flatwoods, which you will see often enough throughout the state, have open forests, 64 varieties of orchids, pitcher plants,

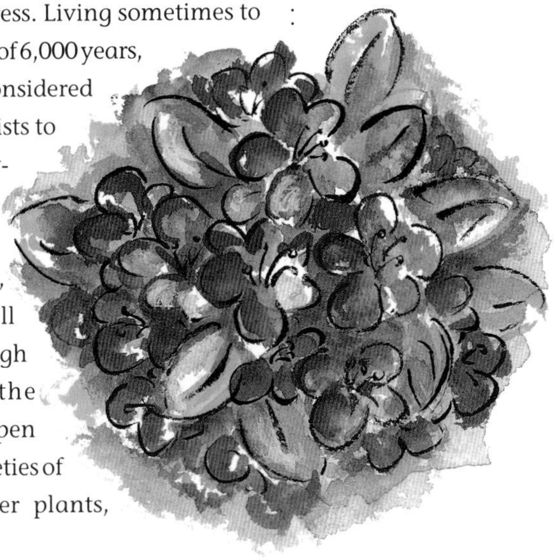

Flora and Fauna

59

A natural survivor – the pitcher plant in a marsh at the Blackwater River State Park.

red lilies, milkwort, and the purple-spiked blazing star.

Scrublands, in Florida's central ridge district and in the coastal sand dunes, has dense growths of saw palmetto, small sand pines, evergreen, live oaks, huckleberries and cactus. In the savannas of Central Florida, you will see water lettuce, yellow American lotus, marine grasses, water hyacinths, Spanish bayonets, seagrapes and cabbage palms. Near the southeast coast is a region of pineland unlike any other in the world. Trees are rooted in soft limestone rock, in a myriad of varieties – cypress, mangrove, mahogany, ferns, aerial plants, and palms.

On Florida's lower coast are dense thickets of red, white and black man-groves. These trees rise from tidewashed sandflats, and have been described as "a forest marching on stilts".

National And State Forests

The best place to see Florida's 314 species of trees is in her forests, which occupy nearly half of her total land area. Some of the most popular Forests include:

• **Apalachicola National Forest**, covering 557,000 acres in the north part of Florida. Primarily a pine hardwood forest, there are miles of rivers for bass, bream, and perch fishing. There is also bear and deer hunting, boating, camping, swimming, and picnicking.

• **Ocala National Forest**, 45 miles west of Daytona is popular with campers, because of two famous springs, **Juniper** and **Alexander** throughout the 366,000 acres. Besides swimming, the park manages an annual large game hunt.

• **Osceola National Forest**, near Jacksonville, has 157,000 acres which are abundant with ponds, sinks, and cypress swamps. You can hunt deer, quail and dove, fish, camp and picnic.

• **Blackwater River State Forest**, north of Pensacola, has 183,153 acres of longleaf pine, juniper, oak, and mixed hardwood trees along clear streams and lakes. You will enjoy hiking alongside the trail that traces Indian and early settler trade routes. There is also fishing, swimming, boating and riding.

• **Withlachoochee State Forest**, 45

Lily pads on the Choctawhacthee Bay near Destin.

Cypress Swamp, filling 2400 square miles. It is not very likely but if you are extremely

miles northwest of Tampa has 113,000 acres of tall dense pines along the Withlachoochee River. Here you can hunt, camp, picnic, fish or go riding on horseback.

And there is more to explore in **Cary**, **Pine Log**, and **Lake Arbuckle** state forests. Cary is a 3,412 acres wilderness in Nassau and Duval counties, Pine Log has 6,911 acres near Panama City, and Lake Arbuckle has 10,000 acres near Bartow.

National Preserves & Parks

Big Cypress National Preserve is the ancestral home of the Seminole and Miccosukee Indians. Set aside in 1974 by Congress as an ecological buffer zone to the adjacent Everglades, the preserve offers sandy islands of slash pines, marshes, forests of dwarf cypress and a few 700 year old giant bald cypress trees.

A ridge of cypress and hammocks separates The Everglades from the Big

lucky, you may catch a glimpse of the state's most highly endangered animal – the Florida panther.

There are no fewer than 50 left in the wild but Florida game commission biologists are experimenting with raising them in captivity. Keep your eyes peeled for two other endangered crea-

A fully bloomed and highly fragrant magnolia in Pensacola.

Birding In Florida

The Everglades National Park

Known all over the world and often regarded as synonymous with Florida wildlife-watching this huge national park covers 5,660 square kilometers of unique wetland habitat. The area is created by a peculiar natural phenomena, the water from the large Lake Okeechobee in central Florida which flows southwards and drains into the Gulf of Mexico in the southwestern corner of the state.

The lake is however only 4.5 metres above sealevel, so the mass of water "creeps" across the pancake flat landscape dropping at only a mere 4 centimeters per kilometer! The result is a "river" which is 80 kilometers wide and 160 kilometers long and which appears like a sea of marshy grasses. This area is the Everglades.

The most important southern part of this area with its associated coastlines and offshore islands is protected in the Everglades National Park.

This vast country is not quite as uniform as it might at first appear. Minute variations in ground elevation dramatically alter the nature of the habitat and the wildlife. On slightly raised areas, islands with patches of tall forest develops. They are termed hammocks, bayheads or willow heads by the locals depending on their soil conditions and the nature of the vegetation. In depressed areas that stay wet all-year round "cypress head" develop, often in conjunction with ponds called "alligator holes" - which are in fact often the haunt of one or more alligators. There is a whole new vocabulary to pick up for anybody visiting the Everglades!

Nearer to the coast tidal, saltwater invades the fringes of the marshes and tropical mangrove forests grow here. Mangroves form a very productive habitat due to the constant flooding of nutritious brackish water and this area is an important habitat for many of the waterbirds that not only feed here but who also seek security by nesting on the remote mangrove islands. The long string of sandy islands south of here leading westwards to Key West lies outside the boundaries of the national park.

The Anhinga in full wing span glory.

The stalky legs of the Snowy Egret.

Timing is important when visiting the Everglades, winter is the most pleasant time of year till April and May when the hot summer season sets in. The summer months are also when most of the 1200 mm rainfall annually falls and mosquitoes come out in numbers. Besides the autumn, winter and early spring is most productive from a birdwatching point of view, many migrant birds flock to sub-tropical Florida at this time of year and they can be seen here next to the local residents.

The Everglades is an easy access location, especially if you rent a car. You travel from Miami south along Route 1 turning west at Homestead into Route 27 which will take you right through the park to Flamingo on Florida Bay.

No, you will not see many flamingos there, as most of the flamingos in Florida are captive birds from the Caribbean Islands which are displayed at tourist attractions as a gimmick! But the park is well-organised with information centres, with rangers acting as guides, a wonderful system of trails into the different habitats and plenty of astonishing birds.

The Great Egret

The Brown Pelican in full flight.

Some Birds to Watch.

Florida is first a heaven for waterbirds. Waterbirds are everywhere and most of them are remarkably tame, the Great Egret which in Europe and Asia is a very shy species impossible to approach within 100 meters. However, in the Everglades it walks along and feeds a few meters off the boardwalks oblivious to the scores of tourists gawking at it.

The egrets can be somewhat difficult to differentiate as apart from the Great Cattle Egret and the local American species the Snowy Egret are also all-white and the Little Blue Heron, Reddish Egret and Great Blue Heron all occur in white phases. The size of the bird and the colour of bill and legs can tell these related species apart. However, there is no way of mistaking the Tricolored Heron or the night herons especially the common Yellow-crowned Night Heron.

The White Ibis is the most common within its family which also includes the Glossy Ibis and Roseate Spoonbill which can be locally common in the western parts of the park. The stork family is represented by the numerous Wood Stork, and the common Anhinga which is often seen sitting in the sun drying out its feathers representing its own family – the darters. There are plenty of ducks and geese in the freshwater segments of the park, especially where there are large pools with free surface water, the rails on the other hand prefer the denser more over-grown parts of the wetlands. The crane family is represented by the Sandhill Crane which is distributed in a patchy fashion over much of North America, the Everglades being a good place to see this large and majestic bird.

In the south and the west coastal parts of the Everglades pelicans are very much in evidence, two species occur: the Brown Pelican which is a perennial resident which stays all year to breed, the White Pelican which only visits during the winter but can locally occur in massive flocks. The pelicans display no fear of humans and can be observed at close quarters when they dive into the waters off the beach for fish or to rest on nearby boating jetties.

The magnificent frigatebirds which are strictly offshore birds are seen flying gracefully over the sea, the species occuring in Florida is incidentally called the Magnificent Frigatebird! There are many different terns occuring in this part of the Everglades and like the white egrets you will probably have to pull out your field guide book to positively identify the different but similar species. However, one member of this family (gulls and terns) stands out as unique, the Black Skimmer which feeds by dipping the lower, much larger mandible of its bill into the surface of the water as it is flying along. At the sandy and muddy shorelines thousands of migrant shorebirds rest and feed during the winter, some like the Sanderling and the Turnstone have come in from their breeding grounds in the high arctic of northern Canada far north of the Arctic Circle.

Apart from the waterbirds look out for raptors – birds of prey of which there are numerous in the Everglades. The fish-eating Osprey does very well here, in parts thanks to artificial nesting poles erected in their prime habitat and very much in use. This species occurs worldwide but you will not find the Snail Kite, also called the

...Birding In Florida

The Ruddy Turnstone.

Everglades Kite, anywhere else in the US as it is a tropical bird which also lives in Central America. There are about 500 of this very specialized and locally endangered bird left in Florida. You are more likely to see a Red-shouldered Hawk perched near the road, and some vultures like the Turkey Vulture are very common. Even the national bird, the Bald Eagle occurs here with a small resident population.

Check out the hammocks and nearby park and woodlands for land birds and you are bound to spot one or several woodpeckers as well as flycatchers, magpies, wrens, finches and many other birds. For the overseas visitor special American families like the tanagers, vireos and mimic thrushes are of course of special interest. For the American tourist from the north it is interesting to note that Southern Florida is

tures living here – the Everglades swallowtail kite and the wood stork.

But if you are a true nature lover, the best place to see 300 bird species, 1,000 varieties of plants, 120 species of trees, 25 types of orchids, acres of sawgrass, and freshwater marsh, and mangrove is at Florida's spectacular

Everglades National Park, along the state's southernmost tip.

Sprawling over 1.4 million acres, the Everglades Park is the largest subtropical wilderness in the United States. Today the federal and state government, the Army Corps of Engineers, the South Florida Water Management District and

the only wintering ground in the US for a large number of northern migrant birds like Lark Sparrow, Brown-headed Cowbird, Ovenbird and many warblers and buntings.

Around the State.

Although the Everglades National Park alone holds enough wildlife to satisfy most nature enthusiasts visiting Florida there are even more places to go to. The Homestead area with its parks, farms and pinelands is good for land birds, even Miami itself has a surprisingly number of birds, check out the causeways to Miami Beach for numerous waterbirds. North of the city the **Loxahatchee National Wildlife Refuge (NWR)** also has many waterbirds as well as Snail Kites, the Lake Okeechobee area just northwest of here is well worth a drive around, watch out for Crested Caracara (in the falcon family), Burrowing Owl and Scrub Jay.

If you visit the Kennedy Space Center in north Florida stop by at nearby **Merrit Island NWR** where you can drive close to Ospreys, Bald Eagles and many herons and spoonbills. On the west coast around the Saint Petersburg Area is the **Suncoast Seabird Sanctuary**, **Fort Desoto Park** and the **Sunshine Skyway Bridge** which are good vantage points to see Florida's famous waterbirds.

Near Fort Myers the **Ding Darling NWR** is well known especially for ducks, the nearby **Corkscrew Swamp Sanctuary** is also rich in freshwater wetland birds. The real adventurous birder can join one of the tours flying or boating out from Key West to the isolated Dry Tortugas

islands, which is the only place in the state to find breeding colonies of typically pelagic birds like the Sooty Tern and Brown Noddy.

More information.

In general American birds particularly Florida birds are very well documented. Scores of talented people paint, photograph and describe wildlife in the US. Roger Tory Peterson pioneered the modern type of identificational field guide to birds with distribution maps and lines marking diagnostic features. His *A Field Guide to the Birds East of the Rockies*, Houghton Mifflin Company, Boston 1980 covers Florida and is still preferred by many American birders although several similar titles have come out in recent years. For the serious birding visitor to Florida, James A. Lane's *A Birder's Guide to Florida*, L & P Press, Denver 1989 is essential luggage, it virtually tells you everything you need to know. All the major wildlife sanctuaries have their own booklets with maps and checklists, several books have been produced about the Everglades alone. For information on accomodation, organised tours, brochures contact the Everglades National Park, PO Box 279, Homestead, Fl 33030, Tel: (305) 247 6211.

For further information on wildlife in the rest of the state write to the Nongame Section of the Florida Game and Fresh Water Fish Commission, 620 South Meridian Street, Tallahassee, Fl 32301. The Florida Audubon Society at Drawer 7, Maitland, Fl 32751 can assist you with information and contacts to local birdwatching groups.

a host of private citizens are working to save and restore this complex and vital ecosystem from human destruction.

Fauna

Florida's incredible variety of natural

habitats are home to numerous species of animals, many of whom are only found here. Here is a brief list of some you may be privileged to see, either in the wild or in a zoo habitat:

• **Black Bears**. The largest of all living mammals in Florida, but the smallest of all American Bear species, there are

The big-billed mien of the White
Pelican at Sea World.

only 1,000-1,500 of these 180-350 pounders remaining in the wild. Loss of natural habitat, poaching, hunting and roadkills have threatened this bear's existence. Living on a diet of berries, roots, honey and grass, and Black Bears mostly live near Big Cypress Swamp and Okefenokee Swamp. Shy and nocturnal, they are not a threat to humans. Unfortunately, hunting for Black Bears is still legal in northern Florida, where some 50 are killed each season.

• **Bobcats**. These 40 to 50 pound feline hunters mostly prowl at night for rabbits, mice, and squirrels in unpopulated areas, but they occasionally raid farms for livestock and poultry. Bobcats are only found in North America.

• **Coyote**. These wily canines eat rodents, rabbits, and sometimes sheep and calves. The females bear 5 to 10 pups per year.

• **Mink**. Living in freshwater marshes, mink eat fish, frogs, turtles, snakes, birds and mice. In the Everglades, mink are protected against hunters by law.

• **Key Deer**. Looking like a real life version of Bambi, the two feet tall, 50 pound Key Deer live on 7,549 acres of the National Key Deer Wildlife Refuge on Florida's Keys, eating Red Mangrove plants. In 1947, there were only 50 left, but protection has save them from extinction. Please be careful while driving through their habitat, as 78 percent of all Key Deer deaths are due to road kills.

• **Opossums**. These marsupials live in the woodlands, eating berries, eggs and insects. Females may bear up to 14 babies once or twice yearly.

• **West Indian Manatees**. Folktales affectionately referred to them as "mermaids", but now they are an endangered species with less than 1,500 left. Weighing in at 1,200 to 3,500 pounds, these slow moving "sea cows" as they are also called, consume a hefty 100 pounds of river grass daily. The Florida Manatee Sanctuary Act of 1978 established a refuge for the manatee, and public awareness has helped protect them against speedboats, divers and hunters. Join the *Save the Manatee Club* by writing 500 N Maitland Avenue, Maitland, Florida 32751; or call 1 800 432 JOIN.

• **Alligators**. Changing little in 200 million years, this egg-laying reptile can grow up to 14 feet long. They do not eat during the winter, but when they do, it is a diet of fish, frogs, birds and snakes. You will be most likely to spot the alligator basking in the sun or submerged just under the water's surface. Alligators are a "Species of Special Concern", since they almost became extinct during the 1960's. Only about 20 percent of their eggs survive to hatch, and so hunting for wild alligators is only permitted under regulated circumstances. On the commercial front, alligators are raised on farms and sold for their meat and skins.

• **Crocodiles.** Found only in North Key Largo and Florida Bay in the Everglades National Park, crocodiles are an endangered species, as only 200 to 400 of them remain in the wild. They resemble alligators but are smaller, with long tapering snouts and two large protruding teeth. Their main diet is fish, small mammals and waterfowl.

• **Gopher Tortoises.** The habitats of these tortoises are gradually being taken over by high rises and boat docks. They have been listed as a "Species of Special Concern".

• **Sea Turtles.** Five species live in Florida's coastal waters: Leatherback Turtle, Green Turtle, Loggerhead Turtle, Kemp's Ridley and Hawksbill. Weighing in at 350 pounds, they subsist on jellyfish, seagrass and seafood. Each year they migrate thousands of miles through the open ocean to reach their beach nesting sites, some of which are located along the Atlantic coast. During June, July and August, walk along the Juno Beach in Jupiter, Florida where you will see these ancient turtles laying their eggs in the moonlight. Local environmental groups sponsor beachside presentations on the turtles during this time. Due to over hunting by man, sea turtles are also an endangered species.

• **Snakes.** Most of Florida's varieties are harmless and eat worms, lizards and frogs. However, keep a sharp eye out for the poisonous ones which can be dan-

An aerial sight at the Metrozoo.

gerous and seek professional medical treatment immediately if bitten.

• **Venomous Snakes:** The Diamondback Rattlesnake, with yellow bordered diamond shaped body markings, and a tail rattle; the Canebrake Rattlesnake, a gray-brown or pink-beige color with dark bands across the body and an orange stripe down the back; the Pygmy Rattlesnake, which is gray with round reddish orange spots and a buzzing rattle and the Cottonmouth Water Moccasin, which is olive brown or black with a dark band from the eye to the jaw. Copperheads and coral snakes are also venomous. It is best to bear in mind that snakes are basically shy creatures and rarely attack unless you frighten or provoke them.

Birds

Florida's population of fine-feathered friends is like none other in the world. You will find many which are so comfortable in their individual habitats, that they may just stroll leisurely across your pathway or alight in a tree next to where you are standing. Birdwatching in Florida presents a rare opportunity to get really close. Here are just a few of the varieties that you are likely to see:

From Pelicans to Herons

• **Pelicans**. You will see them diving into

The pride of the Metrozoo, its white tiger.

Think Florida and pink flamingoes always come to mind.

Alligator Farms

Flavio 'gator wrestlin' a Gatorland.

It is 3pm on Monday at Orlando's **Gatorland**, and time for some good old-fashioned, southern style Gator Wrestlin'.

Fantastic Flavio

Flavio, a strapping, moustached Indiana Jones kind of cowboy, steps bravely into a watery pit of half a dozen, 8 foot long, 160 pound alligators. He grins and waves at us lesser mortals in the stands, and plunges two hands into the thrashing pool: his mind set on grabbing a gator by the tail.

Hissing and lunging, the gator's body language clearly says, "Get your hands off my tail Flavio, or you will become my lunch!"

But Flavio is strong, and fast, and smarter than any dinosaur ancestor, and before the carnivore knows what's happening, Flavio has him dragged up and pinned down inside the moat's miniature sandbox.

"How did I get this job?" Flavio calls out to us. "My mother-in-law sent in my application!"

We giggle nervously, and wonder how sitting on top of an alligator holding his jaw clamped tight and telling jokes can look so easy?

Flavio pries open the gator's jaw to show us 82 very long, very sharp jagged teeth, a big pale pink tongue and a mouth that only a dentist could love.

"Your mother's a handbag," Flavio slyly teases his wily wild pet. (Its probably true as fancy handbags and wallets are sold in the gift shop.)

Now its time for a nap. For the gator, not for Flavio. And certainly not for us, we remain mesmerized in horror, fear and with knotted stomachs, wondering if our beloved Flavio will end up as this gator's snack. Flavio flips the lizard onto his back, and gently strokes his stomach. Up and down, fingers tapping the bulging belly.

"Rock a bye baby, in the tree tops," he croons, a modern Romeo to a prehistoric Juliet.

The gator does not move a muscle. We hold our breath. Can he really be asleep? Or is he waiting for just the perfect moment to lunge at Flavio, and then unleash his fury and devour us all?

Flavio chuckles and tickles the gator's scaly ribs. Like a lazy couch potato watching Sunday afternoon football, he slowly rolls over and silently slithers back into his watery womb.

Screaming with delight and relief, we applaud our hero, who graciously smiles, removes his ten gallon hat, and takes a bow. (Gatorland is one of Florida's largest alligator farms, serving as a breeding and research center for 5,000 alligators and set on 55 acres). The farm also has monkeys, snakes, deer, goats, bears, birds, Pink Flamingos, and Albert, a 300 pound tortoise.

Open daily all year-round at 14501 South Orange Blossom Trail (US 441) Orlando, Florida 32837. Tel: (407) 855 5496.

The Yellow-crowned Night Heron.

the Great Blue Heron, Great White Heron, and of course the delightful shocking Pink Flamingo. They mostly live in shallow bays and mangrove islands and subsist on a diet of fish and frogs. The **Great White Heron National Wildlife Refuge** and the **Key West Natural Wildlife Refuge** has provided them with protection.

the sea along the coast whilst gulping a fish dinner into their roomy swinging pouches. The aggressive pelican also waddles along fishing docks, squawking and begging for bait and fish scraps. Pelicans are a "Species of Special Concern", having declined in recent years from insecticides that ruin the walls of their eggs before they can hatch. Near the town of Sebastian along the Indian River is Pelican Island, the nation's oldest wildlife sanctuary, where pelicans have happily lived since 1905 on 7,000 acres.

- **Cranes**. A graceful creature four feet tall, with a 6-foot wingspan. Females lay two-buff colored eggs in grassy marshland nests. Cranes are a threatened species.

- **Eagles**. Thanks to environmentalists and American Bald Eagle lovers, the population of national bird is increasing in number. Eagles are regal in manner. Of the 1,000 southern Bald Eagles remaining, 700 live in Florida. With a wingspan of almost 7 feet, they thrive on fish and waterfowl.

- **Herons**. Florida has several including

Owls & Ospreys

- **Osprey**. With a dark band across its

The predatory stare of the sleek puma.

Cattle Country

US Route 192 in Kissimmee is an urban sprawl of cheap motels, strip malls, tee-shirt shops, and boxy condominiums, all jammed cheek-to-cheek with barely a wedge of grass in between. But, if you examine the 192 highway sign, you will see that the strip of asphalt has another name: "The Irlo Bronson Memorial Parkway", a tribute to one of Florida's premier cattle barons. And a symbol of a part of Florida most tourists do not know exists.

Do yourself a favor: Take a morning jaunt into the Florida that tee-shirt shoppers never see: go east on 192 to St Cloud and at Vermont Street, take a right until it becomes Canoe Creek Road.

Inhale some of that sweet country air, fragrant with wet grass and yesterday's droppings, and you will feel like you have moved to a different universe. This is Florida's ranch country, acres of lush pastures where cattle munch peacefully and close-knit cattle farming families continue businesses that were begun generations ago.

Cattle country at Kissimmee

The Double C Ranch

Over at the **Double C Bar Ranch**, Leslie and Jimmy Chapman manage their herd of 1000 Brahman beef cattle, as well as their orange groves, a sod grass business, and a retail fencing business down the road. The 3,500 acre ranch was once part of a 20,000 acre ranch started by the Chapman's grandfather, Pat Johnston. Today, they work the ranch much like their ancestors did, putting in long days and wearing a multitude of hats, but supported by moder equipment, computers, fax machines, and beautiful swimming pool out back of their com fortable home.

A typical day for Mr Chapman begins earl in the morning with telephone and paperwor from his home office; then driving his kids to th school bus-stop, back home for more hours c

face, a white breast, and a 5 to 6 foot wingspan, this "sea eagle" flies over its prey and plunges feet first gripping the fish. They frequently build nests in trees, channel markers, or on top of telephone poles.

Another of Florida's "Species of Special Concern", the 1972 ban on DDT helped the Osprey make a recovery.

• **Owls**. Living in holes in open fields or in trees, these nocturnal birds eat snakes, roaches, grasshoppers and rodents. Florida's owls include the Great Horned, Barred, Barn and Burrowing Owl, which has beautiful yellow eyes. Both parents raise their baby owl offspring.

office work, followed by a humid afternoon of doctoring, branding, feeding and moving the cattle, baling hay, planting ryegrass and maintaining fences and farm equipment. Before supper Mr Chapman heads over to another kind of field where he serves as a favorite football and baseball coach. His wife Leslie puts in just as long a day supervising bookkeeping, deliveries, running errands for home and business, getting ready for auctions and maintaining her house, and growing family of four active kids.

Theirs is not an easy life, admits Mr Chapman, who describes his day "as constantly putting out fires", but "there is not a better life anyone could have, away from the rat race, out here in the pasture."

Most tourists do not expect to see tobacco-chewing, manure-booted cowboys in dusty Stetson hats just a few miles from Walt Disney World, but barely 15 miles from the theme park's gates is big business–cattle business. Osceola County happens to be the second biggest beef production county in the tenth biggest beef production state in the United States. And at last count, the cattle population of Osceola county, at 103,000 turned out to be about the same as the human population, at 107,000.

Open Ranges & Grassy Plains

Florida has been cattle country since the Spanish built ranches here in the 17th century. Back then, there were almost limitless open ranges and grassy savannahs where men spent their entire lives on horseback. In the late 1800's, images of the wild west cattle drives, range disputes, outlaws and bad guys, were just as much a part of Florida cow towns up until the 1930's, as in the western part of the US.

The town of Kissimmee once had Western-style saloons, dance hall ladies, gun fights and those John Wayne- type brawls you can now see in most theme park stunt shows.

If you would like to spend a fascinating day "hangin' out" with Florida's cowboys, there are cattle auctions which are open to the public every Wednesday in Kissimmee. Call the **Convention & Visitor's Bureau** for times and locations at 1 800 327 9159.

Silver Spurs Rodeo

Or plan to visit **The Silver Spurs Rodeo** during February and July, which attracts contenders for the "Professional Rodeo Cowboy Association World Championship" every year, and has been featured on the "Today Show" and "Good Morning America." Cowboys compete in calf-roping, steer-wrestling, bronco-riding and barrel-racing.

Farm kids get prizes for the best home-grown cattle and local ladies strut their best "dress western jeans" at the "Miss Silver Spurs" Beauty Contest. Held at the Silver Spurs Arena, 1875 E Irlo Bronson Memorial Parkway, Kissimmee. For tickets, call (407) 847 5118 two months prior to the rodeo.

Of course this is just a brief list. Other Florida birds include egrets, kites, scrubjays, songbirds, vultures, wild turkeys, wood storks, and woodpeckers. Birdwatching in Florida is a favorite sport, so try not to forget your field book, fieldboots and your binoculars!

There are so many varieties of bird and wildlife in Florida. Thanks in a large part to the efforts of the state government which has successfully worked towards public awareness campaigns as well as the establishment of national state parks and historic sites which have managed to conserve a natural way of life for everyone.

Northwest Florida

State Parks & State Historic Centers

Northwest Florida

• **Big Lagoon State Recreation Area** : The sandy beaches and salt marshes of Big Lagoon State Recreation Area provide important habitat for numerous birds and animals. Cardinals, towhees, brown thrashers and nuthatches are commonly observed in the uplands, while great blue herons and many other water birds are frequently seen near Big Lagoon. An observation tower at the east beach area gives visitors a panoramic view of Big Lagoon and Gulf Islands National Seashore across the Intracoastal Waterway.

Swimming, fishing, boating, camping, picnicking and nature study will keep everyone active on the shores of the Intracoastal

Dip into the clear blue waters of the Homosassa Springs.

75

The pristine white pillars of Wesley House in Eden Park.

Waterway and Big Lagoon.

Big Lagoon State Recreation Area is located on C R 292A, approximately 10 miles southwest of Pensacola.

Contact: Big Lagoon State Recreation Area, 12301 Gulf Beach Highway, Pensacola, FL 32507. Tel: (904) 492 1595.

• **Blackwater River State Park:** Canoeing is an activity that appeals to just about everyone and Blackwater River State Park provides the perfect opportunity. Blackwater River, considered to be one of the purest sandbottom rivers in the world, is still in a natural state for most of its length.

Pristine conditions are found in many areas; and nature enthusiasts will enjoy the diversity of plant communities found in the park. Recreational buffs will enjoy camping, picnicking, fishing nature trails, boating and canoeing.

Blackwater River State Park is located 15 miles northeast of Milton, of US 90.

Contact: Blackwater River State Park, Route 1 Box 57-C, Holt, FL 32564 Tel: (904) 623 2363.

• **Eden State Gardens:** The comfortable Gulf coast home of an early Florida lumbering family and its lush surrounding gardens can be discovered at Eden State Gardens.

The grounds, gardens and picnic area at Eden are open daily from 8 am until sundown. The house is open for hourly (9 am - 4 pm) guided tours, Thursday through Monday.

Eden State Gardens is located in

oint Washington, off US 98 on CR 395. Contact: Eden State Gardens, Post Office Box 26, Point Washington, FL 32454. Tel: (904) 231 4214.

Falling Waters State Recreation Area: Falling Waters State Recreation Area derives its name from one of Florida's most notable geological features: a 67-foot waterfall.

Falling Waters Sink Waterfall is a 100-foot deep, 20-foot wide cylindrical pit into which flows a small stream which drops 67 feet to the bottom of the sink.

The water's final destination is not known at this time.Falling Waters contains 155 acres and offers camping, picnicking and nature trails, which guide visitors through the unique plant and geological formations of the park.

Falling Waters State Recreation Area is located three miles south of Chipley, off SR 77A.

Contact: Falling Waters State Recreation Area, Route 5 Box 660, Chipley, FL 32438. Tel: (904) 638 6130.

• Grayton Beach State Recreation Area
Grayton Beach State Recreation Area is located in one of the oldest townships on Florida's Gulf coast.

Recreational activities at this 336-acre park include camping, hiking, swimming, surf fishing and boating. A boat ramp is available on Western Lake. Campfire interpretive programs are available to campers, and a self-guiding leaflet is available for the nature trail. Grayton Beach State Recreation Area is located near Grayton Beach on SR 30-A, south of US 98.

Contact: Grayton Beach State Recreation Area, Route 2 Box 790-1, Santa Rosa Beach, FL 32459. Tel: (904) 231 4210.

• Perdido Key State Recreation Area: Barrier islands protect the Florida mainland from the harsh effects of storms, provide habitat for shore birds and other coastal animals and provide unique opportunities for people to relax and enjoy nature.

Perdido Key State Recreation Area is a 247-acre barrier island near Pensacola on the Gulf of Mexico. The wide, white, sandy beaches and the rolling sea oat-covered dunes make this a pristine oasis along the rapidly developing panhandle.

Perdido Key is located 15 miles southwest of Pensacola, off SR 292.

Contact: Perdido Key State Recreation Area, c/o Big Lagoon State Recreation Area, 12301 Gulf Beach Highway, Pensacola, FL 32507. Tel: (904) 492 1595.

• Ponce De Leon Springs State Recreation Area: Ponce de Leon's "fountain of youth" was probably one of Florida's beautiful natural springs, several of which can be found at Ponce de Leon Springs State Recreation Area. The main spring consists of two flows from a limestone cavity into the Choctawhatchee River and into the Gulf of Mexico. The two flows produce 14 million gallons of crystal-clear water daily.

The spring provides year-round 68 degree water for swimming and sunning. The uplands include nature trails for a leisurely walk or nature study, picnicking and access to fishing.

Ponce de Leon Springs State Recreation Area is located one-and-a-half mile south of US 90 on CR 181–A.

Contact: Ponce de Leon Springs State Recreation Area, Route 2 Box 1528, Ponce de Leon, FL 32455.Tel: (904) 836 4281.

• **Saint Joseph Peninsula State Park:** TH Stone Memorial St. Joseph Peninsula State Park is a 2,516-acre park surrounded by the Gulf of Mexico and Saint Joseph Bay.

Camping, cabins, fishing, hiking, a boat ramp and miles of natural beach offer the outdoor enthusiast an active day or an opportunity for a quiet rest. The park is also an excellent birding area, with sightings of over 209 species recorded. Campfire programs and guided walks are provided seasonally.

Saint Joseph Peninsula State Park is located near Port Saint Joe, off CR 30-E, off US 98.

Contact: Saint Joseph Peninsula State Park, Star Route 1 Box 200, Port St. Joe, FL 32456. Tel: (904) 227 1327.

Central Panhandle

• **Maclay State Gardens:** Alfred B Maclay State Gardens is located in the Tallahassee hills, five-and-one-half miles north of the Florida State Capitol.

The ornamental gardens are the creation of Alfred B and Louise Maclay, who purchased this land in 1923 while visiting the

• **Tallahassee Area**. After the death of her husband in 1944, Mrs. Maclay undertook his dream of creating an ornamental garden for public viewing. The land was donated to the state in 1953. The park is open year-round; however the blooming season is from Jan. 1 until April 30 with the floral peak in mid-to-late March. The park offers picnicking, swimming, boating and nature study in addition to tours of the gardens and the Maclay's former residence. Maclay State Gardens is located one-half mile north of I-10 on US 319.

Contact: Maclay State Gardens, 3540 Thomasville Road, Tallahassee, FL 32308. Tel: (904) 487 4556.

• **Wakulla Springs State Park:** Edward Ball Wakulla Springs State Park is the home of one of the largest and deepest freshwater springs in the world. The springs and the Wakulla River play host to an abundance of wildlife, including approximately 2,000 waterfowl that make the park their winter migratory home. Some of the state's champion trees are located in the park's 1,500 acres of mature upland hardwoods.

Wakulla Springs Lodge and Conference Center offer pleasant, affordable accommodations overlooking the spring. Glassbottom boat tours are operated over the spring when the water is clear. Wildlife observation cruises are available year-round.Picnic areas, nature trails, swimming and snorkeling are allowed in a designated area near the head spring.

Wakulla Springs State Park is located 14 miles south of Tallahassee on S 67.

Contact: Wakulla Springs State Park, 1 Spring Drive, Wakulla Springs, L 32305. Tel: (904) 222 7279.

Ochlockonee River State Park: Pristine Ochlockonee River is the setting for this 392-acre park, just 10 miles from the Gulf coast. Small grass ponds, bayheads and oak thickets provide diverse habitat for wildlife (deer, bobcat, gray fox and extensive birdlife).

Separate riverside camp grounds are offered for park visitors and youth groups with picnicking, fishing and a boat ramp available.

Ochlockonee River State Park is located four miles south of Sopchoppy on US 319.

Contact: Ochlockonee River State Park, Post Office Box 5, Sopchoppy, FL 32358. Tel: (904) 962 2771.

San Marcos De Apalache State Historic Site: Although the history of San Marcos began in 1528 when Panfilo de Narvaez arrived in the area with 300 men, the construction of the first fort built at the confluence of the Wakulla and St. Marks rivers did not begin until 1679. A museum built on the site displays pottery and tools unearthed near the original fort and explains the history of San Marcos.

San Marcos de Apalache State Historic Site is located in St Marks, off SR 363.

Contact: San Marcos de Apalache State Historic Site, Post Office Box 27, St.

A magnificent old yew next to the equally magnificent Gregory Mansion in Torreya State Park.

Marks, FL 32355. Tel: (904) 925 6216.

• **Torreya State Park:** The high bluffs along the Apalachicola River are a rare sight in Florida and that is what makes Torreya State Park special. Steep rises of 150 feet above the river are forested by many hardwood trees and plants more commonly found in the Appalachian Mountains of north Georgia. The park is named after a rare species of Torreya tree that only grows along the Apalachicola River bluffs. The rare yew tree, the US champion-winged elm and many other threatened or endangered rare plants are found in the park.

The park offers a variety of recreational activities including camping, primitive camping, picnicking, nature study and hiking on a seven-mile loop course. Tours are conducted through the historic Gregory House which was built in 1849 and relocated to the park in 1935.

Torreya State Park is located on SR 12, 13 miles north of Bristol.

Contact: Torreya State Park, Route 2 Box 70, Bristol, FL 32321. Tel: (904) 643 2674.

North Central Florida

• **Marjorie Kinnan Rawlings State Historic Site:** "Cross Creek is a bend in a country road by land, and the flowing of Lockloosa Lake into Orange Lake by water." So began Marjorie Kinnan Rawlings' story of her life at Cross Creek. Her home, where she wrote of her Cracker neighbors, her affinity with the land and her Pulitzer prize-winning novel *The Yearling*, is preserved at this historic site.

The house is open from 10 until 11:30 am and from 1 until 4:30 pm, with tours on the half hour. Tour groups are limited to 10 people. The house is closed on Tuesday and Wednesday.

Marjorie Kinnan Rawlings State Historic Site is located at Cross Creek, off SR 325.

Contact: Marjorie Kinnan Rawlings State Historic Site, Route 3 Box 92, Hawthorne, FL 32640. Tel: (904) 466 3672.

• **Olustee Battlefield State Historic Site:** Olustee Battlefield State Historic Site commemorates Florida's major Civil War battle. Union troops under the command of Gen. Truman A Seymour landed at Jacksonville on Feb. 7, 1864 and headed west meeting little opposition. On February 20, a Union force of 5,500 men marched westward from Macclenny. The Confederate line was formed two-and-a-half miles east of Olustee.

The battle lasted for five hours until Union forces began a hasty retreat. Union forces returned and remained in Jacksonville until the end of the war. Battle casualties amounted to 1,860 Union and 946 Confederate soldiers. An interpretive center is open Thursday through Monday.

The battlefield is marked by a trail and signs along the battle lines. A reenactment of the battle is held every February. Olustee Battlefield State Historic Site is located two miles east of Olustee on US 90.

Contact: Olustee Battlefield State Historic Site, Post Office Box 40, Olustee, FL 32072. Tel: (904) 752 3866.

• **San Felasco Hammock State Preserve:** Just a few miles outside of Gainesville is the 6,000-acre San Felasco Hammock State Preserve, an outstanding natural area. The preserve contains impressive examples of a climax mesic hammock with limestone outcrops, sinkholes, springs and 18 other unusual land features.

In addition to self-guided walks, park rangers offer group hikes and horseback rides into the preserve's interior upon request.

Way down upon the Swannee River the Stephen Foster State Folk Cultural Center.

San Felasco Hammock State Preserve is located four miles northwest of Gainesville on SR 232.

Contact: San Felasco Hammock State Preserve, c/o Devil's Millhopper State Geological Site, 4732 NW 53rd Ave, Gainesville, FL 32601. Tel: (904) 336 2008.

• **Stephen Foster State Folk Cultural Center:** On the banks of the famous Swannee River, this center honors the memory of composer Stephen Foster and serves as a gathering place for persons who perpetuate the crafts, music and legends of early and contemporary Florida.

The Secretary of State's Florida Folklife Program sponsors many special events during the year, including the old-fashioned Fourth of July celebration and the Florida Folk Festival. Exhibits in the visitor's center and picnic facilities are available. Stephen Foster State Folk Cultural Center is located in White Springs, off US 41 North.

Contact: Stephen Foster State Folk Cultural Center, Post Office Drawer G, White Springs, FL 32096. Tel: (904) 397 2733.

Northeast Florida

• **Kingsley Plantation State Historic Site:** North Florida, like most of the South, had many plantations which used slave labor to sow and harvest the cotton, corn, black-eyed peas, sugar cane and

Carillon Tower in The Stephen Foster State Folk Cultural Center.

As the sign says "Don't Miss Homosassa Springs – nature's own attraction".

sweet potatoes of early American life. One of the few remaining examples of the plantation system and the oldest plantation house in Florida can be toured at Kingsley Plantation State Historic Site.

The house was built in 1817 on land granted to John McQueen by the King of Spain in 1791. After brief ownership by John McIntosh, the plantation was sold to Zephaniah Kingsley. Under Kingsley's ownership the plantation flourished. Even though Kingsley was married to an African woman and advocated lenient treatment of slaves, he believed that slavery was the method of assuring the success of agriculture in the South.

Kingsley Plantation State Historic Site is located near Fort George, off A1A.

Contact: Kingsley Plantation Stat Historic Site, 11676 Palmetto Ave Jacksonville, FL 32226. Tel: (904) 25 3122.

• **Washington Oaks State Gardens**
The Atlantic Ocean and the Matanza River provide the natural boundarie for Washington Oaks' 380 acres o coastal scenery. Ocean waves hav washed away the sand, exposing coquina rock and creating a picturesqu boulder-strewn beach. At low tide, man shore birds feed and rest around th peaceful tidal pools. Visitors can enjo picnicking, fishing and walking through the ornamental gardens and along the river.

Washington Oaks State Gardens i located three miles south of Marineland ff A1A.

Contact: Washington Oaks State Gardens, 6400 North Oceanshore Boulvard, Palm Coast, FL 32037. Tel: (904) 45 3161.

West Florida

Caladesi Island State Park: Barrier slands lie parallel to the coast and are eparated from the mainland by a shalow bay or sound. They protect the mainand from the high winds and waters of occasional storms which continue to change the shape of the islands.

The most significant thing you'll notice about Caladesi Island is that it is one of the few remaining undeveloped barrier islands on Florida's Gulf coast. The island is accessible by private boat or a scheduled ferry that runs from nearby Honeymoon Island State Recreation Area.

Recreational activities include boating, fishing, swimming, shelling and extensive nature study along the unspoiled island's trails. Private boaters may utilize the 99-slip bayside marina or anchor offshore. Overnight docking s limited to 20 vessels from March through Labor Day. You must register before sundown.

Caladesi Island is located southwest of the city of Dunedin off the Gulf coast.

Contact: Caladesi Island State Park, #1 Causeway Boulevard, Dunedin, FL 34698. Tel: (813) 443 5903.

• **Homosassa Springs State Wildlife Park:** Viewing the harmless, gentle Florida manatee in the wild can be a challenge, but it is an everyday occurrence at Homosassa Springs State Wildlife Park.

Visitors can walk underwater to view these "gentle giants" in the Spring of 10,000 Fish. Other wildlife displays include Florida black bear, bobcats, alligators and an extensive collection of wild birds. Homosassa Springs State Wildlife Park is located in Homosassa Springs, west on Fish Bowl Drive.

Contact: Homosassa Springs State Wildlife Park, 9225 West Fish Bowl Drive, Homosassa, FL 32646. Tel: (904) 628 5343.

Central Florida

• **Lake Kissimmee State Park:** South central Florida was the heart of Florida's frontier cattle country; and the life of early Florida "cow hunters" is explained at the park's re-creation of an 1876 "cow camp."

The park, located on the shores of Lakes Kissimmee, Tiger and Rosalie, offers outstanding fishing, boating and camping opportunities. Nature students will enjoy the 13 miles of hiking trails which showcase white-tailed deer, bald eagles, sandhill cranes, turkeys and bobcats.

Lake Kissimmee State Park is located off SR 60, 15 miles east of Lake Wales.

Contact: Lake Kissimmee State Park, 14248 Camp Mack Road, Lake Wales, FL 33853. Tel: (813) 696 1112.

Southwest Florida

• **Collier-Seminole State Park:** The vegetation and wildlife of the Everglades region of Florida can be studied and enjoyed at Collier-Seminole State Park. The park's tropical hardwood hammock is characteristic of the coastal forest found in the West Indies and the Yucatan. The rare Florida royal palm is a common species in this hammock.

Many threatened or endangered animal species have been seen in the park, including brown pelicans, wood storks, bald eagles, red-cockadaded woodpeckers, crocodiles, manatees, mangrove fox squirrels, Florida black bears and panthers.

Recreational activities include camping, primitive camping, a 6.5 mile nature trail, fishing, a boat ramp and basin and canoeing. Canoes are available for rental at the park.

Collier-Seminole State Park is located on US 41, 17 miles south of Naples.

Contact: Collier-Seminole State Park, Route 4 Box 848, Naples, FL 33961. Tel: (813) 394 3397.

• **Gamble Plantation State Historic Site:** The Judah P Benjamin Confederate Memorial at Gamble Plantation State Historic Site serves as a memorial to a way of life and an economic system that existed before the War Between the States. Gamble Mansion is the only surviving plantation house in south Florida.

The mansion was the home of Major Robert Gamble and headquarters to an extensive sugar-cane plantation of over 3,500 acres. It was designated the Judah P Benjamin Confederate Memorial in 1925 to commemorate its significant history. It is believed that Confederate Secretary of State Judah P Benjamin took refuge in the house after the fall of the Confederacy, until his safe passage to England could be secured.

In 1925, the mansion and 16 acres were saved by the United Daughters of the Confederacy and donated to the state. Today, it is furnished in the style of a successful mid-19th century plantation. The site is open Thursday through Monday, 9 am - 5 pm. Entrance to the mansion is by tour only at 9, 10 and 11 am and 1, 2, 3 and 4 pm. A picnic area is provided.

Gamble Plantation State Historic Site is located in Ellenton on US 301 E.

Contact: Gamble Plantation State Historic Site, 3708 Pattern Avenue, Ellenton, FL 34222. Tel: (813) 722-1017

• **Koreshan State Historic Site:** The remains of an unusual pioneer settlement are preserved on the banks of the Estero River. In 1894, a religious visionary named Cyrus Reed Teed brought his followers from Chicago to Estero to construct a "New Jerusalem." Teed hoped it would become a city of 10 million people practicing the religion of Koreshanity.

A miracle of nature limestone caverns in the Florida Caverns State Park, Marianna.

The tenets of Koreshanity were communal ownership of all property, celibacy and separation of the sexes. Teed believed the earth was a hollow sphere with all life, planets, moon and stars within it.

Upon the death of Teed in 1908, membership began to decline until the four remaining members deeded the property to the state in 1961.

Fishing, camping, nature study, picnicking and boating from the boat ramps are popular activities. Park rangers offer guided walks and campfire programs according to seasonal demand. A self-guided tour book is also available.

Koreshan State Historic Site is located on US 41 at Estero.

Contact: Koreshan State Historic Site, Post Office Box 7, Estero, FL 33928. Tel: (813) 992 0311.

• **Lake Manatee State Recreation Area:** This 556-acre recreation area extends along three miles of the south shore of Lake Manatee, a water reservoir for Manatee and Sarasota counties. The park is mostly mesic flatwoods and sand pine scrub with some depression marshes and xeric hammock.

Recreational activities include camping, picnicking, swimming, fishing and boating. A boat ramp is available; however, boating is limited to less than 20 horsepower. No waterskiing is allowed.

Lake Manatee State Recreation Area is located 15 miles east of Bradenton on SR 64.

Contact: Lake Manatee State Recreation Area, 20007 S R 64, Bradenton FL 34202. Tel: (813) 746 8042.

South Florida

• **Chekika State Recreation Area** Seminole Indian Chief Chekika was responsible for several attacks on settlers during the Second Seminole Indian War (1839 - 1840). Soldiers under the command of Lt. Col. William Harney set out in 16 canoes across the Everglades to find his hideout. The soldiers surprised Chekika and killed him; the raid proved that the Army could carry the war into the inaccessible areas of the Everglades.

Chekika State Recreation Area's 640 acres of tropical hardwood hammock and wetlands lie in the east Everglades region. Over 100 species of birds are observed in the park including heron, ibis, woodstork, hawk and Everglades kite.

Alligator and otter may also be encountered. When the water table is low, endangered Florida panthers are known to use the park. National trail hiking, camping, picnicking, swimming and fishing allow visitors to enjoy the one-and-only Florida Everglades.

Chekika State Recreation Area is located on SR 27, 11 miles north of Homestead.

Contact:Chekika State Recreation Area, Post Office 1313, Homestead, FL 33030. Tel: (305) 252 4438.

• **Indian Key State Historic Site:** Indian Key has played a much larger role

Tomoka a heroic Indian chief, in a park of his own name, Tomoka State Park.

in Florida's history than its appearance would indicate. Through archaeological excavations, researchers discovered that the island was inhabited by Indians for several thousand years prior to the arrival of the Spanish.

The wrecking (salvage) industry found its way to the Keys in the late 1700s when commerce ships began using the Gulf Stream and Bahama Channel, which lie perilously close to coral reefs. In 1831, Jacob Houseman bought the island as a headquarters for his wrecking business.

The island prospered, eventually having a hotel, wharves, warehouses and a permanent population of 60-to-70 persons. In 1836, after disputes with the larger wrecking businesses in Key West, Houseman helped establish Dade County with Indian Key as the county seat. The island's prosperity came to an abrupt halt on Aug. 7, 1840, when the town was burned to the ground by Seminole Indians during the Second Seminole Indian War.

However, the remains of the island's rich history can still be explored. Indian Key is located oceanside of US 1 at Mile Marker 78.5. It is accessible only by private boat or charter boats available at nearby marinas. Three-hour boat tours to Indian Key depart from Indian Key Fill on US 1 at 8:30 am, Thursday through Monday.

Contact: Indian Key State Historic Site, c/o Lignumvitae Key State Botanical Site, PO Box 1052, Islamorada, FL 33036. Tel: (305) 664 4815.

Coral Parks

• **John Pennekamp Coral Reef State Park:** The first underwater state park in the United States, John Pennekamp Coral Reef State Park, covers approximately 70 nautical square miles of coral reefs, seagrass beds and mangrove swamps. These areas were established to protect and preserve a portion of the only living coral reef in the continental United States.

Coral reefs are made up of the skeletal remains of corals, other animals and plants which have been cemented together by limestone secretions and calcareous algae. A coral is a soft animal with a hard, stony skeleton. The surface color is the living tissue of the animal which is less than 1/16 of an inch thick. Reef growth is slow and ranges from 1-to-16 feet every 1,000 years. The park has 53,661 acres of submerged land and 2,350 acres of uplands. The park's uplands are home to many rare and endangered plants.

The park offers swimming, snorkeling, picnicking, camping, fishing and boating from the boat ramp. Concessions within the park offer glassbottom boat tours, a snorkeling tour, scuba lessons and tours, canoeing, motorboat and sailboat equipment rental.

John Pennekamp Coral Reef State Park is located at Mile Marker 102.5, north of Key Largo.

Contact: John Pennekamp Coral

Strictly a sport for the swimmers among us, tubing near Tallahassee.

Reef State Park, Post Office Box 487, Key Largo, FL 33037. Tel: (305) 451 1202.

• **The Barnacles State Historic Site:** Upon entering The Barnacle State Historic Site, a footpath leads visitors to the Coconut Grove of the late 1880s before there was a Miami, before the hammocks were developed and before Biscayne Bay had a bulkhead.

Coconut Grove is the product of a friendship that developed between Charles and Isabella Peacock and Commodore Ralph Munroe. In 1882, Munroe encouraged the Peacocks to build the first hotel on the south Florida mainland.

The hotel was located near here and around it the community began to develop. Soon, the Grove became one of the most spirited, industrious and diversified communities in south Florida.

A strange mixture of Bahamians, Key West Conchs, New England intellectuals and hopeful settlers built a village that has retained its identity to this day.

Today, the early Coconut Grove lifestyle is preserved in Ralph Munroe's home, The Barnacle. Visitors may tour the home he built, picnic on the tropical grounds and tour the boat house where he built his nationally-renowned, shallow draft boats.

The Barnacle is located in Coconut Grove at 3485 Main Highway.

Contact: The Barnacle State Historic Site, Post Office Box 330995, Coconut Grove, FL 33233. Tel: (305) 448 9445.

J ulia Tuttle, often referred to as "the Mother of Miami", predicted that Florida would some day become the crossroads of the world, an international melting pot of faces, faiths and languages. "My prediction may see far-fetched to you", Tuttle told pioneers and entrepreneurs at the turn of the century, " but as surely as the sun rises and sets, all of this will come true."

And it has. During the past 10 years, Florida has gained over 2 million people through immigration, making it the fourth most populous state in the United States. And contrary to the belief that Florida is full of senior citizens, is this little known fact: the population of over 10 million has a median age of 36 years old!

Many immigrant groups have contributed to Florida's development: Native Americans, such as the Miccosukee

People

91

■ ■ ■ ■ ■ ■

Just the two of you, getting drenched side-by-side.

A conch vendor demonstrating his wares.

and Seminole Indians; Cubans, who've brought their dreams and their energy to a new land; Crackers whose heritage extends back to 19th Century settlers; Yankees fleeing the cold and grey skies of the northern United States; blacks, whose ancestors endured the agonies of slavery; and retirees of all ethnic backgrounds, who come to Florida for sunshine and a new lease on life.

Other groups have found their way to The Sunshine State: Key West Conchs, Greeks of Tarpon Springs, Jews of Miami Beach, Minorcans of New Smyrna, the Japanese of Delray Beach, and Vietnamese, who reside throughout the state.

In Miami alone, more than 130,000 people speak some 18 languages other than English or Spanish at home. Leading the top ten list is French/Haitian Creole, followed by Yiddish, German, Italian, Portuguese, Chinese, Sanskrit/Hindi, Tagalog (spoken in the Philippines), and other Indo-European and Arabic languages. Significant percentages of the population also speak Polish, Greek, Hungarian, Russian, Japanese, Korean and Scandinavian.

Meet some of Florida's ethnic residents:

Cubans

Since 1959, nearly half a million Cubans have fled Fidel Castro's communist regime. Each new year since then has brought yet another wave of refugees representing a variety of Cuba's

The totally relaxed Floridian!

social, economic, political and racial strata. By the 1960's hundreds of Cuba's top professionals had relocated in Florida-doctors, lawyers, civil servants, journalists, politicians- many of whom arrived with nothing but their talents, energy, and determination to build a better life.

The exiled Cuban community has endured hardship, poverty, hostility and prejudice. Criticism has been rampant over their frenetic zeal for life, their uninhibited eagerness to live fast, and speak fast, in Spanish of course, and that also has angered and alienated many of Florida's English speaking residents.

But the Cubans' relentless drive to improve their lives, their willingness to work two, even three work shifts a day to create their desired lifestyle has, for some, paid off handsomely.

By 1981, economists estimated that the Cuban section of Miami, called Little Havana, alone generated more than $2.5 billion in annual revenue. Cubans had become sole proprietors of more than 18,000 businesses in Dade County, ranging from small coffee shops, to gas stations, restaurants, stores, factories, car dealerships, garment shops, banks, construction companies, import firms and fishing businesses. Today South Florida has over 20 Cuban bank presidents, and dozens of Cuban company directors and executives.

Hispanics

Hispanics now represent almost 50 percent of the Greater Miami's population, and other Latin immigrants are also calling Miami home. Immigrants from Central and South America, as well as the Caribbean have created a medley of cultures exemplified by the community's calendar of events, which now includes annual festivals celebrating Puerto Rican, Mexican, Nicaraguan, Colombian, and Central American heritages.

African-Americans

The first black to visit Florida is recorded in history as "Little Steven", who ac-

Floridians You Should Know

You probably will never meet them, but consider yourself lucky if you do.

Marjory Stoneman Douglas,
Environmentalist and Author:

At 102 years young, Marjory Stoneman Douglas is still going strong, leading the crusade to preserve the Everglades, working to save the endangered Florida panther and wood stork, and in her spare time at her Coconut Grove home, writing a biography of naturalist and writer WH Hudson.

Her passion for the Everglades began with her 1947 book, *The Everglades: River of Grass*, which brought her international acclaim for its lyrical descriptions of the Everglades history and beauty. The book enabled readers around the world to become aware of the importance of saving this majestic wilderness.

In 1970 when the building of a jetport inside the Everglades was proposed, She organized and served as President of *Friends of the Everglades*, an organization that served as protective watchdog over the "vast glittering openness" as she described the Everglades.

The jetport was never built, and *Friends of the Everglades* now has thousands of volunteer members whose vigilance insures its existence and protection.

In 1983, Douglas received the first "Floridian of the Year" award, commending her "as one who could make things happen without necessarily having the tools of power on hand."

Today, Florida's State Department of Natural Resources Building in Tallahassee bears her name and Governor Lawton Chiles has decreed her April 7th birthday as the start of a two week state celebration of environmental awareness. The tribute is called appropriately enough, "Plant a Tree for Marjory."

Her reaction to all this honor? "How lovely!" So if you can plant a tree, do it.

Carlos J Arboleya
Banker and Civic Leader:

Arboleya is proof that the American Dream of freedom and opportunity is alive and well.

Although his father was a Cuban watchmaker, Arboleya's family encouraged him to pursue his dreams of becoming a banker. Through hard work and determination, he worked his way up to becoming Chief Auditor in the comptroller's division at Cuba's largest bank. However, Castro's confiscation of Cuban banks forced Mr Arboleya to resign his position and leave the country.

He arrived in Miami with only $40 in his pocket. In spite of his substantial banking experience, the only job he was offered in Miami was in a shoe factory, as an inventory clerk. But, this was a minor obstacle. Soon he became bookkeeper, then office manager and finally, vice president and comptroller. This success enabled him to return to banking where he became Vice-President of Miami's Boulevard National Bank. He then joined Fidelity National Bank where he achieved the honor of becoming the first naturalized Cuban exile to become President and Chief Executive Officer of a national bank in the United States.

He then served as President, Chairman and CEO of Flagler State Bank; served as President and Director of Barnett Bank and today is Vice Chairman of Barnett Bank.

What further distinguishes him is the enormous energy and leadership he has given to civic and community activities such as boy scouts, junior achievement, boys clubs, YMCA and dozens of others. For his work with young people he has received Scouting's highest award–the Silver Beaver- and the St George Award–the Catholic Church's highest award.

For his efforts in the field of education, he received the prestigious Horatio Alger Award in 1976. His inspiring rags to riches story is featured in elementary and junior high school textbooks and educational films. Listing all his awards would take its own book.

But when you are walking along Miami's SW 8th Street, take a look at the street sign which also says, "Carlos J Arboleya Boulevard," in tribute to a man who made the American Dream come true for himself, for his family, and for those young people whose lives he continues to touch.

Kenneth Worcester Dow
Art Collector And Benefactor:

Eighty-one year old ponytailed Kenneth Worcester Dow gives new meaning to the word collector. For over 50 years, Dow has travelled the world collecting exquisite paintings, sculpture and decorative arts. He also fell in love with the beautiful city of Saint Augustine, and bought 10 historic houses in the downtown center. This is a man who knows what he likes and buys whatever he likes.

Today he lives in the charming Prince Murat House in S aint Augustine's old quarter, a building once occupied by the nephew of Napoleon Bonaparte and visited by Ralph Waldo Emerson in 1827. Tour bus operators passing the house everyday like to say that descendants of the prince still live in the house, which is not entirely accurate.

Although not related to royalty, he is a "prince" in the true meaning of the word. In 1989, he bequeathed his entire collection, including the 10 St Augustine houses, to the Museum of Arts and Sciences in Daytona Beach. So instead of keeping it all to himself, he has chosen to share his incredible collection of porcelain, pottery, bronze sculpture, paintings and furniture at the Museum in Daytona.

"I just buy the things I like, and I guess I have a good eye," he modestly quips. Since his collection has been cited as "the most important single charitable donation of art in the history of North Central Florida", we can assure you that you are in for an impressive presentation. It is not often that you get to meet a collector of such note, but as he is often busy at the Daytona Museum, say hello to him if you see an energetic gentleman with a moustache and a ponytail.

Bern Laxer
Restauranteur Extraordinaire:
Imagine a restaurant owner so obsessed with perfection that he designs the bread trays, the soup bowls, even creates and test tastes the recipe for his restaurant's home-made banana ice cream.

"Good is not good enough," says Bern Laxer, owner of **Bern's Steak House** in Tampa. "Very good is not good enough. Excellent is not good enough. It is only good enough when its good

enough for me."

Is he ever satisfied? Only if you have the best meal of your life. And come back for another one. It must be working, because they are all standing in line at Bern's Steak House. And although owner Laxer dresses like a high school janitor, his management style is strictly Chief Executive Officer. Called the "Frank Sinatra"of the restaurant industry, he does things his way, whether it is deciding how many cherries go into Black Forest cake or the precise way a waiter should carry a tray. In fact he only hires waiters without experience, so he can train them- HIS way.

Despite his militaristic style, it seems apparent that Mr Laxer's way has turned out to be the best way for his customers, who have been returning to Bern's Steak House again and again ever since it was just a sandwich shop back in the mid 1950s. Renowned for its steak, wine and atmosphere, the restaurant has won Florida's **Trend Magazine's** "Golden Spoon Award" for 24 of the contest's 25 years.

Mr Laxer's business philosophy sounds like a copy from a MBA textbook: Pay attention to the details, make everything the best it can be and give the customer a fair deal. Easy to say, hard to do.

But success is a result of obsession with details, like serving bottles of beer kept cool in a tank of ice water; serving seafood that is caught fresh from one of his kitchen's four 2,000 gallon tanks; serving organic vegetables harvested from Mr. Laxer's own farm, and offering diners a wine book that has more than 7,000 selections priced from $14 to $10,000. If you cannot find the wine that you want in that book, it probably does not exist. (But Laxer will make it for you!)

On request, he is delighted to give you a personal tour of his state of the art kitchen and tell you everything you ever wanted to know, more than you ever wanted to know in fact. But, this is his world and he is an inventor who drives himself and everybody else a little crazy in striving toward perfection.

But it is all for your culinary pleasure, so relax and enjoy Bern Laxer, a Florida treasure who aims to please.

…Floridians You Should Know

Dale Shields
Pelican Man:

It was his failing heart that enabled Dale Shields to fall in love with pelicans.

In 1992, after 25 years in the Midwest car business, Mr. Shields was forced to retire because of heart trouble. He went to Sarasota to mope.

"While fishing at the dock, I saw a pelican lying motionless on the shore. I was feeling sorry for myself, when it slowly blinked an eye at me".

He took the near dead pelican home for some TLC (tender loving care), and soon "George" was healthy again, walking on the beach and flying out to join Shields in his fishing boat.

Dale Shields had helped a single pelican, and in the process found a new lease on his own life. Learning that nine out of 10 pelicans become injured during their lives, he decided that he was the man to rehabilitate them.

In 1985 Shields founded the **Pelican Man's Bird Sanctuary Inc** to rescue and rehabilitate injured pelicans. In 1988, the two acre sanctuary of cages was built on City Island in Sarasota. In 1991, some 6,000 hawks, owls and pelicans were cared for by Shields and his 233 volunteers. They are able to save 95 percent of the pelicans they rescue, which he attributes to the hardiness of the birds. The "enemy is not nature", says the Pelican Man, "the enemy is man. We've encroached on them in every way".

Aside from economic development, our carelessness with fishing lines, pesticides, pollution and fast boats are problems that pelicans must contend with.

Today, thousands of visitors stop at the Sanctuary to visit the recovering pelicans and learn how they can prevent their injury. The educational center holds lectures and demonstrations, which are especially popular with schoolchildren. As we learn more about these precious birds, hopefully fewer pelicans will be injured. But for those that are, Dale Shields. The Pelican Man, welcomes them with open arms and a compassionate heart.

Carrie Meek
Congresswoman:

Who would dream that the granddaughter of a slave and the daughter of a sharecropper could grow up to be a voice in Congress?

From childhood to adulthood, Carrie Meek carried her dreams with her. From sharecropper's daughter to college administrator, to state lawmaker, her perseverance and determination made her dreams come true. In 1992, she was elected to the United States Congress, becoming the first African-American to go to Congress from Florida since Reconstruction some 125 years ago, and the first ever Black woman so elected.

The youngest of 12 children, 66 year old Carrie Meek grew up during the era of segregation, when Blacks were forced to attend separate schools, eat in separate restaurants and drink water from marked fountains. Racism and discrimination touched her own family: her own brother Leroy was shot dead by a white store owner during an argument.

All these experiences made an indelible impression on making her want to dedicate her life to making changes for the good.

After she graduated from Florida's A&M University, no Florida graduate school would admit blacks, so she went to the University of Michigan for her Masters Degree and returned to Daytona Beach to teach at Bethune-Cookman College.

Mary McLeod Bethune, the College's renowned founder, inspired her to "fight for just causes", which she did by working on a federal government appointed committee to plan the remodeling of the inner city–The Model City Program.

"Learning to be competitive, to make deci-

companied Narvaez on his 1527 expedition to Florida. Most Spanish expeditions into Florida had black soldiers, and under Spanish rule blacks lived life fairly freely, as skilled artisans and craftsmen. Both Pensacola and Saint Augustine even permitted intermarriage among Blacks and Spanish.

sions, and to interact with the grassroots people" prepared her for politics she notes.

In 1979, she became one of the first two African-Americans in 95 years to serve in Florida's Senate, a position she held for 13 years. She pushed through more than 60 pieces of legislation to improve public education, health care, affordable housing, civil rights, human services, the environment and women's empowerment.

Now as a newly elected Congresswoman, she plans to focus on creating jobs, fighting for affordable housing, universal health care, fighting for better immigration policies, crime prevention, and issues relevant to the advancement of women.

"I have a full plate ahead of me," says Congresswoman Meeks, "but I feel blessed, challenged, and determined to improve the situation".

Gloria Estefan
Singer/Songwriter Superstar:

You cannot go anywhere in Florida without hearing *Gloria Estefan & Miami Sound Machine.* Their catchy blend of pop, rock, dance and Latin rhythms are part of daily life, blaring out from car radios, boom boxes, clothing stores, shopping mall speakers, MTV music videos and featured at any live performance of any importance.

Songs like "Conga", "Words Get in the Way", and "Rhythm is Gonna Get You" are so delightful, so hypnotic that whatever you are doing you have just got to stop doing it and dance.

Gloria was born in Cuba, but came to the United States with her family when she was two years old. Her father took part in the Bay of Pigs Invasion and was captured and imprisoned in Cuba for over two years. Upon his return, Jose Fajardo served the US Army in Vietnam until 1968.

Her father developed a degenerative neurological disease attributed to Agent Orange, and was bedridden for 12 years until his death. This devastating experience for her and her family was influential in creating her singing career. She turned her heartbreak into music. At first she would only sing for her grandmother, but another Cuban emigre named Emilio Estefan coaxed her into performing with his band, the *Miami Latin Boys.*

She graduated from the University of Miami in 1978, married Emilio, and **Miami Sound Machine** was born.

In the first half of the 1980s they played to standing room only throughout Florida. But things really took off when their 1985 hit "Conga" became a top dance tune at clubs around the United States. And their 1985 Epic album *Primitive Love,* was the beginning of national and international superstardom. The album went double platinum, and was followed by "Let it Loose" (1987) and "Cuts Both Ways" (1989), both of which also went double platinum.

In 1990, she was severely injured in a bus accident, which left her unable to walk for almost one year. She had to endure operations on her spinal cord and underwent intensive physical therapy. However, her childhood experience in overcoming tragedy and pain created a gifted artist not easily deterred. Her spirituality and determination, coupled with the support of her family and the thousands of fans who love her, enabled her to recover within a miraculously brief time.

In 1991, she "used everybody's prayers, feeling that energy focused on me" to produce a new album, *Into the Light,* which she says is "about the love between human beings, the power of collective goodness, and the power of light."

So when you hear the *Miami Sound Machine,* crank it up, way up. And plug into that powerful light.

The Seminole Indians were tolerant as well, demanding little of the runaway black slaves who lived among them. By 1838, of the 1400 blacks living in Florida's swampland with the Seminoles, only 200 of them were slaves, and their only obligation to their masters was to make an annual contribution of corn to

The wacky and whimsical
Floridian!

the farm owner. One runaway named Abraham, proved himself so invaluable to the Seminoles he was freed, and went on to serve as advisor to Chief Micanopy, and later became a leader in the Second Seminole War.

The years of discrimination and segregation against the blacks began in the 1840's when white Florida farmers passed laws requiring all free blacks to have white guardians. Free black sailors had to remain on board ships in Florida ports. When the Civil War broke out, 1200 Florida blacks joined the Union Army, but more than 60,000 slaves still worked for their master's plantations.

After the War, blacks enjoyed an era of new liberalism. Some 19 free blacks served on the state legislature, and Jonathan C Gibbs was appointed Florida's 1868 Secretary of State.

In 1896, Standard Oil millionaire and industrialist Henry Flagler decided to extend his popular East Coast Railway south to what would become the city of Miami. He called on builder John Sewell and his "black artillery" as they were known, who broke ground on the site which foreshadowed Miami's destiny as a tourism mecca. Later that year a group of liberated blacks formed the "colored Board of Trade", to encourage the development of black owned businesses in Miami's Overtown neighborhood.

By the 1940's Overtown became renowned for the major African-Americans brought music and magic to neighborhood nightclubs: Nat King Cole, Cab Calloway, Billie Holiday, Ella Fitzgerald, and Louis Armstrong, all put Overtown's N W Second Avenue on the map as "Little Broadway." The town of Eatonville ran newspaper ads encouraging blacks to "solve the great race problem by securing a home in Eatonville, Florida, a Negro city governed by Negroes."

But discrimination in Florida and the rest of the United States was still alive and well in the 50's and 60's, with bus boycotts in Tallahassee, and demonstrations in Daytona Beach, Jacksonville, and Saint Augustine. Blacks were subjected to humiliating fights over their right to eat at lunch counters and to sit in the front of public buses.

The totally romantic Floridian!

By the 1970's African-Americans were again making political strides, with Jesse J McCrary Jr's appointment as 1978 Secretary of State. Other African-Americans were appointed by Governor Reubin Askew to the state Cabinet, the state Supreme Court, the University Board of Regents, and other important government departments.

From 1950 to 1980, the number of blacks in Florida shot from 600,000 to 1.3 million, making the state sixth in the US in total African-American population. Today Florida's blacks reside for the most part in Jacksonville, Fort Lauderdale, Miami, Orlando, Saint Petersburg, Tampa and Pensacola.

In Tallahassee, thousands of black students attend Florida A&M University, graduating to go on to the business, education and government careers of their choice. Many feel that despite the century of segregation, racism and poverty, they and their families have endured, Florida is still home, and a place where they can realize dreams.

The Black Archives, History and Research Foundation of South Florida holds the records of black contributions to Florida. The Archives have established Dade Country's Black Heritage Trail, and have plans to restore the historic Lyric Theater to recreate Overtown's glory days.

Every year the African Heritage Cultural Arts Center in Liberty City sponsors "Kwanza", the African Thanksgiving Celebration, featuring music, dance, drama and visual arts. February is Black Heritage Month, a celebration of African-American theater, music, poetry and art. And 1994 will mark the sixth anniversary of the South Florida Black Film Festival, with black celebrities such as actor Danny Glover and director Spike Lee. For African-Americans with education, ambition and a willingness to persevere, Florida is a land of opportunity.

Native Americans

Florida's Native Americans are divided into two tribes: the Seminoles, a Creek word meaning "wild" or "ones apart"; and the Miccosukee. The Seminoles live and work mainly on the 42,278 acres Big Cypress reservation, the 35,000 acres Brighton reservation, northwest of Lake Okeechobee; and on a small area in Hollywood, Florida. Miccosukees live on the Tamiami Trail and Alligator Alley reservations, although some have moved to Miami's suburbs.

Since Chief Billy Bowlegs and 3,000 other Native Americans were forced to leave their Florida homes in the late 1800's, Florida's Indians have had to fight for land, respect, and the right to achieve success and prosperity.

The Brighton, Big Cypress and Hollywood Creeks organized into the Seminole Tribe of Florida in 1957; the Miccosukees formed a separate political body in 1962. Each tribe continues to battle with the US Government over land rights and money. The Indian

Claims Commission in 1970 awarded $16 million to the Seminoles, but there has been disagreement about disbursement of the funds between tribe members in Oklahoma and Florida. The Miccosukees are involved in law suits over land claims in Southwest Florida, acreage granted them in an 1845 treaty signed by President James Polk.

Meanwhile, many of Florida's Native Americans struggle to earn a living. Thirty miles west of Miami on the Tamiami Trail, native Miccosukees sustain their way of life at the Miccosukee Indian Village, a commercialized venture with alligator wrestling shows, a restaurant, soda stand, and souvenir shops selling fiber dolls, baskets, bracelets and colorful wooden tomahawks. There is also a model of their old homestead, called chickee, from the days when they had to camp in the Everglades swampland, hidden from government officials trying to evict them.

A number of Seminoles in Brighton have become successful cattle breeders, selling the stock they raise to other farms in Arizona and Texas.

Besides learning English, some Miccosukee children learn a language called Hitchiti in their reservation schools as a way to preserve their Indian heritage. The tribe also promotes their heritage by presenting two annual festivals which celebrate the tribe's culture. The Arts Festival held on the last week of December features native dancers in colorful costumes, alligator wrestling, craft demonstrations, American Indian artists from throughout the United States, and authentic native food. Every year in July, the International Music and Crafts Festival highlights Indian music, dance and native rituals.

Jews

The first Jew to be associated with Florida history was Moses Elias Levy, (1782-1854), a native of Morocco who became wealthy in the Caribbean lumber business. His son, David Levy Yulee was one of Florida's leading political figures from 1836 until after the Civil War.

The first organized Jewish community in Florida was in Jacksonville, in the northern part of the state in the early 1850's. By the 1880's, there were small Jewish communities in Gainesville, Tampa, Deland, Key West, Palm Beach and Ocala. The first wave of Jewish migration from the North was given impetus by the shift of the cigar industry from Havana to Tampa, the opening of the first north-south railroad, and the Spanish-American War, after which a number of Jewish soldiers who were stationed in Florida stayed on, becoming the nucleus of further settlement.

After WW II, with the growth in tourism, they played an important role in the state's economic life, with the construction of luxury hotels, the introduction of light industry, and the expansion of trade and commerce. Another major spur to Jewish settlement in the 1950's and 60's was the US Air Force

Malts, milkshakes, and drive-by diners - an American portrait.

Missile Center at Cape Kennedy, attracting many Jewish scientists and technicians.

Florida's Jewish population has grown to over 593,000, many of whom reside in Miami and Miami Beach, the most heavily Jewish community of its size in the world today outside Israel. In 1988, Ken Triester's provocative Holocaust Memorial was unveiled on Miami Beach by Nobel Laureate and South Florida resident Eli Wiesel.

Gold Coasters, Conchs, Crackers & Yankees

Touring throughout the state, you will hear folks refer to themselves and oth-

The ultimate Floridian pastime - sitting on the beach and be-ing.

ers like "he's a gold coaster", "she's a conch" causing you to wonder what language is being spoken!

Well, "gold coaster" refers to those who live in the prime residential cities of the state, such as Palm Beach, Miami Beach, and Ft Lauderdale. Some of these city folk have second homes in the upper Keys, where you'll most likely hear the term bandied about.

The term "conch" refers to people who are born in the Keys, especially Key West. If they have a family lineage in Key West, they're called "bubbas". Of course, conch also refers to the marine creature living in those pink and pearl hued sea shells, and you'll see the word on many a Florida menu. Usually it's served in a thick delicious soup or fried

up as a crunchy spicy conch fritter.

Then there are the Crackers and the Yankees. According to Floridian autho: Ernest Lyons, "the Florida Cracker is as closely rooted to his pine and palmetto ranchland as the Tennessee mountain-eer to his blue hills. He may rise to be a supreme court justice or a governor, bu his heart stays at the ranch with hi; cows, catch-dogs, and rattlesnakes." So anyone with strong Southern roots whose ancestors earned their living from farming, ranching and lumber milling could proudly wear the Cracker badge

The term Yankee goes back to a nickname the British had for colonist; living in New England before the US became independent. In Florida, the name usually refers to anyone who is rom the northeastern or midwestern area of the United States.

Scots & Greeks

North of Clearwater is the community of Dunedin, established in 1870 by Scottish immigrants. Scottish merchants opened a general store and petitioned the government for a post office named Dunedin, a Gaelic word meaning "peaceful rest." The area became a major citrus producing center, under Count Odet Phillippe, a surgeon who settled in Dunedin in the 1830's and was the first man to introduce grapefruits to the new world. Today the citrus business has disappeared, but the community's Scottish heritage is kept alive with the April Highland Games and Festival, where bagpipes, drums, highland dancing and athletic games turn the town into a huge celebration. You can discover Dunedin's Scottish heritage through a permanent exhibit of drawings and relics at the Railroad Historical Museum. Just a bit north up the west coast is Tarpon Springs, the oldest city on Florida's suncoast, where close to one third of the city's 20,000 inhabitants are descendants of the Greek sponge divers. The fragrant aromas from the Greek restaurants and bakeries, and the sponger's lively conversation in their native tongue give Tarpon Springs a distinctive ethnic flair.

Today, Tarpon Springs has become the largest sponge market in the world, generating annual sales of over $6 million. The beautiful Byzantine style Saint Nicholas Cathedral, built in 1943, serves as a focal point of this lively Greek community. Every year on the 6th of January, more than 30,000 residents and visitors take part in Epiphany, a day of Greek tradition and culture commemorating the Baptism of Christ by John the Baptist.

Retirees

For many of Florida's over 2 million retirees, the living is easy. Some seniors are back in school, others are pursuing the hobbies they never had time for while working and raising families. Others pursue sports, from baseball to swimming to lawn bowling and shuffleboard.

One group of over 60 men and women, called the Silver Haired Legislature, gather each year in the Tallahassee state capital to make recommendations on way to improve laws for other Florida seniors.

But Florida has become a retirement mecca for more than just her warm climate. The state has no income tax, offers homeowners partial exemptions from property taxes, and imposes smaller inheritance taxes than other US states.

You will see retirees in most Florida cities, but the largest populations are along the central Gulf Coast from Tampa to Fort Myers, Fort Lauderdale, Miami area, Palm Beach and Jacksonville.

The US has traditionally been viewed as a melting pot of all the world's cultures, but as one Miamian put it, Florida's religious life is more of a tossed salad. Catholics, Jews, Mormons, Scientologists, Mennonites and African-American Evangelicals are all thrown in together, creating a lively mix of ritual, tradition and individual expression.

Variety of Religion

Madonna and child.

The colorful variety of religion in Florida is testimony to the rich history of this land which has always attracted immigrants in search of such fantastical things as the "fountain of youth" or such simple things as a little winter sunshine. Even the name Florida has religious roots. When Juan Ponce de Leon first landed here in

A church near Tallahassee.

1512, it was during the Catholic Easter season, known in Spain as "Pascua Florida." He chose to commemorate the event by so naming the new land.

Catholicism

Other names bear witness to the deep faith of the Spanish Conquistadors. **Saint Augustine**, home of the first Catholic mission in the region, was thus named because explorer Pedro Menendez de Aviles arrived at that place on August 28, 1565, the day of the Feast of Saint Augustine. The Saint John's River, the San Sebastian, the Castillo de San Marcos and the Maria Sanchez Creek all are named after Catholic events or saints.

Although the Spanish had little success in converting the native population to Catholicism, twentieth century Cuban immigrants brought with them their own distinct form, a colorful mixture of missionary teachings with elements from African and Caribbean religious practices. Catholicism is the oldest form of Christianity, based on the belief of one, omniscient God – the same God of Judaism and Islam.

Unlike Jews and Muslims, Christians believe that Jesus Christ is God's promised son, "the Word made flesh," sent to redeem the world from sin. The Christian view of the world is based on Jewish scripture (known as the Old Testament) and contains a heaven,

ell and a multitude of angels and
oly saints.

Cuban-Americans' Faith

A short jaunt through Miami's **Little
Havana** immediately shows signs of
the Cuban-Americans' faith. Private
gardens often contain small shrines to
Cuba's patron saint the "Virgen de la
Caridad del Cobra" (the Virgin of the
Charity of Cobra), complete with votive
candles, pictures of the saint and perhaps a glass of water to refresh a wandering spirit. Religious stores sell prayer
candles, prints of favorite saints, prayer
books and a variety of medallions and
statues, some with historical roots in
Catholicism, others rooted in Voodoo
and other Caribbean rituals.

Not all of Miami's Catholic community comes from Latin America. The
**Assumption Ukrainian Catholic
Church** at 58 NW 57th Avenue offers a
distinctly Eastern European flavor with
its shiny onion-shaped dome, another
reminder of Florida's rich diversity.

Judaism

Miami Beach has traditionally attracted
a large number of Jewish residents, primarily senior citizens who choose to
retire in the comfort and sunshine of
southern Florida. In 1980, 50,000 senior
citizens lived in the South Beach area,
85% of whom were Jewish. That number

diminished greatly as younger Latin
American families moved to the area in
the late 1980s, lowering the median age
from 67 in 1980 to 44.5 in 1992. Even
though the population of the South
Beach Jewish community has declined
by about 60%, the area still retains a
strong Jewish identity. **Washington
Avenue** is still home to an enormous
number of traditional Jewish delicates-
sens with Kosher meats, pickles and
fresh bagels, but they now share the
space with Latin groceries and trendy
restaurants.

There are Orthodox, Conservative,
Reform, Reconstructionist, and Hasidic
Jewish congregations in the United
States. All are based on the teachings
found in the *Torah* (the first five books
of the Bible) and the Hebrew Scriptures,
yet they vary according to the strictness
in which older laws are upheld. Tradition says that God wrote the Torah
through Moses—who led the Jews out of
slavery in Egypt and gave them the Ten
Commandments. Adherents to this
5000-year-old religion believe in one
God that communicates directly with
his people and follow the doctrine of
"Do unto others as you would have
them do unto you."

Holocaust Memorial

Miami is home to one of the world's
largest populations of Holocaust survivors. In 1984, a group got together with
plans to build Miami's own **Holocaust**

Early Spanish Missionaries

The Spanish Mission System

When the Spanish Conquistadors landed in Florida in 1512 they possessed the same religious zeal that fueled the Catholic Crusades and the Inquisition of 1478. The Spanish monarchy was devoutly Catholic and had just emerged victorious from a 700-year war to drive the Moors and Jews from their land. They sent explorers to the new world with two distinct goals in mind. First was the conquest of lands rumored to be full of unimaginable riches to fill their recently depleted coffers. Yet equally important was the conquest of heathen souls, filling the coffers of heaven, so to speak, with converts to the Catholic faith.

Priest Adventurers

In the 50 years between the discovery of Florida and the first Spanish settlement, priests accompanied each foray into the new land. About 2,000 Spaniards died during these futile expeditions which turned up neither gold nor converts. In 1565 King Philip ordered Pedro Menendez de Aviles to establish Saint Augustine as a base to drive the French Huguenots from their encampment on the Saint John's River. He also sent along a group of priests to set up a mission, settle the land, and befriend the Indians with hopes of converting them to the Catholic faith.

Menedez' Bloody Reputation

Menendez established a particularly bloody reputation for the Spaniards in the battle against the Huguenots. The Spanish sacked Fort Caroline, then promptly disposed of all the men who were not killed in the raid by hanging them from nearby trees. Menendez then met a group of shipwrecked Frenchmen who had been sent to reinforce Fort Caroline. He convinced them to surrender under peaceful terms, then slaughtered each one of them. Three days later, another group of Frenchmen met the same fate at that

spot which still bears the name, "Matanzas," place of slaughter. This bloodbath did little to attract the devotion of Florida's native people who already had a distinct set of religious beliefs and rituals. But despite its bloody beginnings, the missionary system was ultimately successful. By 1566 St. Augustine became the center of a system employing almost 20 missionaries. A church was built, second only in stature to the fort. Within 20 years, other churches were built, priests were learning the native language, and Indians were travelling to Spain to study Spanish and Christian theology.

Church Construction

By 1600 there were more than 80 churches in the mission system, which stretched as far north as Georgia and as far west as Tallahassee. The Spanish missionaries can be credited with translating, "La Doctrina Christiana," into the Yemassee language, the first book written in any language of the North American Indians. All the same, Catholic doctrine wasn't always warmly embraced by local tribes. In 1597, five priests were slain by the Talamato Indians purportedly in protest against Catholic insistence that each Indian marry only one wife, in defiance of the Talamato's age-old custom.

The English Colonists

By the middle of the seventeenth century, the English colonists had captured much of Spanish territory in North America. Although some 13,000 Indians were confirmed by the Bishop of Cuba in 1674 and 1675, the mission system had already began to decay. The Indian population was declining due to the British slave trade, continuous warring and the spread of European diseases such as chicken pox and measles. When the Spanish finally ceded Florida to the British in 1763, they reportedly took the remaining two hundred natives with them to Cuba, leaving the land to the British and the Oconee Creeks, a tribe from the north who would later become known as the Seminoles.

Memorial, a tribute to the six million Jews who died during World War II. The Memorial opened in 1990 at Meridian Avenue and Dade Boulevard with a speech by Nobel Laureate Eli Wiesel, himself a South Florida resident. Built from dazzling white Jerusalem stone around a serene pool of water lilies, the Memorial is a lesson in contrasts, detailing the horrors of the Holocaust while expressing a gentle love for those that were lost.

According to sculptor and architect Kenneth Treister, "the Memorial serves three purposes: to keep alive the memory of the Jewish culture; to create a peaceful place that would give survivors and families of the deceased a place to visit in lieu of the cemeteries that were never built; and to articulate the history and emotions of the Holocaust so it can never be repeated."

Church of Scientology

One of the more controversial religions to have taken hold in Florida is the **Church of Scientology**, headquartered at the former Fort Harrison Hotel in Clearwater. Established in the 1950s by science fiction writer L Ron Hubbard, Scientology is a relatively new religion and claims several million followers world-wide. Scientologists believe in a human spirit called "thetan" said to be a person's true being, reincarnated over an infinite number of lives.

According to Scientologists, thetans migrated over 40 trillion years ago when their planet, Helatrobus, was destroyed by evil means.

Engram Eliminator

Essentially, the thetan's goal is to be free of the confines of the human body. To do this, the Church of Scientology employs an "E-meter," a device devised by Hubbard that works in much the same way as a lie-detector to eliminate "engrams" from the body. Engrams are said to inhibit the free movement of thetans.

Scientology has received a good amount of bad publicity in the national and local media, prompting some of Clearwater's residents to become concerned by its growth in their community. As a result numerous lawsuits have been filed against the Church, the Church counterfiled and the court battles continue.

Greek Orthodox Church

Nearby **Tarpon Springs** houses the Saint Nicholas Greek Orthodox Church, built by the large community of Greek fishermen who came to harvest sponges near the turn of the century. The present church at 36 N Pinellas Ave. was completed in 1943, and is actually a replica of the Saint Sophia Church in Constantinople. Designed in the Byzantine style, with a central dome, smooth arches and a rich and colorful interior, St. Nicholas was built to resemble a jewel box holding rubies, diamonds and other priceless gems. These gems are said to represent the seven sacraments of the Orthodox Christian church.

Like the Roman Catholic Church, the Greek Orthodox Church claims to be the original Christian church founded by Christ which received its mission on Pentecost Day, shortly after Christ's resurrection. Saint Nicholas, the Patron Saint of sailors, was born in Patara, in Asia Minor in AD 300. He was said to be a generous to the poor and a friend of children, secretively helping those in need.

Feast Of Saint Nicholas

Many still celebrate the Feast of Saint Nicholas each year on December 6, when children place their empty shoes in front of the door to find them filled the next morning with gifts and candy. The Christian concept of Santa Claus is believed to have evolved from the celebration of St. Nicholas Day.

Universalist Church

The **Universalist Church** at the corner of Grand Blvd. and Read Street in Tarpon Springs houses eleven large paintings by **George Inness, Jr.**, son of the famous American landscape artist. These eleven paintings were completed between 1897 and 1926 and have held a permanen home in the church since the early 1920s Like his father, Inness possessed a beau tiful ability to capture light and perspec tive in his paintings. The best of thes display a tremendous spirituality an reverence for nature.

Community of Mennonites

A large community of Mennonites car be found near Sarasota with 14 churche and approximately 3,000 adherents Mennonite are a Christian people tha base their beliefs primarily on the Nev Testament. They are staunch pacifist and believe in a life of simplicity an generosity. Perhaps the best knowr Mennonites are the Pennsylvanic Amish, notable for their simple dresse and bonnets, who farm the land an shun modern conveniences like auto mobiles and electricity.

Most Florida Mennonites are pro gressive, and unlike their more con servative Amish counterparts, dress ir modern clothing, drive cars and ever own fax machines and microwaves Mennonites are traditionally expert car penters. A majority of the Sarasota com munity came during the 1960s to worl in the construction boom, but now hold a variety of jobs.

African-American Churches

Numerous African-American churche

can be found throughout Florida's cities. Most are Christian denominations, some are simply store-front churches, others are part of larger organizations such as the Baptists and Methodists. Sunday services in African-American churches are wildly different than services in most white churches. Before the Civil war, religious worship was one of the few means of expression open to African slaves.

Baptist & Methodist Preachers

During camp meetings held by more liberal Baptist and Methodist preachers, blacks were able to develop a religion that kept their African heritage alive. Some services can last the whole day, with exuberance and spontaneity, exclamations of "Amen!" and group movement to distinctively soulful Gospel songs. It is worth noting that Gospel music was one of the first forms of popular music in American churches and gave birth both rhythm and blues, and jazz.

Church of Jesus Christ of Latter-day Saints

The Church of Jesus Christ of Latter-day Saints can be found in Miami, Ft Lauderdale, Orlando, Saint Petersburg and most other major cities. Members (popularly known as Mormons) claim

Memorial Presbyterian in Saint Augustine.

that the original church as Jesus Christ founded it, did not survive its original form, and was restored in the nineteenth century by a modern prophet named Joseph Smith.

Mormons base their beliefs not only on the Christian **Bible**, but also on the **Book of Mormon**, Doctrine and Covenants and the Pearl of Great Price.

These books were either translated by Smith from ancient records or recordings of revelations made by God to Smith through divine revelation. There are over 7 million Mormons and 47 temples world-wide. Temples are considered sacred places of worship and are not open to the general public, but all other meeting places, chapels and halls are open to the general public.

F

lorida has as many festivals as it has beaches, with plenty of events to choose from every month.

If you're planning a visit in January, you would certainly enjoy Tarpon Springs' Epiphany Celebration. Every January 6th, the town's Saint Nicholas Greek Orthodox Church commemorates the baptism of Christ by John the Baptist.

More than 300,000 people visit Tarpon Springs each year for this unique Greek ceremony, which begins with a spectacular Orthodox service, a custom that's remained unchanged for 1,400 years, and culminates with a procession to the bayou where the Archbishop prays for calm seas and safety of sailors with the "Blessing of the Waters".

Bright flags, banners and colorful Greek costumes decorate the town and set the scene for this annual "Glendi", (Greek word for festival). A formal Epiphany Ball caps the evening.

Bite into a delicious, juicy strawberry during the Strawberry Festival.

Festivals

113

Scenes on South Miami beach during Art Deco Weekend.

In February why not kick up your heels at the Silver Springs Rodeo in Kissimmee-Saint Cloud? One of the top twenty rodeos in the nation, Silver Springs is where you can cheer on your favorite professional cowboys as they compete in bull and bronco-riding, steer-wrestling and barrel-racing. Afterwards, The Silver Spurs Quadrille perform their famous square dances on horseback.

The Rodeo takes place at the Silver Spurs Arena, and we suggest you order tickets at least two months in advance. That means some advance planning, but it also leaves you plenty of time to shop for a new cowboy hat.

Florida's spring is bursting with ripe red strawberries and the annual Strawberry Festival in Plant City. Strawberries are served in every way imaginable at this annual festival and fair, in cakes, cookies, pies, milkshakes and whatever

and decorative gourds.

Plant City's location — just 21 miles east of Tampa and 80 miles west of Disney World — makes the Florida Strawberry Festival a convenient, and delicious stop.

Another popular spring event is the world-famous Festival of the States. For over 70 years some 600,000 spectators have gathered in Saint Petersburg for this 17 day Festival. Over 100 musical, artistic, sporting, civic and social activities will give you plenty to see and do.

Baseball lovers will enjoy the Major League Alumni baseball game and a Baseball Breakfast featuring a Major League star. Other highlights include a national high school band marching competition, art shows, auto shows, a road race, and three different food fests.

Proceeds from the Festival of the States go to local and national charities, such as the All Children's Hospital.

There's a Scottish lilt in the Florida air every April as the people of Dunedin don tartans and tune up their bagpipes for the traditional Highland Games. Now in its 28th year, this event kicks off with a Friday night "Ceilidh" (Gaelic word for party) and ends a week later with competitions in athletics, bagpipe playing, and highland dancing. Local beauties compete in the Bonnie Lass beauty pageant.

Members of 60 different Scottish clans from around the country participate in the piping, drumming, storytelling, and sheepherding demonstrations. You don't have to be Scottish to attend

else anyone can think of. The two week Festival features a strawberry recipe contest, a strawberry shortcake eating contest, dog shows, steer grooming contests, 4H demonstrations, as well as top star entertainment.

Another popular aspect of this Festival is the 1850 style Arts and Crafts Village, where craftsmen in period costumes demonstrate unique pioneer skills. Artists from throughout the nation are here displaying collectibles like quail egg jewelry, hand painted sawblades,

Springtime in Tallahassee with the belles.

or enjoy this Festival, but be forewarned — you may return home wearing a kilt!

Next on the Florida calendar is The Fiesta of Five Flags. Each May, Pensacola salutes a rich history by celebrating the diverse cultural influences brought to Florida by the British, Spanish, French, Confederates, and the Americans.

This 10-day festival begins with the Surrender of the City, a re-creation of Don Tristan DeLuna's conquest of Pensacola, and continues with a re-enactment of DeLuna's landing on Pensacola Beach with a 2-day Landing Celebration featuring live entertainment, a sand sculpting contest, and volleyball tournament.

One of the highlights of the Fiesta is the DeLuna Treasure Hunt, in which clues are collected for days on end as participants search for a treasure worth up to $5,000. If you just want to relax, enjoy the parade, concert on the lawn, a living history exhibition, or the traditional flag-changing ceremony.

Every July in Key West, locals and visitors gather for the Hemingway Days Festival, which coincides with the famous author's birthday. A variety of literary and sports-related activities take place, such as a short story competition, an arm-wrestling competition, a storytelling contest, a Papa Hemingway look-a-like contest, and a busy schedule of non-stop parties.

Some people consider the Hemingway Days Festival one of the

Ten Best Summer Festivals in the United States, and it continues to draw crowds from around the world.

September is the month for Saint Augustine's 428th Founding Anniversary in Pensacola. The anniversary celebration is held on the Mission of Nombre De Dios grounds, the original landing site of Spanish Admiral Don Pedro Menendez de Aviles. This one-day celebration features a re-enactment of the landing, and presents a fascinating look into the rich history of the city. High school bands dressed in period costumes are a favorite sight.

November keeps spirits soaring with the two day Florida State Air Fair in Kissimmee-Saint Cloud with a breathtaking air show of aerobatics, and wing walking.

Christmas-time in Florida proves you don't need snow to celebrate with tradition. On Amelia Island, let a Victorian Seaside Christmas spice up your holiday. Activities stretch over the entire month of December, beginning right after Thanksgiving at Ft Clinch State Park, where you'll revisit the Civil War during a candlelit tour of the Fort. Next is the Fernandina Christmas Parade and an island-wide Holiday Bazaar. Down at the docks a 30-foot cedar Christmas tree glows with lights as carollers merrily sing "Joy to the World". Every visitor will delight in the Victorian charm of the Florida style Christmas.

Fort Lauderdale joins in the spirit as well as they transform their tropical city into the annual Winterfest. The festival's highlight is the Boat Parade, a night-time procession of boats elaborately decorated with lights and holiday props. More than 750,000 spectators line the banks of the Intracoastal Waterway to watch this lavish event. Other activities you'll enjoy are the Winterfest Ball, the Blockbuster Bowl Reception, and the exhilarating Light Up Lauderdale, a New Year's Eve celebration complete with fireworks, lasers, and a street fair.

Not all of December's festivities revolve around Christmas. For a different view of the state, why not float in a colorful hot air balloon over the town of Brandon? Over 60 balloons take to the skies every year in Brandon on the second weekend of December.

A favorite aspect of the Brandon Balloon Festival is the Hound and Hare Race, where one balloon lifts off first, and then is chased by the other balloons. A marathon, attracting runners from a variety of states and foreign countries, is another well-attended activity, giving spectators plenty to see both in the air and on the ground.

Rounding out the year is the Miami Orange Bowl Festival, a 10-day run of events in late December highlighted by the King Orange Jamboree Parade on New Year's Eve and the Federal Express Orange Bowl Game on New Year's Day.

Over 100,000 visitors throng Miami during this Festival, cheering on their favorite Big Eight football champions. In addition to football, you can enjoy the Rolex/Orange Bowl International Tennis Championship, the world's top junior tennis tournament, a series of regattas, a 10K race, and a non stop schedule of luncheons and fashion shows.

This brief Festivals Calendar includes only a fraction of Florida's many wonderful festivals. Hundreds more occur throughout the year. For more dates and activities of Florida festivals you would like to attend, contact the Chamber of Commerce or Tourism Department of the city you plan to visit and read on.

January

• *Islamorada Seafood Festival*
Islamorada
January 28-29
Held at the Plantation Yacht Harbor, this festival features the best of delicacies straight from the Gulf of Mexico. Oysters, crab, shrimp, and all kinds of fish will be offered along with an arts and crafts show and other entertainment.
Tel: (305) 664 4300.

• *Art Deco Weekend Festival*
Miami Beach
The magic Miami Beach's historic Art Deco District is the focus of this seven block street festival, which highlights a newly transformed Ocean Drive and includes art, music, and food.
Tel: (305) 672 2014.

• *South Florida Fair*
West Palm Beach

Ahoy there mateys!– A Pirate Festival.

One of the largest fairs in the state featuring musicals, entertainment, exhibits and performances.
Tel: (407) 793 0333.

• *Citrus Bowl And Parade*
Orlando
Top college football teams compete in this prestigious bowl game. More than 70,000 spectators attend the newly renovated Citrus Bowl downtown.
Tel: (407) 423 2476.

• *Edison Festival of Light*
Fort Myers
Commemorating the birthday of inventor Thomas Edison, with two weeks of events, culminating in a Parade of Light.
Tel: (813) 334 2550.

• *BASS Pro-Am Fishing Tournament*
Leesburg

Some 100 professional and 100 amateur anglers compete for cash prizes awarded by the weight of the fish that they catch.
Tel: (904) 787 2131.

• *Hall Of Fame Bowl*

Tampa

The New Year's Day Hall of Fame Bowl brings together top college football teams, a 5 kilometer run and a high school band competition.
Tel: (813) 874 BOWL.

February

• *Everglades Seafood Festival*

Everglades City

February 4-5

This festival is sponsored by the Everglades City Betterment Association and the Everglades City Jaycees. There will be seafood, authentic Indian foods, an arts and crafts show, Indian crafts display and continuous entertainment.
Tel: (813) 695 2555.

• *Around The World Fair*

Miami

February 4-5

Metro Miami's Tropical Park is the site for this extravaganza featuring rides, games, and cuisine from "all around the world."
Tel: (305) 579 2676.

• *Palm Beach Seafood Festival*

West Palm Beach

February 10-12

This event is always held on the second weekend of February and features all kinds of seafood indigenous to the shores of Palm Beach County. There will also be live entertainment and various exhibitions. Tel: (407) 832 6397.

• *Gasparilla Fiesta Of Tampa Bay*

February 11

A month-long series of events, traditional parades, a pirate invasion, 5 and 15 kilometer races, parties, performances and exhibits. The cultural flavor of Italy, Cuba, and Spain is relived in the historic atmosphere of Ybor City. There will also be various ethnic music and Latin dancing. Tel: (813) 223 1111.

• *Greek Food Festival*

Fort Pierce

February 17-19

Authentic Greek cuisine, wines, musical entertainment and folk dancing are featured at this celebration of Greek culture. Tel: (407) 464 7194.

• *Cortez Fishing Festival*

Cortez

February 18

This seafood festival is always held on the third Saturday of February. It features an arts and crafts show with a nautical theme, net–making demonstrations and environmental exhibits. Its highlight is a seafood festival offering the best in the area's delicacies from the sea. Tel: (813) 794 0280.

• *Silver Spurs Rodeo*

Kissimmee

February 16-19

The rodeo will feature professional rodeo cowboys competing in events such as calf roping, steer wrestling, bronco riding, barrel racing and much more.

Ruffles, lace and buoyant spirits
during the festival.

Special rodeo entertainment includes the Silver Spurs Quadrille.
Tel: (407) 847 5118.

• *Speed Weeks*
Daytona Beach
February
A series of races culminating in the Daytona 500 by STP. Begins with Rolex 24 at Daytona , first weekend in February, Busch Clash, second weekend, Daytona 500, third weekend. Tel: (904) 253 7223.

• *USPA Rolex Gold Cup*
West Palm Beach
February 17 - March 12
Sanctioned by the United States Polo Association, this tournament is played on a single elimination basis at a 20-26 goal handicap level.

Tel: (407) 798 7040.

• *Swamp Cabbage Festival*
Labelle
February 24-26
This event is always held on the last full weekend of February and features down home fun with country music, dancing, rodeos, a foot race, quilt showings, authentic Indian foods and the highlight–swamp cabbage prepared in a variety of ways. Tel: (813) 675 1717.

• *Mount Art Festival*
Mount Dora
A jured show with prize money, for best painting, photography, sculpture, glass, and ceramics. About 220,000 art lovers attend each year.
Tel: (904) 383 0880.

• *Coconut Grove Arts Festival*
Coconut Grove
The largest art festival in the US, featuring more than 300 top visual artists and over 50 chefs offering unique ethnic foods. Tel: (305) 447 0401.

• *Florida State Fair*
Tampa
This annual fair held on the first two weeks of February features the best arts, crafts, livestock, entertainment and food found in Florida.
Tel: (813) 621 7821.

March

• *Strawberry Festival and Hillsborough County Fair*
Plant City
March 2-12

This festival celebrates the winter straw-berry harvest with top-name country entertainment, parades, exhibits, the Strawberry Queen contest, and much more. The highlights of this festival are strawberry delicacies and old family reci-pes. Tel: (813) 752 9194.

• *George Island Chili Cook–Off*
Saint George Island
March 3-4
The Saint George Island Chili Cook-Off is a fundraiser held for the Saint George Island Volunteer Fire Department and is sanctioned by the International Chili Society. This event is held annually on the first Friday and Saturday of March. Tel: (904) 670 9810.

• *Pine Island Seafood Festival*
Pine Island
March 4-5
This festival celebrates the largest in-dustry of Pine Island and one of the largest in the state–fishing. It includes seafood concession stands serving shrimp, blue crab, oysters on the half shell, smoked mullet, and much more. Tel: (813) 283 0273.

• *March Carnival Miami Ocho*
Little Havana
The nation's largest Hispanic celebra-tion begins with Carnival Night on March 6, at the Orange Bowl. It ends with the Calle Ocho Festival, March 15, a 23-block party with dance, food, cos-tumed revelers and top Latin entertain-ers. Tel: (305) 644 8888.

• *March Medival Fair*
Sarasota
Crafts, food booths, live theater, jug-

glers, jousting and a human chess match with a medieval theme. Held on the grounds of the Ringling Museum of Art. Tel: (813) 355 5101.

• *March Kissimmee Bluegrass Festival*
Kissimmee
Entertainers in bluegrass and gospel music perform in this event featuring "The First Family of Bluegrass", the Lewis Family. Tel: (407) 896 6641.

• *Port Canaveral Seafood Festival*
Port Canaveral
March 24-26
This seafood festival, held on the Spacecoast, features the finest seafood of the Atlantic. Tel: (407) 459 2200.

April

• *April Delray Affair*
Delray Beach
The oldest street fair in Palm Beach County features arts, crafts, plants, jewelry, painted clothing, festive foods and entertainment. Tel: (407) 278 0424.

• *April Seven Mile Bridge Run Mara-thon*
On race day at 7:30 am, 1,500 runners line up at the east end of the Seven Mile bridge and compete in a race to the other side. Tel: (305) 743 5417.

• *April Bausch And Lomb Tennis Cham-pionship*
Amelia Island
The world's leading women tennis stars converge on the highly acclaimed clay courts of Amelia Island Plantation for this nationally televised tournament.

February is Tampa's Month of Fun

Every February, pirate Jose Gaspar and his rowdy band of buccaneers invade the city of Tampa, triggering a month-long celebration of parades, races, concerts and fireworks. Festivities begin as the world's only fully rigged pirate ship sails into the heart of the city, flanked by hundreds of sailboats and power boats. It is a sight you have got to see to appreciate.

Built entirely of steel, the black-hulled "Jose Gasparilla" is 165 feet long, topped with three steel masts towering 100 feet above deck. With flags flying and cannons booming, the vessel is towed by tugboats along Hillsborough Bay from Ballast Point Pier to the Tampa Convention Center.

Imagine 700 scar-covered pirates on board, decked out in black boots, brightly colored vests, and tricorn hats festooned with feathers, and you have got the picture. The pirates are actually Tampa's business leaders who dress up for the event, and go berserk once they get on board.

Once the "Jose Gasparilla" docks in downtown Tampa, they swarm on shore, claiming the city as their prize and then lead a victory parade stretching over two miles along the city's scenic waterway, Bayshore Boulevard. Do not be surprised if a bawdy buccaneer festoons you with strands of beads and "gold" doubloons, it is all part of the party.

All this madness can be traced back to the antics of the legendary José Gaspar, who prowled the waters of West Florida during the late 18th and early 19th centuries looking for his own treasure.

Today, the Festival hosts more than half a million spectators, who gather on the first Saturday in February for the invasion, parade and street party that goes on from sunrise to sunset.

If you cannot be in Tampa on that first Saturday, the rest of the month offers five other festivals:

February 3-14: you might enjoy The Florida State Fair, featuring turn-of-the-century Florida exhibits, agricultural contests, 120 carnival rides, alligator wrestling and musical entertainers.

February 13: Ybor City celebrates Fiesta Day with dance troupes and musicians, a Krewe of the Knights of Sant Yago Illuminated Night

No prizes for guessing what he is dressed as!

Parade, and delicious Spanish, Cuban and Italian food.

February 15-21: Golfers take to the green for the Annual Senior PGA Tour's GTE Suncoast classic at Cheval Polo and Golf Club.

February 27: Attracts 13,000 runners and wheelchair racers from around the world who meet in Tampa to compete for cash prizes awarded to the winners of the 5K and 15K Gasparilla Distance Classic event.

February 25-March 7: You can taste why Tampa is known as the "Winter Strawberry Capital of the World" at the Florida Strawberry Festival. Good old-fashioned country cooking and some of the biggest stars on the country music scene, make this a great event.

So stop by Tampa in February for the party of your choice. Be sure to check dates and places before you arrive by calling 1 800 44TAMPA, or write Tampa/Hillsborough Convention and Visitors Association, Inc. 111 Madison Street, Suite 1010, Tampa, Florida 33602.

Tel: (904) 261 6161.

• *A Walk Through Time*
Micanopy
Meet Pedro Menendez, the conquistador who surveyed Florida in 1565; a Seminole Indian tribe; confederate cavalry from the early 1860's and enjoy a panoramic view of Paynes Prairie State Preserve. Tel: (904) 466 3397.

• *Florida International Airshow*
Punta Gorda
Features the US Navy Blue Angels and Army Golden Knights in an exciting aerobatics performance. Tel: (813) 639 3720.

• *Sun N Fun EAA Fly-In*
Lakeland
This seven-day event, one of the largest aviation events in the US, features aircraft exhibitions, and aviation demonstrations. Tel: (813) 534 4372.

May

• *Stephen Foster Folk Festival*
White Springs
On the grounds of Stephen Foster State Park, thousands gather to celebrate Florida's early heritage with craft and food booths. Tel: (904) 758 1312.

• *Fernandina Shrimp Festival*
Fernandina Beach
May 5-7
This festival is held in honor of Amelia Island's shrimping industry. Tel: (904) 261 7130.

• *Not Just A Seafood Festival*
Tarpon Spring

May 12-14
This festival takes place along the famous Sponge Docks of Tarpon Springs and features seafood of all kinds, Greek specialties and continuous entertainment. Tel: (813) 937 6109.

• *Pompano Beach Seafood Festival*
Pompano Beach
May 13-14
Over 2,000 seafood lovers sample stone crab, conch, shrimp, lobster and chowders, all prepared by forty of Broward County's finest restaurants. Live entertainment, offshore power boat races, an arts and crafts festival and much more. Tel: (305) 941 2940.

• *Lower Keys Food Fest And Craft*
Sunshine Key
May 20
Always held on the weekend prior to Memorial weekend, this event combines an ethnic foods and seafood festival with a water race for canoes, kayaks, and homemade rafts. Tel: (305) 872 2411.

• **May West Palm Beach**
Palm Beach
Florida's largest jazz, art and water events festivals, along the beautiful Intracoastal Waterway. Two main stages host top entertainment, other activities are crafts, art, powerboat races, water ski shows, fireworks and food.
Tel: (407) 659 5992.

June

• *Taste Of The Bay*

Tampa

June 2-4

This first-time event will feature Tampa area restaurants serving samples of their finest cuisine at the Franklin Square Mall. Also offered will be reggae, jazz and folk entertainment.
Tel: (407) 832 6397.

• Florida Blueberry Festival

Ocala

June 2-4

This festival, held at the Ocala Southeastern Livestock Pavilion, features every blueberry dish imaginable, plus entertainment, and much more.
Tel: (904) 236 2305.

• Fourth Annual Southwest Florida Fair

Captiva Island

June 4

The wine fair is always held on the first weekend of June. There will be seminars, panel discussions and tastings showcasing wines from all over the world. Tel: (813) 275 5758.

• Miami Bahamas Goombay Festival

Coconut Grove

The largest Afro-American heritage festival in the US, celebrating this history and culture of early Bahamian settlers in Miami. Live entertainment, sailing regatta, limbo golf, arts and crafts, the Bahamas Police Band and the Junkanoo Band. Tel: (305) 372 9966.

• Sarasota Music Festival

Sarasota

Sponsored by the Florida West Coast Symphony, this festival brings together top musical artists and introduces newcomers.

Tel: (813) 953 4252.

• Cross And Sword

Saint Augustine

Florida's official "State Play", a symphonic drama depicting the settlement of Saint Augustine by Spanish colonists. Nightly performances except on Sundays. Tel: (904) 471 1965.

July

• Eigth Annual Chili Cook-Off

Fort Pierce

July 8

This cook-off is usually held on the first Saturday after Independence Day. Various organizations and businesses compete for a place in the State Chili Cook-Off. Tel: (407) 461 2414.

• Blue Angels Air Show

Pensacola Beach

July 15 or July 22

The Blue Angels will demonstrate precision flying over the Gulf of Mexico. Spectators gather at the Pensacola Beach Fishing Pier to witness breathtaking maneuvers. Tel: (904) 932 2259.

• Hemingway Days Festival

Key West

July 17-23

This event is always held on the week of Ernest Hemingway's birthday, July 21. Ernest Hemingway spent the entire 1930s in Key West. This week-long festival is held to honor both the man and his works. Highlights include a short story contest coordinated by Lorian Hemingway, a billfish tournament, an arm wrestling contest, a story-telling contest, the Papa Hemingway look-a-like contest and a 1930-theme party at the Hemingway House. Tel: (305) 294 4440.

• *Wira Christmas In July*
Fort Pierce
July 29
Sponsored by WIRA radio station, this off-season Christmas celebration is held to benefit the underprivileged children of Saint Lucie County. There will be a dance with big band sound and an auction. Tel: (407) 464 1400.

• *July Fourth Celebration*
Marathon
July 4
This holiday celebration on Sombrero Beach offers raft races, a volley-ball tournament, watermelon eating contests and a fireworks show at dark. Tel: (305) 743 4386. Also a huge fireworks display in Tallahassee. Tel: (904) 893 0344.

• *Greater Jacksonvile Kingfish Tournament*
Jacksonville
A four day offshore fishing tournament with over $250,000 in prizes and merchandise. Tel: (904) 241 7127.

• *Suncoast Offshore Grand Prix*
Sarasota
Powerboat racing in the Gulf of Mexico for a week, including parades and fireworks. Tel: (813) 923 2721.

August

• *Boca Festival Days*

Boca Raton
August (entire month)
This is the thirteenth year that the community of Boca Raton has come together for a variety of events and public programs. Activities will include the Boca Expo, an arts and crafts fair, barber shop quartet singing, concerts, a sand castle building contest, a fishing tournament and more. Tel: (407) 338 7070.

• *Annual Possum Festival And Parade*
Wausau
August 5
Held to raise money for the betterment of the community and to fund a local scholarship, this annual festival pays homage to one of Florida's most famous critters–the possum. The main menu offers a choice between the baked possum plate or possum hash, with sweet potatoes, corn bread and collard greens. There will also be live entertainment, a parade, a beauty contest, and the possum auction. Tel: (904) 638 0250.

• *Surfside International Fiesta*
Surfside
August 5
As most of this town's visitors are foreign ones, Europeans, Hispanics, and Canadians are paid tribute to through sporting events, an ethnic food fest, music and much more. Tel: (305) 864 0722.

• *Jaycees Bed Race*
Port Saint Lucie
August 27
This event is usually held on the fourth Sunday in August. Sponsored by the local Jaycees, the community enjoys a

watermelon eating contest, pizza eating contest, bikini contest and culminates with the Annual Jaycees Bed Race. Tel: (407) 878 8812.

• **Beach Fishing Classic**
Panama City Beach
Fishing tournament with over $1 million in prizes awarded. Tel: (800) PCBEACH.

• **US American Waterski Association Nationals & US Open**
South Walton
The nation's best waterskiers compete for the national title. Tel: (800) 822 6877.

September

•*Pioneer Days*
Englewood
September 1-4
For the past 34 years, the community of Englewood has celebrated its roots with a festival of food, fanfare and activities. Tel: (813) 474 9158.

• *Augustine's 423rd Founding Anniversary*
Saint Augustine
September 8
Held in honor of the 1565 landing at the Mission of Nombre de Dios, the celebration re-enacts the landing and is followed by a celebration of the Catholic Mass by the Bishop of Saint Augustine. Tel: (904) 824 3355.

• *Pensacola Seafood Festival*
Pensacola
September 15-17 & 22-24

The Pensacola Seafood Festival celebrates one of the city's oldest industries–seafood. It offers a wide variety of seafood entrees, an arts and crafts display and continuous music. Tel: (904) 433 6512.

• *Dupont All American Tennis Championship*
Amelia Island
The uppercrust of tennis vie for one of the nation's top trophies in this prestigious sports showdown on the courts of Amelia Island Plantation. Tel: (904) 261 6161.

• *Destin Cup Sailing Race*
Emerald Coast, Destin
Small sailboat racing gathers several size classes and competitors from around the state and country to compete. Tel: (904) 651 7131.

• *Seaside Institute Concert Series*
Seaside
Internationally acclaimed musicians perform during Seaside's spectacular concert series. Tel: (904) 231 4224.

October

• *Hispanic Hertiage Festival*
Miami
October (entire month)
This festival commemorates the discovery of America by Christopher Columbus and the hispanic contribution to the economic and cultural development of Florida. There will also be folklore displays, an arts and crafts show, food and musical entertainment. Tel: (305) 541

Miami's Latin Quarter:Calle Ocho

If you want to get a feel for the hospitality of the Cuban people then take a drive over to Little Havana in Miami, and stroll along Calle Ocho, SW 8th Street.

Here you can wander past restaurants, fruit stands ("fruterias"), pinata shops, art galleries, and flamenco bars, or purchase a Spanish painting, a guayabera (gauzy man's shirt), a box of hand-rolled cigars, or a handmade guitar. The air is fragrant with palomilla steaks, fried beans and rice ("frijoles negros y arroz"), fried plaintains and seafood paella. Sidewalk stands offer Churros, long spirals of deep fried sweet dough and mango ice cream for dessert.

Café Cubano

Make sure you try the "Cafe Cubano" Cuban coffee, served in a tiny thimble of a cup, best with milk and sugar. They say that one "shot" is equal to three cups of American coffee, so get ready for a major caffeine buzz!

At night the clubs come alive with Latin dance music–merengues, mambos, salsas and tangos; and many also have exciting flamenco shows. Neighborhood theatres put on a variety of productions from Spanish tragedies to Cuban comedies.

"Old" Havana

Little Havana is reminiscent of the style of Old Havana in Cuba: gaslight streetlights, brick sidewalks and shopkeepers eager to chat with you for the rest of the afternoon. Everyone here has something to do, but nobody's in too much of a hurry doing it. You may not hear much English here either, as the main language is definitely Spanish. But, if you know any Spanish, make an effort, the shopkeepers appreciate it. Down at Antonio Maceo Park, elderly Cuban men are engrossed in very serious business: playing dominoes. This is their club, but they hardly look up if you wander in to watch. Just do not interrupt with any questions!

Two blocks east of the park is Cuban Memorial Boulevard, an avenue dedicated to the heroes of the Bay of Pigs invasion. At Flagler Street and 17th Avenue is the "Plaza de la Cubanidad", where a water sculpture by local Cuban artist Tony Lopez features the faces of important Cuban Patriots. And at Little Havana's edge, on the Miami River is José Marti Park, with a waterfall, swimming pool, picnic benches and a small cafe.

Originally known as Riverside, Little Havana was first settled by Cuban immigrants in the 1920s, and you can still see the Spanish-Mediterranean- style apartment buildings built alongside bungalow-style single family homes. Since 1959, nearly half a million Cubans have fled Fidel Castro's communist regime and Little Havana has provided a comfortable home for many of them.

A Hispanic Celebration

Presented every year in March, Carnaval Miami/ Calle Ocho is the largest Hispanic celebration in the United States and the major Latin celebration of the year in Miami. There are nine days of festivities with events like the "Paseo" parade along Flagler Street, fireworks displays at Bayside, "Calle Ocho: Open House"–the world's largest block party (attracting more than one million people) and a special night at the Orange Bowl.

In October there's the Hispanic Heritage Festival, showcasing Spanish and Latin arts and crafts, folklore and featuring live entertainment and international foods.

In May the International Hispanic Theater Festival hosts theater companies from around the world who perform award winning productions by Hispanic playwrights.

The "Festival 20 de Mayo" celebrates Cuban Independence Day, while the Latin Orange Festival on New Year's Eve and the Three Kings Day Parade in early January kick off the new year.

Before you plan to attend any of these events, be sure and check dates and places by contacting the Greater Miami Convention & Visitors Bureau at 1 800 642 6448 or by writing them at 701 Brickell Avenue, Suite 2700, Miami, Florida 33131.

5023.

• Pioneer Day
Mayo

October 14

This event is always held the second Saturday of October in City Park. Activities include an arts and crafts show, a food festival, bluegrass music, and more. Tel: (904) 294 2536.

• Lake Wales Pioneer Day
Lake Wales

October 28

Emphasizing historic Lake Wales, this celebration is held in honor of the Florida pioneers and their traditional craft-making skills, old-fashioned "cracker" foods and down-home entertainment. Tel: (813) 676 2317.

• Confederate Garrison Weekend
Fernandina Beach

October 29-30

Witness the lifestyle of the Union Soldier at the historic site of Fort Clinch. Tours are offered through the fort to see re-enacters portraying the Union soldiers. Tel: (904) 261 4212.

• Sixth Annual Maritime Festival
Saint Augustine

October 6-8

This event is always held on the first weekend of October. The highlight of the celebration is the two-day seafood festival offering everything from stone crab and blue crab to mackeral and flounder. This festival will also feature waterfront activities, games, art shows, sail boat races and a costume ball. Tel: (904) 829 5681.

• 11th Annual Destin Seafood Festival

Destin

October 7-8

The Destin Seafood Festival will include live entertainment, a sky diving act, arts and crafts demonstrations and the best seafood the Gulf of Mexico has to offer. Tel: (904) 837 624.

• Seafest '89
Jacksonville

October 13-15

Seafest '89, sponsored by the Southbank Riverwalk, is a festival featuring seafood restaurants and other organizations serving a variety of seafood specialties. There will also be live entertainment. Tel: (904) 396 4900.

• Floride State Chili Cook-Off Championship
Marco Island

October 14

Sanctioned by the International Chili Society, this one-day event features chili teams from all over the State of Florida competing for trophies and prizes. Winners of the competition will go to California to compete in the International Chili Cook-Off. There will also be live country/western music, a parade, beauty contest and more. Tel: 1 800 237 4173.

• Boggy Bayou Mullet Festival
Niceville

October 20-22

Seafood and international foods, an arts and crafts festival, sporting entertainment, a beauty pageant and much more. Tel: (904) 678 1615.

• Brandon Balloon Festival
Tampa

October 20-21

Everything goes during Art Deco Weekend.

Every third week of October, balloonists converge in Brandon and traverse the treetops of the city in a colorful array of balloons. Spectators are treated to balloon rides, special events, a Halloween Ball, and national and local entertainers. Tel: (813) 251 4115.

• Bone Valley Fossil Society's Fossil Fair
Mulberry

October 20-22

This fossil fair gives the public a chance to learn more about the past through lectures, field hunts and displays of collections. Food and entertainment will also be available. Tel: (813) 425 1125.

• Fantasy Fest '89
Key West

October 23-29

Always held on the final week of October, this Halloween festival celebrate's the city's unique lifestyle with costume parties, top-name recording artists in open concerts, the Old Town Street Fair, displays by world-renowned mask makers and numerous other activities. The celebration closes with the Night Time Grand Parade–a procession of marching bands and over 40 floats stretching down Duval Street.Tel: (305) 294 4440.

• North Florida Air Show
Lake City

October 27-28

The North Florida Air Show is a two-day event featuring some of the top acts in the air show industry. All proceeds go to local charities such as the Ronald McDonald Houses of Gainesville and Jacksonville, and the Columbia County Association for Retarded Citizens. Tel:

(904) 755 4844.

• Guavaween Extravaganza
Tampa

October 28

Guavaween is always held on the Satur day closest to Halloween. Parading down Seventh Avenue, locals come together to poke fun at some of the aspects of life in Tampa and Ybor City. The Mama Guava Stumble Parade floats are the wildest and zaniest floats to be found anywhere. This public frolic is led by the Grand Marshall, "Mama Guava," a spoof representative of VM Ybor's attempt to grow guavas in the area.Tel (813) 248 3712.

• Seaside Halloween Masquerade Ball
Seaside

October 28

This outdoor ball is held at The Dock on the Gulf of Mexico. Participants dress in outrageous fashion in celebration of All Hallow's Eve and vie for best costume Tel: (904) 231 4224.

• Haunted House
Miami

October 30-31

Those who dare come out on All Hallow's Eve won't want to miss the Haunted House at the Gold Coast Railroad Museum in Miami, a likely place to find spirits of the past, ghosts and goblins. Tel: (305) 579 2676.

• Tenth Annual John's Pass Seafood Festival And Art Show
Madeira Beach

October 27-29

This seafood festival will be held in conjunction with a jured art show and will feature restaurants from John's Pass Village and Boardwalk. Tel: (813) 391 3373.

Island Oktoberfest
Big Pinekey
October 28
The Island Oktoberfest is a celebration of Fall festivities, ethnic entertainment and a raffle and much more. The highlight are German and local delicacies. Tel: (305) 872 2411.

November

Fifteen Annual Harvest
Miami
November 18-19
Held at Tropical Park in downtown Miami, it celebrates the pioneers of Florida with an arts and crafts show, food concessions, historical re-enactments, an antique machinery exhibit, livestock exhibition, and more. Tel: (305) 579 2676.

• 26th Annual Florida Seafood Festival
Apalachicola
November 3-4
This is the state's oldest seafood festival, held to honor the area's thriving seafood industry on Apalachicola Bay. Local merchants, fishermen and the chamber of commerce come together to put on one of Florida's finest and largest seafood festivals. Tel: (904) 653 8051.

• Sixth Annual Taste Fair Of Bonita Springs
Bonita Springs
November 5

The community and restaurants of Bonita Springs prepare their favorite specialties and family recipes to be sampled by everyone in this Taste Fair. The samples are sold by the Olde 41 Business Association as a community fund raiser. Tel: (813) 992 8678.

• Sixth Annual Taste Of The Town
Fort Myers
November 6
Over 50 area restaurants offer a taste of their specialties. Presented by the Junior League of Fort Myers, this festival will feature food, beverages, and a contest between the area's waiters and waitresses. Tel: (813) 936 8547.

• Fourth Annual Chili Cook-Off
Pensacola Beach
November 25-26
This chili cook-off is always held the weekend after Thanksgiving. Chili cooking competitions in various categories, an arts and crafts show, games and more. Tel: (904) 934 3777.

• Florida Trail Association Fall Meeting
Longwood
November (TBA)
The Florida Trail Association is responsible for Florida's wonderful hiking trails. Each year the association hosts lectures on hiking, the outdoors, workshops on outdoor activities, wilderness safety, and other important topics. Entertainment includes camping, wilderness hikes, campfire sing-a-longs, square dancing and much more. Tel: (904) 383 5318.

• Fort Myers Sand Sculpture Competition

Fort Myers

November (TBA)

This is a family event where natural art is featured as teams of families, organizations, senior citizens groups, businesses and children under ten years of age compete by building their own sand creations. Tel: (813) 482 5811.

• *83rd Annual Florida State Air Fair*

Kissimmee

November 3-4

Held on the first weekend of November at the Kissimmee Municipal Airport.

Two days of exciting aerial performances by a thrilling stunt jet team is featured. Food concessions are available. Tel: (407) 933 2173.

• *10th Annual Fall Festival*

Goulds

November 4

Promoting community spirits and the holiday season. There will be an arts and crafts exhibition, food concessions, musical entertainment and historical tours. Tel: (305) 258 0011.

• *Deerfield*

Deerfield Beach

November 10-12

The sixth annual Deerfest promises a carnival-style atmosphere featuring rides, games for kids and arts and crafts. Tel: (305) 427 1050.

• *Light Up Orlando*

Orlando

November 11

Orange Avenue comes to life as six main entertainment stages offer a myriad of performers. Over 30 food concessions line the street and cook up all kinds of seasonal cuisine. Tel: (407) 849 2221.

• *Fort Myers Beach Swing Bridge Festival*

Fort Myers

November 17-19

This festival commemorates the old swing bridge that used to run from the mainland to Estero Island. There will be a small carnival complete with a mini midway, food and entertainment. Tel: (813) 463 3412.

• **Cane Grinding Harvest Festival**

Live Oak

November 17-26

This Thanksgiving celebration at the Spirit of the Suwannee Park features a grand Thanksgiving feast, fiddlers and bluegrass music. Tel: (904) 364 1683.

December

• *Ye Olde Madrigal Christmas Feaste*

Captiva Island

December 16

This "feast" is held on the third Saturday of December. With a six-course meal served in traditional 16th and 17th century style.

People will be costumed in period attire and there will be Madrigal singers providing entertainment.

• *Winter Festival And Celebration Of Lights*

Tallahassee

An explosion of sights and sounds, including ice skating, twilight parade, Jingle Bell Run. Tel: (904) 222 7529.

Madness and mayhem are all part of the festivities in Florida during Art Deco Weekend

Winterfest Boat Parade
Fort Lauderdale

More than 100 decorated boats ply the waters of the Intracoastal Waterway from Port Everglades to Commercial Boulevard. Tel: (305) 767 0686.

Orange Bowl Festival
Miami

The Federal Express Orange Bowl Classic, pitting college football's top team and featuring the New Year's Eve King Orange Jamboree Parade. Also tennis, sailing regattas, road races and fashion shows. Tel: (305) 642 1515.

• Victorian Seaside Christmas
Amelia Island

A Victorian spice adds to Christmas fun, with horse-drawn carriages, strolling carolers and luminary lined streets. Tel: (904) 277 0717.

• Charlotte County Christmas Parade
Punta Gorda

The first Saturday in December, thousands of people line the streets of downtown to watch marching bands and Christmas floats. Tel: (813) 627 2222.

Florida in the 1990's is a lot more than oranges, palm trees, and sandy beaches-it's an international center of culture and art. From Miami's famous Book Fair, to Jacksonville's free jazz festival, Florida offers a dazzling array of innovative museums, galleries, concerts halls, symphonies, opera, dance, and theater.

Northeast

■   ■   ■   ■   ■   ■

Renovation of a historic hotel in the Art Deco District.

Jacksonville, in Florida's northeast corner, is a regular stop for such diverse artists as Mikhail Baryshinikov, Luciano Pavarotti, Michael Jackson, and the Rolling Stones. Classical music lovers rave about the resident Jacksonville Symphony, which performs more than 100 concerts each season led by conductor Roger Nierenberg.

Fun and art converge each year during "Arts Mania", Northeast Florida's largest arts festival featuring dance, theater, music and visual arts. And

Arts & Culture

135

speaking of visual arts, Jacksonville was the only East Coast city to showcase the magnificent "Ramses II: The Pharaoh and His Time" international exhibition. Jacksonville's Art Museum is well known for its excellent permanent collection ranging from Chinese and Korean porcelains to the works of modern master Pablo Picasso.

Just an hour southward along the coast brings you to the nation's oldest city, Saint Augustine, settled in 1565. Here you'll discover a glittering collection of 19th century decorative arts, period glass and antiques in the fascinating Lightner Museum.

Northwest

From Tallahassee's San Luis Archaeological and Historic Site westward to the Space Age and Flight exhibits at Pensacola's National Museum of Naval Aviation, Florida's Panhandle boasts a combination of old-fashioned Southern hospitality and a delightful array of cultural attractions.

At the **Museum of Florida History** in Tallahassee, you can tread through time, from the prehistoric Mastodon era to the excavation site of a Spanish-Indian village. Around the corner stop in for a tour of the historic Old Capitol, where art exhibitions are regularly on display.

In Panama City and Pensacola, catch a touring Broadway play, Moscow's famed Bolshoi Ballet, or an Alvin Ailey American Dance Theater performance.

The Panhandle's resident groups, the Pensacola Symphony Orchestra, the Northwest Florida Ballet and the Pensacola Jazz Fest, continue to earn accolades for their artistic excellence. If you're an architecture buff, visit Pensacola's Seville District, which features a rare concentration of Creole and Victorian buildings, all listed on the National Register of Historic Places.

Central Florida

From the natural beauty of the Bok Tower botanical gardens, where moonlit carillon recitals fill the air, to the largest US collection of Louis Comfort Tiffany's Art Nouveau works in Winter Park's Morse Museum of American Art, Central Florida is a world of beauty and art. In Lakeland, Florida Southern College boasts the largest collection of Frank Lloyd Wright buildings ever constructed in one place. Also in this area is the Polk Museum of Art, known for its collection of contemporary works by Florida artists.

Over in Orlando, at the **Orlando Museum of Art** is a fine collection of 19th and 20th century American art. The Southern Ballet Theater is an innovative young company, where rising young dancers and choreographers present both traditional classical ballet as well as innovative styles of modern dance.

The power of concentration – a mime statue during Art Deco Weekend.

Central East

lorida's central east coast is a fascinating blend of high technology and wildfe, existing side by side. In the same ay you can venture into the space age y touring Kennedy Space Center's paceport USA, or wander among birds nd alligators at Merritt Island National Wildlife Refuge.

There is culture here too, in Melbourne, where the Maxwell C King Center for the Performing Arts provides a 2000 seat theater for major music, dance and theatrical productions, as well as a Black Box Experimental Theater or more intimate performances.

Over in Cocoa Village, is The Porcher House, a unique example of 20th century Classical revival architecture, interpreted in local coquina rock.

Central West

You might expect that a place settled by Cuban cigarmakers, circus families, and a railroad tycoon would be filled with a interesting mix of arts and culture. You'll find this to be true in Central West Florida.

The world class Tampa Bay Performing Arts Center and the Ruth Eckerd Hall in Clearwater, feature the best in cultural entertainment with an international array of performing arts programs. The Museum of Fine Arts, home

Modern art and artistes at the Metro Dade Cultural Center.

to Georgia O'Keefe's magnificent "Poppy", and the Florida Craftsmen Gallery showcase two sides of the visual arts in Saint Petersburg. And Tampa's Ybor City provide glimpses of the lives of earlier settlers from Latin America.

Mambo, merengue, salsa, flamenco, would you care to dance? Ybor City takes you back in time to the days of cobblestone streets, ornate iron grillwork, hand-blown glass, and hand-rolled cigars. The old exclusive private clubs are still there, where workers once gathered in the evenings to sing, dance and enjoy each other's company. Today the clubs are in renovated buildings, home to hardworking artistic entrepreneurs, painters, dancers, sculptors, wood workers and writers.

You'll discover centuries of visual arts history in the astonishing collection of surrealist paintings at St. Petersburg' Salvador Dali Museum, as well as in the galleries of Baroque works by master like Rubens and Van Dyck at the Ringling Museum of Art in Sarasota. Next to the Ringling Museum is Ca'd'Zan, John an Mable Ringling's magnificent mansion as well as a delightful museum of circus memorabilia.

Just steps from the Ringling Museum complex is the Asolo Center for the Performing Arts, home of the Asolo Theater Company, a regional Equity theater in operation for more than 30 years. The $15 million Mediterranean Rivival style building is graced by a 19th century opera house, whose interior was transported from Dunfermline, Scotland

South West Art

It was in the serene Gulf Coast territory of Southwest Florida that Thomas Edison and his two neighbors, Henry Ford and Harvey Firestone, formulated plans for a technological revolution. At Edison's winter home, now a popular spot for visitors, the phonograph, the motion picture camera and projector, the teletype, the swimming pool, prefabricated housing, synthetic rubber, and dry cell batteries were invented or perfected.

Today the new Philharmonic Center for the Arts in Naples is a major performance venue, with a year round schedule of theater, dance, and music

t the Collier County Museum, also in Naples, you'll delight in handicrafts like perfectly modeled miniatures of Florida Native Americans and Spanish Explorers.

Perhaps for you, Florida's most spectacular art will have been created by Mother Nature, at The Everglades, a watery wildnerness described by environmentalist Marjorie Stoneman Douglas as " a vast glittering openness...under dazzling blue heights of space."

South East Art

Although much of cosmopolitan South Florida moves to the beat of salsa, reggae, and rock and roll, in some places you can feel the Old World rhythms.

Wander through the Addison Mizner designed ornate archways on North Avenue in Palm Beach, one of America's most elegant and most expensive shopping districts. Continue your artistic journey at the Norton Gallery of Art in West Palm Beach, home to artistic treasures by Brancusi, Matisse, Renoir, Picasso and Braque.

Take in a performance of Palm Beach's Ballet Florida, the Greater Miami Opera, or the Philharmonic Orchestra of Florida, directed by maestro James Judd. In Miami, Michael Tilson Thomas conducts the young energetic New World Symphony, America's national training orchestra. There's also Edward Villella's critically acclaimed Miami City Ballet, where top notch danc-

ers perform cutting edge choreography.

In Miami Beach, stroll along Ocean Drive where Art Deco, Streamline and Modern style buildings in cool pastels recreate the stylized ambience of the 1930's. Or walk through outdoor sculpture gardens in downtown Miami, where artists like Claes Oldenburg and Coosge van Bruggen display outdoor art as part of the Metro-Dade Art in Public Places collection.

At the popular Coconut Grove Playhouse, regional theater spotlights dramatic classics, as well as original productions reflecting the multicultural vitality of South Florida.

North of Miami in downtown Fort Lauderdale the Broward Center for the Performing Arts features two state-of-the art theaters and a community hall grouped around a central courtyard, located along the north bank of the New River. Over at the stunning Fort Lauderdale Museum of Art is one of Florida's best art collections, emphasizing modern painting and sculpture under the banner of CoBrA, a group of artists from Copenhagen, Brussels and Amsterdam.

If you love art, music, and dazzling theater and dance, you're in for a cultural treat in Florida.

Patrons & Creators

Florida is fortunate to count many internationally acclaimed art patrons and artists among its citizens, whose ex-

Send in the clowns...

traordinary achievements have helped put Florida on the map as "a state of the arts."

Here are a few of the state's renowned art patrons and artists.

• **Ray Charles, 1930:** An exceptionally talented musician and performer who grew up in Florida, Ray Charles has been called "the genius of soul" and is considered a living legend in the world of modern music. Charles began playing the piano at age five and attended the St. Augustine School of the Deaf and Blind, where he received musical training. In 1949, he began recording for different record labels and touring extensively throughout the United States. Some of his best known hits include "Georgia On My Mind" and "Hit the

Road Jack", as well as his acclaime version of "America the Beautiful."

His many memorable appearance on television, in films, and nightclub have made him famous worldwide, a have his 11 Grammy awards.

• **John D MacDonald, 1916-1986:** A internationally recognized author fror Sarasota, MacDonald's novels, short sto ries, and articles prominently featur Florida's culture and environment. Hi twenty-two "Travis McGee" books, set ir Florida, are one of the most substantic series in the history of the detective nove genre.

• **Zora Neale Hurston, 1901-1960:**
Born in Eatonville, Florida, Hurston wa a noted novelist, folklorist, and anthro pologist who traveled throughout Florid

ollecting and writing stories of rural eople. A recipient of Guggenheim and osenwald fellowships, her most prominent works include "Mules and Men","Dust Tracks in the Road", and Their Eyes Were Watching God." atonville annually holds the Zora Neale urston Festival, a tribute to her lasting terary accomplishments.

George Firestone, 1931: As Florida's 0th Secretary of State, Firestone has een a Florida resident since 1936. He rved in the House of Representatives nd the Senate before being elected Sectary of State in 1978. As Chief Cultural fficer of Florida, Firestone established goal for Florida to be recognized as the State of the Arts." Under his leadership, upport for the arts increased more than ,200 percent and Florida currently ranks econd nationally in arts funding.

Marjorie Kinnan Rawlings, 1896-953: Rawlings was a well known writer the 1930's and 1940's, drawing mate-al for her stories from Florida's Cross reek and Alachua County. In 1928, onvinced that the Florida wilderness ould allow her to concentrate on her riting, she purchased sight unseen an range grove with an old farmhouse at bordered on the murky Cross Creek. he won the Pulitzer Prize in 1939 for The Yearling", about a boy and his ove for a deer in the Florida scrub coun-y.

Robert Rauschenberg, 1925: One of e truly influential artists of the 20th entury, Rauschenberg's works are in-uded in major museum collections throughout the world. Rauschenberg was a primary figure during in the modern art world of the 50's and 60's and today his Rauschenberg Overseas Cultural Interchange facilitates intercultural exchange between emerging and well known artists.

- **Tennessee Williams, 1911-1983**: Williams, whose name has been synonymous with American theater since production of "The Glass Menagerie" in 1945, adopted Key West as his home in 1949, living there for over thirty years. He was active in productions of his work in the Miami area, notably Coconut Grove Playhouse, and at Studio M. During his time in Florida, Williams received some of the highest honors awarded to contemporary writers, including the Pulitzer Prize for "Cat On A Hot Tin Roof."

- **Ernest Hemingway, 1899-1961**: Hemingway moved to Key West in 1928, and lived there until 1940 where he wrote many of his most famous works, such as "A Farewell to Arms", "For Whom The Bell Tolls", and "The Snows of Kilimanjaro." In 1954, he became the fifth American to win the Nobel Prize for Literature. He also was awarded a Pulitzer Prize for his novel, "The Old Man and the Sea."

- **John N Ringling, 1866-1936**: A celebrity of circus fame, Ringling amassed a fortune through his entertainment interests and business ventures. He and his wife built a magnificent museum adjacent to their Sarasota Bay home to house their collection of 17th and 18th

As if juggling itself is not enough, juggling on stilts.

century Baroque art. Ringling willed the museum, the residence and the estate to "the people of the State of Florida", and today the newly renovated John and Mable Ringling Museum of Art remains one of the premier museums of the South.

• **Duane Hanson, Sculptor, 1925**: A leading figure in contemporary sculpture, Duane Hanson adopted South Florida as his home in 1965. The style he calls "superrealism" caught the attention of the art world in the 1960's and drew popular and critical accolades. Hanson uses polyester, resin, vinyl, bronze, and fiberglass to explore his artistic vision of everyday individuals. Record breaking exhibitions and inclu-

sion in major collections throughou the world, illustrate his prominence i 20th century art.

For your cultural pleasure, here ar some artistic offerings that will enric your visit to Florida.

Daytona Beach

Museums

• **Museum of Arts and Sciences an Planetarium** has an outstanding co lection of Cuban art, an American Wing Prehistory of Florida Wing, Frische Sculpture Garden, Giant Ground Slot skeleton and educational starshow 1040 Museum Boulevard. Tel: (904) 25 0285.

• **Ormond Memorial Art Museum a Gardens:** Permanent collection c Malcolm Fraser paintings. Garden gc zebo in a park setting: 78 E Granad Boulevard. Tel: (904) 677 1857.

Performing Arts

• **Seaside Music Theater:** Musicals, chi dren's theater. Daytona Beach Commu nity College Theater Center. Building 8 Tel: (904) 252 6200.

• **Daytona Playhouse: Comedy** an drama. 100 Jassamine Boulevard. Te (904) 255 2431.

• **Bandshell Concerts**: Jazz, easy lister ing, big bands, barbershop performance at the Daytona Beach boardwalk. Te (904) 258 3106.

Fort Lauderdale

Museums

• **Museum of Art**: Twentieth Centur realism, pre-Columbian, North Amer

The stunning interior of Vizcaya – a villa on the James Deering Estate in Miami.

:an Indian, West African tribal, Oce-
anic art. Two hundred works from the
Glackens Collection. 1 East Las Olas
Boulevard. Tel: (305) 525 5500.
• **Museum of Archaeology**: Artifacts
from the Tequesta Indians. 203 SW First
Avenue. Tel: (305) 525 8778.
• **Museum of Discovery and Science**:
Hands-on science and high-tech crea-
ivity exhibits. Dinosaurs, sharks, in-
ects. IMAX Theater. 231 SW 2nd Av-
nue. Tel: (305) 462 4116.

Art
• **Broward Art Guild**: Juried exhibitions.
Workshops with Duane Hanson, Miles
Batt. 713 East Broward Blvd. Tel: (305)
764 2005.

Theater/Music
Broward Center for the Performing

Arts: Broadway plays and musicals,
concerts, symphony, opera, dance. Two
theaters. 201 SW 5th Avenue. Tel: (305)
522 5334.
• **Parker Playhouse**: Broadway plays.
Children's theater performed by adult
Equity actors. Holiday Park. Tel:(305)
764 0700.
• **Off Broadway on East 26th Street**:
Contemporary, original theater produc-
tions. E 26th Street. Tel: (305) 566 0554.
• **Fort Lauderdale Children's Theater**:
Local youngsters star. Tel:(305) 763
6901.

Jacksonville
Museums
• **Cummer Gallery of Art**: Two thou-
sand item permanent art collection on

the Saint Johns' River. Beautiful formal gardens. 829 Riverside Avenue. Tel: (904) 356 6857.

• **Jacksonville Art Museum**: Contemporary, classic art. Chinese and Korean ceramics. Pre-Columbian artifacts. Major travelling exhibits. 4160 Boulevard Center Drive. Tel: (904) 398 8336.

• **Museum of Science and History:** Hands-on science exhibits, live animals, planetarium. Telescope observation. Downtown Riverwalk. Tel: (904) 396 7061.

Music

• **Jacksonville Symphony**: 50 concerts led by Conductor Roger Nierenberg. Florida Theater and Civic Auditorium. Tel: (904) 354 5547.

Theater

• **Alhambra Dinner Theater**: Broadway-style shows with top stars. Dinner buffet. 12000 Beach Boulevard. Tel: (904) 641 1212.

• **Florida Theater**: Plays, symphonic and rock concerts, ballet and modern dance, children's theater, in a magnificently restored 1920s theater. Downtown. Tel: (904) 355 5661.

•**Theater Jacksonville:** Oldest producing civic theater in the US Drama, comedy, musicals, children's theater in a deco period playhouse. 2032 San Marco Blvd. Tel: (904) 396 4425.

Key West
Theater

• **Tennessee Williams Fine Arts Center**: Plays, concerts, performing arts, dance. Florida Keys Community College. 5901

Junior College Road. Tel: (305) 296 9081

• **Red Barn Theater**: Popular plays new works by local playwrights. 319 Duval Street. Tel: (305) 296 9911.

• **Waterfront Playhouse**: Plays by loca and guest playwrights, directors. Mallory Square. Tel: (305) 294 5015.

Miami
Museums

• **Art Museum at Florida Internationa University**: Contemporary Hispanic Ar and a permanent collection of North and South American artists. American Art Today series featuring critics, lec tures and art park tours. University Park SW 8th Street. Tel: (305) 348 2890.

• **Bass Museum**: Permanent collectior of Old Masters paintings, sculpture, tex tile. The period furniture is the mos comprehensive in Southeast Florida 2121 Park Avenue. Tel: (305) 673 7533

• **Center for the Fine Arts**: Designed by architect Philip Johnson, major exhibit: from collections around the world. 101 W Flagler Street. Tel: (305) 375 3000.

• **Cuban Museum of Arts & Culture** Two hundred paintings and drawing: by renowned Cuban artists. 1300 SW 12th Avenue. Tel: (305) 858 8006.

• **Miami Youth Museum**: Magic, fan tasy and hands-on exhibits for the whole family. Bakery Centre, 5701 Sunse Drive. Tel: (305) 661 2787.

• **North Miami Center of Contempo rary Art**: Contemporary art by Florida artists. Lectures, discussion, films and studio tours. 12340 NE 8th Avenue. Tel (305) 893 6211.

Theater

Actors' Playhouse: Off Broadway style productions at South Florida's second largest professional equity theater. 8851 SW 107th Avenue, Kendall. Tel: (305) 595 0010.

Area State Company: Contemporary classics, original productions in an intimate setting. 645 Lincoln Road. Tel: (305) 673 8002.

Coconut Grove Playhouse: Innovative, original productions presenting world, national and regional premieres. 3500 Main Highway, Coconut Grove. Tel:(305) 442 4000.

Florida Shakespeare Theater: Elizabethan drama, contemporary classics, children's theater. 232 Minorca Avenue, Coral Gables. Tel: (305) 446 1116.

Greater Miami Broadway Series: National touring productions of hit Broadway shows. Jackie Gleason Theater, 1700 Washington Avenue, Miami Beach. Tel: (305) 673 8300.

M Ensemble Company: The best in contemporary African-American theater. 174 E Flagler Street. Tel: (305) 377 2322.

The Minorca Playhouse: Home to the Florida Shakespeare Theater, and hosts other theater and dance companies. 232 Minorca Avenue, Coral Gables.Tel: (305) 446 1116.

Dance

• **Miami City Ballet**: A world class professional company under the direction of Edward Villella. Dade County Auditorium, 2901 W Flagler Street. Tel: (305) 532 4880.

• **Ballet Flamenco La Rosa**: Traditional and modern flamenco dance with live music in a theatrical setting. 1040 Lincoln Road. Tel: (305) 672 0552.

• **Ballet Theater of Miami**: A professional ballet company that gets rave reviews. 1809 Ponce de Leon Boulevard, Coral Gables. Tel: (305) 442 4840.

• **Freddick Bratcher and Company**: Jazz, modern, classical and narrative dance. Dance Tracks, 5788 Commerce Lane, South Miami. Tel: (305) 448 2021.

• **Momentum Dance Company**: Fifty performances of contemporary dance. Special children's series, lecture demonstrations and open rehearsals. Gusman Center for the Performing Arts, 174 E Flagler Street. Tel: (305) 673 3331.

Music

• **Greater Miami Opera**: A 52 year old world class opera company with guest artists from the world's great opera houses. Dade County Auditorium, 2901 W Flagler Street. Tel: (305) 854 1643.

• **The New World Symphony**: America's only orchestral academy and renowned guest conductors and solo artists. Under the direction of Artistic Director Michael Tilson Thomas. Gusman Center for the Performing Arts, 174 E Flagler Street, and Lincoln Theater, 555 Lincoln Road. Tel: (305) 673 3331.

• **Florida Philharmonic Orchestra**: Classical music, pop concerts, children's programs under the direction of conductor James Judd. Gusman Center for the Performing Arts. 174 E Flagler Street. Tel: 800 2261812; Jackie Gleason Theater, 1700 Washington Avenue,

Miami Beach. Tel: (305) 673 7311.

Orlando Area

Museums

• **The Cartoon Museum**: Thousands of cartoonists' drawings, comic books and magazines. 4300 Semoran Boulevard. Orlando. Tel: (407) 273 0141.

• **Central Florida Railroad Museum**: A restored 1913 depot with 3,000 antiques, whistles, switchlights and train memorabilia. 101 South Boyd Street, Winter Garden. Tel: (407) 656 8749.

• **Cornell Fine Arts Museum**: Old Master European paintings, 19th century American paintings, graphics, bronzes. Rollins College campus, Winter Park. Tel: (407) 646 2526.

• **Fort Christmas Museum**: Maps, weapons, pioneer artifacts at an 1837 fort built during the Second Seminole Indian War. Route 420, 24 miles east of Orlando, Christmas. Tel: (407) 568 4149.

• **Morse Gallery of Art**: Impressive collection of Tiffany-stained glass windows, paintings, jewelry, lamps. Also exhibits on Maxfield Parrish and Frank Lloyd Wright. 133 Welbourne Avenue, Winter Park. Tel: (407) 644 3686.

• **Orange County Historical Museum**: Exhibits on Orange County's development from the Seminole Wars to the present. 812 East Rollins Street, Orlando. Tel: (407) 898 8320.

• **Orlando Museum of Art**: Permanent pre-Columbian Gallery, 20th century American and African art. Loch Haven Park, 2416 North Mills Avenue, Orlando. Tel: (407) 896 4231.

• **Orlando Science Center**: Exhibits on health, astronomy, physical science and Florida's natural history. Loch Haven Park, 810 East Rollins Street, Orlando. Tel: (407) 896 7151.

• **Osceola Center for the Arts**: Historical Society Museum on Osceola County history. Also monthly art gallery showings and theater productions. 2411 East Irlo Bronson Memorial Highway, Kissimmee. Tel: (407) 846 6257.

Dinner Theater Shows

• **Arabian Nights**: Chariot races, Royal Lippizzans, a unicorn and Arabian horses. Prime rib dinner. On US 192. Tel (800) 553 6116.

• **Asian Adventure**: Visit famous sights of the Orient with explorer "Orlando Joe". Oriental meal. 5225 International Drive. Tel: (407) 351 5655.

• **Brazil Carnival**: Native artists perform South American dances and music. Brazilian dinner. 7432 Republic Drive, Orlando. Tel: (800) 821 4088.

• **Capone's Dance**: Song and comedy in a speakeasy setting with an Al Capone Italian feast. 4740 W Highway 192. Tel (407) 397 2378.

• **Fort Liberty Ropers**: Gun fighters, Indians, cowboys, singers and dancers. Western meal. 5260 US 192 West, Kissimmee. Tel: (407) 355 151.

• **King Henry's Feast**: Comedy, magic, juggling, swordfighting at King Henry's summer estate. Dinner. Tel: (407) 351 5151.

• **Mardi Gras**: Masquerade ball, Dixieland Jazz, and a Latin American carnival. Four course banquet. Mercado Shopping Village on International Drive

Orlando. Tel: (407) 351 5151.

• **Medieval Times**: Tournament games, jousting matches, sword combat in an 11th century European castle. Dinner Feast. Highway 192, Kissimmee. Tel: (407) 239 0214.

• **Sleuth's Mystery**: An exciting whodunnit with mystery characters. Dinner. Republic Drive, Orlando. Tel: (407) 363 1985.

Sarasota

Museums

• **The John and Mable Ringling Museum of Art**: Baroque masterpieces and modern art in an Italiant villa. Adjacent to the state art museum are circus art galleries and Ringling's lavish mansion, Ca'd'Zan. 5401 Bay Shore Road. Tel: (813) 355 5101.

Theater

• **Asolo Theater Company**: Contemporary and classic theater from a 30-year old professional company. 5555 N Tamiami Trail. Tel: (813) 351 8000.

• **Florida Studio Theater**: New works with a New Play Festival each May. 1241 N Palm Avenue. Tel: (813) 366 9796.

• **Golden Apple Dinner Theater**: Musicals and dining. 25 N Pineapple Avenue. Tel: (813) 366 5454.

• **The Players of Sarasota**: Dramas, comedies, musicals by community theater actors. 838 N Tamiami Trail. Tel: (813) 365 2494.

• **Theater Works, Inc.**: Comedies, musicals, dramas. 1247 First Street. Tel: (813) 952 9170.

• **Van Wezel Performing Arts Hall**: Touring theater productions, dance performances, children's programs, classic, jazz and pop concerts. 777 N Tamiami Trail. Tel: (813) 953 3366.

Dance

• **Sarasota Ballet of Florida**: Contemporary and classical ballet under direction of choreographer Eddy Toussaint. Tel: (813) 954 7171.

Film

• **Sarasota French Film Festival**: Screening of new films, seminars, panel discussions, social events with French film stars. 5555 N Tamiami Trail. Tel: (813) 351 9010.

Music

• **Florida Symphonic Band**: Broadway scores, Sousa marches, band concert works. Outdoor concerts and 4th of July concert. 709 N Tamiami Trail. Tel: (813) 955 6660.

• **Florida West Coast Symphony**: Classical music in Bach and Beethoven. String Quartet, Wind Quintet, Brass Quintet and New Artists Quartet. 709 N Tamiami Trail. Tel: (813) 953 4252.

• **Jazz Club of Sarasota**: Concerts and jazz jams culminating in a 3-day jazz Festival each April with top US jazz musicians. 61 Pineapple Avenue. Tel: (813) 366 1552.

• **Sarasota Opera Association**: Four operas annually under the leadership of Victor de Renzi, including an American premiere. 61 N Pineapple Avenue. Tel: (813) 953 7030.

Call ArtsLine for 24-hour a day information on Sarasota's cultural scene.

Tel: 359 ARTS.

Tallahssee

Music

• **Tallahassee Symphony Orchestra**: Masterworks season features Mozart, Bartok, Back, Bernstein, Ginastera and Gershwin. FSU Ruby Diamond Auditorium, College Avenue and Copeland Street. Tel: (904) 224 0461.

• **Monticello Opera House**: Turn-of-the-century opera house featuring jazz, music of the Americas, and swing bands. Twenty-three miles east of Tallahassee on US 27, Monticello. Tel: (904) 997 4242.

Theater

• **Civic Center**: Contemporary concert artists, family shows, sporting events and Broadway plays. 505 W Pensacola Street. Tel: (904) 322 3602.

• **Florida State University Mainstage**: Student/faculty performances in theater productions. FSU Fine Arts Building. Copeland Streets. Tel: (904) 644 6500.

• **The Nucleus Entertainment Group**: Florida Hysterical Society: Comedy and mystery dinner theater shows. Live radio drama with audience participation. Call for location. Tel: 904 877 2633.

• **Tallahassee Little Theater**: Community theater productions of comedy and drama. 1861 Thomasville Road. Tel: (904) 224 8474.

Tampa

Theater

• **American Stage**: Shakespeare, drama, comedy and children's theater by a resident professional company. 211. 3rd Street, St Petersburg. Tel: 813 822 8814

• **Mahaffey Theater**: Broadway shows, ballet, symphony concerts, Disney or Ice, pop and rock concerts. Bayfron Center 400 1st Street South, St Petersburg Tel: (813) 892 5767.

• **Ruth Eckerd Hall**: 2200 seat auditorium with ballet, drama, music and c children's touring theater company Richard B Baumgardner Center for the Performing Arts, 1111 McMullen Booth Road, Clearwater. Tel: (813) 791 7400.

• **Tampa Bay Performing Arts Center** 2400-seat Festival Hall, 900-seat Playhouse, and 300-seat Jaeb Theater offer Broadway shows, opera, music and dance. 1010 N MacInnes Place, Tampa. Tel: (813) 221 1045.

• **Tampa Players**: Classic, contemporary and recent Broadway plays by a professional nonprofit acting company. Call for locations. Tel: (813) 229 3221.

Dance

• **Tampa Ballet**: Classic and contemporary ballet, including a December performance of "The Nutcracker". Call for location. Tel: (813) 221 6253.

Music

• **Florida Orchestra**: Masterworks series with outstanding guest soloists and a Pops Series conducted by Skitch Henderson. Tampa Bay Performing Arts Center, Bayfront Center, and Ruth Eckerd Hall. Tel: (813) 286 2403.

• **Tampa Bay Opera**: Classic operas such as *Carmen*, *Die Fledermaus*, and *Turandot*. The season runs from October through April. Clearwater. Tel: (813) 538 0775.

A harpist creating sweet soothing music from his strings.

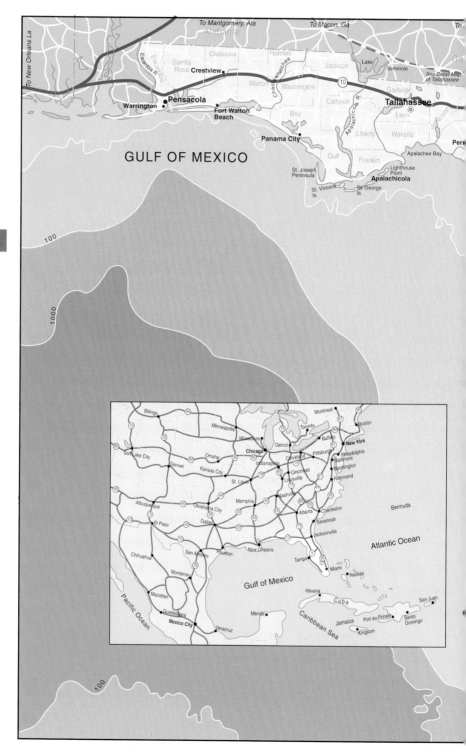

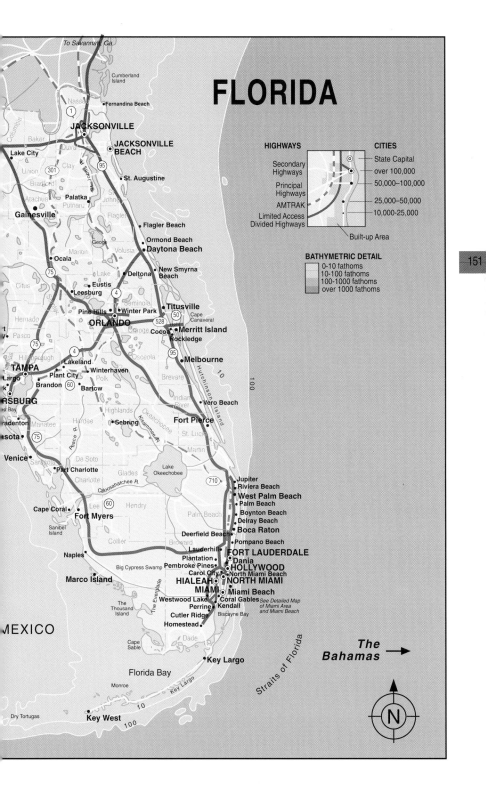

FLORIDA

HIGHWAYS

Secondary Highways

Principal Highways

AMTRAK

Limited Access Divided Highways

CITIES

- State Capital
- over 100,000
- 50,000–100,000
- 25,000–50,000
- 10,000–25,000

Built-up Area

BATHYMETRIC DETAIL

- 0-10 fathoms
- 10-100 fathoms
- 100-1000 fathoms
- over 1000 fathoms

To Savannah, Ga

Cumberland Island

Nassau
Fernandina Beach

JACKSONVILLE

Lake City
Baker
Duval

JACKSONVILLE BEACH

Union
(301)
Clay
Bradford
Atachua
Palatka
Putnam

St. Augustine

Gainesville

Geoge

Flagler Beach

Ocala
Marion
Volusia

Ormond Beach
Daytona Beach

Lake
Deltona
New Smyrna Beach

Eustis
Leesburg
(4)
Seminola

Citus

Hernado

Pine Hills
Winter Park
ORLANDO
(50)
Titusville
Cape Canaveral

Cocoa
Merritt Island
Rockledge
(528)

Orange

Pasco

(75)
(4)
Osceola

TAMPA
Lakeland
Winterhaven

Hillsborough
Plant City
Polk

Largo
Brandon
(60)
Bartow

RSBURG

a Bay

radenton
Manatee
Hardee

sota
(75)

Highlands
Sebring

Melbourne

Brevara

Indian River

Vero Beach

Okeechobee

Fort Pierce

St. Lucie

Venice

Sarasota

Port Charlotte
Charlotte

De Soto

Glades

Lake Okeechobee

Martin

(710)

Cape Coral
Lee
(60)
Fort Myers

Hendry

Jupiter
Riviera Beach
West Palm Beach
Palm Beach
Boynton Beach
Delray Beach
Boca Raton

Sanibel Island

Collier

Deerfield Beach
Pompano Beach

Naples

Broward
Lauderhill
FORT LAUDERDALE
Plantation
Dania
Pembroke Pines
HOLLYWOOD

Big Cypress Swamp

Carol City
North Miami Beach
HIALEAH
NORTH MIAMI
MIAMI
Miami Beach

Marco Island

Westwood Lake
Coral Gables
Perrine
Kendall
Cutler Ridge
Homestead
Biscayne Bay

See Detailed Map of Miami Area and Miami Beach

The Everglade

The Thousand Island

Dade

MEXICO

Cape Sable

Florida Bay

Key Largo

Monroe

Key Largo

Straits of Florida

The Bahamas →

Dry Tortugas
Key West

N

ew places in the world offer the diversity of Central Florida, which includes the cities of Winter Haven, Lake Wales, Lakeland, Mulberry, Baseball City, Kissimmee, Orlando, Winter Park and Ocala to name but a few.

Within Central Florida you can waterski, golf, fish, stroll through incredible gardens, see 10 million year old fossils, visit racehorse and cattle farms, shop for antiques or compact disc players, eat dinner with Arabian knights or wild west cowboys, sleep in a budget motel or a Victorian B&B, get Goofy's autograph, see a 3D Muppet movie, and carry ET on your bicycle over a city skyline into outer space.

If you have got the energy, Central Florida has the fun.

Meet Mickey and Minnie Mouse. ©The Walt Disney Company.

Central Florida

153

Winter Haven

Winter Haven is right in the middle of Florida's P o l k County, just south of Inter-

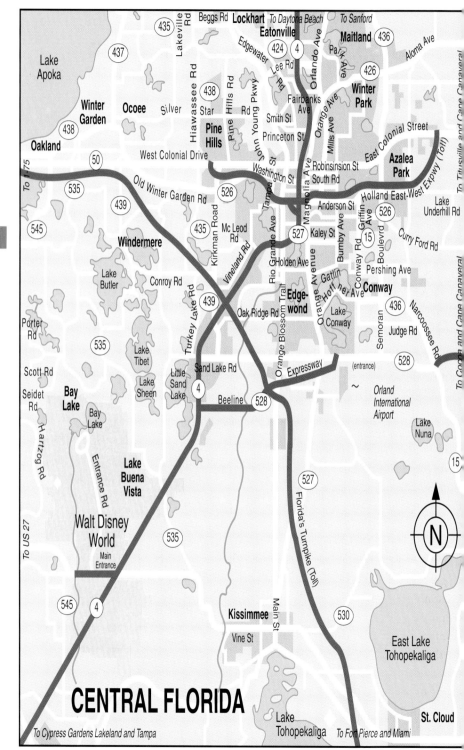

CENTRAL FLORIDA

154

Lake Apoka

437

Winter Garden

Ocoee   Silver

438

Oakland

438

To I-75

50

535

439

545

Windermere

435

439

Lake Butler

Conroy Rd

535

Porter Rd

Lake Tibet

Scott Rd

Seidet Rd

Bay Lake

Lake Sheen

Little Sand Lake

Hartzog Rd

Bay Lake

Entrance Rd

Lake Buena Vista

Walt Disney World

Main Entrance

535

To US 27

545   4

Lakeville Rd   Beggs Rd   **Lockhart**   To Daytona Beach   To Sanford

435

Eatonville

Edgewater   424   4   **Maitland**   436

Lee Rd   Orlando Ave   Park Ave

Hiawassee Rd   438   Star   Fairbanks Ave   426

Pine Hills Rd   Smith St   Orange Ave   Mills Ave   **Winter Park**

John Young Pkwy   **Pine Hills**   Princeton St

West Colonial Drive   Tampa St   Robinsinsion St   East Colonial Street

Washington St   South Rd   **Azalea Park**

526   Magnolia Ave   Anderson St   Holland East-West Expwy (Toll)   Lake Underhill Rd

Kirkman Road   435   Mc Leod Rd   527   Kaley St   15   526   Curry Ford Rd

Vineland Rd   Rio Grande Ave   Bumby Ave   Griffin Ave   Conway Rd   Boulevrd   Pershing Ave

439   Holden Ave   Orange Avenue   **Conway**

Turkey Lake Rd   Oak Ridge Rd   **Edge-wood**   Gatlin   Hoffner Ave   436

Orange Blossom Trail   Lake Conway   Semoran   Judge Rd

Sand Lake Rd   Expressway   (entrance)   528

4   Beeline   528   ~   *Orland International Airport*   Lake Nuna   15

527

Kissimmee   Florida's Turnpike (Toll)   530

Vine St   Main St   **East Lake Tohopekaliga**

CENTRAL FLORIDA   N

Lake Tohopekaliga   **St. Cloud**

To Cypress Gardens Lakeland and Tampa   To Fort Pierce and Miami

To Trusville and Cape Canaveral   To Cocoa and Cape Canaveral

Looks so easy, at the water skiing show in Cypress Gardens.

state 4 in the center of the state. Polk County has over 600 freshwater lakes, numerous rivers, streams, dozens of golf courses and two state parks, making this an ideal place for fishing, hiking, canoeing, camping and golfing.

Winter Haven is also the "Water-ski Capital of the World" as you will see at **Cypress Gardens** in Winter Haven, off US Route 27. Some of the best water ski champions in the world perform at the Gardens' famous ski shows. The theme park also has 223 acres of beautiful flower gardens, museums, rides for children, a model railroad, and pretty "Southern Belles" posing for pictures in frilly pastel hooped gowns. Call Tel:

(813) 324 2111 for information.

How did Polk County became "the black bass capital of the world"? Stop into the **Museum of Fishing** just down the street in Winter Haven, open Monday through Friday from 9-4pm to find out!

If you like antiques, the Antique Mall has 20 shops of Americana, primitives, glass and toys.

Lake Wales

Just south of Winter Haven on US 27 is **Lake Wales**, and **Bok Tower Gardens**, a peaceful 128-acre garden of ferns,

The Bok Singing Tower at Lake Wales.

palms, oaks, pines and flowers. A marble and coquina stone tower houses a carillon and there is a recital every day at 3pm. Bok Tower is a wonderful place for a romantic picnic or just a quiet stroll, and not touristy like many of Florida's "theme" parks. Call Tel: (813) 676 1408. If you want to camp, fish or hike through woods, drive over to Camp Mack Road and spend a day at **Lake Kissimmee State Park**. There is also a "frontier cow camp" here, with demonstrations of how Florida cowboys herded cattle back in 1876. Tel: (813) 696 1112.

Lakeland

West of Winter Haven is Lakeland. In the northeast part of Lakeland on State Route 33A (off I-4) is another state park, **Teneroc State Reserve**, where you can choose from five ponds stocked with large mouth bass. It can get crowded here especially on weekends, so make reservations at Tel: (813) 665 2421.

Polk County has over 25 golf courses and eight of them are here in Lakeland! Some of the courses open to the public include **Cleveland Heights Golf & Country Club** at Tel: (813) 682 3277 (27 holes) and **Skyview Golf & Country Club** at Tel: (813) 665 4008 (18 holes).

Mulberry

Head south of Lakeland on Route 37 and you will come face-to-face with an 18 foot, 10 million year old Baleen Whale inside the **Mulberry Phosphate/Fossil Museum**. Housed in an original 1899 wooden structure, the museum also has 3,000 other petrified fossils, many of which were found within 50 miles. It is open from Tuesday-Saturday, 10-4:30pm. Tel: (813) 425 2823.

Baseball City

From Mulberry, head east on route 60 and north on 27 to **Baseball City**, where the Kansas City Royals have Spring Training. Or head back into Winter Haven and watch the Boston Red Sox at the **Chain 'O Lakes Complex.**

Polk County publishes an excellent

Kissimmee with attractions of its own, curving country roads and peaceful green pastures.

outdoor recreation guide listing everything from canoe outfitters, to water ski schools, fishing lakes, boat rentals, stables, and golf courses. It is free at Tel: 1 800 828 POLK (7655).

Kissimmee-Saint Cloud

Kissimmee-Saint Cloud is located near Florida's best known attractions, such as Walt Disney World, Sea World, and Universal Studios. The main drag through town, Route 192 or Vine Street, is a blur of wall-to-wall discount shops hawking everything from T-shirts to sportswear to household appliances. Choose from over 29,000 accommodations, from low budget motels to furnished 4-bedroom houses. It is a highly commercial area with fast food, discount shopping and family accommodations.

But just east of Kissimmee, in and around Saint Cloud on Canoe Creek Road (Rt. 523), are curving country roads, peaceful green pastures and many of Florida's top cattle farms.

Kissimmee has special events going on all year: Art and bluegrass festivals, rodeos, air fairs, off-shore boat races, basketball tournaments and livestock shows.

In June and July 1994, Kissimmee-Saint Cloud will host the World Cup Soccer Championship, the largest single sport spectacle in the world. Over 100,000 national and international fans

A relaxing life.

are expected.

Free schedules of all events and maps are available from the Convention and Visitors Bureau at 1925 E Irlo Bronson Memorial Parkway, (Rt 192) or call Tel: 1 800 327 9159.

Just west on 192 from the visitor's center is the **Osceola County Stadium** where the Houston Astros work out in Major League spring training. Next door is the **Silver Spurs Arena** which always has something fun going on, especially the annual Rodeo held the end of every February.

Continue west on 192, and you will not run out of things to do:

• **Airboat Rentals**, that take you through Lake Tohopekaliga's backwaters and cypress swamps. Tel: 407 3672.
• **Fun 'N Wheels**, go-karts, bumper cars and water slides. Tel: (407) 870 2222.
• **Pirate's Island Adventure Golf**, 18-hole miniature golf with a swashbuckling theme. Tel: (407) 396 4660.
• **Medieval Life**, a medieval village, with craftsmen, birds of prey, a dungeon and torture chamber. Tel: 1 800 327 4024.
• **Alligatorland Safari Zoo**, 10 acres of gators, birds and exotic cats. Tel: (407) 396 1012.
• **Water Mania**, 38 acres of raft rides, speed slides, a wave pool and two children's water playground. Tel: 1 800 527 3092.

South of 192 on Rt 531 is the **Flying Tigers Warbird Air Museum**, which was originally a WWII aircraft restoration facility and today is an interesting collection of historic planes and arti-

facts. 231 N Hoagland Boulevard, Tel: (407) 933 1942.

Get the idea? There are hundreds more theme parks, water parks, go-kart racetracks, miniature golf courses in this area, as well as balloon rides, wax museums, airboat rides, a winery, an environmental study center, stables, pioneer center, and the **Tupperware "Awareness Center"**, where you can learn new ways to store leftovers in those handy plastic containers!

Evening Entertainment

Kissimmee has a number of theme restaurants which serve up mediocre food, but have amusing music and dance theme shows appropriate for the family. Spend the evening with Arabian horses Tel: 1 800 553 6116; Calvary soldiers and Comanche Indians Tel: 1 800 776 3501; Celebrity impersonators Tel: (407) 396 7469; Dixieland musicians Tel: 1 800 347 8181; Medieval knights Tel: 1 800 432 0768 or dance to your favorite 50's and 60's rock n' roll hits, Tel: (407) 396 6499 .

Orlando

Some 14 million visitors vacation in Orlando every year, enjoying the tremendous diversity of entertainment. This is where kids can get close to their favorite movie and television characters, and where even the most serious

Sliver Springs

Spot the Tricolored Heron at Silver Springs – more welcome than a tarantula.

Visiting Silver Springs in Ocala is an unusual experience, because the park rangers, jeep tour guides and riverboat captains truly love the park, and delight in showing you "their" animals.

Of Claws & Stings

For example, meet the handsome park ranger over in the outdoor amphitheatre who's doing a "Creature Feature" demonstration. He is holding a 4" black African scorpion underneath a video camera, so the audience can get a closer look on the overhead television monitor at the beast's "fascinating claws and stinger". That scorpion is posing on the ranger's hand like a small town beauty queen, and they BOTH are having a great time. (Kids: do not try this trick at home.)

Next up: a furry Chilean tarantula. Leisurely

she crawls onto his hand, and under the video camera we see "her beautiful eyes". Bug-eyed little kids are muttering "yuk", and the adults in the audience are shaking their heads in disbelief, squirming like– well, little kids.

This is definitely the closest you will ever get, or want to get, to any of these critters. Not everyone has our ranger's passion for bug demos, but do not tell him that. Secretly we all wish we had his courage!

Then our "Creature Feature" guide asks for a volunteer. One brave teenaged girl walks on stage, dons a vest, and allows the tarantula to pose on her shoulder.

But before shooting a photo, our ranger has a last detail : out of the vest pockets he pulls first a giant African toad and a hissing Madagascar cockroach.

Gently, he places each into her hands. By now she is too frozen with fear to move as he snaps a polaroid for her vacation album. Mum-

ling "thank you", she numbly takes the photo and returns to her parent's arms. Will this girl need intensive bug therapy?

Is this anyway to run a nature park?

Wait, it gets better.

Head over to the Lost River Voyage, where a glass-bottom boat glides you over 80-foot clear as glass springs, bubbling up from caves below. Giant mullets undulate through the air bubbles. You are peering down into an unspoiled, wild Florida, the way it was thousands of years before all the tourists showed up.

It is beautiful and peaceful out here, floating past gators stretched out on fallen logs, orange spider monkeys screeching from trees, red-eyed green headed wood ducks quacking by, 2000 pound horned Scottish bulls grazing on the riverbanks.

Black anhinga birds balance on rocks, holding their wings open to dry in the humid 90°F sunshine. No cages, no roller coasters, no T-shirt shops. Just Mother Nature at her best!

Ode To Silver Springs

On the way back to the boat pier, our river boat captain Barbara Clemmons, a pretty mother of four, asks if she might share one of her poems about her feelings for Silver Springs.

Slowly she recites:

In the glow of morning an Osprey sings,
To begin a new day out over the springs.
The Red-tailed Hawk gives a warning cry,
As a Great Blue Heron goes sailing by.
The monkeys swing quietly over the grass,
"Leave us be" is all they ask.
The gators roar deeply upon the bank,
No longer endangered, it's man they thank.
A majestic Eagle tilts her wings,
In silent thanks to Silver Springs.
So I ask you today my friends,
Join hands with us, so this won't end.

Is this any way to run a nature park? You decide. Silver Springs, one mile east of Ocala on State Route 40. Open seven days from 9-5:30 pm. Tel: 1 800 234 7458.

adults can enjoy the wonderful sensation of being a child again. All that is really needed here are shorts, sneakers and a camera to catch those happy chocolate-smeared faces. A full wallet does not hurt either.

Most tourists are so overwhelmed by the number and diversity of Orlando's theme parks and attractions they just short circuit after a few days. This is not a place to relax! In fact, the intense stimulation and whirlwind nature of it all leaves some families so exhausted, they need a vacation after their vacation. It takes a lot of energy to have this kind of fun. Wise travelers will schedule some "down time" at the hotel pool, in-between mad dashes to "just one more ride"; or make plans to spend a few days at the east or west coast beaches and parks before heading home. Do not leave without seeing the "real" Florida–the birds, beaches, parks and wildlife.

Here's a brief look at some of Orlando's most popular attractions:

Church Street Station in downtown Orlando is an entertainment, dining and shopping complex with five showrooms featuring live Dixieland jazz, country western, rock 'n roll, and the famous **Rosie O'Grady's Good Time Emporium**. Open seven days. 129 W Church Street. Tel: (407) 422 2434.

Gatorland has over 5,000 alligators and crocodiles, a train ride, an observation tower over a breeding marsh, birds, reptiles and one of Florida's most entertaining Gator Wrestlin' shows. There's a new educational show called

Spaceship Earth "geosphere" at the World EPCOT Center.

"Snakes of Florida". Try smoked gator ribs at the snack bar. 14501 S Orange Blossom Trail. Tel: (507) 855 5496.

"Go Bungee" is a new thrill in Florida, where you can jump 150 feet off a crane, to dangle and swing from a 9-inch thick 40-foot bungee cord. Not for wimps. Major Boulevard. Tel: (407) 354 0036.

Orlando Museum of Art, just a few minutes from Church Street Station, is known for its excellent Pre-Columbian collection, as well as 19th and 20th century American, and African art. At 2416 N Mills Avenue. Tel: (407) 896 4231.

Orlando Arena in the downtown Orlando Centroplex is a 15,000 seat arena home to the city's basketball team,

the "Orlando Magic" and football team, the "Predators". The Arena also schedules concerts, ice shows, tractor pulls and rodeos. Tel: (407) 849 2562, ext. 3112.

"Rock on Ice" is one of Orlando's newest entertainments, a roller rink where you and the kids can skate to rock 'n roll favorites. This is great family fun for those rare rainy days or at night after dinner. At 7500 Canada Avenue. Tel: (407) 363 7465.

Sea World is Orlando's world renowned marine life park with killer whales, dolphins and several new exhibits: "Mission: Bermuda Triangle" takes you on a "scientific" expedition, and "Shamu's Happy Harbor", a 3 acre get wet water maze play area for kids.

For overheated parents, **Anheuser-Busch** has a lush new Hospitality Center serving up ice cold beer. At 7007 Sea World Drive. Tel: (407) 363 2200.

Universal Studios is one of Florida's newest and most entertaining theme parks, where you can go behind the scenes of your favorite movies, stroll though actual movie street sets, take a ride with ET and travel Back to the Future in a glitzy sportscar. Nickelodeon Studio tapes the game show, "Double Dare" here, and you can be part of the studio audience. At 1000 Universal Studios Plaza, just off Kirkman Road. Tel: (407) 363 8000.

Walt Disney World Magic Kingdom Park, Epcot Center, Disney-MGM Studios, Typhoon Lagoon, and Pleasure Island are what millions of tourists come to Florida for. **Magic Kingdom** has over 45 attractions in "magic lands"; **EPCOT** has educational and entertaining exhibits on international countries and futuristic subjects; **Disney-MGM Studios** takes you into the world of television and feature films; **Typhoon Lagoon** is a water theme park; and **Pleasure Island** is a nighttime family park with music, clubs and theme restaurants. Special prices on four day and five day passes. Tel: (407) 824 4321.

Wet 'n Wild is a 25-acre park with water rides, slides and waves. There is a terrific beachwear shop here too. At 6200 International Drive. Tel: (407) 351 3200.

If you need a day of rest, hop on a Gray Line bus for an Orlando city tour

"Wet 'n Wild" fun in Orlando.

through historic neighborhoods, parks, science center, historical museums and Museum of Art, with lunch at Church Street Station. Tel: (407) 422 0744.

The Orlando/Orange County Convention and Visitor's Bureau has a new "Orlando Magicard" which provides 10-50 percent discounts at 85 area attractions, hotels, restaurants, auto and RV rental firms and retail shops. To order the card, call Tel: 1 800 551 0181 or write the Bureau at 7208 Sand Lake Road, Suite 300, Orlando Florida 32819. Tel: (407) 363 5800.

Winter Park

Just a few miles north of Orlando at the

Universal Studios

Are you a movie fan? Do you count ET, King Kong, Alfred Hitchcock, Yogi Bear and Lucille Ball among your closest friends? Then plan to spend an entire day at Florida's most spectacular and technologically advanced movie theme amusement park.

Universal is also a working motion picture and television production studio center, so you can be part of a television audience or watch a feature film crew in action on a very real looking "New York City" or "San Francisco" street set.

Here are some of the most exciting rides:

"ET Adventure"–Your mission is to help ET return home to his Green Planet in another galaxy. So climb aboard your bicycle, and soon you will be up in the tree tops, escaping police cars and gliding over a valley of bright city lights and then, into outer space. In minutes your bicycle arrives at the flower gardens and bubbling streams of the Green Planet, and ET waves goodbye, calling out your name in thanks. This ride is so much fun, you will want to go on it two or three times!

"Back to the Future...The Ride"– Climb inside your sleek eight passenger DeLorean sports car and rocket into the future at 21 million jigowatts. Your stomach roller coasters as the car lurches, dips and careens around fiery volcanoes and hungry dinosaurs. This ride is intense, but thrilling.

"Kongfrontation"–You will ride a New York Trolley through real flames and past a howling, angry life-sized King Kong. Yes he is a hairy ape!

"The Beetlejuice Graveyard Revue"–A funky, rock 'n roll pyrotechnical dance show where Dracula, Wolfman, the Phantom of the Opera and Frankenstein rouse the dead and raise the roof. You will walk out whistling.

"EarthQuake, The Big One"– Ride a California subway train into an underground tunnel. Suddenly the earth cracks around you, fires

A "Miami Vice" stunt show at Universal Studios.

break out and the city floods your train. This will cure you from ever moving to California.

"GhostBusters"– A nerdy MC selects audience members to receive "ghost busting training" and the show gets wild after that. At the "Ectoplasmic containment center", ghosts leak out and soon the stage is a rousing song and dance number with slime, holograms, lasers, lights and smoke. Lots of fun, even if you are afraid of ghosts.

These are just a few of the more creative rides and shows. But walking around is entertaining too. Out front of **Mel's Drive-In** along

intersection of Routes 50 and 436, is a charming town of 100-year old oaks, sprawling mansions, elegant boutiques and quiet lakes. Once heralded as *THE* resort for wealthy northerners, Winter

Park boasted of having more millionaires per capita than any other city in Florida. Though that reputation has moved to other Florida towns, Winter Park offers a delightful day of estate

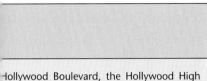

Hollywood Boulevard, the Hollywood High Tones croon your favorite 1950s and 60s dance tunes, like *Under the Boardwalk* and *Why Do Fools Fall in Love?* Inside, Mel's serves up tasty french fries and thick chocolate milkshakes.

Over on **Plaza of the Stars**, fans are watching "I Love Lucy" reruns, screaming at "Alfred Hitchcock's Art of Making Movies", and getting queasy at "The Gory, Gruesome & Grotesque Horror Make-Up Show." And do not forget to look in on "The Funtastic World of Hanna-Barbera", creators of those cartoon characters Yogi Bear, Fred Flinstone and George Jetson.

On the backlot, are true-to-life street sets, from New York's sidewalks to a New England village, from the Garden of Allah to Angkor Wat. And there is also a replica of shops from Hollywood's ritzy Rodeo Drive, complete with movie stars' names immortalized in the sidewalk.

If you like stunts, you will get a big kick out of the "Wild, Wild, Wild West Stunt Show", a gun-slinging, fist-swinging, roof-toppling, comedy spoof of wild west wranglers.

If you want to see how you measure up as a "star", the "cinemagicians" at the Screen Test Home Video Adventure will put you on the Big Screen with the Starship Enterprise crew. You can take this video home if you want to make sure no one else will ever see it!

Or just be a member of the audience at "Double Dare", Nickelodeon Studios' popular game show, which tapes new episodes at Universal Studios throughout the year. Get ready for a big dose of slime and goo at these crazy tapings.

At **Universal Studios**, 1000 Universal Studios Plaza, off Kirkman Road, Orlando. Tel: (407) 363 8000.

viewing, shopping and dining in excellent restaurants.

Start your tour of Winter Park with the "Scenic Boat Tour" folks, by taking East Morse Boulevard east until it deadends at Lake Osceola. Climb aboard the 15-passenger excursion boat and head out into Lake Osceola, Lake Virginia and Lake Maitland, connected by narrow 127-year old canals. From here you can see the manicured grounds of beautiful million dollar estates, one of which has 250 wild peacocks wandering through the grounds. Float through forests of bamboo, banana trees, cypress trees and orange Chinese pagoda flowers, past black cranes sunning on backyard piers. Scenic Boat Tour captains charmingly narrate the hour long boat trip with an amusing mixture of Florida history and local gossip. Tel: (407) 644 4056.

After the boat trip, walk back up Morse Boulevard and turn left onto Center Street. At the corner of Center and Welbourne (just walk for one block) you'll come to The Morse Gallery of Art. Step inside to a world of color and light, for this is the rarest collection of Louis Comfort Tiffany windows, blown glass, paintings, pottery and lamps in existence. Morse Gallery also displays other art nouveau artists like Frank Lloyd Wright and Maxfield Parrish. A tiny gem of a museum with a splendid gift and book shop. At 133 East Welbourne Avenue, Winter Park. Tel: (407) 644 3686.

If you are ready to shop or have lunch, walk one block west to Park Avenue where there are elegant boutiques and restaurants. If you spot a young brunette wearing a diamond tiara walking through Central Park, say hello to

Golf Country.

Leanza Cornett, the 1993 Miss America, who was Miss Winter Park until she happily claimed her crown in Atlantic City.

Ocala

Now that you are relaxed from Winter Park's warm southern hospitality, take a drive 80 miles north on Route 75 to Ocala, a town with thoroughbred race horses, five star golf resorts, crystal clear Silver Springs, and a downtown Historic District of 1880-1930 Queen Anne homes.

Horse Country

The Florida Thoroughbred breeding industry, generating over $1 billion yearly in revenue, has produced 33 North American champions, 26 millionaires, 10 Breeders' Cup, and 11 Classic winners. Ocala's rolling green pastures, divided by miles of curving white fences and huge oaks, is home to many of these sleek race horses. Some farms welcome visitors, but ask that you call before stopping by.

Here is a partial listing of horse farms. The Ocala/Marion Oaks Chamber of Commerce can give you the entire list at Tel: (904) 629 8051. Or write them at PO Box 11206, Ocala, Florida 34473.

Florida Stallion Station, Tel: (904) 629 4416.

Franks Farm, Tel: (904) 245 2495.

• **Live Oak Stud**, Tel: (904) 854 2691.

• **Ocala Stud Farm**, Tel: (904) 237 2171.

• **Good Chance Farm**, Tel: (904) 245 1136.

(Good Chance is home to "Gate Dancer" the winner of over $2 million in races. He gets $25,000 for any foal that he sires).

Golf

The Ocala area has nine superb golf courses, some of which are open to the public. Again, contact the Chamber of Commerce for a complete listing. Here are a few that you might try:

• **Marion Oaks Golf and Country Club** is a par 72 public course and teaching center. 4260 SW 162nd Street Road, Marion Oaks. Tel: (904) 347 1271.

• **Huntington Golf Club** is also public, par 72, with 18 holes and a teaching center. At 14525 SW 67th Avenue, Marion Oaks. Tel: (904) 347 3333.

• **Ocala Golf Club** is a par 72 public course with a driving range. At 3130 NE Silver Springs Boulevard, Ocala. Tel: (904) 622 6198.

• **Pine Oaks of Ocala Golf Course** is a par 72 public course with three nine-hole courses and a driving range. Also a restaurant. At 2201 NW 21st Street, Ocala. Tel: (904) 622 8558.

Jungles, Jeeps & Wildlife

One mile east of Ocala on Route 40 is a

The Incredible World Of Disney

Be dazzled by the splendid sights seen in the Kodak Pavilion.

Disney World is actually made up of three parks: The Magic Kingdom, EPCOT and the new Disney-MGM Studios. Because the parks are spread out with so much to see, most tourists spend at least three to four days here. You can purchase a one day one park pass, or the more economical four day or five day passes which allow access to all three parks. Here is a brief rundown on what you can find here:

The Magic Kingdom Park

The best spot for getting a hug from Mickey, Goofy or Donald Duck is over at Mickey's Hollywood Theatre in Mickey's Starland to the northeast part of Magic Kingdom. Or walk down Main Street, USA where there are frequent parades with dancers, singers and 40-foot balloons. It is a non-stop party, where delighted kids are mesmerized.

Then choose from (or your kids will drag you

to): Fantasyland, Liberty Square, Frontierland Adventureland or Tomorrowland. **Fantasyland** is a whirl of Mad Hatter giant tea cups, sailing underseas with Captain Nemo on a submarine dashing through the woods with Snow White or a 3D fantasy film flight.

Liberty Square is rollercoasting through Gold mine, exploring caves with Tom Sawyer and kicking up your heels at the Diamond Horseshoe Jamboree. The newest ride here Splash Mountain, hurls you 87 feet down into splashing pool, as Brer Rabbit and 68 other animated characters sing and dance in a musical extravaganza.

Frontierland cruises you down a river aboard a steam-powered stern wheeler and lures out the ghosts at Haunted Mansion.

Adventureland is where kids search for treasure amid St Caribbean pirate coves and sing along with Enchanted Tiki Birds.

And **Tomorrowland** has Space Mountain an exhilarating (not for kids only) roller coaster ide inside a galaxy of stars and planets and American Journeys, an emotional film about the beauty of the United States.

Epcot

This $1.1 billion park helped transform Disney World into a major resort when it opened in 1982. Tourists love the mix of thrill rides, futuristic exhibits and international pavilions. You could easily spend several days just enjoying EPCOT (Experimental Prototype City of Tomorrow), which is divided into "World Showcase" and "Future World."

World Showcase: Eleven countries are represented in pavilions here, each reflecting the architecture, cuisine, merchandise and entertainment of that land's people and culture. Visit Mexico, Norway, China, Germany, Italy, America, Japan, Morocco, France, the United Kingdom and Canada. There are excellent films at the China, French and Canada buildings, but all the pavilions are interesting.

Future World: A fascinating look into the future at eight pavilions: Spaceship Earth, a 180 foot high "geosphere" unveiling the history of human communications; Communicore, presenting the history of computers; Universe of Energy, a multi-image journey where theater cars take you on an energy odyssey; Wonders of Life, where you discover the mysteries of birth; Horizons, a journey through the lifestyles of the 21st century; World of Motion, a ride through the evolution of transportation; Journey into Imagination, an exploration with "Dreamfinder" and "Figment" of the creative process. The Land, presenting film about man's relationship with the land, as well as a song and dance salute to good nutrition. And do not miss the Living Seas, where you can travel to the bottom of a 5 million gallon saltwater world to visit with sharks, manatees and dolphins.

Disney-MGM Studio

This is a fun movie theme park, that most people can see in half-a-day. Highlights include:

A Goofy embrace.

• Jim Henson's Muppet Vision 3D: A delightful 3D film with "audio-animatronics" figures, special effects and of course, Kermit and Miss Piggy.
• Star Tours: A realistic ride aboard a "star speeder" to planet Endor, where the moving seats give you the sensation of hurtling into outer space.
• The Great Movie Ride: A nostalgic tour through the sets and footage of your favorite movies like *Sound of Music, Singing in the Rain, Tarzan, Star Wars* and of course, *The Wizard of Oz.*
• Indiana Jones Stunt Spectacular: A first class live production of daring stunts, runaway trucks and explosions. Extras for the show are selected from the audience, so try not to be shy. If you are on a short time schedule, put this show first on your list, it is truly wonderful.

There is a lot more going on, including a live song and dance show with *The Little Mermaid, Beauty and the Beast* and just opened, *Aladdin's Royal Caravan*, a parade performance with Prince Ali, Princess Jasmine and a 26-foot genie! For Walt Disney World information and tickets, call Tel: (407) 824 4321, or Tel: (407) 934 7639.

national landmark nature park where you can happily spend an entire day.

In an outdoor amphitheater, a park ranger is showing the audience live scorpions, bats, furry tarantulas and a hissing Madagascar cockroach.

Over at **The Jeep Safari,** 15 tourists bump along through an open air nature preserve waving at porcupines, boars, tapirs, sloths, parrots, golden eagles, rhesus monkeys and gators.

At the petting zoo, other visitors feed Kimba and Cayma, graceful 18-foot high giraffes, who stand proudly over their new born "Baby".

And then there is the reason that tourists travel to Silver Springs from all over the world: The Jungle Cruise, a glass bottom river boat which glides along the Fort King Waterway over pure fresh water springs fed by the Silver River. Over a green grassy bottom just 6 feet deep, you soon float out over clear crystal springs, peering 60-80 feet down at giant mullets swimming below.

Along the banks of the springs is a wildlife sanctuary of alligators, African crown cranes, apes, llamas, ostrich, zebra, Scottish bulls and great blue herons.

Silver Springs is one of Florida's most beautiful and uncommercial nature parks. Thankfully there are few t-shirt shops here, and the staff have an unusual enthusiasm for their park and their animals. After you've been here for a few hours, you will also fall in love with the animals. Open seven days from 9-5:30pm. Tel: 1 800 234 7458.

A giant tree puts everything in perspective.

Suntanned fishermen competing with brown pelicans for that perfect catch; palm trees framing dazzling sunsets; elegant red-roofed Spanish-style homes and shopping malls; peaceful islands strewn with millions of tiny shells. These are the images of Southwest Florida, in cities like Naples, Fort Myers and the Sanibel-Captiva Islands.

Southwest Florida

173

A birds-eye view of a wharf scene, Fort Myers Beach.

Naples

Driving into this picture postcard perfect 11 square mile city, you may mistake it for a golf course. Most of the lovely wide boulevards are perfectly manicured with emerald green grass. Naples 21,000 residents take great pride in the city's pristine appearance, and also keep a loving lookout for their wildlife as well. Beaches post signs on what to do if you hook a pelican by mistake, and the nearby **Conservancy** is a haven for injured birds and animals.

Alligators sun on the banks of canals as golfers play five-

Naples, Florida like its cousin in Italy is great for relaxing and letting the mind drift away.

star courses. Brown pelicans, gulls and herons wade along the seashore next to bronzed sunbathers. Wildlife and humans peacefully coexist.

Although life seems quiet here, Neapolitans love to party: there are annual fishing tournaments, swamp buggy races, polo matches, canoe races, beachside jazz and an annual Tropicool Music Fest. Besides having more golf holes per capita than anywhere else in the world, there are acres of farmland to pick your own citrus, tomatoes, corn and strawberries. How is that for town and country living combined?

Your first stop should be at **The Naples Fishing Pier** over at Gulf Shore Boulevard and 12th Avenue South. Ask anyone for directions, they will know

the way: the Pier was built back in 188 and is a favorite fishing spot for loca and tourists. From here you can appr ciate Naples' 10 miles of alabaste beaches, lined with elegant privat homes, and sleek high rise condomin ums.

Try to arrive at The Pier no late than 8:00am. By then, some 50 fishe men will be reeling in snook, snappe redfish, grouper, and mackerel that the have caught for lunch. Just 50 feet from the pier, dolphins kick up their flipper and brown pelicans glide over the wave scouting for their own lunch. It is hard tell who is more skilled at fishing–th birds or the folks with high-tech tack boxes, but everyone at The Pier enjoy themselves to the max.

After an hour or a morning on The Pier, step onto the adjacent gorgeous white beach for a day of sunning, swimming and picnicking. Naples is blessed with fabulous beaches, all open to the public. Even streets in exclusive residential neighborhoods within the city lead to public beaches, providing street parking for visitors. These folks know how to make a stranger feel welcome.

If you are not in the mood for a day at the beach, head over to Naples City Dock at Crayton Cove on Naples Bay and rent a boat in the marina. There are all types of boats and day packages, from huge deep sea cruisers, sleek sailing yachts and small powerboats that will speed you out to the fabled 10,000 Islands in the Gulf of Mexico. Call Tel: (813) 434 4693 for reservations.

Up for something unusual? Spend some time browsing through two very unique museums: The Collier Automotive Museum and Frannie's Teddy Bear Museum.

The Collier, over at 2500 South Horseshoe Drive, has a vast collection of high performance automobiles displayed like Tiffany jewels. Gary Cooper's 1935 Dusenberg gleams alongside ten Rolls Royces and dozens of Bentleys, many of which have been shown at New York's Museum of Modern Art. Next door is a $1/4$ mile "exercise" track where you can see these beauties in action, as maintainence professionals prepare them for upcoming car races. Call Tel: (813) 643 5252 for hours and schedules.

You see teddy bears coming and going at **Frannie's Teddy Bear Museum**, just east of the city at 2511 Pine Ridge Road. Some tourists like to bring their own teddies to visit the 1,800 bears housed in very creative displays. Bears range in size from one inch to 8 feet in height, including the famous "Goldilocks and her Three Bears", patriot bears, polar bears, Count "Bearacula", an officious "Beard of Directors", and of course, Winnie the Pooh. A Museum for bear lovers of all ages, with a staff that is happy to share "beary" special anecdotes with you. Call Tel: (813) 598 2711.

Driving west on Pine Ridge Road, take a left at Goodlette Frank Road where you will see signs directing you to **The Conservancy** at 1450 Merrihue Drive. Devoted to protecting and preserving nature and wildlife in Southern Florida, The Conservancy is a fascinating natural science museum where you can get eye-to-eye with snakes, loggerhead turtles, sea creatures and bald eagles. Nature trail walks and free boat trips add to the educational fun. Call Tel: (813) 262 0304.

If you are into shopping, plan a few days for browsing through some of Florida's most delightful boutiques, offering everything from silk dresses to cowboy boots to daring swim wear. Galleries have a wide spectrum of art, from Pre-Columbian gold treasures to paintings and sculptures executed by locals and Old Masters. One favorite shopping area right near The Pier, is "Third Street South", where over 100 shops are nes-

The Conservancy: Walk On The Wild Side

Inside the Conservancy's Natural Science Museum in Naples, a wide- eyed kid stands eye-to-eye with a Florida rattlesnake that is bigger than he is. Another kid wanders through a forest of stuffed black bears, panthers and armadillos. Over at the saltwater tank, an excited group of children are making fast friends with sea urchins, starfish and horseshoe crabs. It is a toss-up over who is getting wilder at the Conservancy, the kids or the wildlife?

For over 25 years, The Conservancy and their 3,000 volunteer members have worked to protect the beaches, waterways, islands, fisheries and wildlife of Collier County. They have done a spectacular job. With the help of biologists, botanists, land planners and economists, The Conservancy has proven to commercial developers that they can financially benefit when projects include precious natural resources, instead of destroying them.

The Conservancy welcomes visitors to their wooded complex in Naples, which includes the Natural Science Museum, self-guided nature trails, and an outdoor aviary where injured owls, ospreys, hawks and bald eagles are rehabilitated. The Nature Store offers a fine selection of animal toys, gifts and books.

If you are lucky you may glimpse some manatee and mangrove birds on the Conservancy's free 45-minute boat ride along the tidal lagoon and the Gordon River.

There is always something interesting going on around here: wildlife experts give talks on "sneaky snakes" and "tracking the Florida Black Bear". There are square dancing and fish fry nights, sunset bike tours through the Everglades, and Barrier Island canoe trips.

Just a few miles south of Naples on Shell Island Road, is Rookery Bay, an estuary of 9,400 acres, where wading birds, fish and shellfish thrive in rivers and streams that meet the sea. The headquarters and research facilities of the Department of Natural Resources, and The

Conservancy's Briggs Nature Center are here. Browse through the nature center's estuarine exhibits and marine aquariums or sign up for lectures like "The Estuary Scavenger Hunt", "Snack with the Blue Crab" and "The Endangered Manatee." Out behind the nature center you can walk along the half mile boardwalk.

The best way to learn about Rookery Bay is to get out in a boat or canoe into the estuary and see the wading birds, fish and shellfish. The Conservancy staff naturalists offer guided field trips several times each day. There are also guided walks through the forest fringing the bay where you will learn the difference between red, black and white mangroves, and see some of the animals that live within them.

The Conservancy has been immensely successful in land preservation, acquiring more than 25,000 acres of environmentally endangered land. They were instrumental in the Federal Government selecting Rookery Bay as one of the 11 US sanctuaries mandated by Congress to be set aside for research and education.

They persuaded the state of Florida to acquire and protect 13,500 acres of wetlands and islands surrounding Marco Island, by offering a commercial developer other equally workable sites. And in addition to building and operating the Naples Nature Center and the Rookery Bay Briggs Nature Center, the Conservancy has been a leader in saving endangered species like the loggerhead sea turtle and protecting the popular snook sportfish from becoming overfished. More than just a nature center and museum, The Conservancy is an inspiring environmental role model for making sure our children have a future world to enjoy. The center has demonstrated what a group of enlightened, caring citizens can accomplish, when they decide that wildlife and human beings can live together in a way mutually beneficial way.

The Conservancy, Inc. At 1450 Merrihue Drive, Naples. Tel: (813) 262 0304.

tled in cozy arcades and courtyards. It is so pretty here, you might not make it inside the stores! In the same neighborhood is "Fifth Avenue South",

another excellent shopping area where you can find antiques, books, electronics, furniture, jewelry and clothing.

Not many tourists know that Naples has one of Florida's leading symphonies and the city is the Gulf Coast home to the Miami City Ballet. Both perform at the spectacular **Philharmonic Center for the Arts**, at 5833 Pelican Bay Boulevard, which also has other musical and theatrical performances year round. Call Tel: (813) 597 .111 for schedules.

After some great fishing, boating, beaching, golfing and shopping, save some energy for Naples' nightlife.

Fort Myers

Forty miles north of Naples on Route 41 or I-75, is Fort Myers, with more beautiful beaches, wildlife, sea shells, fishing, and and water sports, and fascinating history.

Are you a baseball fan? Then drive over to **The Lee County Sports Complex** on Six Mile Cypress Parkway in south Fort Myers, and cheer on The Minnesota Twins during their spring training. This open-air stadium with an old-fashioned steeple seats 7500 fans. There is also an 8 acre lake stocked for fishing, as well as soccer and softball fields, bicycle paths and a playground. Call Tel: (813) 335 2284 for training schedules.

Just a few miles north on Cypress Parkway is the "Six Mile Cypress Slough Preserve", a 2,000 acre wetland ecosystem. It is so peaceful strolling along the boardwalk trail, winding through ancient cypress trees and slash pine. You

Shrimp boats hard at work in the open seas.

have to look carefully to see the herons, egrets, wood storks, roseate spoonbills, woodpeckers, alligators, racoon, red-shouldered hawks and wild turkeys, but they are there in this mysterious swamp. A beautiful, intimate look at the "real" Florida.

North On Cypress Parkway

Continuing north on Cypress Parkway, the street name changes to Oritz Avenue, where you will see signs for the **Nature Center and Planetarium** of Lee County. Families with young children will find this center a delight, as volunteers help them to "pet" snakes, baby alligators and turtles. Outside you can

Thomas Edison: The Man & His Mansion

Seat of genius, Thomas Edison's winter home in Fort Myer.

A 1930 magazine ad for Edison's electric light bulb touted his marvelous invention as: "The Sun's only Rival".

Who was this man who worked 20 hours a day and created over 1,000 patents for inventions that changed the world?

Besides The Light Bulb

Besides the electric light bulb, Edison invented electric motors, electric appliances, batteries, phonographs, telegraphs and the motion picture projector, the "Kinetoscope." And many many more practical products that are part of modern life.

Edison built the first in-ground swimming pool at his Florida home, but never swam in it. He spent hours on his gazebo pier with a fishing pole that had no bait on it, so "it won't disturb my thinking." He worked so late into the night in his lab that he would take naps on his desk the next day. His wife Mina finally put a cot there because she thought his cat naps on his des table top were "ungentlemanly."

Fort Meyer

Thomas Alva Edison, genius inventor and sel absorbed individualist, fell in love with For Myers in 1885, when it was just a sleepy tropica village along the bamboo-lined banks of th Caloosahatchee River. He purchased 14 acres c waterfront estate, built a gracious ramblin home and in 1886 made it his lifelong winte home. There is no better way to get a sense of man's character than to visit his castle, an touring Edison's winter home offers a fascina ing insight into the mind of the man.

You will be guided through the incredibl gardens that he and Mrs Edison planted: lemor mango and orange trees, palms, bamboo, Ch nese cinnamon, clove, tea, allspice, papyru

trees, sugarcane, coconut palms, and Mina Edison's beloved lily pond. You will see where he kept his electric boat, the gazebo where he "dreamed" with an empty fishing pole, and the largest Indian Banyan tree in the United States, a gift from his friend Harvey Firestone.

His home is lovely, with overhanging porches, white wicker furniture, and French doors on the first floor instead of windows. The interior, decorated with early American furniture, handpainted porcelain, floral wallpaper and Mina's baby grand, emanates a feeling of the glittering social world they were part of, entertaining captains of industry and international friends.

Edison's chemical lab is a Frankenstein movie set, with tables and cabinets overflowing with hundreds of odd-shaped flasks and murky bottles. Here Edison experimented with the idea of turning goldenrod into rubber, some of his research becoming the basis for today's synthetic rubber industry.

The Edison Museum

The 7,500 square foot **Edison Museum** is a testament to the prolific results of his life: hundreds of phonographs, batteries, the ticker tape machine, movie projectors, light bulbs, talking dolls, children's furniture, and hundreds of other inventions. There's also Edison's beloved Model-T Ford, a gift from Henry Ford. The culmination of a lifetime of inventiveness, genius and hard work.

Across the street is Henry Ford's winter home, where they were neighbors from 1863 to 1947. You can also tour this home, seeing Ford's 1914 and 1917 Model Ts and his 1929 Model A which are parked in the garage as if he may go out for a spin any minute.

Visiting Edison's home, garden, laboratory and museum is a delightful way to get to know one of America's most beloved and influential inventors, Thomas Edison and the winter home of his neighbor and famous friend, Henry Ford.

The Edison-Ford Winter Estates, at 2350 McGregor Boulevard, Fort Myers. Tel: (813) 334 3614.

visit the bird aviary, full grown gators and a Florida bobcat. The gift shop has wonderful toys and an excellent book selection. Tel: (813) 275 3435.

From here, go North on Ortiz, and take the ML King Boulevard west to McGregor Boulevard before returning left. At 2350 McGregor you will come to Thomas Edison's elegant 14-acre riverfront estate, his winter home for 45 years. Edison's home, lab and experimental gardens have been beautifully maintained and are a must-see, during your Fort Myers visit. Next door and part of the tour, is the winter home of Edison's very famous good friend, Henry Ford. Tel: (813) 334 3614.

Most tourists come to Fort Myers for the beaches, fishing, and water sports on the beautiful Gulf Of Mexico. Over at Fort Myers Beach, sail the high seas in the *Eagle*, a 68-foot schooner; watch for dolphins from the *Pelican Queen*, a 40-foot pontoon; or dance and gamble on board the 165-foot *Europa FunKruz*. At the Time Square area along the beach, you can go parasailing, rent a jet ski, or charter a deep sea cruise.

You are not likely to run out of things to do in Fort Meyers.

Scintillating Sanibel

In her best selling book, *A Gift From the Sea*, author Anne Morrow Lindberg shares the magic of the Sanibel and Captiva islands: "Rollers on the beach, wind in the pines, the slow flapping of

Captiva offers hours of stress free golfing at the South Seas Plantation.

herons across sand dunes, drown out the hectic rhythms of city and suburb. One falls under their spell.. one becomes...open, empty as the beach erased by today's tides..."

Connected to the mainland by a three-mile long causeway, Sanibel and Captiva are worlds away from Fort Meyers city and suburban life. Although Sanibel has gotten over-civilized with hardware and grocery stores and dozens of restaurants among the Australian pines, it is still a charming peaceful island where wildlife and people get along together.

On The Gulf Side

On the Gulf side on **Bowman's Beach Road**, you will find superb shelling at Bowman's Beach. Stroll along the soft beige sand and pick out your own special pink, peach, grey, and white "gifts from the sea." The gulls, ibis, egret, and pelicans are so tame that they will march

drive past otters, alligators and raccoons, living among the seagrape, salt myrtles, red mangrove and sabal palms. The visitor center will outfit you with walking and driving maps. Tel: (813) 472 1100.

Captivating Captiva

Captiva is much less developed than Sanibel and even quieter. You can spend days just peacefully on the beaches or taking picnic boat cruises to **Cabbage Key** and **Useppa Island**, to explore historic inns, nature trails, and see some of the "old Florida" style homes. Tel: (813) 472 7549.

Of Sailing & The South Seas

If you have got too much energy to relax on the beach, why not learn to sail at the "Offshore Sailing School" at the **South Seas Plantation Marina**? The owner is Steve Colgate, an Olympic and America's Cup veteran. The school offers courses for beginners, advanced, racing, and bareboat cruising. Tel: (800) 221 4326. Or perhaps you would rather ogle those "gifts from the sea" from an underwater point of view. Also at the South Seas Plantation on Sanibel-Captiva Road, is Pieces of Eight Dive Center, a PADI dive operation, with snorkeling and diving excursions to coral reef ledges, ship wrecks and deep "blue holes". Tel: (813) 472 9424.

right along with you, darting into the water's edge, looking for their own "gifts."

At Sanibel's southern tip, is a pier and beach which is delightful for fishing, shelling and bird watching. A couple of "pet" pelicans live on top of the pier roof, and are enormously interested in any extra fish you might hand up. If you have not had your fill of wildlife by now, plan to spend some time at the **JN Ding Darling Wildlife Refuge**, located on the Sanibel/Captiva Road. The refuge has excellent footpaths, winding canoe trails, and a five-mile long scenic

Nesting sea turtles, peach-colored seashells on snow white beaches, 43 golf courses, umpteen tennis courts, 60 marinas with international yachts, superb art and science museums, Greek and Scottish villages, 361 days of sunshine a year, and every land and water sport ever invented. This is the Saint Petersburg/Clearwater area, called Florida's Pinellas Suncoast.

■ ■ ■ ■ ■ ■

The curve of the bay and waterside living along Don Caesar, St Petersburg.

Heading north on Route 41, watch for signs to Route 19 Skyway into Saint Petersburg. Like a fantasy yacht sailing into heaven, this incredible Skyway bridge draws you up... up... up... into the blue sky until you think you are driving into the clouds, instead of into a modern city. But soon you're speeding down the other side, exhilarated from this unusual Saint Petersburg

Saint Petersburg & Tampa

183

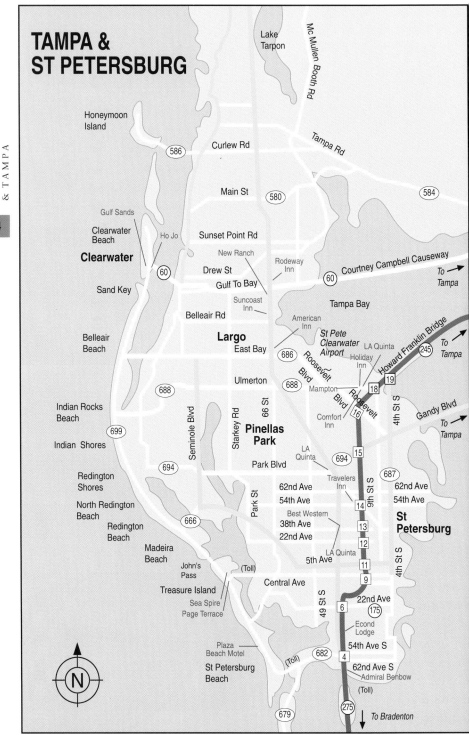

TAMPA &
ST PETERSBURG

Lake
Tarpon

Mc Mullen Booth Rd

Honeymoon
Island

586

Curlew Rd

Tampa Rd

Main St

580

584

Gulf Sands

Clearwater
Beach

Ho Jo

Clearwater

60

Sand Key

Sunset Point Rd

New Ranch

Rodeway
Inn

Drew St

Gulf To Bay

60

Courtney Campbell Causeway

To
Tampa

Belleair Rd

Suncoast
Inn

Tampa Bay

Largo

East Bay

American
Inn

St Pete
Clearwater
Airport

LA Quinta

Howard Franklin Bridge

To
Tampa

Belleair
Beach

686

Roosevelt Blvd

Holiday
Inn

245

Ulmerton

688

Mampton

Roosevelt Blvd

18

19

Indian Rocks
Beach

688

Comfort
Inn

16

4th St S

Gandy Blvd

To
Tampa

699

Seminole Blvd

Starkey Rd

66 St

**Pinellas
Park**

LA
Quinta

694

15

687

Indian Shores

Park Blvd

Travelers
Inn

9th St S

62nd Ave

694

54th Ave

Redington
Shores

North Redington
Beach

62nd Ave

14

**St
Petersburg**

Redington
Beach

666

54th Ave

Best Western

38th Ave

13

22nd Ave

12

Madeira
Beach

LA Quinta

5th Ave

11

4th St S

John's
Pass

9

(Toll)

Treasure Island

Central Ave

49 St S

6

22nd Ave

Sea Spire

Page Terrace

175

Econd
Lodge

54th Ave S

Plaza
Beach Motel

4

62nd Ave S

St Petersburg
Beach

(Toll)

682

Admiral Benbow

(Toll)

679

275

To Bradenton

N

welcome.

Continue to 275 north and then 175 west into downtown Saint Petersburg. Follow signs to The Pier at 800 Second Avenue. Park in the lot and walk (or take the complimentary bus) down to the Pier, a beautiful spaceship-like building filled with shops, restaurants, an aquarium, and from the top observation deck, a superb city view. Sprawling before you are Saint Petersburg's yacht-filled marinas, the growing downtown skyline, residential neighborhoods and the glistening waters of Tampa Bay.

On the Pier street level, you can rent scooters, rollerskates, bicycles and wave runners. Or hop aboard one of the cruise ships for a lunchtime float out into the Bay.

After a morning at The Pier, head back west to Beach Drive and turn right, where you will see **The Museum of Fine Arts**. An intimate Mediterranean villa-style museum, the Fine Arts has a diverse collection, ranging from antiques, to Steuben crystal, African art, Rodin sculptures and paintings by Monet, Renoir, Cezanne and Gauguin. At 225 Beach Drive NE. Tel: (813) 896 2667.

Continue south to 3rd and 11th Avenues and you will see the **Salvador Dali Museum**, the largest collection of work in the world by the famous Spanish artist. Dramatic and compelling, Dali's work is not easily understood, with its intense colors, three dimensional figures, and often perverse images melting into bizarre, nightmarish shapes.

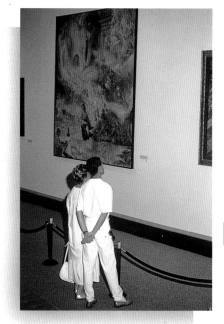

Feast your eyes on the genius and emerge stimulated, Dali Museum.

His subject matter delves into man's darker side: alienation, difficulty in relationships, paranoia, familial estrangement. In his writings, Dali revealed that "the only difference between myself and a madman is that I am not mad." You will definitely leave his Museum stimulated. Take the free guided tours which are helpful in learning about this eccentric genius' life and work. Dali Museum, at 1000 Third Street South. Tel: (813) 823 3767.

If you are travelling with kids, try not to miss **Great Explorations**, just down the street at 1120, 4th Street South. A unique "hands-on" museum involving art, exploration, brain teasers, a touch tunnel and physical strength tests, there is also a fantastic creepy crawly

Scenes at the pier, Saint Petersburg.

Tarpon Springs: Sea Sponges, Parks & Miracles

Bounty from the seas – the multi-functional sea sponges.

In his rust-colored rubberized suit, bronze shoulder pads and metal helmet, Diver Dionysus Angelis looks like a frog from another planet. But here in Tarpon Springs, Dionysus is dressed for work, in the Greek town which is once again becoming "The Sponge Capital of the World."

Tarpon Springs owes its beginnings to real estate businessman John Cheyney, who invested in sponge harvesting here, and to Greek sponge buyer John Corcoris, who with his two brothers were the first of 2,000 Greeks who helped the Tarpon Springs sponge industry become a $3 million international business by 1936.

Today, natural sponges continue to be in high demand throughout the world, and Tarpon Springs is a busy center of sponge dive boats, sponge processing factories, sponge museums sponge shops and of course Greek festivals and food. The city has become a favorite stop for tourists who enjoy the friendly small town atmosphere, irresistible food, and plenty of Mother Nature nearby.

Downtown on Dodecanese Boulevard, you can climb aboard the Saint Nicholas VII, a Mediterranean-style sponge boat, and head out along the Anclote River for a sponge diving demonstration. Twisting on his heavy metal helmet, the diver's suit is pumped up with air. Slowly he sinks to the sea floor below the water, a black air tube his only lifeline. All you can see are bubbles floating to the water's surface. With a hook he spears the sponge, puts it in his basket, and passes it up to the waiting boat. Just like in the old days, it is totally a tedious labor intensive job. But for Diver Dionysus and Captain Angelo, it's all part of their day's work.

Sea Sponge

Back at the dock, boats unload bundles of sea sponges from giant green nets into dockside shops where tourists take home sponges of every size and shape. Some people use them as planters, for washing cars, or for relaxing in the bath.

Across the street, Chef Andy Salivaris at **Mykonos Restaurant** is serving up delicious home-cooked Greek-style shrimp in garlic, panfried squid, pickled octopus and for dessert, some sweet and flaky *baklava*.

Tarpon Springs' downtown area has been nicely restored with brick tree-lined sidewalks, benches, banners and old-style street lamps. Many of the old buildings now house dozens of antique shops, art galleries and studios, cafés, a bank, a bed and breakfast inn and specialty shops.

Over at the old **City Hall** on Pinellas Avenue, the **Cultural Center** hosts programs, concerts, and exhibits.

The old **Atlantic Coast Line Railroad Station** at the corner of Tarpon Avenue and Safford Avenue is now home to the Historical Society, as well as a newly formed Model Railroad Association. Stop by to see the miniature railroad, as well as reproductions of historic buildings and Sponge Docks.

Few visitors to Tarpon Springs are aware that the city has two spectacular parks: Fred Howard Park and Anderson Park.

Fred Howard Park, on the west side of town on the Gulf of Mexico, has picnic tables nestled among pine and palm forests, superb fishing and a beautiful quiet beach. At 6:00am, runners, dog walkers, bikers and fishermen are out enjoying the gorgeous coastline. So are the gulls, egrets and black anhinga birds. Stop by any time, but do stop by!

AL Anderson Park on the east side of town, is right on Lake Tarpon. Pristine fields of green grass, palm and pine woods and a delightful kid's playground by the lake makes this a wonderful park for fishing, picnicking or just for a quiet stroll.

Driving Through The Streets

Driving through the residential streets of Tarpon Springs, you will see many homes from the early

Old Greek sponger reminiscing on the ole days.

1900s located along twisting and turning bayous. Some homes have water for backyards, where lucky residents can keep their fishing boats.

Over at 113 Hope Street is Saint Michael's Shrine, a tiny Greek Orthodox chapel with stained glass windows, a few pews, religious portraits and a simple altar. According to local legend, the shrine was built by the Tsalickis family because of the miracle they experienced.

Their son, Steve Tsalickis became so ill as a child that he was close to death. But while praying to a religious painting of Saint Michael from Greece, Steve received divine instructions that his mother was to build a shrine to the Holy Saint. Mrs Tsalickis agreed and Steve was immediately healed. Today the lovely shrine is open for all to visit, and Steve Tsalickis is alive and well, managing Paul's Restaurant in Tarpon Springs. It is all part of Tarpon Springs' magic, a place of history, heart, and hope.

Skiing without skis!

reptile zoo. Tel: (813) 821 8992.

Any trip to Saint Petersburg calls for plenty of time at the beach, two of which have been named by *Conde Nast Traveler Magazine* as among the Top 10 beaches in the United States. The beaches stretch for 28 miles along the Pinellas Suncoast, which includes communities like **Clearwater Beach**, **Saint Pete Beach**, **Treasure Island**, **Madeira Beach**, **Indian Rocks Beach**, **Dunedin** and **Tarpon Springs**.

Besides sunning and people watching, you can spend several happy days on these gorgeous beaches snorkeling, windsurfing, surfing, parasailing, jet skiing, waterskiing, sailing and scuba diving. Just head east of Saint Petersburg, and settle on the beach you like best.

They are all winners.

When you are ready to dry off, there is an extensive public park system that showcases the area's diverse ecosystem: amber sea oats along the Gulf of Mexico, stands of pine, cypress and mangroves and inland trails that weave through jungle-like hammocks. There are 14 county parks to choose from, where you can take photographs, bicycle, camp, canoe, fish and hike. Some of the more popular ones are **Anderson Park** and **Brooker Creek Park** in Tarpon Springs; **Lake Seminole Park** in Seminole; **Sawgrass Lake Park** in Pinellas Park; **Veterans Memorial Park** in Bay Pines; **Boyd Hill Nature Trail** in Saint Petersburg, and **Moccasin Lake Nature Park** in Clearwater. To get a complete list of parks and facilities, contact Pinellas Suncoast Convention & Visitor Bureau, Florida Suncoast Dome, One Stadium Drive, Suite A, Saint Petersburg, Florida 33705. Tel: (813) 892 7892.

Two of Pinellas's Suncoast most unusual communities are Dunedin and Tarpon Springs.

Dunedin was settled by the Scots in 1870. Her ancestors still celebrate that fact each April with The Highland Games with bagpipes and drum competitions, highland dancing, athletic games and other Scottish traditions, making this a fun time to visit.

Tarpon Springs is a Greek fishing village that was once the sponge capital of the world. There is still a flourishing sponge industry here, with many companies exporting worldwide. For tour-

Wonderful World of Reptiles, Science & Dolphins

is Sunday at the **Great Explorations Museum Reptile Zoo**, but nobody here is taking the day off.

A palm-sized hairy tarantula crawls along a jagged tree branch heading for a water bowl swim. A black thigh-sized 8 foot long boa constrictor slides up his glass wall greeting you eye-to-eye. A tomato-red Madagascar frog hops over to a green Gecko lizard, trying to start a conversation. And a lady reptile keeper over at the corner "touch table", calmly strokes the smooth scales of a 5 foot long king snake, telling awed kids how this friendly snake eats poisonous rattlesnakes and rats.

It is relatively easy to become mesmerized by this cast of lively critters. You are so close and they're so active, it is kind of creepy crawly and scary, in a totally wonderful way. This zoo is a dream come true for any kid that ever put a critter in his jeans pocket.

The **Reptile Zoo** has educational entertaining shows going on all the time like, "Snakes, Dragons and Folktales", "Wildlife Magic Show" and "Captain Cool's Liquid Nitrogen Show".

The Zoo is part of the Great Explorations Museum, an interactive, hands-on museum about science, art, thinking and physical strength. Robert Miller, an artist displaying his work here, gives his interpretation : "Blobs, spots, specks, smudges, cracks, defects, mistakes, accidents, exceptions and irregularities are the windows to other worlds."

Great Explorations challenges you to explore those other worlds, the inner realms of your own perceptions, creativity and feelings.

Dance in front of a video camera, where your body is a silhouetted pattern of color and motion and is projected larger than life on a big black screen. Crawl through a 90 foot long pitch black tunnel: were you excited or afraid? Test out your problem-solving skills with computerized brain teasing games.

After a morning of reptiles and science, head 35 miles northeast to Clearwater, where Sam the Atlantic bottlenose dolphin is hard at work painting t-shirts. Sam was rescued from Tampa Bay by the marine scientists at the **Clearwater Marine Science Center** when he became very ill. Today he lives happily in a 260,000 gallon pool where he works with handicapped children and calms other marine animals arriving for treatment. Although he has a liver condition and is visually impaired, Sam has become quite celebrity for his artistic abilities. Put a paintbrush in his mouth and wow! Salvador Dali and Peter Max watch out! Sam's artful t-shirts are sold at the science center gift shop, to help raise funds for their continued research and support of the animals.

The Clearwater Marine Science Center is a non-profit organization dedicated to the rescue and rehabilitation of injured marine life. Most of the animals are treated and released, but some permanently live here .

Meet Max and Adam, rare Kemp's Ridley sea turtles; Mo, a loggerhead sea turtle, Sybil, a deaf dolphin; Atlantic stingrays, Nurse sharks and cat sharks. It is a totally impressive family.

In the lobby are beautiful coral reefs, tanks of fish and sponge displays. There's a "Sea-o-rama" Room displaying dozens of fish and sea shells found in the Gulf and around the world. And a touch tank where kids can get friendly with sea creatures.

During the summer months, The Center monitors 11 miles of local beach, from Redington Shores to Caladesi Island, making sure that they are safe places for the loggerhead sea turtles to lay their eggs.

The Clearwater Marine Science Center has delightful exhibits and educational classes all year round, so stop by at 249 Windward Passage, Clearwater. Tel: (813) 441 1790 to say hello to Sam, and get one of his original t-shirts.

Great Explorations is at 1120 4th Street South, Saint Petersburg. Tel: (813) 821 8885.

sts there are sponge diving tours, sponge hops and fabulous Greek food. Try not to miss out on the fresh calamari, shrimp, dolmades and baklava for lunch! There are also some great antique shops in Tarpon Springs.

If you have more time, head over to Indian Shores, (just west of Seminole, on

Gulf Boulevard, right on the oceanfront) and visit the **Suncoast Seabird Sanctuary**. Founded in 1971 by zoologist Ralph T Heath Jr, The Sanctuary is the largest wild bird hospital in the United States, working to rescue, repair, recuperate and release sick and injured wild birds. The Sanctuary has been featured on network television and in major environmental magazines, and is a *don't* miss on your trip to the Saint Petersburg area. At 18328 Gulf Boulevard, Indian Shores. Tel: (813) 391 6211.

Tampa

Wealthy glamourous Americans once socialized at Henry Plant's exquisite 1891 Tampa Bay Hotel. Today it is the **University of Tampa**, where students from around the world make plans for the future, in domed ballrooms of the past.

Don Vicente Martinez Ybor built his Ybor City in Tampa into the "Cigar Capital of the World". Today Ybor City is a revitalized urban neighborhood of offices, galleries, museums, shops and restaurants.

Pirate José Gaspar, last of the late 18th century buccaneers, once terrorized the coastal waters of West Florida, robbing treasure-laden merchant ships. Today, Tampa celebrates his demise by the **USS Enterprise**, with Gasparilla Day, when city leaders dress as pirates board the Jose Gasparilla ship, and Tampa becomes a month-long party of parades, music, dancing and international

As the sign reads "Suncoast Seabird Sanctuary" with their mascot pelican

cuisine.

These are all images of Tampa, city where history, international cultures and entrepreneurs celebrate the past, the present and the future.

Plan to spend at least a week here possible because Tampa is one of Florida's most fascinating cities.

Touring Tampa

Start out in Ybor City, the former "cigar capital of the world." Take I-4 to the Ybor City exit, go south on 21st street. Turn right on Palm Avenue (10th Ave.) go west and turn left on 13th Street to 8th Avenue where you will see Ybor Square. From here you can take a free

Boat-building on the Dark Continent, Tampa.

$^1/_2$ hour guided walking tour past the factories where workers hand-rolled cigars; wander past Cuban and Italian clubs, where cigar workers socialized and see the homes where they lived. The tour ends at The **Ybor City State Museum** at 1818 E 9th Avenue, where wonderful historic photographs tell Ybor City's story. After the tour, browse through Ybor City's boutique and antique shops, art galleries, book stores and have lunch at the **Columbia**, the world's largest Spanish restaurant.

From here, get back on I-4 west to I-75 towards Tampa, and take the Ashley Street exit. Take Ashley to Kennedy Boulvard, turning right where you will see domes, minarets and pinnacles rising 50 feet into the sky. This is the former Tampa Bay Hotel built by railroad magnate Henry Plant for the social elite of the 1890s.

On the front veranda where the barons of industry and their very refined wives once took afternoon tea, you can now hear the buzz of University of Tampa students conversing in French, German, Italian, Japanese and yes, English. It is truly fascinating to wander through the hallways, ballrooms, gardens, and the Henry B Plant Museum, trying to imagine those very glamorous days of old. At 401 West Kennedy Boulevard, Tampa. Tel: (813) 254 1891.

USA Today lauded Tampa as the "Sports Capital of the USA" and for good reason. The Cincinnati Reds and The New York Yankees spring train here in

Cedar Key

If you do not want to fish, you can always shop or eat at the shops and restaurants along the fishing pier, Cedar Key.

It is amazing that no one has turned Cedar Key into a kitschy tourist town. It is just a tiny laidback weathered old fishing port on the Gulf of Mexico, where scruffy locals and unfashionable tourists reel in trout, redfish, mullet, sheepshead, grouper, snapper and pompano.

Inside **Hammock House Gift Shop** over on 1st Street, there is a huge bulletin board with polaroid snapshots of the results: tanned happy fishermen and women holding up gleaming fish as big as they are. Forget the designer tackle boxes, isn't catching fish what its all about?

Cedar Key has no glitz or glamour, just downhome folks who do not care that some of the portside buildings are shacks on stilts, looking like they can tumble over at the slightest breeze. Try not to worry, most of these windswept two-story wooden buildings have faced severe storms since the 1840s, and they are certainly not about to fall down now.

Today, they are simple but comfortable hotels, seafood restaurants with Gulf views, trendy art galleries, real estate offices, and ok, a few kitschy T-shirt and shell gift shops.

March. The Tampa Bay Buccaneers compete in the National Football League at **Tampa Stadium** from August to December. Greyhounds race in parimutuels at **Derby Lane**, thoroughbred horses race at **Tampa Bay Downs**, and

Tampa's fastest ball games take place at **Tampa's Jai-Alai Fronton** all year round. And newly arrived: National Hockey League games feature Tampa Bay Lightning.

Not enough? How about golf, fish-

Start with a visit to the **Cedar Key State Museum**, just north of town on Museum and Whitman Drive. They have interesting exhibits on the town's history and a nice shell collection.

Cedar Key was settled in the early 1840s, but flourished with the 1861 completion of the cross state railroad from Fernadina, which allowed the shipment of lumber and turpentine by land or sea. During the War between the States, supplies were shipped in and out from Cedar Key, and salt was locally made to send to the Southern armies. After the war, Cedar Key continued to prosper by shipping lumber until the 1880's when seafood became the town's main industry.

The need for deeper harbors caused the decline of the port, as well as the exploitation of the oyster beds. Cedar Key's last industry, manufacturing brushes and brooms from palm fiber, ceased with the discovery of plastics.

But decline never lasts long in Florida as there are just too many entrepreneurs who envision opportunities to begin again. And so in 1991, Project OCEAN (Oyster Clam Educational Aquaculture Network) began in Cedar Key, where training is being provided by the Federal Job Training Partnership Act teaching the techniques of shellfish farming. Oysters and clams are raised from seed to harvest under protective conditions, so local fishermen can study the process and establish their own commercial enterprises. Sounds like we are sure to be hearing from Cedar Key again real soon.

Meanwhile, the town is a popular spot for those who do not need any more entertainment rather than sitting on the pier–fishing. Some times there seem to be more pelicans and gulls than people–who arrive at dawn with plastic buckets, plenty of bait, and wide-rimmed straw hats against the blinding sun.

Besides visiting the Museum, and wandering through the town's shops, you might like to spend a day at **Cedar Key's National Wildlife Refuge**, which was established in 1929 by President Herbert Hoover.

The refuge consists of offshore islands loated within five miles of Cedar Key, ranging in size from 1 to 165 acres. Many of the islands are nesting areas for white ibis, egret, cormorants, heron, osprey and brown pelicans. This is a good place to see lots of Florida plantlife: forests of cabbage palm, red bay, live oak, saw palmetto, wild olive, prickly pear and Spanish bayonet. If you are a snake lover, there are whole families of them on Snake, North and Seahorse Keys. (On second thought, why not visit your favorite snakes at the zoo?)

The only way to visit the Refuge is by boat, which you can easily lure at the Cedar Key City Marina. Island beaches, except Seahorse Key, are open to the public, and the boats will drop you off for a day of collecting shells, birdwatching, picnicking and taking pictures. If you have been trying to get away from crowded beaches, and close to the "real" Florida, this is your big chance.

Or if you are in the mood for a terrific party, plan to be in Cedar Key from April 17 to18 for the Sidewalk Arts Festival or on October 17 to 18 for the Seafood Festival. Hundreds of artists and seafood lovers come from all over the country to attend these festivals, and it is a great way to fall in love with Cedar Key, as you most certainly will.

Cedar Key is 50 miles west of Gainesville. From I-75 take Route 24 west, and watch for signs to Cedar Key. For information on current festival dates, write to the Cedar Key Chamber of Commerce, at PO Box 610, Cedar Key, Florida 32625. Tel: (904) 543 5600.

ing, tennis, marathon running? There is even a skydiving school for those with fearless hearts.

Complete sports, events schedules and city maps are free from the Tampa/Hillsborough Convention and Visitor's Bureau at 111 Madison Street, Suite 1010, Tampa. Fl 33601-0519. Tel: (813) 223 1111. Call, write or stop by when you arrive.

If you have wanted to see Florida's manatees throughout your travels

A flamingo paradise at Busch Gardens, Dark Continent.

through the state, **Tampa's Lowry Park Zoo** just opened the $3.3 million "Pepsi Manatee and Aquatic Center".

Inside cool, dimly-lit underwater viewing rooms, you can watch and fall in love with these gentle creatures! Undulating and spinning through the water, these 2,000 lb. "sea cows" play, flirt, hug each other, nibble plants and every few minutes, stick their blubbery-mouthed faces above the water for air. A narrator explains how they live, why they have become endangered, and what you can do to protect them.

Manatee Mania

This is one of the few places in Florida where you can see manatees close-up and underwater, and a must-see if you love wildlife. The Zoo also has elephants,

Drive. Tel: (813) 223 8130.

Theater & The Performing Arts

Save some energy for Tampa's nightlife. The **Tampa Bay Performing Arts Center** is one the largest arts complexes in the US and always has two or three broadway and theatrical shows going on. At 1010 N MacInnes Place. Tel: (800) 955 1045.

The **Tampa Theater** is a restored 1926 movie palace with feature films, concerts and special events. 711 Franklin Street. Tel: (813) 223 08981. Tampa is also home to **The Florida Orchestra**, at 1211 N Westshore Boulevard. Tel: (813) 286 2403; **New Playmakers.** Tel: (813) 972 1177; **Spanish Lyric Theater**. Tel: (813) 223 7341; **Tampa Oratorio Society**. Tel: (813) 988 2165 and **The Tampa Players**. Tel: (813) 229 3221.

A Big Future!

Tampa city leaders are gearing up for a big future. Within the next few years at the Port of Tampa, you will be able to visit a new state-of-the-art 120,000 square foot **Florida Aquarium**, a $25 million **Music Dome Amphitheater**, a shipwreck/treasure museum and a high-tech motion theater, all built along Tampa's scenic waterfront.

So stay tuned for more Tampa-style innovation and fun.

birds, reptiles, black bears, wolves, alligators and other animals. **Lowry Park Zoo**. At 7530 N Boulevard, Tampa. Tel: (813) 935 8552.

Tampa has many excellent museums, including **The Museum of Science & Industry**, 4801 E Fowler Avenue. Tel: (813) 985 5531; **The Children's Museum of Tampa.** Tel: (813) 935 8441; **The Museum of African-American Art** at 1308 N Marion Street. Tel: (813) 272 2466; and **The Tampa Museum of Art** at 601 Doyle Carlton

Sarasota

199

From around the world travellers come for Sarasota's sunshine, and the serenity of relaxing along miles of beautiful beaches in a shady cabana.

But if creativity and artistic inspiration are your idea of a vacation, then you have come to the right city, for Sarasota is also a treasure chest of culture: art, music, dance, theater, opera and film; as well as a mecca of fascinating museums, gardens and wildlife.

Stunning Italian Renaissance-style villa seen in the Ringling Mansion.

Touring Sarasota

Begin your exploration of the city at **The John and Mable Ringling Museum of Art**, off U S Route 41, two miles north of downtown. Within this stunning Italian Renaissance-style villa, is one of the nation's finest collec-

The best type of fishing, bare-bodied, half-submerged and in the presence
of competing fowl – a pelican!

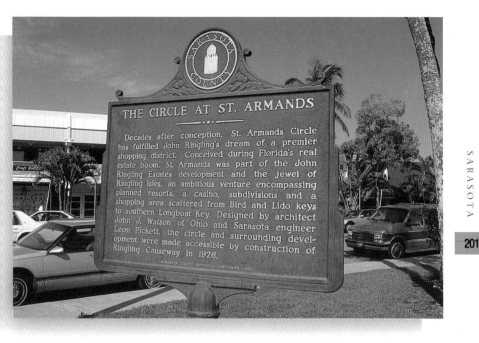

THE CIRCLE AT ST. ARMANDS

Decades after conception, St. Armands Circle has fulfilled John Ringling's dream of a premier shopping district. Conceived during Florida's real estate boom, St. Armands was part of the John Ringling Estates development and the jewel of Ringling Isles, an ambitious venture encompassing planned resorts, a casino, subdivisions and a shopping area scattered from Bird and Lido keys to southern Longboat Key. Designed by architect John J. Watson of Ohio and Sarasota engineer Leon Pickett, the circle and surrounding development were made accessible by construction of Ringling Causeway in 1926.

SARASOTA COUNTY HISTORICAL COMMISSION, 1988

Read the sign and then shop on.

ions of Old Master paintings, including magnificent murals executed by Peter Paul Rubens. The beautifully land-caped courtyard holds a replica of Michelangelo's David, bubbling fountains and a spectacular view of Sarasota Bay.

On the same grounds, you can wander through John and Mable Ringling's unusual home, **Ca'd'Zan** (House of John), a 30-room mansion modeled after a Venetian palace. Stairs from the outdoor marble terrace lead to the waterfront where Mable Ringling once kept her Italian gondola!

Next door, **The Circus Galleries** hold a delightful collection of parade wagons, photographs, costumes and colorful posters from the early days of the internationally renowned Ringling Brothers Circus. Try not to miss the charming photos of Emmett Kelly and Tom Thumb. At 5401 Bay Shore Road. Tel : (813) 355 5101 or (813) 3511 660.

Just south of the Ringling Museum grounds are the **Sarasota Jungle Gardens**, where you can stroll through 10 acres of jungle trails and tropical gardens. They also have a petting zoo for the kids, a shell and butterfly museum, and frequent bird shows. At 3701 Bay Shore Road. Tel : (813) 355 5305.

If you are a serious plant and flower lover, continue south on US 41 to **Marie Selby Botanical Gardens**. Overlooking Sarasota Bay, this is a world renowned orchid and display garden, which specializes in air plants. Take a tour through

Insider's Guide To Sarasota's Beaches

On the deckchairs, before getting onto the waves.

With so many sugar sand beaches bordering the crystal blue Gulf of Mexico, here is a guide to help you find the Sarasota beach that suits your mood:

• **Manatee Public Beach**: Off Gulf Drive in Holmes Beach on Anna Maria Island, this is a place for everyone: families, teens and retirees. There is adequate parking, showers, lifeguards, a food bar and volleyball nets.

• **Palma Sola Causeway**: Further east on Manatee Avenue, it is much noisier with jet skiing, boating and more of a "party " atmosphere.

• **Cortez Beach**: Back south along Gulf Drive near the town of Bradenton Beach, is a good fishing spot, with miles of wide sandy beaches.

• **Coquina**: Next door, has trees, shelters and great shelling. This is a good cookout spot, with barbecue pits and picnic tables. You will see a lot of family reunions here.(Or have your own!)

• **North Lido Beach**: Lido Key has beautiful Australian pines and is great for long walks.

• **Lido Beach**: A little further south, it has a playground, dressing rooms, pool and pavilion.

• **South Lido Park**: Has nice views of Siesta Key and Sarasota city and is a good spot for a picnic.

• **Siesta Key Beach**: On Siesta Key, it is wide and long, and Sarasota's most popular–oft crowded with teens and families. Parking a picnic areas are available.

• **Turtle Beach**: At Siesta's Key's south end, th beach is more secluded, with boat ramps, she ters, picnic tables and volleyball nets. From he you can cross on foot to the north end of Cas Key to "Palmer's Point", a pretty, private spc

• **Nokomis Beach**: Further south this beach is nice place for quiet walks.

• **North Jetty Park**: At the south end of Cas Key, boasts excellent surfing and fishing.

• **Venice Municipal Beach**: On Venice Aven near downtown Venice, you might discov some shark's teeth; a coral reef a quarter m out which is popular with scuba divers.

• **Caspersen**: South of Venice, a long remo beach with seashells and a nature trail throug marshes, mangroves and tidal flats.

• **Manasota Beach**: On Manasota Key at th west end of Manasota Bridge, has a picturesqu boardwalk that meanders through mangrove

• **Gasparilla Island**: Across the bridge to Bo Grande, south of Englewood, boast seven mil of gorgeous pristine beaches. The toll is $3.2 to cross the bridge, but it is really worth if yc are looking for peace and serenity.

he stately **Payne Mansion**, which
ouses the **Museum of Botany**. Plants
re offered for sale in the gift shop. At
11 S Palm Avenue. Tel : (813) 366 5730.

Drive west across the Ringling
'auseway, turn right and you will see
gns for the **Mote Marine Aquarium**.
here are dozens of tanks containing
olorful local marine life, as well as a
ving mangrove and seagrass exhibit;
harks, rays, an extensive shell collec-
on and a "touch tank" filled with horse-
hoe crabs and sea urchins. At 1600 City
sland. Tel : (813) 388 2451.

Just across the parking lot from the
quarium is where Dale Shields, the
Pelican Man", keeps his Bird Sanctu-
ry. Dale and hundreds of volunteers
ave rescued and rehabilitated over
2,000 birds. Stop by and see some of
our favorite fine-feathered friends and
neet the man who has devoted his life
o them. Tel: (813) 955 2266.

If you love horses, then take a trip
ast of downtown to **Herrmann's**
ipizzan Ranch**, where you will see
rained stallions performing intricate
outines. From downtown, take Fruitville
Road east to the end; go left on Verna, go
ne and a-half miles to Singletary Road.
urn right and drive three miles. Call
irst, because the horses tour through-
ut the year. Tel: (813) 322 1501.

*Everyone gets dressed for
medieval madness.*

pate in The Medieval Fair held on the
grounds of the Ringling Museum. Fair
maidens, knights in shining armor, jugglers, jesters, musicians and magicians,
swordsmen and serfs, all celebrate a day
in the Middle Ages. The highlight of the
fair is a human chess match, played out
on a giant lawn chessboard. Food, music, costumes and lots of revelry. Call the
Ringling Museum for exact dates. Tel:
(813) 355 5101.

Medieval Times

ry to plan your visit to Sarasota in early
March, when you will be able to partici-

Flair For Drama

Few tourists know that Sarasota has
long been regarded as the "Cultural

The founders of Rome immortalized on the grounds of the founder of one of the best circuses in the world.

Center of Florida". During a visit here, there are a mind-boggling number of cultural choices: opera, ballet, professional and amateur theater, choral and instrumental performances. Broadway hits or world premieres of experimental productions. Attend an art gallery opening to see avant garde art, photography and classic paintings.

Sarasota has a 24-hour Arts Line you can call for events and schedules at Tel: (813) 359 ARTS.

Just to give you an idea of some of what you can find:

The Asolo Center for the Performing Arts (next door to the Ringling Museum on Rt 41 north) is a new theater and educational complex that houses the Scottish Dunfermline Opera House,

restored as the new home for the Asolo State Theater, a professional repertory company. Also at the center is the Asolo tour company, Florida State University Asolo teaching conservatories and television production facilities. Schedule and tickets: Tel: (813) 351 8000.

The purple mirrored **Van Wezel Performing Arts Hall**, designed by the Frank Lloyd Wright Foundation, is on Sarasota Bay and offers performances by the Florida West Coast Symphony, the Florida Symphonic Band, touring Broadway shows, and one-man shows and celebrity lectures. At 777 N Tamiami Trail. Tel: (813) 953 3366.

The historic 1920's **AE Edwards Theater** is home to the 35-year old Sarasota Opera, which presents four full

Solving Marine Mysteries

There is, one knows not what, sweet mystery out this sea, whose gently awful stirrings em to speak of some hidden soul beneath". oby Dick by Herman Milville.

In 1955, a young marine biologist named Dr genie Clark received a phone call that changed r life. It was the wealthy Mrs Vanderbilt lling to ask Dr Clark if she would be interested "starting a place where people can learn ore about the sea."

For Eugenie Clark the opportunity was a eam come true and so she and her orthopedic rgeon husband moved from New York to orida. She began her marine studies at the lab e called "Cape Haze Marine Laboratory", a ne-room, 12 foot by 20 foot wooden "field ation" with one sink and no air conditioning, Gasparilla Sound.

Diving along the red reef near Boca Grande ss, she began to discover and catalogue Gulf arine life: three-inch long blennies, giant manta ys, cow nose rays and sharks. She became a oneer in shark research, learning to keep them ve in captivity in order to study their ability to rceive color and shapes.

Other marine scientists heard about her ork and came from Africa, Germany, Italy, ael, England, France, Denmark and Japan to sit the laboratory.

Fast forward to 1992.... Now named **Mote arine Laboratory**, after William R Mote whose vestments and business acumen rescued the b from financial problems, and now located in odern quarters on City Island in Sarasota, ote Marine has become a national leader not ly in shark research, but also in marine and vironmental research.

Visiting scientists from the most prestigious stitutes in the world come to work with Mote ientists, to study and protect the Gulf and its untiful marine life.

The Lab has been featured in international levision documentaries and in magazines and e US Congress has named Mote Marine Laboratory as THE "Center for Shark Research". ational and international scientific conferences, well as public lectures and educational pro-ams are held in the new 450-seat Science ducation Center.

The research taking place at Mote has the potential to affect all our lives:

• Mote's ongoing studies exploring the shark's and skate's resistance to cancer may lead to the prevention of cancer in humans.

• Mote scientists are successfully growing redfish in freshwater, to prevent this popular saltwater food from becoming overfished.

• Working with Mexican biologists, Mote scientists are tracking the migration patterns of mackerel in the Gulf and helping to provide information in managing international fisheries.

• Other studies look at the effects of chemicals and pollution on the marine environment. And Mote was instrumental in winning Sarasota the federally funded "Sarasota Bay National Estuary Project" to improve Gulf waters.

In 1992, Mote was chosen by the US Congress and the Environmental Protection Agency as the lead agency for "The Year of the Gulf of Mexico", a nationwide study of issues affecting the Gulf of Mexico such as marine debris, freshwater inflow, nutrient enrichment, living aquatic resources, public health, toxic substances, coastal and shoreline erosion and habitat degradation.

Mote has been involved in a 20-year study of the dolphins in Sarasota Bay, learning about dolphin behavior, life cycles and social interaction. The Lab is currently monitoring the return of two dolphins to Sarasota Bay. Named Misha and Echo, they had been held in captivity in California to see how they readapt to their natural home.

You can learn first-hand about the Lab's research and accomplishments by visiting the Mote Marine Aquarium in Sarasota. There is a 135,000 gallon shark tank, where sharks, rays, giant grouper live. The horseshoe and hermit crabs, skate embryos and starfish live in the 30-foot touch tank. Other tanks thrive with lobsters, octopus, sea horses and sea turtles.

It is a friendly entertaining Aquarium that shares the innovative work going on Mote Marine Laboratory, making the exciting world of the sea more accessible to everyone.

Mote Marine Aquarium, City Island Park, 1600 Ken Thompson Parkway, Sarasota. Tel: (813) 388 4441 or (813) 388 1986.

Sarasota's Saint Armands Circle boasts of the best shoppping for miles around

length operas each year, such as **Carmen** and **The Barber of Seville** and **Il Trovatore**. They often features international opera stars in leading roles. At 61 North Pineapple. Tel: (813) 953 7030.

Also downtown at the corner of Palm and Coconut Avenues is the **Florida Studio Theater,** where you can see experimental drama, play readings of "works in progress", and the "Festival of New Plays", which premiers the works of rising playwrights from around the country. At 1241 N Palm. Tel: (813) 366 9796.

If you have the opportunity to see Sarasota's **Ballet of Florida**, you are in for a rare treat. The Artistic Director/ Choreographer Eddy Toussaint has created some powerful and innovative bal-

lets, especially for two of the company stars, Sophie Bissonnette and Den Dulude, a masterful husband and wi duo who give new meaning to the wor "passionate". Tickets at Tel: (813) 95 7171.

Music, Film & Circuses

Sarasota has arts festivals going on a year-round, but here are some you migh like to schedule your trip around:

In April, The Jazz Club sponsors th Sarasota Jazz Festival, which brings to gether internationally known artists wh perform for three nights at Van Weze Hall. Call for the schedule at Tel: (813 366 1552.

In June, at The **Music Festival of Florida**, students from the US and abroad perform with faculty artists in chamber ensembles and as soloists with the Festival Orchestra. Tel: (813) 953 .252.

In November, France comes to Florida during the five day **Sarasota French Film Festival** with American and world premieres of new French films, seminars, luncheons and galas. Screenings are held in the **Sarasota Opera House**. Tel: (813) 351 9010, ext 4300.

And if you are in Sarasota in late December, you are invited to attend a star studded new season premiere of the Ringling Brothers and Barnum & Bailey Circus. Shows are in Venice, about 17 miles south of Sarasota. Schedules and tickets, at Tel: (813) 484 0496.

Sarasota's Barrier Islands

After a few days of all this activity and creative stimulation, you will be ready for relaxing on Sarasota's soft sandy beaches and lazing in the lovely turquoise Gulf of Mexico waters. Sarasota has three barrier islands where you can get as relaxed as you want: Siesta Key, Longboat Key, and Lido/St Armands Key. Each with its own distinct personality and style.

Siesta Key: Being just a few minutes from downtown Sarasota gives Siesta Key a combination of suburban/tropical resort feel.

Restaurants, shops, churches and professional offices are located on narrow streets shaded with overhanging tree branches of Spanish moss. Sea oats grow along the white sandy beaches. The private lawns are a blaze of colorful flowers. It is truly like a small town, with a festive party atmosphere.

Siesta Key residents tend to be painters, photographers and writers, mixed in with young working families, and retired couples. Along Ocean Boulevard, you can jog, and cycle **Siesta Key Public Beach**, (the most popular), you can walk for miles along the Gulf of Mexico, or rent a boat south of the Stickney Point Bridge.

Longboat Key: Nicknamed "The Park Avenue of Sarasota", it is a narrow 12-mile island with million dollar homes, exclusive golf and tennis resorts, chic boutiques, and two of its very own weekly newspapers! You can settle into a beach cottage or elegant resort here and spend a week (or the whole summer!) just beachcombing, fishing, golfing, dining and checking-out novels from the library located next to the Town Hall. The **Longboat Key Art Center** hosts fairs, festivals, teas, suppers and dances, which is a good way to socialize with your fellow islanders.

Lido Key: This is the best known of Sarasota's offshore islands and is easily reached by a modern four-lane causeway that crosses Sarasota Bay, traversing St Armands Key. Lido has lovely beaches, great restaurants and nightclubs popular with the hip "gotta dance til dawn" set.

Try another sport - scuba and open up a whole new world!

St Armands Key is where most tourists like to shop, dine, "see and be seen". St Armands Circle has dozens of charming stores, casual restaurants and lots of outdoor cafés. At the center of the circle is a quaint little park built by John Ringling, where there is often a fashion or arts show.

Shopping

Speaking of fashion, St Armands is one of Florida's most delightful shopping districts. It is a circle, intersected by John Ringling Boulevard and the South/North Boulevard of Presidents. Fanning out from the circle are dozens of boutiques: costume and fine jewelry, animal-print African skirts, supple Italian designer handbags, funky Australian shirts, elegant tailored cashmere sweaters, casual tennis and golf sportswear and the latest exotic swim suits.

Art galleries and gift shops feature treasures like sculpted glass, contemporary paintings, Jon Wolfard lamps, Pueblo pottery and Southwest prints.

In downtown Sarasota, stroll along the street where Rudolph Valentino, Mae West, and F Scott Fitzgerald browsed back in the 1920's: Palm Avenue. Here you will find fine *objets d'art* from around the world: French and English antiques, designer furniture, contemporary glass, porcelain, silver and bronzes, paintings, sculpture, graphics, Italian 18K jewelry and Hartmann luggage. Bring your credit cards if you shop at Palm Avenue.

Sports

If you are more of a sports lover than a culture creature, you will not be bored in Sarasota. In March, during Spring Training, you can cheer on the Chicago White Sox at **Ed Smith Stadium**, at 12th Street and Tuttle Tel: (813) 953 3388 and the Pittsburgh Pirates at McKechnie Field, at 1750 Ninth St West, Bradenton. (just north of Sarasota).Tel: (813) 748 4610.

In February, Sarasota hosts the Seniors PGA Chrysler Cup at Prestancia Tournament Players Club, at 4409 Tournament Players Club Drive. Tel: (813) 924 5776. The competitors often include Arnold Palmer and Lee Trevino. And of course, there is excellent golf all year-round here on the 23 manicured golf courses, many with sparkling lakes. Most of the upscale resorts have tennis courts, boats and deep sea fishing charters.

Scuba Diving

Scuba diving is popular in Sarasota. Two PADI five-star dive shops in Sarasota are: **Florida Down Under Inc.** At 5714 Clark Road, Tel: (813) 922 3483; and **Ocean Pro Dive Shop**. At 2259 Bee Ridge Road. Tel: (813) 924 DIVE.

The Sarasota Convention & Visitor's Bureau will send you complete current sports, arts, and special events information. Write to 655 N Tamiami Trail, Sarasota. FL34236. Or call Tel: 1 800 522 9799.

Southern Florida

Ultra modern skyscrapers designed by IM Pei and Philip Johnson, stand proudly among classic Florentine Renaissance and art deco buildings. The largest cruise port in the world is surrounded by a fascinating mix of Latin, Haitian, African-American and Jewish neighborhoods. Downtown in Miami's booming business districts, you are apt to hear more Spanish, Portuguese, and Japanese than English. And there is always a festival of art, music and culture going on, from "Goombay", the largest black heritage festival in the US, to Coconut Grove's Arts Festival, to world film premieres at Miami's Film Festival.

The fabulous Miami Beach.

City Tour

The best way to meet Miami and some of her neighborhoods, is to hop on the Old Town Trolley for "The Magic City Tour" at Bayside Marketplace, lo-

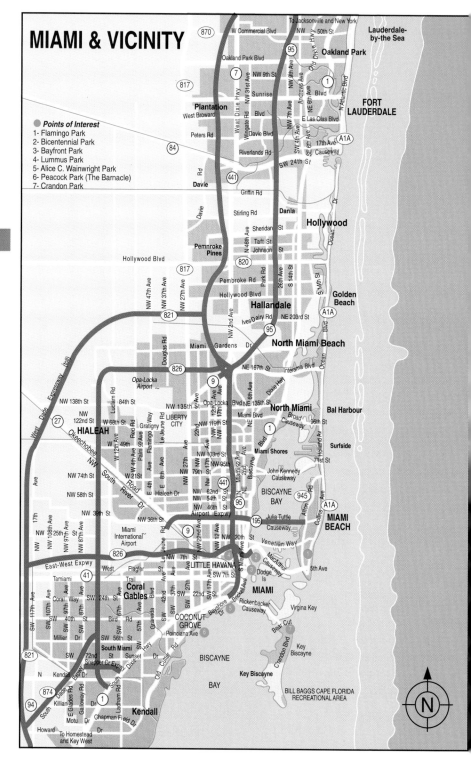

MIAMI & VICINITY

Points of Interest
1- Flamingo Park
2- Bicentennial Park
3- Bayfront Park
4- Lummus Park
5- Alice C. Wainwright Park
6- Peacock Park (The Barnacle)
7- Crandon Park

To Jacksonville and New York

Lauderdale-by-the Sea

870

W Commercial Blvd

NW 50th St

Old Dixie Hwy

95

Oakland Park Blvd

Oakland Park

817

7

NW 9th St

NW 31st St

NW 8th Ave

NE 6th Ave

Andrews Ave

1

Blvd

Plantation

West Broward

Sunrise

NW 7th Ave

E Las Olas Blvd

FORT LAUDERDALE

West Dixie Hwy

Wingate Rd

Blvd

Peters Rd

Davie Blvd

SW 4th Ave

SE 6th Ave

17th Ave

N Atlantic Blvd

84

Rd

Riverlands Rd

Causeway

A1A

441

SW 24th St

Davie

Griffin Rd

Rd

Davie

Stirling Rd

Danla

Sheridan St

Hollywood

Pemroke Pines

N 46th Ave

Taft St

Johnson St

Hollywood Blvd

820

Pembroke Rd

Park Rd

26th Ave

S 14th St

S 14th St

Golden Beach

817

NW 47th Ave

NW 37th Ave

NW 27th Ave

Hollywood Blvd

Hallandale

Ives Dairy Rd

NE 203rd St

A1A

821

NW 2nd Ave

95

North Miami Beach

Blvd

Ocean

Douglas Rd

Miami Gardens Dr

826

NE 167th St

Interama Blvd

Opa-Locka Airport

9

Opa-Locka Blvd

NW 135th St

6th Ave

NE 135th St

North Miami

Bal Harbour

NW 138th St

Ludlam Rd

84th St

12th Ave

17th Ave

Dixie Hwy

27

NW 122nd St

W 68th St

Gratigny Rd

Le Jeune Rd

NW 119th St

Miami Blvd

96th St

Broad Causeway

Okeechobee

NW 12th Ave

Palm St

Flamingo

22nd Ave

NW

NW

NE

1

Surfside

HIALEAH

W 49th St

W 4th Ave

Red Rd

E 8th Ave

NW 103rd St

NW 17th Ave

Miami Ave

Miami Shores

71st St

NW 74th St

South River Dr

W 21st

NW 79th St

NW 95th

2nd

Biscayne

John Kennedy Causeway

NW 58th St

Hialeah Dr

NE

441

945

A1A

NW 39th St

NW 62nd St

95

BISCAYNE BAY

Collins

NW 17th Ave

NW 108th Ave

NW 25th St

NW 97th Ave

NW 87th Ave

Miami International Airport

NW 36th St

NW 54th St

NW 46th St

Airport Expwy

195

Julia Tuttle Causeway

Alton

MIAMI BEACH

826

East-West Expwy

Le Jeune Rd

9

NW 22nd Ave

NW 12th Ave

NW 20th St

Venetian Way

A1A

Tamiami

41

West

Flagler

NW 7th Ave

LITTLE HAVANA

SW 7th St

St Miami Ave

MacArthur Causeway

5th Ave

Coral Gables

Trail

SW 24th Ave

SW 67th Ave

SW 42nd Ave

SW 37th Ave

SW 22nd

SW 22nd St

Brickell Ave

Dodge Is

MIAMI

SW 117th Ave

SW 107th Ave

SW 97th Ave

Coral Way

Coral Way

Bird Rd

Granada Blvd

SW 57th Ave

Bayshore Dr

Rickenbacker Causeway

Virgina Key

SW 40th Ave

SW 87th Ave

Miller Dr

SW 56th St

COCONUT GROVE

Poinciana Ave

Bear Cut

SW 72nd St

South Miami

SW Sunset Dr

Old Cutler Rd

US Dixie Hwy

6

Crandon Blvd

Key Biscayne

821

SW Snapper Cr Expwy

BISCAYNE

Key Biscayne

874

Kendall Dr

South Dade

E Glades Rd

Galloway Rd

1

Dr

BAY

BILL BAGGS CAPE FLORIDA RECREATIONAL AREA

94

Killian

Motu Dr

Ladham Rd

Chapman Field Dr

Dr

Howard

To Homestead and Key West

Kendall

N

A horse-drawn carriage and a ride around the Biscayne Bay area.

cated at the eastern edge of downtown on the Bay, at Flagler and Biscayne Boulevard.

Bayside Marketplace is a huge lively indoor/outdoor complex of shops and restaurants on the waterfront, where you can take a leisurely walk, shop and have a snack before climbing onto the open air Trolley.

The 90-minutes narrated Trolley Tour takes you through some of downtown, south over the Rickenbacker Causeway to Key Biscayne, then along South Miami Avenue and Bayshore Drive into Coconut Grove, west into Coral Gables and Calle Ocho and ends up back at Bayside Marketplace. You can stop off at some of the attractions and museums, or take the entire tour

and go back to the neighborhoods and sights that most interest you. To find out the many highlights on the tour just read on:

Downtown Miami

The trolley passes the city's hi-tech rapid transit systems, The Metrorail and Metromover, 1910 buildings next to 1993 sleek-mirrored highrises, and million dollar condominiums.

You may recognize the **Atlantis** with its middle floor cut out for a garden of cloud level palm trees, as the building featured in the opening title sequence of the popular television series, "Miami Vice."

Miami Beach: Pretty Buildings, Pretty People

Detail from an etched glass window in the historic Art Deco District.

Sipping champagne curbside at the historic Colony Hotel, the passing parade is captivating: Ponytailed young musclemen wearing diamond earrings glide by on skateboards, as long-legged girls in white lycra shorts strut their bronzed sun-bleached stuff.

A gleaming 1958 purple, gold and black Packard parked out front competes for attention with dragoon tattooed arms, flirtatious shoulders, and sculpted buttocks peeking out of very short shorts. A red head in a leopard catsuit studies the menu as a motorcycle macho studies her.

Ocean Drive at 10:00pm is awash in pink, blue, red and purple neon reflecting off sun-burned flesh. The soft evening is a hypnotic aroma of salty air, sweat, Chanel No.5 and anticipation.

Sounds like quite the scene, doesn't it? That is Miami Beach – the "American Riviera", where tourists rub elbows with models, movie stars and muscle men.

Serving as an appropriate backdrop to all this beauty is the **Art Deco District**, an architectural treasure of 800 buildings in art deco, streamline, modern and Spanish Mediterranean Revival styles.

Walking through the Deco district, from 6th to 23rd streets, and the Atlantic Ocean west to Lennox Court, you will see a stunning variety of architectural images: decorative columns, arched windows, clay barrel tile roofs, rough stucco walls, wrought iron and spindled gates guarding picturesque courtyards. Glass windows and doors are dramatically etched with tropical birds, fish and plants.

The Modern-style buildings are more simply decorated, with bands of colors called "racing stripes", cantilevered window shades called "eyebrows" and rounded corners. Aluminum, chrome, neon lights and glass block accessorize the look.

If you are interested in the area's history, take a free walking tour on Saturday morning with one of the local historians. Meet at **The Miami Design Preservation League's Art Deco Welcome Center**, at Leslie Hotel, 1244 Ocean Drive. Tel : (305) 672 2014 if you need to check their schedule, but reservations are not required. There are also excellent brochures and free maps at The Miami Beach Chamber of Commerce, at 1920 Meridian Avenue. Tel (305) 672 1270.

The District's history and beauty has made it an immensely popular location for fashion and feature film shoots. Every corner has its share of camera crews and curvaceous cover girls. This in-turn has created new business for modeling agencies, photography studios, recording studios and graphics companies. Artists moving here in droves are giving Miami Beach a New York Soho-style nickname – SoBe, for South Beach.

You can watch artists working at **The South Florida Art Center** over at 810 Lincoln Road. Tel : (305) 674 8278. Over 85 artists work and exhibit here, in media ranging from painting, sculpture, printmaking, glass, jewelry, clay and art-to-wear. This is the perfect place to discover an affordable one-of-a-kind piece, and meet the artist who created it.

Lincoln Road is home to the **Colony Theater**, **The New World Symphony** and the **Lincoln Theater**. Watch the **Miami City Ballet** rehearsing through their street side window, near where actors from **Area Stage** rehearse their next performance. The **Jackie Gleason Theater** over on Washington Avenue brings in the latest Broadway hits and the **Bass Museum of Art** features contemporary European, American and Hispanic art.

If you love art, historic architecture and very beautiful people, then Miami Beach will

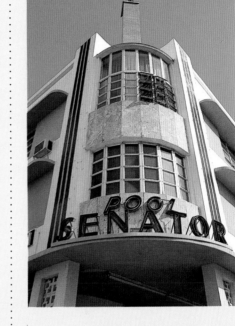

Towering fascades of art deco buildings will keep you craning your necks as you walk around Miami Beach.

Art around every corner.

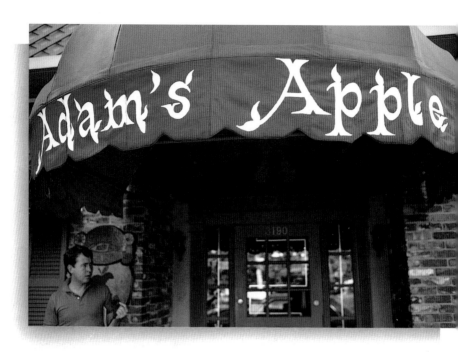

Adam's Apple in Coconut Grove.

Key Biscayne

Crossing over the causeway named after WWI flying ace Eddie Rickenbacker, you will see dozens of massive cruise ships headed for glamorous destinations out of the Port of Miami, the largest cruise ship port in the world. Get a glimpse of Fisher Island, an "island" neighborhood for the very wealthy, where residents get to their homes by ferry.

Key Biscayne is well known for **The Miami Seaquarium**, home to Lolita, the 10,000 pound killer whale, and Flipper, everyone's favorite television star dolphin. There are dozens of aquarium tanks here with Atlantic Ocean and Caribbean Sea marine life and daily shows with dolphins, sea lions and of course, Lolita and her pals.

Coconut Grove

Crossing back over the Australian pine and Cabbage palm-lined Causeway, the tour goes south along S Miami Avenue past the **Miami Museum of Science and Space Transit Planetarium**. There are over 150 hands-on exhibits of rare and unusual natural history specimens. A $5 million expansion program will add new science galleries and increase the planetarium's space, so be sure and stop in if you are a star gazer.

Continuing south, you will pass

The castle-like facade of the Coral Gables church in Miami.

Vizcaya Museum and Gardens, a gorgeous Italian Renaissance-style villa with formal gardens, elegant European furniture, and some very unusual decorative arts. Built in 1916 at a cost of $22 million, Vizcaya was the winter retreat of industrialist James Deering, who clearly spared no expense in his pursuit of luxury.

Coconut Grove's commercial street, Main Highway, is lined with art galleries, vintage clothing and antique jewelry boutiques, trendy sidewalk cafés, restaurants and a blur of shoppers, skaters, joggers and sightseers. There is elegant sportswear and evening wear at MayFair Shops and the European village style "Coco Walk", and the IN crowd is decked out in designer duds at **Johnny Rockets**

Hamburger Café.

Residents and tourists alike can look forward to February's Coconut Grove Arts Festival, when the town turns into a sidewalk art party, with the streets jammed with the latest works by top local and national artists.

And the famous **Coconut Grove Playhouse** always has a crowd at their popular theatrical productions.

Coral Gables

Your trolley tour continues west into Coral Gables, which is also called "The City Beautiful" for its formal Spanish–style entrances, gates, fountains, plazas, and exclusive estates, many with

The town goes wild on Art Deco Weekend.

backyard canals where sleek yachts are parked, waiting for the next floating dinner party.

Coral Gables has strict "beauty" regulations. For example, if you want to paint your house, the color of the paint must be selected from the approved city "color" book (only pastels are featured!). Another rule: you must keep your lawn

properly mowed, or the city will do it and send you a large bill for their service! This town is serious about maintaining its "beauty queen" reputation, and the results are well worth the effort.

The trolley passes George Merrick's magnificent apricot–hued **Biltmore Hotel**, built in 1926 as a posh playground for beauty queens, movie stars

glades, sunken gardens and a rare plant house. After your trolley tour you can come back here and take another relaxing tram ride through the gardens.

Calle Ocho

Heading north of Coral Gables and back east, the trolley wends along Calle Ocho, or S W 8th Street, the primary commercial street in Little Havana.

The brick sidewalks, gaslight streetlights, and outdoor markets are reminiscent of old Havana in Cuba. During the 1960s, over 500,000 Cubans fled Fidel Castro's communist regime from Cuba to Miami, and this is the neighborhood where many of them have settled.

Domino Park

Today, Cubans live throughout the Miami area, but this neighborhood has maintained its Latin flavor. You can stroll past Cuban food markets and bakeries, and stop at a sidewalk stand for some "café cubano", a tiny cup of strong Cuban coffee mixed with milk and sugar that is equivalent to three regular cups of American coffee! You will also notice that Spanish is the language of choice in Calle Ocho. At night the Spanish restaurants come alive, serving fresh seafood, white beans and fried sweet plantains, as flamenco dancers swirl onstage in gorgeous red satin and lace

and celebrities of the era. Johnny Weismueller, (remember "Tarzan"?), was one of the pool lifeguards, so that gives you an idea of the fun that went on. The Hotel has recently undergone a $38 million rehabilitation and is once again open for tourists.

Another attraction worth visiting in Coral Gables is the **Fairchild Tropical Garden**, 83 acres of rainforest, exotic palms, cyads, vine pergola, palm

Be borne aloft an elephant as you survey the Miami Metrozoo, and all its residents.

costumes.

At 14th Avenue is **Domino Park**, where 60 year old Cuban men fiercely compete in daily domino games. The trolley makes a brief stop on Calle Ocho, so wander into this park if you want to pick up some tips and hints.

Back to Bayside

On your way back to Bayside Market-place you will cross over the historic Miami River, where cargo ships cruise by with heavy loads of refrigerated railroad cars. The Miami River is the oldest natural landmark in southeast Florida, and was named "Miami", meaning "sweet water" by early Indian

inhabitants.

Today, it is a busy commercial ar-tery and an international point of entry.

Other Miami Attractions

Just north of Bayside on Biscayne Boul-evard is the nation's only police mu-seum, the **American Police Hall of Fame**. In a building that used to house the Miami FBI, are displays of SWAT trucks, an electric chair, jail cell and stockade and a memorial with the names of 3,400 law enforcement officers who died in the line of duty.

Further north in the neighborhood of Hialeah, is the **Hialeah Race Track** at 2100 East 4th Avenue. Originally

The Holocaust Memorial

What brings tears to your eyes are those haunting photographs of innocent children. Etched into black granite walls, their enormous eyes stare at you from haggard faces, asking, "Why were we chosen to be murdered? What did we do to suffer such agony?"

Walking through **The Holocaust Memorial** at Dade Boulevard and Meridian Avenue in Miami Beach is a deeply emotional experience. It is impossible to understand how the Nazis could have succeeded in killing over 6,000,000 Jews, including 1,500,000 Jewish children, while the world watched and did nothing.

It began in July, 1937 at the German Buchenwald Concentration Camp, where intellectual Jews and anti-Nazi dissidents were interned. By September 1938, in his drive toward the "Aryanization" of Germany, Adolf Hitler had ordered the confiscation of property owned by Jews, the removal of Jews from all public and professional positions, the closing of Jewish businesses, and the expulsion of 17,000 Jews holding Polish citizenship to Poland. On November 9, 1938, during "*Kristallnacht*", (night of broken glass), 30,000 Jews were arrested without cause, 191 synagogues were destroyed and 7,000 shops had their windows shattered and looted. The unique Jewish culture, tradition, centuries of learning, and contributions to society, were to be abruptly erased.

On January 20, 1942, Hitler unveiled his "Final Solution to the Jewish Question", a plan calling for camps equipped with gas chambers and special crematoria, where Jewish men, women and children would be put to death and disposed of. They would be herded naked, like animals, into chamber "showers", to be sprayed with deadly Zyklon B gas. The corpses would be burned in ovens, their bones sold for fertilizer, their hair used to manufacture military blankets, and their body fat to be made into soap.

Hitler's plan was executed in death camps throughout Poland and Germany, and by 1944, 6,000,000 Jews had been annihilated. In the worst human catastrophe in modern history, an entire people and their age old culture were almost entirely wiped out. Walking through the sculpture garden of The Holocaust Memorial, you wonder at the depth of human hatred that

such a tragedy could have taken place. And you are thankful that Miami's Jews cared enough to create a memorial as witness that it did happen, so future generations will never forget.

The Memorial is designed so that you embark upon a symbolic journey into the universe of the Holocaust, past sculptures of families clinging to each other, horrific photographs set into stone, dimly lit narrow tunnels, and a black granite wall etched with victims' names.

The first sculpture is of a mother with her two children, fearfully clinging to each other as the signs of the Holocaust first appear. Anne Frank's message tries to give them hope: "...In spite of everything, I still believe that people are really good at heart."

In a semi-circular colonnade of Jerusalem stone columns are a series of black granite slabs etched with photographs of the tortured victims. Poetic inscriptions tell the story of their fate, asking questions that have no answers.

There is a beautiful **Garden of Meditation**, where a water lily pond set against a backdrop of palm trees reflects the blue skies and white clouds. Inside The **Dome of Contemplation**, the sun projects a star of David in front of an eternal memorial flame. A stone tunnel with names of the death camps carved into its walls leads to a stunning giant sculpture: an outstretched arm reaching into the sky, tattooed with a number from Auschwitz, rises from the earth, the final attempt to live of a dying person. Desperate human figures covering the arm are life-sized, and as you stand close to their faces, you can almost hear their cries. You want to grasp their hands, to take them away from this hell. But, there is nothing you can do to take away the agony of history.

Kenneth Triester, the Memorial's architect and sculptor of this unique bronze wrote, "The totality of the Holocaust cannot be created in stone and bronze...but I had to try. The rich diversity of the European culture, now lost, can not be expressed...but I had to try. Six million moments of death cannot be understood...but we all must try." If you are Jewish, you will have good reason to visit The Holocaust Memorial. If you are not, you will have even more of a reason.

An aerial view of the architecture in the business district of Miami.

constructed in 1925 for dog races, *jai-alai* and an amusement park, this lushly landscaped French Mediterranean Revival-style complex was rebuilt in 1932 for horse racing. It is truly a pleasant way to gamble.

Southern Miami

The southern area of the city has three very popular attractions:

• **Parrot Jungle and Gardens.** 11000 S W 57th Avenue, Greater Miami South, has some of the world's most beautiful birds, flowering tropical plants, baby primates and a petting zoo. Tel: (305) 666 7834.

• **Miami Metro Zoo.** 12400 S W 152nd Street, Greater Miami South, has rare white Bengal tigers, koala bears and 300 exotic birds and a petting zoo. This is one of the largest cageless zoos in the nation and a great way to get "up close and personal" with the animals. Tel: (305) 251 0400.

• **Monkey Jungle.** 14805 SW 216th Street, Greater Miami South. At this zoo, you are caged and the monkeys are free to roam! Fun shows with trained chimpanzees and monkeys. Tel: (305) 235 1611.

Sports with a View

There are dozens of golf courses in the Miami area to choose from, but the

Water, water everywhere and all for your swimming and sunning pleasure.

The prospect of reaping booty from ship wrecks will have all you prospective plunderers signing up for PADI and NAUI courses!

Strike up the band on Church Street.

links at **Key Biscayne Golf Course** offer panoramic views of Biscayne Bay and fairways that weave through mangroves. At 6700 Crandon Boulevard, Key Biscayne. Tel : (305) 361 9129.

There are dozens of Marinas in the Miami area that charter boats of every size, for fishing, cruising, gourmet dining, dancing, and gambling.

You can cruise for an hour in Biscayne Bay, take a day cruise to the Bahamas, or take a luxury liner to any country in the world.

Other Sports

Dive to Miami's undersea wrecks, or sky

Boas, sequins and bikinis – Miami's nightlife is sizzling.

dive at 150 miles an hour in a two – person parachute. Tour Miami by motorcycle, bicycle or scooter; spend the day waterskiing or check into a five-star spa for a workout and some pampering.

With its sub-tropical climate, 15 miles of sandy beaches and azure waters, the Miami area will keep you very busy, both indoors and out.

Miami Nightlife

Take an afternoon nap during your visit to Miami, because there is lots going on after sundown, theater, dance, music, festivals and special events – from Broadway hits to Spanish Flamenco, there is sure to be an evening event that cap-

Latin American Connection

It was Julia Tuttle, the "Mother of Miami", who predicted that Miami would some day become the crossroads of the world, an international community, and the world's busiest seaport linking North America to the Caribbean and Latin America.

Miami's Hispanic presence goes back more than 200 years to Florida's second Spanish period, following the British defeat in the American Revolution. The Spanish Crown was left to its own devices in Florida, granting land to settlers in "Cayo Biscaino" (Key Biscayne) and the *Rio nombrado de agua dulce* (the Miami River). Architectural reminders of this early Spanish influence are as much a part of Miami's flavor as the 14 Cuban coffee bars that offer up steaming strong "café cubano" on Calle Ocho in Miami's Little Havana.

Nearly half a million Cubans have fled Fidel Castro's communist regime since 1959. The second largest exodus arrived in 1980, when Castro allowed 125,000 Cubans to head for the U S in the Mariel boatlift, known as the ***Freedom Flotilla***.

Many of these exiles joined their families in Little Havana, a 3.5 square mile neighborhood of Cuban restaurants, *fruterias*, *pinata* shops, art galleries and *flamenco* bars. *Bodegas* offer exotic delicacies like *yuca* (ripe plantains), while record stores spin Latin dance tunes for the *merengue*, *mambo*, *salsa* and *tango*.

Spicy Fare

At Antonio Maceo Park, known as Domino Park, elderly Cuban men gather to enjoy their favorite game. Nearby, the Bay of Pigs monument at the **Cuban Memorial Plaza** pays tribute to Brigade 2506, reminding both locals and visitors of the Cubans' exile to Miami. The Plaza is a gathering site for many of the Hispanic community's festivals, including Carnaval Miami, the nation's largest Hispanic celebration, with over one million people attending each year. The nine days of festivities include a parade, fireworks display at Bayside, and "Calle Ocho: Open House", the world's largest block party, with plenty of dance, top Latin entertainment

Public outdoor chess game in Little Havana.

and food.

Speaking of food, if you love Latin cuisine, Little Havana is the place to come. Mom and pop restaurants serve *moros y cristianos* (black beans and rice), *palomilla* steak and *fritas*, the Cuban variety of a hamburger. Or try a Cuban sandwich: crispy Cuban bread, honey-baked ham, pork, Gruyere cheese, pickles and butter. Not dietetic, but delicious!

At dinner, there are more Latin specialties to tempt your palate: *masas de puerco* (fried pork), *arroz con pollo* (chicken and rice) and *paella* (seafood with seasoned rice). For dessert, try *churros* (long spirals of deep-fried sweet dough), *flan* (a creamy custard with a caramelized crust), or mango ice cream, along with a thimbleful of "cafe Cubano". You will dance til dawn on this sugar and caffeine high.

After dinner, many of the restaurants in Little Havana have backroom nightclubs with delightful foot-stomping, hand-clapping *flamenco* shows. Or you can catch a neighborhood theatre production, ranging from Spanish tragedy to Cuban comedy. If you are there in May, the **International Hispanic Theater Festival** hosts theater companies from around the world who perform award winning productions by Hispanic playwrights.

As Greater Miami's Latin community has grown-Hispanics now represent almost 50 percent of the area's population. It has also diversified to include immigrants from Puerto Rico, Mexico, Nicaragua, Colombia and Central America. They all have their own festivals and foods for you to enjoy. With future plans to develop Little Havana into a 60-block Latin Quarter, the neighborhood will continue as Miami's Latin American connection – a world renowned showcase of Latin culture and hospitality.

Everyone becomes outdoorsy once they hit Miami Beach.

tures your attention. Consider:

• **Jackie Gleason Theater**. 1700 Washington Avenue, Miami Beach. Tel: (305) 673 8300. Broadway hits.

• **Actor's Playhouse**. 8851 SW 107th Avenue, Kendall. Tel: (305) 595 0010. Florida's second largest professional equity theater, presents off Broadway style productions.

• **Coconut Grove Playhouse**. 3500 Main Highway, Coconut Grove. Tel: (305) 442 4000. World, national and regional premieres of original productions.

• **Miami City Ballet**. Dade County Auditorium, 2901 W Flagler Street. Tel: (305) 532 4880. Classical and contemporary repertoire of dance, directed by the famous Edward Villella.

• **Greater Miami Opera**. At the same address as the Miami City Ballet. Miami's 52-year old world class opera company, boasts international guest artists.

• **The New World Symphony** : At the Gusman Center for the Performing Arts, 174 E Flagler. Tel: (305) 673 3331. Renowned guest conductors, solo artists, and America's finest young musicians perform under the direction of Artistic Director, Michael Tilson Thomas.

Another Brief Look

There is also a terrific free booklet you can get that lists entertainment, sightseeing, maps, shopping ,dining and lodging called "***Destination Miami & The Beaches***." Just write to the Greater Miami Convention & Visitors Bureau.

Fort Lauderdale's gorgeous red roofed Spanish mansions along the islands and canals jutting into The Intracoastal Waterway show why the city is known as the "Venice of America." Then, there are those 23 miles of wide sandy beaches, stretching enticingly along azure Atlantic waters, with ocean cruisers, yachts, fishing boats and jet skis on the horizon. Sunseekers from all over the world come to Fort Lauderdale to get bronzed, reel in some big fish, play golf, tennis, shop, and get in on the 24- hour a day party. More than 42,000 yachts are registered in Fort Lauderdale, hence her other nickname, "Yachting Capital of the World."

On the way to the great, wide expanse of beach.

231

Water Tour by Taxi

Start out your Fort Lauderdale tour by w a t e r taxi. It is the easiest, most fun way to see the

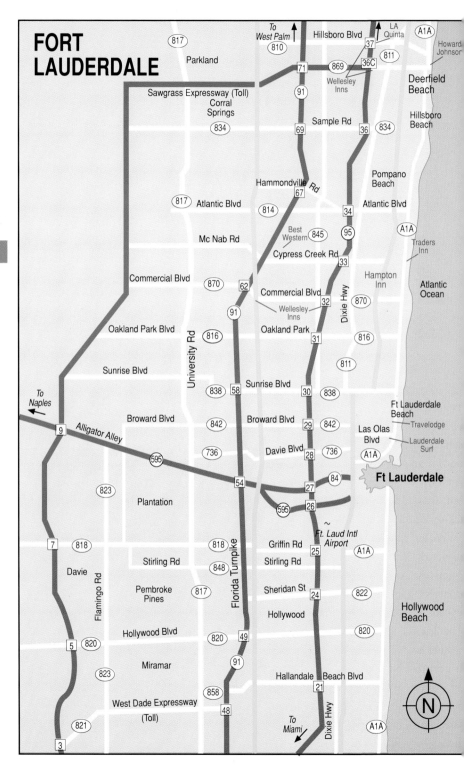

Hangin' out during spring break.

ty and neighborhoods and to get in
ᴉe mood for the town that advertises
self as "Where the Fun Never Sets." Just
ᴇad for any dock or marina side restau-
ᴉnt hop on board the open-air taxi
ɔat. Or call Tel: (305) 565 5507 for a
ᴄk-up and they will come to get you.

Water taxis go anywhere within
ᴉe nearly seven miles of Intracoastal
ᵃaterway, between Port Everglades and
ᴉe city's Commercial Boulevard, up the
ᴇw River or Fort Lauderdale's down-
ᵂn. Incredible mansions are located
ᴉ these islands along the canals, some
ᴉth ornate Roman columns, wrought
ɔn Romeo & Juliet balconies, arched
ɔor to-ceiling windows, marble bird
ᵃths, glamourous outdoor terraces and
odern art under shady palm trees on

perfectly manicured front lawns. Some
folks know just how to live!

Everyone in this neighborhood has
a sleek yacht floating in their
"backyard." With names like **Insatia-
ble**, **Bob's Retreat** and **Monkey Business**, you get an idea of their owner's
personalities, (and what they did to get
those yachts). Even the yacht gas stations are spiffy, with attendants pump-
ing gas from the lower dock, while on
the upper deck, captains and their mates
enjoy great views and snacks .

Water taxis are an inexpensive scenic mode of transportation to and from
many of Fort Lauderdale's hotels, restaurants and shops. You can hop off
and on, or relax for a few hours and
tour.

*Hire boat and rod and strap
yourself in for deep sea fishing.*

Ships: Cruising & Fishing

Fort Lauderdale's Port Everglades is the world's second largest cruise port, with most five-star ships departing for the Caribbean and points south. You can cruise for a day, an evening, a week or 100 days on glamourous cruise lines like Cunard, Holland America, Royal Viking and Sun Line, to name just a few of the 25 major lines. Two of the more popular day cruises are on *Discovery I*, Tel: 1 800 749 7447 and *Seaescape*, Tel: 1 800 432 0900.

Charter boats with names like *Tom Cat*, *Naughty Girl* and *Intoxication* are available for deep-sea sport fishing, where you may be lucky and reel in sailfish, dolphin, wahoo, tuna or kingfish. Three primary centers for charter boats are Fort Lauderdale's **Bahia Mar Yachting Center**, 801 Seabreeze Boulevard, Fort Lauderdale. Tel: (305) 764 2233; **Cove Marina**, just south of Hillsboro Boulevard in Deerfield Beach. Tel: (305) 427 9747 and **Fish City Marina**, on Highway A1A and Hillsboro Inlet in Pompano Beach. Tel: (305) 941 8222.

If you are dreaming about Florida's famed largemouth bass, maybe you should see a psychiatrist! Or rent a 14 foot flat-bottomed *Johnboat* at *Sawgrass Recreation Marina*. Tel: (305) 389 0202 or **Everglades Holiday Park**, Tel: (305) 434 8111, both in West Broward.

Ships: Underwater Wrecks

Just one mile off the Fort Lauderdale beach in 97-feet of crystal clear water lies the *Mercedes I*, a 197-foot German freighter that's become a hot spot for coral, barracuda, angel fish, sea turtles and the scuba divers who love photographing them.

There are dozens of other wrecks you can dive along to the 23-mile long reef, with names like *Wreck of the Rebel*, *Ancient Mariner*, and *Houseboat Wreck*. The reef varies in depth from 15 feet to 100 feet, making it good for either snorkelers or divers. Average visibility is 40 to 60 feet, but on some days it can reach 100 feet.

The extensive sinking of old vessels

Butterfly World

Suddenly you're in a world of gossamer wings, each delicate pair unlike the other. The rainbow color combinations are infinite: red and black, blue and pink, orange and white, yellow and brown. And the patterns a geometric delight of stripes, dots, rectangles and owl's eyes.

This is Fort Lauderdale's Butterfly World, a live butterfly park that's the largest in the world. It began as the hobby of Ronald Boender, who collected butterflies while growing up on his family farm in Illinois.

Boender moved to Florida in 1968, and after retiring from a successful career as an electrical engineer, decided to pursue his hobby full time. By 1984 he had established the MetaScience Company which farmed butterflies for sale to universities and zoos.

When Boender visited London's Butterfly House, he decided that he wanted to build a butterfly house in America that would be not only a park for tourists, but also become a center for research and education.

In 1988, Boender's dream came true: Butterfly World opened its doors, as the first U.S. center for butterflies, and has since established itself as the most complete facility of its kind worldwide, dedicated totally to the preservation of butterflies and their habitat.

You can stroll along flower lined pathways inside the "Paradise Adventure" aviary where clouds of butterflies fly, feed and bask in Florida's sunshine. Between this aviary and the Tropical Rain Forest are fragrant flower filled hanging baskets where butterflies drink nectar. At the pupa emerging cases are the different stages of a butterfly's development; one may emerge right before your eyes.

In the Tropical Rain Forest, thousands of exotic butterflies and free flying birds soar through waterfalls and lush dense foliage. Every few minutes there's a light tropical shower. Along the banks of the lake is a blooming botanical garden, with spectacular water lilies. Part of the garden has 20 different varieties of roses.

The Museum and Insectarium is an amazing collection of thousands of mounted butterflies, moths, spiders, wasps and exotic beetles from all over the globe. For any kid who ever went out bug hunting, this museum is a dream come true. Especially beautiful are the brilliant Blue Morpho Butterflies, from the heart of the Amazon Basin. Stop for a snack at the outdoor Butterfly cafe, and pick up some home garden books and butterfly nick knacks from the Caterpillar Canopy gift shop. Want your own butterfly world? The plant shop has all the native nectar and food sources you'll need to turn any warm weather backyard into a haven for butterflies. Maybe you will discover a species they do not have at Butterfly World.

Butterfly World. 3600 W. Sample Road, Coconut Creek. Tel: (305) 977 4400. Take I-95 north out of Fort Lauderdale, exit Sample Road and go miles west. Just west of the Florida Turnpike, look for Butterfly World signs and turn left.

has helped rebuild the once eroded reef, renewing fish and coral life. Keep your eyes peeled for octopus, butterfly fish, and even the huge tuna and sailfish.

At **Bahia Mar Resort & Yachting Center** there is a Pro Dive package with hotel rooms and diving. Tel: 1 800 772 DIVE; **The Bahia Cabana Beach Resort** has Weekend Diver packages. Tel: 1 800 BEACHES and **The Best Western Marina Inn & Yacht Harbor** has a package with Lauderdale Undersea Adventures. Tel: (800) 327 8150.

Land Sports

If you are more of a landlubber, Fort Lauderdale is one of the Southeast's premiere golf centers, with more than 50 courses, on lush greens interspersed with lakes and tree-shaded hammocks.

Don't they have houses down here?

Some of the most popular include **Bonaventure**, with two par 70 and par 72 courses set in the midst of lakes and waterfalls.Tel: (800) 327 8090; **Grand Palms**, a 505-acre resort community built around a golf course and lakes, Tel: (800) 327 9246; **Rolling Hills Resort and Country Club**, with an 18-hole par 72 and 9 hole par 36 course. Tel: (800) 327 7735 and **Palm-Aire**, the posh Pompano Beach spa resort with four 18-hole courses. Tel: (800) 327 4960.

There are 550 tennis courts in the Fort Lauderdale area, but a sampling includes: **Marina Bay & Resort**, 2175 State Road 84. Tel: (305) 791 7600; **The Tennis Club**, 600 NW 19th Street. Tel: (305) 763 8673 and **Bonaventure Racquet Club**, 357 Racquet Club Drive. Tel:

(305) 389 8666.

The Greater Fort Lauderdale Convention & Visitors Bureau has a complete listing of golf and tennis courts in their free *Official Visitors Guide*, so write them at 200 East Las Olas Boulevard, Suite 1500, Fort Lauderdale 33301. Tel: (800) 22 SUNNY, ext. 711.

Shopping

Shopping in Fort Lauderdale is fun because of the diversity of goods, ranging from simple cotton t-shirts to designer gowns, to garage sale "treasures".

Las Olas Boulevard in the heart of the downtown area has shops and galleries that include European antiques,

Swapshop – lifestyle store for adults, mini-Disneyland for the kids and fun for everyone.

riginal needlepoint and clothing designs, paintings, sculpture, country-rench fabrics, Southwest furnishings, rts, crafts and gourmet foods. There is ven a beauty salon for cats!

Sawgrass Mills, an enormous mall, as over 200 brand name and designer utlets, specialty shops and restaurants. f you come by motorcoach, the mall's isitor department will give you gift ertificates for even more discounts.

If you love flea markets, head for he **Fort Lauderdale Swap Shop** at 3292 V Sunrise. The seven day a week market as live entertainment, a giant carousel nd acres of second-hand treasures. Who nows what goodies you will be able to ake home? Read a copy of the *Visitor's* *uide* to find out where else to shop!

Beaches

People-watching is unrivaled on Fort Lauderdale beaches: lanky Germans, matronly Russians, svelte Canadians, petite Asians, long-haired biker-types, college students in teeny-tiny bikinis... The only rules here are to hang loose, and make your own good time.

On the Fourth of July, the Lauderdale Sandblast attracts thousands of sun worshippers who competitively create elaborate sand sculptures. During the rest of the year the beautiful beaches are party playgrounds, as well as quiet havens where you can walk for uninterrupted miles, accompanied only by the surge of the incoming sea.

In 1893, Henry Morrison Flagler, a partner with John D Rockefeller in Standard Oil, took one look at this lovely palm-tree lined island and decided that Palm Beach was the perfect winter escape for America's rich and beautiful. And so on February 11, 1894 he opened the world's largest, most lavish resort, the Royal Poinciana Hotel, and ever since Palm Beach has been home to the glamorous and the glittering ever since.

Palm Beach

239

Living in vast palatial estates that give new meaning to the word "grandeur", are the moguls, entrepreneurs and captains of industry that own and direct America's Fortune 500. Their philanthropic wives are

West Palm Beach is exactly as you fantasized with polo and poodles.

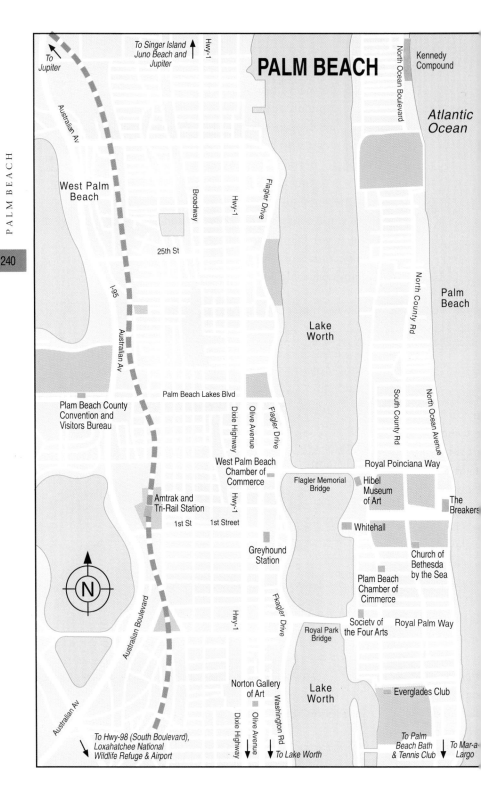

A magnificent skyline of a magical city, West Palm Beach.

ust as hardworking, organizing opu-
ent charity balls that raise millions for
organizations like The Cancer Society,
Heart Association, Red Cross and Cystic
Fibrosis.

You can tell a lady is from Palm
Beach because she wears her pearls even
while walking the dog! And, Palm Beach
homes have two entrances, one for resi-
ents and guests, and another for "serv-
ce", the maids, butlers, caterers, gar-
eners and pool cleaners that arrive
aily to help out around the house.

In-between taking care of business,
ttending fund-raising parties, playing
olo, golf, tennis, spa workouts, shop-
ing, and for some, consultation with
esident psychics, Palm Beach families
work hard to maintain their high stand-

ards in business, arts and culture. America's elite have "simple tastes": they want
only the best. And they can afford it.

Touring Palm Beach

Palm Beach County is a 2,000 square
mile community of 37 municipalities
stretching for 47 miles along the Atlantic coast, from Jupiter in the north to
Boca Raton in the south.

You might like to spend a few days
exploring Palm Beach, as the town has
fascinating museums, and historic resort hotels with excellent golf, tennis
and water sports. A good way to get
acquainted with this posh neighborhood, is to start out on the bike trail

Worth Avenue

The Via Mizner, the basis for the elegent shopping of Worth Avenue.

Somehow it seems appropriate that the man who transformed Worth Avenue from a sleepy thoroughfare to the world's most famous shopping street was somewhat of a shopper himself. Architect Addison Mizner smuggled Klondike gold from California, stole silver and furniture from abandoned churches in Antigua, and financed his worldwide wanderlust by wheeling, dealing and gambling. What a life!

By the age of 46, Addison Mizner had studied architecture in the Far East, Central America and Europe, and established himself as a "society architect", designing pleasure palaces in New York for the wealthy and powerful.

So when his friend Paris Singer invited him to Palm Beach in 1918 for a vacation, naturally Mizner was happy to head south in search of new adventures.

Singer had been toying with the idea of building a "convalescent club", sort of a social hangout for rich folks with winter blahs. With

doctors and dance directors on staff...

Singer gave Mizner *carte blanche* to desig what became **The Everglades Club** on Wort Avenue. Mizner went to work, placing livin spaces next to patios, cloisters and loggia letting the air and sunshine flow through th interiors. He knew the power of Mother Natur to cure almost any winter ailment.

A wing of the club facing Worth Avenu contained maisonettes for guests on the to floor. On the street level were Worth's Avenue very first shops, albeit not the deluxe ones the are today.

Before the Everglades Club even opened i 1919, Palm Beach lovers were clamoring fo their own Addison Mizner blueprints. He wa commissioned to build resorts for numerou socialites including Palm Beach society's grand dame, Mrs Edward Stotesbury. Mizner Indus tries in Palm Beach flourished.

For his own home, Mizner created a "Spa

sh fortress", a five-story building he christened *Villa Mizner*, filled with treasures he had acquired in Spain and Central America. He built a bridge between his residence and his offices, creating an alleyway between Worth and Peruvian Avenues, "Via Mizner", which became the basis for today's elegant Worth Avenue shopping district.

Picturesque Old Spain

Mizner proudly described his shopping village as, " ...A row of tiny shops at Palm Beach, with the picturesqueness of Old Spain-the narrow streets of Granada. Characteristic are the light stucco walls in pastel tints, topped with tile roofs, weathered cypress woodwork, and the inevitable coconut tree."

Via Mizner is still a charming alleyway, now lined with fine art galleries, and "the light stucco walls in pastel tints" house more than 200 world-famous specialty shops, posh department stores, gourmet restaurants, and art galleries. Set amidst lush gardens and sparkling fountains are internationally renowned names like Cartier, Van Cleef & Arpels, Bottega Veneta, Gucci, Louis Vuitton, Saks Fifth Avenue, Brooks Brothers, Polo Ralph Lauren, FAO Schwarz, Calvin Klein, Chanel, Ungaro, Escada, Hermes, Jaeger, Krizia, Lanvin, Ferragamo and Valentino. It would take a life time to visit them all, and for the rich and famous who shop here–it is a major occupation.

Exotic, Sophisticated & Chic

Blending the exotic ambience of sub-tropical Palm Beach with the sophisticated chic of Manhattan and the celebrity sparkle of Beverly Hills, Worth Avenue is a shopper's delight if you have deep pockets and unlimited credit lines. For those of us who can only window shop, it is still a heavenly "kingdom of thingdom".

Addison Mizner, shoppers of the world salute you for a job well done!

Worth Avenue, Palm Beach, Florida. Worth Avenue Association. Tel: (407) 659 6909.

The Intracoastal waterway and bridge which enables the passage of yachts and other seaworthy vessels.

along the Intracoastal Waterway that winds behind many of Palm Beach's incredible estates. The trail starts at the Society of Four Arts, runs for several miles and is quite lovely, with Lake Worth on one side and opulent homes, sculpted trees, and backyard pools on the other.

You can rent a bicycle from the **Palm Beach Bicycle Trail Shop**, at 223 Sunrise Avenue, and they will direct you to the trail. Tel: (407) 659 4583.

After an hour or so on the trail, head into downtown Palm Beach and tool along Worth Avenue where you will see the top designer boutiques of the world displaying the best of everything, from Chanel suits to Cartier jewelry to Louis Vuitton handbags.

Henry Flagler: The Man Who Dreamed Of Florida

Henry Morrison Flagler had big dreams, but even he could not have imagined how those dreams would impact on Florida's future.

Flagler envisioned that Florida's "wilderness of waterless sand and underbrush" could become a vacation paradise, and he devoted his life to achieving this vision. His ambition and hard work took him in spectacular leaps from being the son of a Presbyterian minister, to overcoming the failure of his Michigan salt production business, to becoming the multimillionaire partner with John D Rockefeller in their Standard Oil Company.

On a trip to Saint Augustine in 1883 with his second wife Ida, Flagler was so impressed with its charm and potential, he decided to build the fabulous Ponce de Leon hotel, which opened to great fanfare in 1888, and was followed by the equally luxurious Cordova and Alcazar Hotels. To make transportation convenient for his important guests, Flagler purchased and modernized the Jacksonville, Saint Augustine and Halifax River Railroads, making it possible to board a pullman train in New York and ride all the way to Saint Augustine. By 1894, the railroad reached to a point just across Lake Worth from Palm Beach, and the fashionable and wealthy came in droves to party at the exquisite Royal Poinciana Hotel, the largest wooden hotel in the world. Across the island on the ocean shore, Flagler bought a hotel called the Palm Beach Inn, which he enlarged, renovated and renamed The Breakers. Though it was destroyed by fire in 1903 and again in 1925, it was rebuilt on a greater scale. Today, **The Breakers** is an award-winning luxury oceanfront resort that the National Register of Historic Places describes as "culturally significant in its reflection of 20th century grandeur." The hotel's exterior was patterned after the Villa Medici in Rome, the fountain, similar to the one in the Boboli Gardens in Florence. The main lobby, graced by frescoes and decorated vaulted ceilings, overlooks the central Mediterranean courtyard of splashing fountains, like the inner gardens of the Villa Sante in Rome.

Along the courtyard are magnificent Mediterranean and Venetian Ballrooms where bejeweled American and European society min-gle at elegant fashion shows and black tie galas.

At 3:00pm every Wednesday, Palm Beach historian Jim Ponce leads a tour through The Breakers, and it is probably the most delightful way to hear Henry Morrison Flagler's story from within the setting of his exquisite hotel.

Just a few blocks from The Breakers is **Whitehall**, the magnificent marble mansion that Flagler built for his third wife, Mary Lily Kenan in 1901. Her portrait graces the music room, where she is wearing another wedding gift from Flagler, a hip length strand of $500,000 pearls.

Mrs Flagler was noted in the Guiness Book of Records as a woman who in a 12-year period never wore the same dress twice! There were so many social functions one could don a different gown four times daily. You can see some of her gowns displayed in her upstairs dressing rooms.

Whitehall is an intimate look at Flagler's love for all things magnificent. The huge entrance hall, 110 feet long and 40 feet wide, suggest the atrium of a Roman villa, covered by a baroque ceiling like those of Louis XIV's Versailles. The Italian Renaissance Library has walls of walnut and regal family portraits. The opulent Louis XIV Music Room where Mrs. Flagler gave singing recitals has a copy of Guido Reni's "Aurora" painted on the recessed dome ceiling. There is a Swiss Billiard Room, a Louis XV Ballroom, Elizabethan Breakfast Room, Francis Dining Room, and endless luxuriously decorated suites and guestrooms, many coupled with the Flagler's original furnishings. In the backyard is **The Rambler**, Henry Flagler's private railroad car, built to his specifications in 1886.

Flagler's railroad eventually extended well beyond Palm Beach, reaching to Miami and by 1912, Key West, where he declared to throngs of well wishers, "Now I can die happy, my dream is fulfilled." Less than 18 months later, he did die, having begun Florida's development that millions from around the world can enjoy today. Tours of The Breakers with historian Jim Ponce, Wednesdays at 3:00 pm. 1 South County Road, Palm Beach. Tel: (407) 655 6611.

Tours of Whitehall, The Henry M Flagler Museum, Whitehall Way at Coconut Row, Palm Beach, Tuesday to Saturday 10:00-5:00 pm, Sunday noon- 5:00 pm. Tel: (407) 655 2833.

The vaulted ceilings of the award winning luxury hotel, The Breakers.

Croquet with all-whites and mallets on the grounds of the Breakers.

Sports Galore

Golf and tennis are king in Palm Beach County, with more than 140 golf courses and 1,100 tennis courts. But, you can also spend time fishing, playing polo, croquet, horseback riding, watching *jai alai,* dog racing, baseball, basketball, auto racing, Olympic swimmers, charter a yacht or cruiser, or hunt for rabbit, quail and deer in the wildlife management areas.

Here are a few suggestions:

• **Golf**: More than 70 hotels in Palm Beach County participate in the "Golf-A'Round" program, which allows guests to play a round of golf at different courses at reduced prices. This is a good way to experience the diversity of the county's 145 courses. Ask your hotel if they are part of this program or get more information from the Palm Beach County Convention & Visitors Bureau at Tel: 1 800 554 PALM.

If you would like to take golf lessons, the Academy of Golf at the **PGA National Golf Club** offers three-day courses from November to May and two-day courses from June to October. At 1000 Avenue of the Champions. Tel (407) 627 1800.

The Executive Women's Golf League, founded in 1991 in West Palm Beach, has chapters nationwide. If you are a member you can play at special rates at Jupiter Dunes and Emerald Dunes. Call Tel: (407) 694 2820 for more membership information.

• Tennis: Tennis pros Chris Evert, Steffi Graf and Jennifer Capriati have made Palm Beach County the hot spot for tennis. Many pro-am tournaments are held here such as the Chris Evert/Phar-Mor Pro-Celebrity Tennis Classic. There are more than 1,100 courts in Boca Raton, Boynton Beach, Delray Beach, Jupiter, Lake Park, Lake Worth, Lantan, North Palm Beach, Palm, Tequesta and West Palm Beach. Call the Visitors Bureau for the complete list at Tel: 1 800 554 PALM. Or just drive around, there is a tennis court on almost every corner!

• Fishing: With the Gulf Stream less than two miles offshore, your chances are excellent for catching marlin, pompano and kingfish. Lake Okeechobee, the second largest body of freshwater in the US is loaded with large mouth bass, bream, crappie and catfish.

• Polo: Sunday is THE day to watch the "sport of kings" from December to April. Head over to the **Palm Beach Polo & Country Club**, at 13198 Forest Hill Blvd. in Wellington. Tel: (407) 793 1400; or the **Royal Palm Polo Sports Club**, 6300 Clint Moore Road, Boca Raton. Tel: (407) 994 1876. And when celebrities like Burt Reynolds and Loni Anderson are in the stands, people watching becomes its own sport.

• Croquet: The US Croquet Association is headquartered here, as are 16 croquet clubs. A full-time staff gives lessons all year round. From October through May a three-day croquet school is offered.

Tel: (407) 627 3999. Try something new!

• Horseback Riding: You can rent horses for trailriding at several private stables and many parks. If you want to see some Olympic style riding, go to the **Palm Beach Polo Equestrian Club**. Tel: (407) 793 1400. Or plan to be here during The Florida Winter Equestrian Festival. Call Tel: (407) 793 5867.

• Jai Alai: In West Palm Beach, place your bets on this very fast game at the **Palm Beach Jai Alai Fronton**, at 1415 45th Street. Call Tel: (407) 844 2444.

• Dog Racing: This is the sixth largest spectator sport in America, and you can find out why at the **Palm Beach Kennel Club**, at 1119 N Congress Avenue, West Palm Beach. Tel: (407) 683 2222.

• Baseball: The Atlanta Braves and Montreal Expos work out in Spring Training starting in March at the **West Palm Beach Municipal Stadium.**

• Auto Racing: Moroso Motorsports Park on the Beeline Highway offers drag racing, stock car racing and mudbogging. Tel: (407) 622 1400.

• Water Sports: Swim your laps at one of four Olympic class pools at **Boca Raton's Mission Bay Aquatic Training Center**, at Glades Road. Tel: (407) 488 3632.

Enjoy the World and National Waterski Championships at **Okeeheelee Park** in West Palm Beach. You can also take waterski lessons yourself as well as classes in windsurfing and parasailing.

Rent sailboats, powerboats and canoes at area parks and marinas. Try **Club Nautico Powerboat Rentals** for cruising and fishing boats, and scuba diving trips at Tel: (407) 627 1138. **Canoe Outfitters** will get you put together with canoes, maps, etc. for self-guided all day outings on the Loxahatchee River, South Florida's only designated wild and scenic river. Tel: (407) 746 7053.

Museums & Galleries

Palm Beach County is rich in history, art and culture. Plan to spend some time at some of these museums and galleries:

The **Ann Norton Sculpture Gardens** in West Palm Beach has a stunning collection of Ann Norton's monumental sculptures, as well as a Tropical Garden with 200 species of palms. Tel: (407) 832 5328.

The **Boca Raton Museum of Art** exhibits national and international artists, both world famous and unknown, which change every four to six weeks. Tel: (407) 392 2500.

The **Children's Museum of Boca** at Singing Pine is a learning center with hands on exhibits. Tel: (407) 368 6875; and the **Children's Science Explorium** nearby also has science exhibits that kids can experiment with. Tel: (407) 395 8401.

The **Henry Morrison Flagler Museum** in Palm Beach, the $2.5 million marble palace he built in 1901, has many original Victorian furnishings from when it was a luxury hotel from 1925 to 1959. Tel: (407) 655 2833.

Marinelife Center of Juno Beach in Loggerhead Park has live sea turtles and other marine life of the area. Sign up here for beach walks to see the turtles laying and hatching their eggs in June and July. Tel: (407) 627 8280.

Complex Culture

Japanese culture in Palm Beach? Stop in at the **Morikami Museum of Japanese Culture** in Delray Beach. Five acres of gardens, bonsai trees, Ro Pond and exquisite nature trails. Tel: (407) 495 0233

The **Norton Gallery of Art** in West Palm Beach has a prestigious collection of French Impressionists, post-impressionist masterpieces, renowned American art and an impressive Chinese collection. Tel: (407) 832 5194.

If you are a history buff, visit **Pahokee Museum** in Pahokee to learn about the city's earliest pioneers. There is an interesting celebrity profile of country western singer Mel Tillis, a Pahokee native. Tel: (407) 924 5579.

The **Society of the Four Arts** in Palm Beach is a fascinating cultural complex of architectural landmark buildings. A museum, theater, library, auditorium and gardens host cultural events from December to April. Tel: (407) 655 7226.

The **South Florida Science Museum** in West Palm Beach has the largest public-use telescope in South Florida, an aquarium, the Aldrin Planetarium, Native Plant Center, Light and Sight

...all, and Science Theater. Tel: (407) 832 ...988.

The Arts

...rom theater, to music, opera and dance, ...'alm Beach County offers first- rate the-...trical entertainment. To find out what ...s showing, call the ArtsLine for current ...ultural events at Tel: 1 800 882 ARTS.

A sampling for you to choose from: The new **Raymond F. Kravis Center ...or the Performing Arts** has a 2,200-...eat concert theater, and a 300-seat ...black box" theater presenting dance, ...heater and music greats like Leontyne ...'rice and Ella Fitzgerald. Tel: (407) 833 ...300.

Caldwell Theater Company in Boca ...aton presents contemporary and clas-...ic plays, comedy and musical revues. ...el: (407) 832 2989.

Jupiter Dinner Theater in Jupiter ...eatures Broadway and movie stars in ...riginal and well known productions ...nd includes dinner. Tel: (407) 746 5566.

...**Royal Poinciana Playhouse** in Palm ...each, billed as "the most glamourous ...heater in the country" features top stars ...n Broadway hits and concerts. Tel: (407) ...59 3310.

...**Ballet Florida** presents classical and ...modern dance performances. Tel: (407) ...59 1212.

...**Boca Raton Symphonic Pops** in Boca ...aton, is an 85-member orchestra play-...ng jazz, swing, pops and classical. Tel: ...407) 393 7677.

Urns and pillars accent Henry Flagier's Museum and home.

• **Miami City Ballet**, among the 10 largest US dance companies, performs throughout Florida and worldwide. Tel: (407) 488 7134.

• **Palm Beach Opera** in Palm Beach produces three operas each year with major artists under conductor maestro, Anton Guadagno. Tel: (407) 833 7888.

• **Florida Philharmonic Orchestra** in West Palm Beach, is a professional symphony orchestra featuring major guest artists and conductor James Judd. Tel: (407) 659 0331.

This is just a brief listing of what is available, so please call the ArtsLine for complete arts and culture events in Palm Beach County.

Cruising Highway A1A along Florida's east coast past the **Lobster Shanty** restaurant, and **A Kick in the Pants** surf shop, past peaceful marinas, soaring pelicans, smiling joggers and miles of serene beaches, one will feel like all is right in the world.

Ahead is **Daytona Beach**, with its famous hard-packed driving beach and "the most famous race track in the world". Then onto Florida's Space Coast, where space shuttles and wildlife coexist on the same island, where glamourous cruise ships leave the third largest US port for offshore adventures, and charming historic towns, where life on the main street is much like it was in the good old days.

Spaceport USA, The Rocket Garden at the NASA Kennedy Space Center.

Daytona Beach

Daytona Beach, all 23 hardpacked miles of it is a happenin' place. A red convertible speeds by carrying a bronzed

Speeding through the waters near the Stuart Intracoastal Waterway.

blonde in a white bikini, who waves to the world like a newly crowned beauty queen. A pick-up truck advertises boogie boards, umbrellas, and popsicle-colored floats for rent. A toothy grinning dinosaur peeks his head from the sand, pleased to be this morning's sand sculpture winner. And down at the Pier the joyland arcades, kiddie carousel rides and oyster bars are full of tanned tourists. Everyone is happy, and whats not to be happy about?

For $3 you can drive up and down along the beach, all day checking out whatever you want to check out. Or park alongside the miles of already parked cars. The day's activities are up to you. Fly a kite, ride a bike, charter a boat for deep sea fishing, go sailing,

surfing, jet skiing, or watch some svelte champions show you how it is really done. Or just relax in one of those sand chairs, as the waves wash over your winter weary body. There is really lots to do–including nothing.

Feeling a little too earth bound? Head over to the 100 year old **Ponce De Leon Inlet Lighthouse** on South Peninsula Drive and climb the 203 steps for an exhilarating view of sprawling private homes sited along the glorious Atlantic Ocean. There is also a video presentation next door on the area's history, a museum, gift shop, and picnic tables. Just a short walk from the ocean is the **Halifax River**, an intracoastal waterway, where you can cruise on the cheerful yellow and white **Dixie Queen**

Riverboat, modeled after a turn-of-the-century paddlewheeler. Lean over the deck, yes, those are dolphins playing in the wake, dancing to that snazzy Dixieland jazz playing on board. You can take a day river cruise trip to Saint Augustine. Or just enjoy dinner served at sunset.

After a few days of beaching and cruising, you will probably be too relaxed to even get dressed anymore. Spending day after day padding around in nothing but a bathing suit does that to you. How about some excitement, something to speed up that sluggish pulse? Get yourself over to **Daytona International Speedway**, the high banked 2.5 mile oval track where the bravest of the brave zoom around trying to beat the clock and the odometer. The Speedway is home to the world famous Daytona 500 car race held every February. Other months the "speedweeks" feature stock car and sports car races, as well as motorcycle races.

During the week after Christmas, there are go-kart races. In between races, you can tour the track in a van and see what it feels like to be a speedster. Take a close look at those tread marks. Call Tel: (904) 248 0055 or (904) 253 RACE for schedules and tickets.

Ready for some culture? Daytona's **Museums of Arts and Sciences** is one of Florida's hidden treasures. Located at 1040 Museum Boulevard in the Tuscawilla Nature Preserve, the Museum houses an eclectic collection: a skeleton of a 13-foot tall, 130,000 year old Giant Ground Sloth, an Arts in America Wing with furniture and paintings from 1700 to 1910, and a Cuban Museum spotlighting 200 years of Cuban culture, from 1759-1959. The Cuban collection is delightful, with vivid paintings, prints, sculpture, decorative arts and photography of Cuban life, that will leave you with a better understanding for the creative immigrants that have had such a positive impact on Florida.

The Museum also houses a planetarium and an outdoor nature trails. A certain don't miss especially if you are an art lover. Call Tel: (904) 255 0285 for schedules of current exhibits.

Mother Nature

Aside from beaches, the race track and a five-star museum, Daytona Beach is close to some spectacular state parks and wildlife refuges.

DeLeon Springs State Park, (take the A1A to US 92 and follow State Road 17 to signs), has ancient cypress and oak trees, native birds, Indian burial grounds and an old Spanish sugar mill, where you can cook pancakes on your table griddle. Rent canoes and paddleboats for a trip on the springs. Tel: (904) 985 5644.

Also in DeLeon Springs, just south of the park off Highway 17, is the **Lake Woodruff National Wildlife Refuge**. Here you can see southern bald eagles, manatees, alligators, wood storks, ospreys, ring-necked ducks and dozens of

Merritt Island: Wildlife Refuge

Have you ever stroked a baby alligator between the eyes? Fed popcorn to albino catfish? Or have you ever been within touching distance of a four foot great blue heron as he devoured his fish dinner?

If this sounds like your idea of a good time, plan a day at **Merritt Island National Wildlife Refuge**, a unique sanctuary located within sight of Kennedy Space Center shuttle launch pads. Start out at the Visitor Information Center where the park ranger will introduce that baby gator and give you maps to find the great blue heron and all his other relatives.

Birdlife abounds on Merritt Island, over 280 species including gulls, terns, sandpipers, herons, egrets, ibises, pelicans and osprey. Keep a sharp eye out for soaring eagles, dancing reddish egrets and the colorful Roseate Spoonbill.

Early Morning & Late Afternoon

Early morning and late afternoon are the best time to observe the birds, in the shallow marshes and along the beaches and dunes. Take a 40-minute drive along Black Point Wildlife Drive, a beautiful dusty road that snakes through watery marsh and pine flatwoods. Stop wherever you like to get out and photograph the waterfowl and wading birds. Another road, Max Hoeck Creek Wildlife Drive, follows a railroad through a marsh and uplands just west of Playalinda Beach. If you would rather hike, the Oak Hammock Trail is a 30-minute loop through a hardwood hammock. At Turtle Mound, a short self-guiding trail leads to the top of an Indian shell mound, where you can enjoy a beautiful view of the Atlantic Ocean and Mosquito Lagoon.

Mosquito Lagoon and the Indian River, with their shallow brackish water and dense aquatic grass beds, provide ideal fishing spots for mullet, redfish, trout, crabbing, clamming and shrimping. On the island's interior there is also freshwater fishing, which requires a license that you can get at the Visitor's Center. Along the Atlantic Ocean off the beaches you can also enjoy good surf fishing for bluefish, whiting and pompano. Or rent a canoe and go paddling

The Great Blue Heron stalking its territory.

through the peaceful streams.

Backcountry camping is permitted in certain seasons, as is hunting for ducks and coots. Both of which require permits.

You might enjoy a day at Playalinda or Apollo Beaches. Both have parking areas and crosswalks to the beach over native dune vegetation. The currents can get rough here, and you have to watch out for stinging jellyfish, and Portuguese man-of-war. During the summer if you experience one of violent lightning thunderstorms, get out of the water and wait out the storm under a shelter.

These are natural beaches without modern conveniences like hot dog stands and shower rooms. Only Apollo Beach has running water. But if you are seeking solitude, sun, sand, sea and plenty of wildlife, this is Florida at her most beautiful. From Titusville, take Route 406 east to route 402 and follow signs to Merritt Island National Wildlife Refuge Visitor Information Center. Tel: (407) 867 0667.

The Space Shuttle, Spaceport USA, NASA Kennedy Space Center.

other species. Fishing is allowed, and as well as limited hunting. Tel: (904) 985 4673.

The **Blue Springs State Park** (go south on State Road 17 and follow signs), is also a good spot for manatee watching from November through to March. You can get quite close to photograph them from the observation platform. Tel: (904) 775 3663.

Space Coast

South of Daytona is known as Florida's Space Coast because the NASA Kennedy Space Center Spaceport USA is here, as is the US Astronaut Hall of Fame, and US Space Camp of Florida. However the 72 mile area also has exceptional wildlife, from sea turtle nests on Melbourne Beach, to alligators and bald eagles at the Merritt Island National Wildlife Refuge. And there is also lots to do in the towns of Titusville, Cocoa, Cocoa Beach, Melbourne and Melbourne Beach.

Titusville

The **NASA Kennedy Space Center** is the main attraction here and a fascinating place to spend the day. For more details see p 256 of this chapter. Tel: (407) 452 2121.

Next to the Kennedy Space Center entrance on the NASA Parkway (State route 405) is the **Astronaut Hall of**

Kennedy Space Center

As 13,000 aerospace employees head for research labs and administration buildings, bald eagles, frisky otters and tall white egrets rise and shine for another busy morning at the Kennedy Space Center.

Everyone has seen the thrilling sight of a shuttle blasting heavenward in a cloud of smoke and fire on television news programs. But few know that on the 140,000 acre grounds of the Kennedy Space Center, there are more endangered and threatened species of wildlife than at any other refuge in the United States.

Back in the early 1960s when NASA needed a location large enough to support the Saturn V moon vehicle, they chose this 220-square mile portion of Merritt Island, a then desolate spit of land that enabled launches to take place without danger to nearby communities, over water instead of land. The sub-tropical climate allowed year-round operations. Soon after, NASA's concrete and steel structures began sprouting above the marsh and scrublands that were home to towering trees and hundreds of species of animals.

To preserve the wilderness, in 1963 NASA turned the management of all non-operational areas of the Kennedy Space Center over to the US Fish and Wildlife Service. A short time later, the Canaveral National Seashore and Merritt Island National Wildlife Refuge were established.

So, when you visit the Kennedy Space Center, you are apt to see two of our nation's symbols: a regal southern bald eagle circling skyward in front of the United States flag on the enormous **Vehicle Assembly Building**. It is truely a moving sight, seeming appropriate that exploration into worlds unknown is taking place in the same neighborhood as those who already know how to fly. A visit to the Kennedy Space Center is a fabulous learning experience for adults and children alike.

Two narrated bus tours give you an inside view of what goes on here. On the "Red Tour" you will see the massive six million pound crawler/transporters that carry Space Shuttles from the Vehicle Assembly Building to the launch pads. Stand next to an authentic **Saturn V** rocket for a family portrait. And the most interesting is the ride out to **Launch Complex 39,** where NASA prepares and launches the space shuttles. If you are lucky, perhaps a shuttle will be awaiting its launch when you are there.

Black-winged birds soar around the shuttle patiently waiting in its grey skeletal launch tower, as if to say "Fly, fly, gleaming metal bird. And return home with tales of your discovery!"

If you take the "Blue Tour", you will see **Cape Canaveral Air Force Station**, and the sites where America's first astronauts were launched in the Mercury and Gemini programs. You will also stop at the Air Force Space Museum to see their collection of missile and space memorabilia.

All tours begin and end at the Visitor's Centers, called **Spaceport USA**, which also holds many interesting exhibits. Climb aboard the *Ambassador*, a 68-ton replica of a space shuttle orbiter, and get an astronaut point of view from within. Walk through **Satellites and You**, an exhibit that uses animatronics and interactive videos to show how satellites affect our everyday lives. Browse through the **Gallery of Spaceflight**, chronicling the history of human space exploration; and the **NASA Art Gallery**, displaying 250 paintings commissioned by NASA art program artists. Outside is a most unusual giant playground for kids: the **Rocket Garden**, where eight rockets including *Juno* and *Saturn* are on display. Also tracking antennas, a lunar module, and an Apollo launch tower. And the **Astronauts Memorial** is a tribute to the courage and spirit of the US astronauts who gave their lives to further the exploration of space.

Movies you will enjoy:

• *The Boy From Mars*: An award-winning film that tells the tale of the first human born on another planet who makes a journey to the "foreign" planet earth.

• *The Dream Is Alive:* An IMAX film where you join shuttle astronauts in pre-flight training aboard the space shuttle in orbit and on a breathtaking launch and landing.

• *Blue Planet:* Another IMAX film, shot by crew of five space shuttle missions from 300 miles above earth. This film unveils the environmental effects of man and nature on our own home, Spaceship Earth.

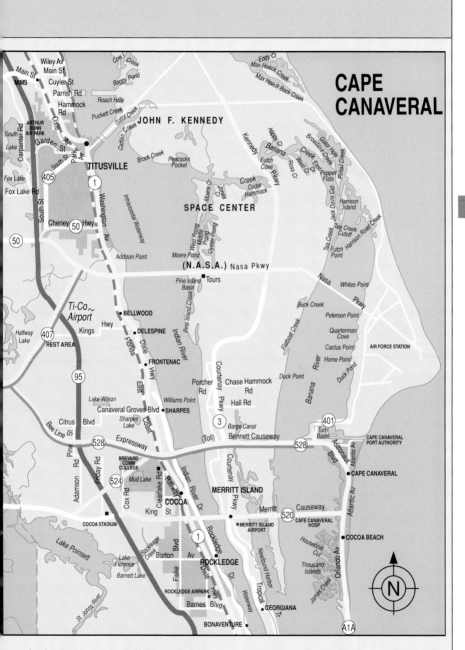

CAPE CANAVERAL

A day long visit to Kennedy Space Center and Spaceport USA is a thrilling way to experience the unusual combination of free roaming wildlife and state-of-the-art space technology.

Located one hour east of Orlando, off State Route 405, NASA Parkway, seven miles east of US1. Use exit #78 off I-95. Tel: (407) 452 2121 for more information.

Tame seagulls being fed at Cocoa Beach.

Fame, a museum showcasing the accomplishments of American first team of seven astronauts. It is fun to get to know these men on an individual basis, learning about their backgrounds and personalities through videotapes, photographs and professional mementos.

Part of the museum is a unique training program to encourage young kids to pursue careers in space, science and technology. It is called the **US Space Camp Florida**, a five-day spring and summer camp sessions where 4th-7th grades build and launch their own model rockets, experience weightlessness and conduct a simulated space shuttle mission. Talk with the campers or sign up your own family at Tel: (407) 269 6100.

West of Spaceport on the main-

land, between State Route 405 and State Route 528 is the **Valiant Air Command Museum**. Here you will see some of America's vintage warplanes, such as the Flying Tigers that flew with the Chinese Air Force to thwart the Japanese invasion of the mainland. Over 350 historic warbirds can be spotted here Tel: (407) 268 1941.

Just off I-95 between State Route 46 and State Route 50 is the National Historic District of downtown Titusville Along the main street you can walk past buildings from the late 1800s and early 1900s that are now home to a historical museum, offices, florist shops, antique shops and "eateries". The town often holds festivals like the Space Fest that combine artistic and technical aspect of the space program. Last year the Cosmic Electronic Music Man was there. Who knows what they will come up with next! Tel: (407) 269 7363.

North of Titusville, cross east over the Indian River on State Route 402 and follow the signs to the **Merritt Island National Wildlife Refuge**. This is a very special refuge where you can drive or walk through habitats for hundreds of bird species, alligators and other wildlife. The best time to visit is from October through April. Stop in first at the Visitor Information Center for maps, brochures and some terrific wildlife books. Tel: (407) 867 0667.

On the easternmost coastline of the Refuge is the **Canaveral National Seashore Playalinda Beach** where hundreds of giant sea turtles annually arrive to lay their eggs on these undeveloped, secluded stretches of seashore. Boardwalk crossovers allow you to walk amongst the dune vegetation plants without damaging them. Tel: (407) 867 2805.

Cocoa & Cocoa Beach

South of Titusville on US Route 1 is the city of Cocoa and Cocoa Beach.

Local shopkeepers and the city of Cocoa got together to recreate the old downtown area as it was years ago in 'olde Cocoa Village." The **Village Playhouse**, originally built as a vaudeville theater, and later used as a movie house, has been restored and is now used for live productions. You can tour **Porcher House**, formerly the home of citrus grove owners, or take a town walking tour with guides from the Brevard Museum. It is good fun to browse through the craft and clothing shops.

Speaking of **Brevard Museum**, plan to stop here if you are interested in Florida History–there are exhibits on the 15th century Spaniards who colonized the state and artifacts from the native Americans who lived here. Kids will enjoy "The Discovery Room", with lots of touchy-feely objects. Next door are 22 acres of nature trails. Tel: (407) 632 1830.

Also in Cocoa on the **Brevard Community College Campus** is a planetarium, with multimedia programs, space memorabilia, and a giant telescope to give you a bird's eye view of the heavens. Tel: (407) 631 7889.

If you would like to get a bird's eye view of alligators, drive over to the **Lone Cabbage Fish Camp** on State Road 520 at the St Johns River. They will take you out in a nine passenger airboat to visit the gators, birds and cypress trees. Their fish camp is an excellent place to catch freshwater fish like bass and catfish. There is also a family dining room serving up alligator tails, frog legs and raw oysters. Tel: (305) 632 4199.

Drive east across the Hubert Humphrey Bridge and Merritt Island Causeway (route 520) and you will reach a whole different universe. Along the beach are hundreds of inexpensive family motels, fast food dives, and ticky-

Daytona Raceway

Thrills and spills on the Daytona Speedway.

Daytona International Speedway is without doubt the only place in Florida you can get a " metal sandwich". And sometimes it's "full of mustard".

That is race talk and only applies to cars moving well over the speed limit. If three cars are zooming side-by-side on the steep 31° banked curve, that is called a "metal sandwich." If they make it through the curve without crashing, they "went to lunch." If not, they have gotten "full of mustard."

That is just some of the inside lingo you will learn during the 30 minute Speedway tour which goes out onto the backstretch and along the 97,900 seat grandstand. If you are lucky, you will be guided by Sandy Sanders, a very funny and knowledgeable race car enthusiast. Driving along the wide smooth race track at a pokey 30 miles per hour, it is hard to imagine what it would be like to be jammed in with 42 gleaming slices of rubber and metal careening

around at 200 miles per hour just inches from the ground.

Sandy will give you a bit of Daytona Speed way history. In 1902, RE Olds and Alexande Winton, competed in a car race against each other out on the hardpacked stretch of Daytona Beach. They both won, tying at 57 miles pe hour. The following year, Winton set a record a 68 miles per hour. In those days, that was fast

In 1903, the Florida East Coast Automobile Association was formed to promote permanen local beach racing. For the next 30 years, na tional and international drivers came to Daytona Beach to set world race car records. In 1935, Si Malcolm Campbell of England set a world record of 276 miles per hour, in his 30 foot long V-12 engine, *Bluebird*.

Bill Tuthill, who was curator of Daytona's Museum of Speed described the 1935 run in his book, *Speed on Sand*: "After the shock wave, al heads turned. Now the car was out of sight ir

out the country, like Indianapolis 500 winner Ben Shaw, midget racing champion Bill Schindler, international racing star Major Goldie Gardner and Palm Beach millionaire Jack Rutherfurd.

Twelve thousand fans saw the Frank Lockhart Memorial Race, which was the last event before WWII temporarily halted beach activity. France led the first 20 laps, but the race was won by Smokey Purser, another top racer of the day.

On The Racing Map Again

By 1946, Daytona was on the racing map once again, and Bill France had brought stock car racing to the forefront, becoming a full-time promoter along the way. The Daytona 200 motorcycle classic in 1947 attracted the largest crowd in the history of the beach, paving the way for that summer's successful stock car race. Later that year France and a group of top race car drivers and enthusiasts formed the National Association for Stock Car Racing (NASCAR) which would become the world's largest racing organization . By 1955, France had formed the Daytona Beach Motor Speedway Corporation, and the State of Florida had developed a Speedway Authority to build an ultra modern facility near Daytona Airport. In 1959, the gates opened to reveal the huge 2.5 mile trioval field, and a twisting infield road course suitable for all types of motor racing. One of the most famous sports facilities in the world, the Daytona International Speedway is the host for most of the world's major motor racing events. Some of the more well known races are: The 24 hour Rolex 24 and the Daytona 500 by STP, both part of "Speed Weeks" in early February; Speedway's Camel Motorcycle Week in early March; Daytona Beach Spring Speedway Spectacular (a car show and swap meet), end of March and the Pepsi 400, stock car race on July 4.

There is some type of high speed activity every day for more than four months of the year, so call the Speedway offices for a current schedule. When they are not holding races, take the Speedway tour, which is almost as much fun. Tel: (904) 254 2700.

the other direction, obscured by a swirling sand. We did see a big blue ball of flame that hung in midair for a second and also disappeared. That earshattering blast and the eerie ball of flame when Campbell cut the throttle are the only memories I have as an eye-witness of the fastest run ever made on the world famous measured mile".

By 1936, a new race car enthusiast had entered the scene, a man who would some day create the future of auto and motorcycle racing in America.

From Model-T To Ferraris

His name was William Henry Getty (Bill) France. He started out racing his father's Model-T and by 1938 was organizing and promoting major race events on the 3.2 mile Daytona Beach course, which he and his partners improved by adding clay to smooth out the turns. Races were sanctioned by the American Automobile Association, with a $5,000 winners purse, which attracted many of the big race names through-

tacky T-shirt shops. Down at **Cocoa Beach Pier**, which stretches for 840 feet out over the Atlantic Ocean, there is a great view of the ocean, beach and throngs of sun worshippers who come in every size and shape. The Pier is a historic landmark and a good spot to hang out your fishing line, or just hang out. Tel: (407) 783 7549.

Do not miss a trip to **Ron Jon Surf Shop**, a mind-boggling store stocked with swim suits, t-shirts, beach bikes, surf boards, boogie boards, jet ski, water ski and scuba diving gear. Anything you need to have fun with in the water, they have got. The shop is Cocoa Beach's claim to fame since 1963, and you are bound to see giant billboards advertising Ron Jon all over the state. Tel: (407) 799 8888.

Port Canaveral Cruise Line

Port Canaveral, at the north end of Cocoa Beach, is the third largest cruise passenger port in the US An estimated 1.5 million passengers sailed from this port during 1992. Here is a run-down on cruises you might enjoy.

• **Premier Cruise Lines**-The Big Red Boat: Premier Cruise Lines, the official cruise line of Walt Disney World, offers three and four-night cruises sailing from Port Canaveral to the Bahamas. The Star/Ships Oceanic and Atlantic depart Monday and Friday for Nassau, and an out island, Salt Cay.

The Star/Ships Majestic sails Thurs-

A rare dolls' Museum in Melbourne.

day and Sunday for the Abaco Islands in the northern Bahamas, making stops at Green Turtle Cay, Man-O-War Cay, Treasure Cay and Great Guana Cay.

Premier's Cruise and Walt Disney World Week combine the cruise with a free stay at Disney, including hotels, park admissions, tours at Kennedy Space Center and a one week rental car. Tel: (800) 888 6759.

• **Carnival Cruise Lines**: Carnival Cruise Lines offers three and four-night cruises to the Bahamas. The *Fun Ship Carnivale* departs Port Canaveral on Thursdays for a three night cruise to Nassau, and on Sundays for a four night cruise to Freeport and Nassau. Carnival also has cruise and land packages, some of which provide complimentary airfare from 28

Window shopping in Melbourne will unearth some unusual treasures.

ities to Port Canaveral. Tel: (800) 327 373.

Europa Cruise Lines: The Europa Star has six hour day and evening cruises, with dining, a casino, movies, and musical entertainment. Special supervised activities for children. Tel: (407) 799 400.

Portside Fun

If you just want to enjoy the sights and sounds of this busy deep water port, you do not have to go on board a cruise ship. There are three public parks, bicycle paths, boat launch ramps and coral reefs for fishing. If you do want to head to sea, there are plenty of charter boats

if you want reel in some mackerel, sailfish, marlin, wahoo or tuna.

Melbourne

Like Titusville and Cocoa, downtown Melbourne on the banks of Crane Creek has lovely turn-of-the-century buildings that are now galleries, restaurants, boutiques, book, jewelry and craft stores, and antique shops. You can walk for a block or two along the tree-lined streets over to the harbor and watch the boats coming and going. Or just sit on a park bench and watch the world go by. Tel: (407) 724 1741.

One of the town's newest entertainment facilities is the **Melbourne Grey-**

hound Park, where many of the top racing kennels send their stars to the post. Watch the action from the Winner's Club Dining Room. Located at Wickham and Sarno Roads. Tel: (407) 259 9800.

The **Brevard Art Center and Museum**, at 1463 N Highland Avenue, has decorative arts, ethnographic works, photography, experimental art and touring art exhibitions from major collections. Tel: (407) 242 0737. The **Space Coast Science Center** nearby, 1500 Highland Avenue, has hands-on exhibits, classes, workshops, lectures, films and field trips. Tel: (407) 259 5572.

A Real Dragon?

On the southern tip of Merritt Island, north of the Eau Gallie Causeway is a very unusual sculpture that Tampa sculptor Lewis Vandercar created in 1971. A 100-foot dragon long made of 20 tons of concrete and steel oversees the goings-on along the Indian and Banana Rivers. Four hatchlings were added in 1982. Legend has it that hundreds of years ago a dragon rose out of the river to chase away mainland enemies attacking island Indians. Maybe he will bring you better luck. Tel: 1 800 771 9922.

The 12-mile stretch from Melbourne Beach south to Sebastian Inlet is the largest nesting area in the United States for endangered sea turtles.

You can participate in a Turtle Walk

to watch loggerhead, green and leatherback turtles laying their eggs by calling the **Brevard Turtle Preservation Society** at Tel: (407) 676 1701 Reservations are mandatory, and walk usually last from 9:00pm to midnight from May through October. Egg laying takes place from May to August afte which you can see the brand new baby hatchlings making a run from the shore into the Atlantic Ocean.

Sebastian Inlet State Recreation Area

Beside turtle watching, the **Sebastian Inlet State Recreation Area** is a 576 acre State Park in Melbourne Beach where you can swim, surf, boat, fish camp and scuba dive. It is a beautifu place with crashing waves and a dra matic shoreline. Tel: (407) 984 4852.

Fresh Eel

The **Indian River Lagoon**, a 160-mile mixture of fresh and saltwater, runs eas along the Titusville and Melbourne areas. The most diverse estuary in the United States, the Lagoon has more than 4,000 species of animals, includ ing 700 species of fish and 310 kinds of birds. You might see manatee in the area. Spend some time sailing, power boating, wind surfing, fishing or enjoying Mother Nature's splendor Tel: (800) 771 9922.

Gone clamming on Indian River at Sebastian Inlet.

Welcome to historic Saint Augustine.

When Don Pedro Menendez de Aviles founded Saint Augustine in 1565, he surely had no idea that this would become the oldest permanent European settlement in North America, or that 423 years later people from all over the world would be drawn to its charming coquina buildings, hibiscus gardens and the brooding stone fortress of Castillo de San Marcos.

A bird's-eye view from the Saint Augustine Lighthouse Museum.

Saint Augustine

267

Through The Centuries

Through the centuries, Saint Augustine has been an illusory pot of gold at the end of the rainbow for all manner of explorers who journeyed here via Spanish galleon, 19th century railroad and 20th century cars and jets.

A tourist visiting Saint Augustine at the turn of

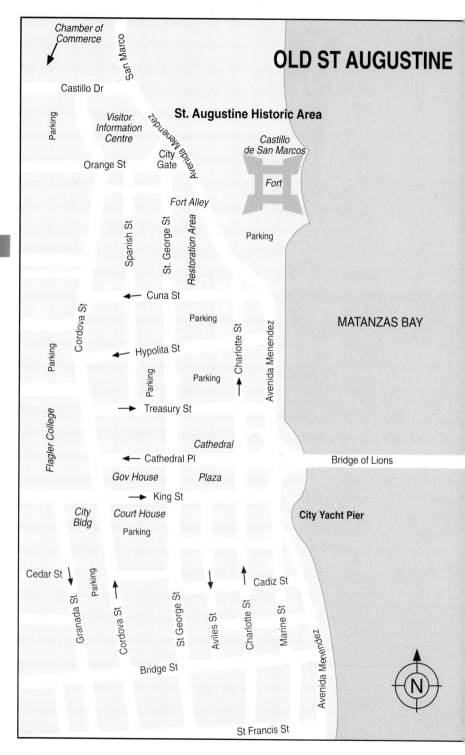

Chamber of Commerce

San Marco

OLD ST AUGUSTINE

Castillo Dr

Parking

Visitor Information Centre

Avenida Menendez

St. Augustine Historic Area

Castillo de San Marcos

Orange St

City Gate

Fort

Fort Alley

Parking

Spanish St

St. George St

Restoration Area

← Cuna St

Parking

Cordova St

Charlotte St

Avenida Menendez

MATANZAS BAY

← Hypolita St

Parking

Parking

Parking

→ Treasury St

Flagler College

Cathedral

← Cathedral Pl

Gov House

Plaza

Bridge of Lions

→ King St

City Bldg

Court House

City Yacht Pier

Parking

Cedar St ↓

Granada St

Parking

Cordova St

↑

↓

↑ Cadiz St

St George St

Aviles St

Charlotte St

Marine St

Avenida Menendez

Bridge St

N

St Francis St

Cannons boom and smoke fills the air during a historical interpretation of the Castillo de San Marco.

he century, summed up her feelings about the city in this letter home to a riend: "I drive over hard shell roads and go yachting. I dance. I play tennis. I fish. In short, the day is always too short in Saint Augustine. And oh, Evelyn, some of the gowns that are worn here! It is Paris come to Florida..."

Except that Parisian gowns have long been replaced by shorts and t-shirts, days in Saint Augustine are still wonderful, and still too short.

Touring Saint Augustine

Start at the **Saint Augustine Visitor Information and Preview Center**, 10 Castillo Drive (at the corner of San Marco Avenue). The center is a good place to organize your activities, and will provide free maps and information on the many attractions, historic sites, restaurants and accommodations. There are also historical exhibits and an audiovisual program on Saint Augustine's history. Tel: (904) 824 3334.

There are a number of options for getting around the city:

• **Saint Augustine Sightseeing Trains** are open-air trains that operate on a 15 to 20 minute pick-up schedule over a seven mile tour route. There are stop-off privileges at major attractions and a narrated lecture throughout the tour. Complimentary pick-up and return for city motel guests. 170 San Marco Avenue. Tel: (904) 829 6545.

Saint Augustine's Lightner Museum

Not many museums in America have concerts, but at Lightner Museum in Saint Augustine there's one every day in the Music Room. Lightner volunteers Phyllis and William Van Marter have restored all the Museum's 1870-1920 instruments, and you'll be delighted by the music they play.

Imagine a complete orchestra in one instrument! The German Orchestrion, made in 1874, has a 45 note piano, three ranks of pipes, a glockenspiel, cymbals, snare drum, and a base drum. The sweet shrill Violano-Virtuoso plays a piano and a violin. And the charming tinny Nickelodeon belts out ten hits from 1900 like "In Your Eyes". If you love really old tunes, this room is where it's at.

The Lightner Museum and its collection of "relics from America's Gilded Age" was a gift to Saint Augustine by Chicago publisher Otto C. Lightner, founding Editor of Hobbies Magazine.

The Museum is inside the magnificent Spanish style building of the former Alcazar Hotel, built in 1888 by Henry Flagler, as part of his grand plan to establish St. Augustine as the American Riviera. Hotel architects were John M. Carrere and Thomas Hastings who later designed the New York Public Library and the interior of the Metropolitan Opera House. Interior decorator was Louis Comfort Tiffany, whose brilliant stained glass windows and lamps now grace a special room in the Museum.

The Alcazar Hotel was host every winter season to 25,000 glamourous guests during the years 1889-1896. But as Flagler extended his railroad to Palm Beach and began to build lavish resort hotels further south, much of the Alcazar' business went south as well. By 1931, the doors of the Alcazar were closed.

On a visit to Saint Augustine, Chicago publisher Otto Lightner noticed the empty Alcazar and offered to buy it to display his growing collection of antiques, curios, art, glass windows and architectural decor. Lightner paid $125,000 to the City for the hotel, and St Augustine's private citizens made an additional $25,000 payment. Lightner Museum opened January 1, 1948.

After Lightner's death the museum was without operating and maintenance funds and had to close in 1971. During the next three years the people of Saint Augustine put their time and expertise to good use, spending hundreds of hours cleaning, repairing, organizing, cataloguing and arranging exhibits. Carpentry students constructed cabinets, glass company employees worked nights and weekends building exhibit covers, parents and children plastered painted, wallpapered and decorated.

St. Augustine citizens were determined to save their beloved museum and on August 12 1974 their champagne glasses were proudly raised at the Lightner Museum public reopening.

Today Lightner Museum is still one of St Augustine's many treasures, and a fascinating afternoon for any visitor to the city. 75 King Street. Tel: (904) 824 2874.

• **Saint Augustine Historical Tours** are open-air trolleys that have much the same tour route and stop-offs as the trains. Discount package tours are available at the 167 San Marco office, where you can park free for the day. Tel: (904) 829 3800.

• **Colee's Sightseeing Carriage Tours** show you the city by horse and buggy, and are a little more personal than the train or trolley. On Bayfront near the Fort Castillo de San Marcos entrance. Tel: (904) 829 2818.

• **Mary Way Jacobs** provides walking tours and special event planning at 212D San Marco Avenue, Suite 151. Tel: (904) 829 5598.

• An enjoyable way to learn some history while taking in the city skyline is a **Matanzas Bay Cruise** on *Victory II* and

An ancient sight next to an ancient site – a horse and buggy parked outside Florida's oldest house (1700s).

Victory III. The cruise departs from the City Yacht Pier just south of the Bridge of Lions downtown. Tel: (904) 824 1806.

Attractions & Sights

You can easily spend several days wandering around Saint Augustine, hopping on and off the train, trolley or carriage, or walking the quaint streets. Some of the attractions and historic sights are more interesting than others. So if you just have one day, be sure to see these:

"The Dream of Empire" at the Museum Theater, 5 Cordova Street, is an ideal place to begin. A 35mm feature film that cost $3 million and took seven years to make, the "Dream" unveils the poignant story of Spain's struggle to found Saint Augustine and will prepare you for seeing the rest of the town.

The "Oldest" Wooden Schoolhouse

From here, walk east on Orange Street to St George Street, a quiet relaxed walking mall closed to vehicles. The street has row-after-row of houses built in the middle 1700s that are now shops selling cigars, gifts, sportswear, books, jewelry,

The ageless charm of the Mission Chapel Shrine of Our Lady of Leche.

handicrafts and pottery. Starting out on the north end, you will first come to the **Oldest Wooden Schoolhouse**, a cypress and cedar frame building used as a billet for city guards and as a private day school. Across the street is the restored **Spanish Quarter**, a collection of historic houses, gardens, and guides in colonial clothing, that will give you a sense of this thriving 1740 community.

Next door is **Saint Photios National Greek Orthodox Shrine and Chapel**, a magnificent chapel of exquisite Byzantine-style frescoes of apostles, saints and Jesus Christ; and exhibits depicting the life of the Greeks who came to America in 1768.

Continue south on St George past King Street and turn left at Artillery

Lane to the **Oldest Store**. There are more than 100,000 mementos of yester year here, such as steam-powered trac tors, red underwear, Gibson Girl corsets and high-wheeled bicycles.

The Lightner Museum

Now walk back north on St George and turn left at King Street to the **Lightne Museum**, at the corner of King and Cordova Street. This was originally the old Alcazar Hotel built in 1888 by Henry Flagler. It is still a grand building where you can wander through three floors o cut crystal, Tiffany glass, American European and Oriental art, a Victorian village and hear a concert of delightfu antique mechanical musical instru ments.

East At The Bridge

From here, walk southwards on Cordova and go east at the Bridge, and one block south to St Francis Street. Here is the **Oldest House**, a 250-year old Spanish colonial house with patio, museum and gardens.

The historians here will really make Saint Augustine history come alive through stories of the house's original families.

From the Oldest House you can hop back on the train, trolley or carriage and head over to the **Castillo de San Marcos** the oldest masonry fortification in the

Saint Augustine Gives New Meaning to "Old"

school regulation from 200 years ago warns, Women teachers who marry or engage in nseemly conduct will be dismissed." Times vere tough back then, as you'll see at Saint ugustine's "oldest wooden schoolhouse in the JS" on Saint George Street. A bell rings as you nter the cozy little box, sunlight streaming hrough the windows.

Students in period dress sit on hard benches, eading shared textbooks as the "professor" ctures. Heat came from the fireplace, and the itchen was a separate building where teachers ad to cook everyone's lunch!

Built of red cedar and cypress, and put ogether with wooden pegs and handmade ails, "the oldest wooden school house" was ome to the schoolmaster and his wife who ved upstairs. Talk about job loyalty!

And then there's Saint Augustine's "oldest ouse", which was occupied by Spanish settlers the early 1600's. The first documented family ving in the house were the Gonzalez who lived ere until Florida was ceded by Spain to Eng-nd in 1763 and the town's 3000 Spanish esidents had to leave.

Major Joseph Peavett, a well to do retired ritish officer was the next owner, making the terations still part of the house today. Peavett ied in 1783 and his 56 year old widow Mary emarried 28 year old John Hudson, a young ish adventurer described as a "profligate wast-

rel". Hudson quickly lost the fortune that his wife had spent her life acquiring, and to pay off his debts, the house was auctioned to a newly arrived Spaniard, Geronimo Alvarez. The Alvarez family and descendants lived in the house for almost 100 years, as Florida became part of the US in 1821, and endured the Seminole and Civil Wars.

In 1918, the Saint Augustine Historical Society acquired " the oldest house," and today historians give spellbinding tours telling about the oldest house and the adventures of the people who loved it.

A few blocks from the oldest house is Saint Augustine's "oldest store museum". The nucleus of the Museum's contents were actually taken from the attic of the old store's warehouse. But this place is a mind boggling selection of "yesterday's mementos", like steam powered tractors, Gibson girl corsets, high wheeled bicycles and animal powered treadmills. Lots of fun for nostalgia buffs.

Whether you're young or old, Saint Augustine's "oldest wooden schoolhouse", "oldest house", and "oldest store museum" are interesting windows back in time.

The Saint Augustine Historical Society answers historical queries and invites membership at 271 Charlotte Street, Saint Augustine. Tel: (904) 824 2872.

nited States.

Built from 1672 to 1695 of coquina, shell rock formation found locally on nastasia Island, it served as the princi-al defense system during the 235 years f Spanish domination in Florida.

Never captured, the Castillo is now National Park Service National Monu-ent, and its views of Matanzas Bay are e perfect way to end a day at Saint ugustine.

Sports & Recreation

If you are going to be in the area for more than one day, there are 45 miles of white sandy beaches for relaxing, picnicking, or taking the challenge in volleyball. Two favorites are **Coquina Beach** at the southernmost end of St Johns' County, with huge statue-like rocks, and **Anastasia State Recreation Area**, where you can also camp over-

Drive through or better still trot through Spanish Moss-draped trees
on Magnolia Avenue.

night and hike on nature trails.

Local marinas rent graceful sailboats, charter boats for deep sea ocean fishing, power boats for big mouth bass fresh water fishing in the St Johns', and equipment for water-skiing and windsurfing. Or just throw a line out from the new 640 feet pier at Saint Augustine Beach, or cast from the shoreline for sea trout.

St Johns' County

St Johns County is the world headquarters for professional golf and tennis, with famous courses like **The Stadium** and **Marriot's Sawgrass**, which *Golf Magazine* rated as one of the top 100 courses in the US. There are three major public tennis facilities with 22 courts with night lights.

Festivals

Saint Augustine hosts more than a dozen festivals a year, from the Columbus Day Weekend Seafood Festival, to Cracker Day, a salute to the cattle industry; to Saint Augustine's Folk Festival which features two days of music at the **Saint Augustine Amphitheater**. Contact the Visitors Center. Tel: (904) 824 3334 to find out what festival is going on when you are there, or write Saint Augustine/ St Johns County Chamber of Commerce, One Riberia Street, Saint Augustine, FL 32084 to plan ahead.

Jacksonville

With 20 miles of broad beautiful family beaches, fine art and science museums, the historic Fort Caroline and one of the country's top zoos, Jacksonville is one of Florida's great undiscovered vacation spots.

Water taxi across the mighty Saint John's River, shop for antiques, tour a Navy ship, or enjoy a play in a restored 1920 theater. Florida's "First Coast" is home to The Players Championship, the Professional Golf Association, and the Association of Tennis Professionals. And although Jacksonville is ranked as one of the top ten growing business cities in the US, this town still manages to party all year round, with festivals celebrating everything from Jazz to Shakespeare to Country Music to a 15 kilometer River Run.

Jacksonville Landing, a horseshoe-shaped marketplace.

Touring

Start your city tour at **The Jacksonville Landing**, a horseshoe-shaped indoor/outdoor

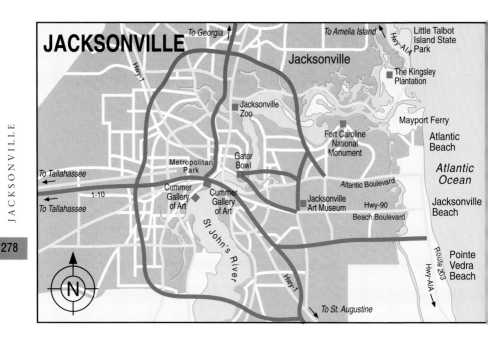

marketplace located on the Northbank of the Saint Johns River, at the foot of the Main Street Bridge. Home to dozens of well-known retail shops like Banana Republic, The Sharper Image and riverfront restaurants, The Landing is a popular location for both locals and tourists. A shooting fountain, strawberry-shaped street lamps, and brick walkways create a picturesque scene along the mighty Saint Johns River. History markers laud famous citizens like author Harriet Beecher Stowe (*Palmetto Leaves*) and poet/composer James Weldon Johnson (*Lift Every Voice and Sing*). Other plaques recount 100 years of riverboat history, a romantic era of elegance when steamboats chugged up and down the Saint Johns, transporting wealthy vacationers who dined in saloons wearing gowns and top hats, and slept in wood-panelled staterooms. In 1830, travelling by steamboat from Savannah, Georgia to Jacksonville took 34 hours!

Today, girls in neon-colored lycra shorts jog along the river, as families with tots in strollers enjoy the cool breezes and spectacular river views.

From The Landing take a river taxi and head for the Southbank of the Saint Johns River. Your first stop will be the 1.2 mile long **Riverwalk**, a boardwalk featuring restaurants, shops, a marina, the **Jacksonville Navy Memorial**, and the **Friendship Fountain**, one of the world's largest. At night it is especially pretty when the Fountain's colored lights reflect in the River waters.

Behind the Fountain is the **Museum of Science and History**, where you can see star shows and musical laser demonstrations at the Alexander Brest Planetarium, a Civil War ship,

The Riverwalk- a boardwalk featuring restaurants, shops, a marina and a fountain.

and a multimedia presentation on "Ribbon of Life: The Story of the Saint Johns River."

After you have explored this area, you might enjoy a longer river cruise. Choose from paddleboats, gondolas and narrated lunch/dinner sightseeing cruises aboard *The Viking Sun*, the *First Lady of Jacksonville*, or *The Annabel Lee*. A river cruise is a great way to appreciate the city skyline of modern white and green mirrored office buildings. You will cruise under Jacksonville's beautiful bridges, like the **Dames Point Bridge** which glows with fiber optic tubes. You will also go past **Metropolitan Park**, a 23-acre grassy park with a canopied pavilion where many free festivals are held, like Shakespeare at the Met and the famous Jacksonville Jazz Festival.

South of downtown on the river is **Fort Caroline**, the site of the first US Protestant settlement. You can explore the 1564 fort, hike along nature trails and also picnic here.

After a river cruise, head to the Southbank side of downtown to the historic **San Marco District**. Here red brick and red-roofed homes line wide boulevards with stately oaks and palmettos. In the heart of this residential neighborhood is a charming shopping area with antiques, books, gifts and restaurants. And the oldest continually producing civic theater in the nation, **Theater Jacksonville**, a 311-seat deco period playhouse.

Jacksonville Beaches

White stretches of pristine white beaches and vast expanses of bathing beauties grace Jacksonville's beaches.

At first it seems like the same old sun, sand and sea you see everywhere in Florida.

But after a few minutes of walking along Jacksonville Beach you realize that people actually LIVE HERE.

Over there a blonde bombshell, aged 6, is chasing her shaggy brown mutt back home. Grandma, pushed along in a beach wheelchair with giant orange wheels, is laughing over something her doting daughter said. A group of giggling teens carrying book bags gossip on their way home from school. A retired couple, still obviously in love, ride by on their bikes, gazing at the blue horizon and each other.

Oh sure there are a few hot numbers in teeny bikinis and muscled Adonis-types, but for the most part these are family beaches, lined with gracious two-story balconied homes. There are swing sets in the front yard, which just happens to be the Atlantic Ocean.

And that gives Jacksonville's beaches a whole different feel. Friendlier. Comfortable. Not a place where you have to impress anybody with a perfect tan. Anyone you smile at here will smile right back. And they are happy to tell you anything you want to know about their city.

The beaches are divided into three communities: Jacksonville Beach, Neptune Beach, and Atlantic Beach.

Jacksonville Beach Pier

The **Jacksonville Beach Pier** near 1st Avenue is a great spot for fishing and you can get rods, reels and bait here. Over on Third Street is The **American Lighthouse Museum**, where you will find lighthouse models, artifacts, paintings and photos. In this beach area you will find public golf courses, tennis courts, arts and crafts galleries, antiques, a 19th century railroad depot and a 1911 steam locomotive and an

oceanside boardwalk, seawalk, with shops and restaurants.

North is sleepy **Neptune Beach**, a small residential community with a few hotels and seafood restaurants.

Where Atlantic Boulevard meets the ocean lies **Atlantic Beach**. Another quiet spot of private homes and seafood hangouts. To the north is the **Kathryn Abbey Hanna State Park**, 450 acres of campgrounds, picnic areas, beaches, salt and freshwater fishing.

The "In" People

So if you are looking for the beautiful people, the *in* crowd, those size-two models that pose for *Sports Illustrated* "Swimsuit Issues", do not come to Jacksonville's Beaches. What you will find here are teen boys on brightly colored surfboards trying to ride gently curling waves. Scruffy dogs, laughing grannies and giggling schoolgirls.

Happy families that are pleased to share their beaches with your family. For a couple of days at least......

Before you leave the downtown area, plan to visit three very fine museums: the **Cummer Gallery of Art**, which exhibits medieval to contemporary paintings, sculpture, jade, ivory and French period furniture at 829 Riverside. Tel: (904) 356 6857; the **Jacksonville Art Museum**, which boasts collections of Oriental porcelain and pre-Columbian artifacts at 4160 Boulevard Center Drive. Tel: (904) 398 8336 and the **Alexander Brest Museum**, which houses collections of ivories, Steuben glass and Royal Danish porcelain at Jacksonville University, 2800 University Boulevard North. Tel: (904) 744 3950, ext 3374.

In addition to all this city activity, you can have a great day at the **Jacksonville Zoological Park**. Take I95 north out of downtown Jacksonville, exit at Heckscher Drive and follow signs to the Zoo.

There are over 700 animals here, ranging from ostriches and wildebeest to kangaroos, parrots, white rhino and giraffes. There are few fences, and lots of open parkland which allows you to get really close to the animals. A delightful gift shop sells animal-theme clothing, jewelry, cards and books. Tel: (904) 757 4462.

From the Zoo, you are only 15 minutes away from the world famous **Anheuser Busch Brewery**. Turn left back onto Heckscher Drive, take Route 17 north 2 miles and turn left at the signs to the Brewery.

If you love beer, you will enjoy the

View of Jacksonville's business district.

tour, which demonstrates the step-by-step process to beer making, from mashing, brewing, cooling, fermenting, filtering and bottling. And naturally, **The Hospitality Room** serves up cold delicious samples on tap. This Brewery turns out 12 million 12 ounce bottles and cans of beer every 24 hours so they are never likely to run out!

If you want to learn about life on a Florida plantation in 1792, take a drive over to the Kingsley Plantation, the state's oldest remaining plantation. Take Route 17 south–also called Main Street—at Heckscher Drive go left, which becomes 105 north. Drive for 30 minutes until you see signs to the Kingsley Plantation. A backwoods road through hanging oaks and sable palmettos twists

and turns for several miles before you reach the Plantation. You will come upon remains of several "slave cabins", and onto the main property where the owner Zephaniah Kingsley became a rich man from the labors of his 200 slaves who farmed sea island cotton, sugarcane, sweet potatoes and citrus from 1813 to 1839.

The Plantation is part of the Timucuan Ecological and Historic Preserve and the park rangers give interesting daily tours of the house and grounds. Its rather disturbing coming face-to-face with this aspect of American history–white men owning, exploiting, and fathering children with black slaves–but it is something that anyone with a conscience should experience. 11676 Pal-

Jacksonville Zoo

t is early in the morning, but the critters at acksonville Zoo are already mighty busy.

A 6-foot high brown and white anteater sniffs and scratches the dirt, looking for one of the 30,000 ants he will eat today.

A dark brown chimp screeches secrets to his buddies as they cavort like kindergardeners on their water-surrounded island.

Master, a 16 year old Bengal tiger, paces around his swimming pool, looking for breakfast. And, a red-legged male Masai ostrich chases after his wildebeest neighbors–just for fun.

The only ones taking it easy are Paco and Salsa, a pair elegant jaguars who laze in the already sizzling sun, before settling down for a mid-morning snooze.

Few fences and the open parkland of acksonville Zoo make it real easy to get "up close and personal" with their 800 wild animals.

Walk up the pathway onto a boardwalk stretching over "The African Veldt", an 11-acre recreation of an African savannah. Patterned after the Serengeti Plain in Tanzania, you can gaze out over vast fields of grazing wildebeest, great horned kudu, elan, gazelle and a very aggressive red-legged Masai ostrich.

In the southeast corner of the veldt is *Mahali Pa Simba*, (Place of the Lion), where the most famous big cats live. The boardwalk allows you to view them from afar, closer into their habitat and nose-to-nose from the ground.

The **Okavango Trail** features animals such as African crocodiles, porcupines, caracal lynx, blue duikers and kirk's dik-dik found in the Okavango River region of southern Africa.

Take the kids to the **Okavango Village Petting Zoo** where they can get friendly with pygmy goats, dwarf zebu, miniature horses and Sardinian pygmy donkeys. A little different than most petting zoos with their sheep and calves.

At the **Chimpanorma**, it is hard to tell who is more excited, the chimps or the kids who watch wide-eyed. Marabou storks and rare Pondicherry Vultures hang out in the aviary, and alligators swim mostly submerged in the dense watery Florida wetland habitat.

At 11:30am on weekdays and at noon and 2:30pm on weekends and holidays, the Zoo presents "Elephant Encounter", where elephant keepers bathe their pachyderms and answer questions posed by curious visitors. Another ecologically oriented show, "Animals and Us", is presented on weekends and holidays at 11:00am, 1:30pm and 3:30pm. The stars here are a Bateleur Eagle, a Scarlet Macaw, a Boa Constrictor, a Barred Owl, a Screech Owl, a Black Vulture, an Armadillo and an Andean Condor. Habitats, diet, environmental status and unique characteristics are highlighted.

The Zoo opened back in 1914 with an animal collection that consisted of just one Red Deer fawn. The first major purchase was an Asian Elephant bought with money raised by local schoolchildren. Their growth and city support since then has been phenomenal. Now home to over 800 reptiles, birds and mammals, the zoo has been nationally lauded for accomplishments like being first to breed Toco Toucans in the Western Hemisphere; breeding the most black jaguars in captivity; being first to breed the Aldabra Tortoises in the Northern Hemisphere and being the first to breed Pondicherry Vultures in the Western Hemisphere.

If you are visiting Florida's First Coast, and hear the call of the wild, the answer is just a few miles from downtown, at the Jacksonville Zoological Park. 8605 Zoo Road. Tel: (904) 757 4463.

netto Avenue. Tel: (904) 251 3537.

On a lighter note, you might like to drive from here back onto Heckscher Drive watching for signs to the Mayport ferry just down the road. Turn left into the ferry auto load, and enjoy a 10 minute ride across the Saint Johns River on board *The Black Beauty Special* ferry. It is truly a colorful sight, with tugs pushing crane barges, fishing boats speeding along and gulls screeching overhead as they dive into the river for lunch.

Driving off the ramp and right onto

A1A you will come to the US Navy's **Mayport Naval Air Station**. Call if you would like to tour the base and aircraft carriers. Tel: (904) 246 2922.

Culture

Jacksonville presents a number of theatrical and musical choices. Here are some of them:

• **Alhambra Dinner Theater**, a buffet and show. Tel: (904) 641 1212.

• **Florida Community College** presents Broadway musicals and plays. Tel: (904) 632 3373.

• **The Florida Theater**, hosts over 100 events yearly. Tel: (904) 355 2787.

• **River City Playhouse**, adult and children's theater. Tel: (904) 388 8830.

• **Theatre Jacksonville**, drama, comedy, musicals. Tel: (904) 396 4425.

• **Saint Johns River City Band**, Sunday afternoon concerts in Metropolitan Park with the Jacksonville Symphony Orchestra. Tel: (904) 354 5547. And try not to forget the free October Jazz Festival, with Jazz greats from around the world.

Tour Assistance

Maps and information on self-guided walking tours of downtown Jacksonville, Riverside, Avondale, and San Marco are available by calling Tel: (904) 353 9736. Information on all attractions, festivals and events is available from The Jacksonville Convention & Visitors Bureau, at 6 East Bay Street, Suite 200. Tel: (904) 798 9148.

Great Getaway

If you want to get far away from the city, drive north for 35 minutes from Jacksonville to Amelia Island, a beautiful island 13 miles long, 2 miles wide with only one town–Fernadina Beach.

The only US location to have seen rule under eight flags, this Island was locked in the Victorian age when Henry Flagler's Southern railroad detoured around Amelia. Historians say "the French visited, the Spanish developed, the English named, and the Americans tamed" the island.

It is a wonderful place to spend a day or a week. Sweeping sandy beaches are framed by magnificent dunes fringed with sea oats; salt marshes are home to a myriad of birds; ancient live oaks draped in Spanish moss hang over sun-dappled paths and the streets are lined with gracious Victorian mansions.

Accomodation

There are a number of quaint bed and breakfasts, as well as 5-star golf resorts. And the port's shrimp fishing fleet guarantees an abundance of fresh seafood. For more information contact The Amelia Island Tourist Development Council, PO Box 472, Fernadina Beach, FL 32034. Tel: (904) 261 3248.

Into the blues at the Jazz Festival in Metropolitan Park.

Northwestern Florida is famous for its friendly "southern" hospitality, fascinating history, and natural beauty: astonishing sugar-white sandy beaches, rolling dunes, emerald green water, native palms, graceful magnolias and moss festooned oaks. The pace is much calmer than in the rest of the state, but people still get a lot done each day. It is just that with an average of 343 sunny days each year, nobody seems to get into a bad mood.

Rent a sailboat along the Gulf Coast at Panama Beach.

Panama City Beach

You are in for some spectacular driving along Florida's Panhandle coastline Highway 98. Twisting and turning through miles of dense cool forests, the road is eerily shady, then blinding with streams of yellow sunshine. As you approach Panama City you begin to see the Gulf of Mexico's emerald green waters, and finally you are ambling along the 27 magical miles of snow white sugary sand beaches called the Panama City Beach.

Why they have been called "The World's Most Beautiful Beaches", will be immediately obvious. The sand is fluffy and powdery, and looks like sugar. The dazzling whiteness reflects the heat of the sun, so the sand stays cool on even the hottest days.

When you walk, tiny quartz granules squeak under your feet.   Like a child you will want to grab it in great handfuls, roll in it, be buried up to your ears in it. Certainly the thought of wearing shoes in this fabulous stuff will definitely be out of the question.

Flocks of shorebirds scurry along the water's edge, darting into the waves to gulp down another fish or two. They are happy if you want to tag along. But you will be lured into the water too before long: warm, clear and heavenly bluegreen.

Some folks are swimming, others windsurf and another contented group sits in low rise chairs, chatting about everything and nothing as waves wash over them. Ahh... this is what letting go is all about.

Fishing

If you have got to add a little challenge and adventure to your vacation, the waters around Panama City and Panama City Beach are chocked with a wide variety of fish, including red snapper, black grouper, king mackerel, cobia and amberjack. You can fish from charter and party boats, or from Panama City's 1,642 feet Pier, the state's longest pier. There are also lots of bridges, and jetties where you can wet a line, and of course there is shore casting.

Fishermen from all over the world come here from March through November for inshore trolling in the bay and just off the beaches. This is a good time to snare spanish and king mackerel, bluefish, barracuda, bonito, jack crevalle and dolphin fish. Blackfin tuna are in the water all year round.

Or you may want to try your luck with deep sea bottom fishing from "party" boats that hold from 25 to 100 people. They make day trips out, and will furnish you with tackle, bait, ice and lots of advice! See if you can reel in some red snapper, scamp, warsaw, grouper, amberjack and triggerfish.

There are dozens of charter boats to choose from, but here's a list to get you going:

• **Born to Boogie Charter**: At slip 36 in the Treasure Island Marina on the eastern most side of Panama City Beach. Fast 30 foot center console fishing boat. Tel: (904) 235 3255.

• **Box Full Fishing Charter:** Fly fishing, wade fishing, Gulf and bay fishing with Captain Buddy Dortch. Tel: (904) 769 8370.

• **Captain Anderson's Marina:** At Thomas Drive and North Lagoon Drive, this is where you can choose from deep

A Shell Island getaway for shell hunters.

sea cruisers, charter fishing boats, dinner/dance cruises and dolphin viewing cruises. Tel: (904) 234 3435.

• **Captain Blood Light Tackle Fishing:** This is an alternative to deep sea fishing, along the inshore Gulf and calm bay water. Four, six or eight hour trips for one to three people. Tel: (904) 785 6216.

Diving

If you would rather be in the deep than on it, the **Hydrospace Dive Shop** next to the Treasure Ship and at the foot of the Hathaway Bridge is one of the Gulf Coast's largest dive operations. You can take a half day resort course; or sign up for one of the six dive boats that make half and full day charter trips. Tel: (904) 234 9463 or (904) 234 3036.

Shell Island Getaway

Ready to play Robinson Crusoe? Why not take a boat trip out to Shell Island, a 7 $\frac{1}{2}$ mile long, 1 mile wide barrier island just south of Panama City Beach? With no residents other than other tourists out for the day, Shell Island is a beautiful slice of deserted sandy beach perfect for swimming, relaxing and searching for sea shells.

Several charter operations in Panama City and Panama City Beach run cruises to Shell Island:

Saint Andrews State Recreation Area

Definitely for the nature lover – the Saint Andrews Recreation Area.

At the east end of Thomas Drive is one of Panama City Beach's greatest secrets: a beautiful recreation area with rippling snowy white sand dunes, pristine beaches fringed with wild sea oats, and secluded nature trails. This is Saint Andrews, 1,063 peaceful acres of beaches, dunes, pinewood, marshes and the wildlife that calls them home. On overload from amusement park frenzy? Or just looking for a little more privacy than the noisy beaches? Then spend the day here at Saint Andrews. Bring along a bucket and collect scallops from the grass flats on the park's Bay side; or grab a net and scoop up those blue crabs scurrying through the grass flats in Saint Andrews Bay. Both make great eating. (Just make sure the crabs are not egg bearing females-check for bright orange eggs on their underside- and return those mother to the water). Winding nature trails throughout the park have signs pointing out interesting foliage. Keep your eyes open for wading waterbirds and snoozing alligators.

If you have a non-gasoline operated boat, you can take it into Gator Lake. There is also a boat ramp for launches into the Gulf of Mexico

The fishing is fabulous here, whether you choose saltwater angling in the Gulf, head for the bay's brackish water, or toss your bait to Gator Lake's freshwater fish. In the spring, you can count on reeling in bluefish, speckled trout, redfish, flounder, cobia, pompano, king and Spanish mackerel. Summer offers schoolie, speckled trout, flounder, bonita, jack crevalle, Spanish and king mackerel.

In Autumn look for redfish, Spanish and king mackerel, pompano, bonita and flounder. Winter will yield sheepshead and black drum. There are beautiful picnic areas throughout the park, swimming in the Gulf and behind the jetty, a concession stand, bathhouses, and a campground. Most facilities are handicapped-accessible. One of Florida's most popular parks, the Saint Andrews State Recreation Area is a peaceful easy getaway from the hustle and bustle of Panama City Beach. East end of Thomas Drive. Tel: (904) 234 2522.

The Ashley Gorman: Cruises Saint Andrews Bay to Shell Island with four hour long narrated tours, passing the Port Panama City harbour and Audubon Island watching pelican, seagulls and dolphin add to the fun. Docked at Sun Harbour Marina, east end of Hathaway Bridge. Tel: (904) 785 4878.

Captain Anderson's Marina: Cruises to Shell Island with three hour long sightseeing trips. They also have glassbottom boats, dinner boats, and a seafood market. At 5550 N Lagoon Drive, Panama City Beach. Tel: (904) 234 3435.

The Glassbottom Boat: Daily sightseeing trips to Shell Island, with the added attraction of seeing under the sea on the way out. At Treasure Island Marina, Thomas Drive, Panama City Beach. Tel: (904) 234 8944.

The Island Star Sightseeing Cruise: Sightseeing cruises and snorkeling/sightseeing cruises off Shell Island. You can rent snorkel gear from them. Also narrated cruises of Saint Andrews Bay. At Rude Roy's Marina, west of Hathaway Bridge. Tel: (904) 235 2809.

Family Fun

Panama City Beach is perfect for families with hyperactive kids. In addition to the beautiful beaches and diverse watersports, there are amusement parks, mini-golf courses, go-kart raceways, water parks, a zoo, a greyhound race track, a marine park, state park and the largest roller skating facility in the

United States.

Drive along Front Beach Road in Panama City Beach and you will be bombarded with dozens of family fun choices. Here are a few of the attractions:

• **Coconut Creek Mini-Golf and Gran Maze:** Journey through caves and waterfalls testing your skill on two mini-golf courses. Next door at Gran Maze, race against the clock to find your way through a giant size maze. 9807 Front Beach Road, Panama City Beach. Tel: (904) 234 2625.

• **Gulf World:** A Marine amusement park with sea lion, dolphin and penguin shows. Also stingrays, parrots. 15412 Front Beach Road, Panama City Beach. Tel: (904) 234 5271.

• **Jellybeans Skate Park:** A 1/4 mile roller skating track around a lake with dips and curves. Rock 'n roll music and light shows. Great place for a birthday party. 12202 Middle Beach Road, across from Shipwreck Island. Tel: (904) 233 0010.

• **Miracle Strip Amusement Park:** More than 30 rides, including a 2,000 foot roller coaster and a 40-foot swinging Sea Dragon. 12001 Front Beach Road, Panama City Beach. Tel: (904) 234 5810.

• **Shipwreck Island Water Park:** Northwest Florida's largest waterpark, with a "Rapid River Run", "Wave Pool" and "Tadpole Hole". Across the street from Miracle Strip Amusement Park. Tel: (904) 234 0368.

If you and the kids cannot find enough to do in Panama City and

Those Funny, Friendly Shorebirds

Look closely, there is a smile on the faces of these Laughing Gulls.

Whoever said a dog is man's best friend never strolled along the ocean surrounded by a flock of friendly funny shorebirds. They watch your every move and always stay just out of reach, but it is patently clear that they love your company.

Voracious Eaters

Darting in and out of the shimmering sea, these voracious eaters are never sated. No matter how many fish they gulp down, it is never enough. You will be even more popular of course, if you have brought along a treat to share. And once you have fed one bird, he broadcasts it to the whole neighborhood, and soon the entire flock waddles along after you for miles and you are forever referred to as "The Pied Piper of Pelicans".

For a city slicker not used to hanging out with these aggressive feathered friends, it can be a little intimidating at first. But after awhile it feels natural to have your winged pals around all day. They are great entertainment.

Gulls

The black wingtipped gulls are the biggest eaters: they consume so much junk along the beach that they have earned the nickname "health officers of the coasts." Of course they prefer small fish, mollusks and crustaceans to beach leftovers, but they will take anything they can get, including another gull's food. And what a racket they make during food fights as they screech with indignance.

Terns look like gulls, but are smaller and more graceful, dive bombing into the water for fish. Somehow they rarely miss with that 20/20 vision and those streamlined bodies.

The osprey, or fish hawk, looks like an American bald eagle, but this bird is slimmer, smaller and white on the underside. Their technique is just the opposite of the tern: they hit the water feet first, and snare their catch with their sharp black talons.

Brown Pelicans

Brown pelicans are sort of gawky looking, usually perched on a pier waiting for leftovers from some generous fisherman. They do pretty well on their own though, pointing that long thin beak into the water and scooping up to three gallons of water and unlucky fish. It is important to make sure that these very tame birds do not swallow your fishing hook, so take great care to keep your line away from where they swim. If you do hook a pelican by accident, gently walk the bird to shore, cover with a jacket to keep it calm and carefully take the hook out. If the pelican is injured or bleeding, take him immediately to the nearest wildlife rehabilitation center.

Egrets & Herons

You can spot egrets and herons, because they have that "royal" attitude. The great blue heron has dark blue/grey plumage and a black long-feathered crown that bestow him with a regal appearance as he hunts for small snakes, mammals and fish. The white great egret is spectacular, with dozens of delicate fluffy feathers extending from shoulder to tail during the mating season. And the snowy egret holds his plumes erect on his head and neck like a gorgeous fan. These lovely birds were once almost hunted to extinction, as their plumage was "the feather in a lady's cap". Fortunately state and federal laws have banned hunting, saving these magnificent birds from complete destruction. Imagine almost losing an entire bird species to fashion!

As you cavort on the soft sandy beach with your shorebird buddies, try not to forget to say hello to the comical sandpipers, those tiny frisky birds that play tag with the waves and your heartstrings.

Panama City Beach, then you are just not looking!

Pensacola

Built between bayous where red cliffs and golden bluffs face Escambia Bay, Pensacola is one of Florida's hilliest cities. Founded over 400 years ago, it is also one of Florida's oldest. The lack of high rises and the blocks of beautifully restored homes, make this a favorite city for both young families and military retirees.

In fact Pensacola was cited as one of "The 50 Healthiest Places to Live and Retire in the United States" in a 1991 guide by Norman D Ford. We feel it offers a great deal for tourists as well.

Beaches

Those same amazing beaches of Panama City are here as well, more than 40 sun-drenched gorgeous miles, stretching from Perdido Key to the tip of Navarre. The beaches are part of The Gulf Islands National Seashore, a coastal treasure which encompasses 100,000 acres of protected land and water.

Pensacola Beach is located on Santa Rosa Island, part of a chain of natural barrier islands that protects the mainland of Florida, Alabama and Mississippi. Here you will find every type of accommodation from luxury hotels to condominiums to quaint beach cottages.

Historical Pensacola

In 1559, Tristan de Luna founded a colony of 1500 settlers near where Pensacola Naval Air Station is today. Though he enthusiastically reported back to his King Philip II that it was "the best port in the Indies", after two years the colony was destroyed by a hurricane and abandoned.

A Variety of Conquerors

During the next four centuries, Pensacola flew under Spanish, French, British, Confederate and the United States flags.

Today Pensacola, Florida's "First Place City", honors its historic past, renovating homes and avenues that are now listed on the National Register of Historic Places.

The Seville District was once a thriving maritime center, with fishing, shipping and naval stores serving as their economic backbone. Others worked in lumber mills, brickyards, railroad and the military.

Wandering through town you can see the different architectural styles, from Frame Vernacular to Folk Victorian to Creole style. When the Spanish captured Pensacola in 1781, they retained the original British layout of the streets here, but changed the street names to Spanish, which is how they remain today.

"Shotgun" House

Over on East Zaragoza Street, is the **Moreno Cottage,** called a "shotgun" house because a shot could be fired through the front door and exit the back without hitting anything, the entire structure being just one room wide!

Walking to East Government Street, you will see the 1896 **Saint Michael's Creole Benevolent Association Meeting Hall,** where the Creoles socialized.

And they met in the hereafter as well, in **Saint Michael's Cemetery,** which contains nearly 3,000 marked graves of priests, patriarchs, slaves and settlers of all religions.

West of the Seville Historic District is the Palafox Historic District, the commercial heart of Old Pensacola. From 1900 to 1920, this area saw a building boom of hotels, office buildings, City Hall and over a dozen consulates of foreign countries. Although many of the original buildings were lost to fire, hurricanes and demolition, you can still see a large number of the historic structures.

Glamour & Elegance

Imagine evenings at the glamourous **San Carlos Hotel** over at Palafox and Garden Streets, considered in 1910 to be one of the finest hotels in the South. Businessmen, military personnel and local families dined there, especially after theater on Sunday evenings when a female orchestra played classical music.

The 1925 **Vaudeville Saenger Theater** on Palafox Place opened its first night with Cecil B. Demille's epic film, "The Ten Commandments." Today, the elegant Spanish Baroque architecture and Renaissance exterior ornamentation has been restored to its former glory, and now hosts the Pensacola Symphony, First City Dance and Pensacola Opera.

North of Palafox is **The North Hill Preservation District,** with 50 blocks containing over 500 homes that were once the site of British and Spanish forts. In fact residents still unearth the occasional cannonball while digging in their gardens!

Residential Historic Districts

One of the most intact residential historic districts in Florida, you will see an incredibly diverse collection of architectural styles: Queen Anne, Neoclassical, Tudor Revival, Craftsman Bungalow, Art Moderne and Mediterranean Revival.

Walking through the quiet elegant streets, listen very carefully. There is an energy to this neighborhood, a feeling of accomplishment and pride. It seems that the prominent businessmen, politicians, physicians, and lawyers who were lucky to call this place home are still around, in spirit anyway.

The historical Seville quarter in Pensacola.

There is shopping at Quietwater Boardwalk, dining at oyster bars or swank French restaurants and of course non-stop music at the pink shell-shaped boardwalk stage. The horizon is a blur of boats: fishing boats, sailboats, cruising yachts, catamarans. And then there are the parasailors, up there in the big blue with the birds' eye view...

On Santa Rosa Island you can explore **Fort Pickens**, built in 1829. There are campgrounds, picnic areas, nature and bicycle trails, a boat ramp and a fishing pier.

Navarre Beach is much less developed than Pensacola Beach but no less lovely, with its four miles of crystal water and wind-swept dunes. This beach is bordered on the west by 12 miles of **Gulf Islands National Seashore Park**, and on the east by 22 miles of **Eglin Air Force Base**, making it one of the largest pristine coastal areas in the state.

Perdido Key Beach separates the quiet water of Big Lagoon on its northern shore from the Gulf Of Mexico to the south. From certain vantage points, you can enjoy two waterfront views!

At **Johnson Beach**, you will find a lifeguard, showers, restrooms and picnic tables, as well as nature trails. And if you love fresh seafood, this is where it goes right from the sea into your stomach with the chef as middleman!

Touring Pensacola

If you can tear yourself away from these spectacular beaches, there are a number of interesting sights to explore:

• **The Zoo**: A natural habitat with landscape houses more than 600 exotic animals, including two of the largest lowland gorillas in captivity. Kids will enjoy the petting zoo, safari train, puppet shows and elephant rides. Eight miles east of Gulf Breeze on Highway 98. 5701 Gulf Breeze Parkway. Tel: (904) 932 2229

• **The National Museum of Naval Aviation**: An indoor/outdoor museum with over 100 Navy, Marine Corps and Coast Guard planes, as well as personal mementos from historic battles, flight logs vintage instruments and flight gear. Four A-4 Blue Angels "Skyhawks" are suspended in a dazzling seven-story glass and steel atrium. South of Pensacola at the Naval Air Station. Tel: (904) 452 3604. (Also at the Naval Air Station explore the first Spanish built fort, **Fort Barrancas**).

• **The Wildlife Rescue and Sanctuary Park**: Send some get well wishes to birds and mammals recovering from illness and injury here. The lucky ones will be released back into the wild, but the animals that must stay in the sanctuary have a pretty good life too. Ten miles east of Gulf Breeze, on Highway 98.

• Historic **Pensacola Village**: Several museums, historic houses, and the Colonial Archaeological Trail. Museums include The Museum of Industry, the Museums of Commerce and the TT Wentworth Jr Florida State Museum. Homes are French Colonial and the 1871 **Dorr House**, home to a successful lumer baron. The Trail leads you to a Garrison Kitchen, the government House and a British Well site. Downtown Pensacola in the Seville District. Tel: (904) 444 8905.

Pensacola Museum of Art: A 1906 building originally serving as Pensacola's jail and courthouse, now hosts art shows like "Works by Warhol" and "Florida Watercolors". Handicapped accessible. 407 South Jefferson Street. Tel: (904) 432 6247.

Saenger Theater: Showcases a variety of touring artists as well as The Pensacola Symphony, First City Dance, the Choral Society and the Pensacola Opera. 118 South Palafox. Tel: (904) 444 7699.

Nature around every corner in Pensacola.

Parks & Views

In addition to all these manmade attractions, Mother Nature offers some beautiful sightseeing as well. Plan to take in the views from bluffs and shorelines:

Fort Pickens National Park: A three mile hiking/bicycle trail. 1801 Gulf Breeze Parkway. Tel: (904) 934 2600.

Naval Live Oaks National Park: One major hiking path in a figure-eight pattern. Same address and telephone as above.

NAS Nature Trail: A two mile nature trail overlooking the beautiful Bayou Grande. At the US Naval Air Station. Tel: (904) 452 2535.

• **Big Lagoon State Park:** With three trails, each 1/2 mile long. Boardwalks through woods and marsh. 12301 Gulf Beach Highway. Tel: (904) 492 1595.

• **Bay View Park:** A 3/4 mile walking path with fitness stations. Tel: (904) 435 1788.

• **Bay Bluffs:** Elevated boardwalk provides a breathtaking 30 minute cliff stroll overlooking Escambia Bay. These 20,000 year old cliffs are unique in the entire state of Florida. At the intersection of Scenic Highway and Summit Boulevard. Tel: (904) 435 1770.

• **Edward Ball Nature Walk:** Walk along a mossy elevated boardwalk around a fresh water bayou. University of West Florida. 11000 University Parkway, behind Building 13, Blue Parking Lot 20. Tel: (904) 474 3000.

At the junction of Florida's panhandle and peninsula are lush rolling hills dotted with plantations. In spring, tree-canopied streets and gardens, are ablaze with dogwood, camellias and roses.

This is Tallahassee, Florida's capital city, home to the "Walkin' Lawtons", Governor and Mrs Lawton Chiles who walked 1,003 of Florida's beautiful miles. A high intensity university center where passion for the Florida State University "Seminoles" and Florida A&M's "Rattlers" football teams knows no bounds. Festivals with names like "Summer Swamp Stomp" and "Tunes in the Dunes". Exciting performances by The Tallahassee Symphony, the Civic Ballet and the Florida State Opera. And some of Florida's most unusual museums.

From historic pow-wows to contemporary power plays, Tallahassee has been Florida's capital center for more than

Three kids, a butterfly net and a long afternoon along Canopy Road.

Tallahassee

299

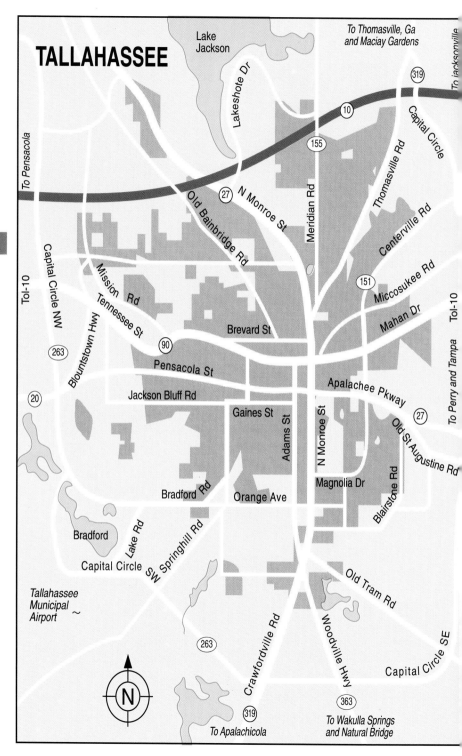

TALLAHASSEE

Lake Jackson

To Thomasville, Ga and Maciay Gardens

To Jacksonville

Lakeshote Dr

319

10

Capital Circle

155

27

N Monroe St

Thomasville Rd

Meridian Rd

Centerville Rd

To Pensacola

Capital Circle NW

Old Bainbridge Rd

Miccosukee Rd

151

Tol-10

263

Mission Rd

Tennessee St

Brevard St

Mahan Dr

To Perry and Tampa

90

Pensacola St

Apalachee Pkwy

20

Blountstown Hwy

Jackson Bluff Rd

Gaines St

Adams St

N Monroe St

27

Old St Augustine Rd

Bradford Rd

Orange Ave

Magnolia Dr

Blairstone Rd

Bradford

Lake Rd

Springhill Rd

Capital Circle SW

Old Tram Rd

Tallahassee Municipal Airport ~

Capital Circle SE

Crawfordville Rd

Woodville Hwy

263

N

319

363

To Apalachicola

To Wakulla Springs and Natural Bridge

Take the Old Town Trolley for your day's trek.

ight centuries. Through it all, the city as managed to maintain its genteel harm and southern hospitality.

City Touring

nside the 22-floor New Capitol Building on Duval Street, stop at the Visitor nformation Center who will give you ree maps and information on the city.

Just a few blocks away at the north-vest corner of Jefferson Street and Adams treet, board The Old Town Trolley for a ree city tour. Tallahassee is one of the ew cities in the US with free trolley tours and this will give you the best orientation for places you would like to go back o later.

Some of the tour highlights:

• **The Old Capitol**: First opened in 1845, the lovely building has been restored to its 1902 appearance, with red-candy striped awnings, stained glass dome and classic rotunda.

• **The New Capitol**: A modern 22-story building housing the Legislative and Executive branches of Florida's government. From February through March you can view lawmakers in action. The top floor observatory offers beautiful panoramic views of the city and her rolling hills.

• **Vietnam Veteran's Memorial**: Commemorated in 1985, two black marble pylons depict the names of Florida's Vietnam casualties.

• **Museum of Florida History:** Features

Tallahassee Museum of History & Natural Science

For real life chills down your spine and natural history at its
natural best – a rattlesnake round-up.

Few museums in the United States are as enter-taining and eclectic as this one: an elegant plantation house, an historic black church, and a one room schoolhouse are sited in a clearing right next to a natural habitat where panthers, bobcat, gray fox and alligators freely roam. And down the road is the Big Bend Farm, an 1888 farmstead with mules, cows, a buggy house, a smokehouse and a syrup shed. Throw in *John Henry*, the Museum's 1919 Model-T and **The Discovery Center**, a kid's playground of micro-scopes, computers and puppet shows, and you have got a most unusual education center. If you just cannot have fun here then maybe you are taking life too seriously.

The Museum's theme is "exploring Florida's natural and cultural history, providing the set-ting in which communities of people and wild-life have historically interacted." It sounds a little complicated in theory, but in reality it somehow works.

The wildlife exhibits are wonderful becau animals are in large natural habitats instead zoo cages. Many of them are the ones that yo would not see often throughout the state.

Meandering along the outdoor raise wooden platform, it is a thrill to peer into th woods and catch sight of a Florida panther, th official state animal that is unfortunately on th brink of extinction. Fortunately the museur has been successful in breeding panthers an has produced two litters of their kittens b parents Osceola and Florida.

Another animal rarely seen by humans is th Florida Black Bear. Here you can see Cheste the Museum's shy bear who spends most of h days secretly nestled amongst tree branche while his mate Annie looks on from below.

Also wandering about their habitats are re wolves, whitetail deer, mallards, wood duck Canada geese, otters, gray foxes, turtles an alligators.

Bird watchers will enjoy the **Birds of Prey Aviary**, a giant-tent like structure where Southern bald eagles, Red-tailed and Red Shouldered Hawks, Barred Owls, Ospreys and Great Horned Owls live. There is also an indoor **Bird Room**, where you can relax behind three walls of glass along the shore of Lake Bradford and watch native birds dining at the feeders.

Historical Buildings, Churches & Discoveries

The historical buildings are also fun to visit: **The Bethlehem Missionary Church**, built around 1937 it is one of the state's oldest black churches. The **Bellevue Plantation House**, built around 1850 is the former home of Catherine Murat, great grandniece of George Washington, whose husband was the Prince of Naples and a nephew of Napoleon Bonaparte. The **Concord Schoolhouse** was used in the 1870s as a one-room schoolhouse for children of former slaves. And the **Transportation Pavilion** houses a 1919 Model T-Ford, a Studebaker spring wagon and next door, a bright red 1924 train caboose.

Kids love **The Discovery Center** where they can play computer games, crawl through a 12-foot high oak tree, try on Victorian clothes, peer through microscopes and giggle at puppet shows.

Festivals hosted by the Museum tend to be as off-beat as the place itself. In July there's "Swamp Stomp", a day of "knee-slappin', toe-tappin', leg-shakin', hand-clappin' musical fun".

August is "Tell-Ahassee Tale Tellin' Time", when the Museum stage comes alive with tales, myths, legends, lies, stories and lessons, unveiled by local and national storytellers. And September brings the Native American Heritage Festival, a get together of Seminole, Miccosukee, Choctaw and Creek tribes who celebrate their native dances, arts, crafts and history.

If you are not much of a history, wildlife or festival fan you will be after a visit here, at one of Florida's most unusual museums. Tallahassee Museum of History & Natural Science. 3945 Museum Drive. Tel: (904) 575 8684.

The columnaded Knott House.

exhibits on Indian artifacts, sunken Spanish galleon treasure, a nine foot high mastadon and prehistoric Florida.

• **Florida State University**: Home of the mighty Seminoles football team, and 25,000 students.

• **Florida Supreme Court**: A neo-classical style building with Doric portico and dome, dedicated in 1948.

• **Adams Street Commons**: An old town square block of shops and restaurants.

• **Park Avenue Historical District**: A lovely flowering, tree-lined promenade of historical homes. **Knott House**, built c.1843, has a delightful collection of antique furnishings, each given an identity through poems written by the owner

Dusk hits the water at Maclay Gardens.

Luella Knott.

• **First Presbyterian Church**: The oldest church structure in Tallahassee, built in 1838.

• **Old City Cemetery**: Established in 1829, it contains the graves of many pioneers, slaves, confederate and federal troops.

Country Touring

Ask the Visitor's Center to give you driving maps to Tallahassee's famous canopy roads. Low sprawling oaks draped with Spanish moss create dramatic emerald tunnels of dancing sunlight on these special roads: Miccosukee, Centerville, Old Saint Augustine, Me-

Museum of Florida History

Ever wondered what it is like to steer a steamboat down a wide rushing river?

At the Museum of Florida History you can climb aboard the *Hiawatha II* and find out. A two-story forward section of the steamboat proudly stands in the Museum, complete with stateroom, captain's cabin, wheelhouse and passengers dressed in turn-of-the century clothing. Audio dramas, slides, and photographs help set the scene. Take the wheel as captain and see how you fare!

How about rummaging through "Grandma's Attic", a treasure trove where you can see and touch clothing, furniture and books from the old days.

Next to the attic is a campsite, showing the "Tin Can Campers" who came to Florida in droves from the north during 1920s real estate booms. And over there: a huge mastodon skeleton presides over all this history, looking much like his original million year old self. Well sort of....

These are just some of the fascinating exhibits at the Museum, which is located right in the heart of downtown Tallahassee. Instead of glass cases filled with yellowing books, letters and documents like most history museums, this one really brings Florida's history alive with exhibits you can touch, smell and hear. There are artifacts from an 18th century Spanish shipwreck, Civil War flags, Seminole Indian clothing, dugout canoes, battleships and a nuclear powered sub. Two blocks east at Jefferson and Monroe Streets is another museum site, **The Old Capitol Building**. The center of Florida's history and culture, this building will show you the restored Senate and House Chambers, the Supreme Court, the Governor's Suite and a photo exhibit on Florida's political history.

Continue your Museum tour across the street at the state's oldest surviving bank building, **The 1841 Union Bank**. Here are exhibits on territorial Tallahassee, Florida's African-American heritage and a display of historic coins and currency.

Just 10 minutes west at the corner of Mission and Ocala Roads is another aspect of the museum that is not an exhibit. The **San Luis Archaeological and Historic Site** is a former

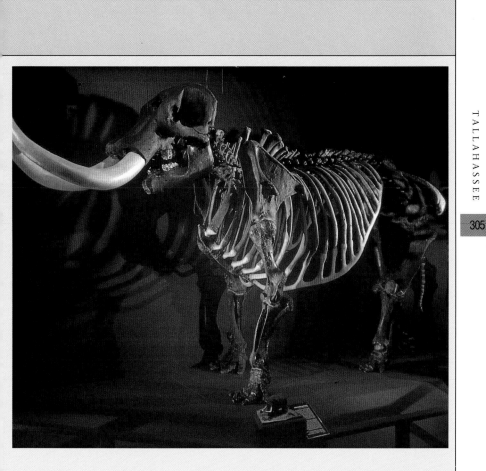

Ancient bones at the Museum of Florida History

17th century Spanish mission and Apalachee Indian townsite where full-scale excavations go on all year round. You can walk through the townsite, which consists of a **Visitors' Center, Spanish Religious Complex, Apalachee village** and **Council House, Town Plaza, Spanish Village** and **Fort**, and the Research Laboratory where artifacts are housed.

The Old Capitol, The Union Bank, and San Luis Archaeological Site are all part of The Florida Museum of History, and spending a morning exploring them will give you an exciting look at the state's fascinating history.

From September through May, the Museum offers Saturday Workshops which are open to the public. These workshops focus on arts and crafts relating to Florida history, such as: calligraphy, oral history, knot-tying, paper-doll making, flintknapping, kite making and creating Victorian Christmas ornaments.

At noon you can listen to an historical lecture at the "Gallery Hour", which range from topics such as Florida's state seal to archaeological activities held at San Luis. And if you are shopping for unusual gifts, the History Shop has a delightful selection of reasonably priced educational, practical and whimsical items.

The Museum of Florida History, RA Gray Building, 500 S Bronough Street, Tallahassee. Tel: (904) 488 1673.

Another old mansion in Wakulla Springs.

ridian and Old Bainbridge.

On Centerville Road 12 miles north of downtown, stop in at **Bradley's Country Store**, a tiny weathered tin box of a place, with a couple of gas pumps out front. Country western tunes are playing on the radio as owner Frank Bradley oversees the production of his famous seasoned sausage. You can also pick up some unusual southern delicacies: hogshead cheese, liver pudding, country grits and red beans and rice. Tel: (904) 893 1647.

A little further north on Thomasville Road are the **Maclay State Gardens**, with 200 varieties of flowers surrounding the 1930 winter home of New York financier, Alfred B Maclay. Rent a canoe, fish, hike the nature trails or take a swim. 3540 Thomasville Road. Tel: (904) 487 4556.

If you are interested in Indian lore head west to **Lake Jackson Mounds State Archaeological Site**, one of the area's most significant prehistoric ceremonial centers of the Lake Jackson Indians, who were forefathers to the Apalachee tribes. 1313 Crowder Road. Tel: (904) 562 0042.

Lake Jackson Indians, who were forefathers to the Apalachee tribes. 1313 Crowder Road. Tel: (904) 562 0042.

Near the intersection of Tennessee Street and Ocala Road is the **San Luis Archaeological and State Historic Site**, a 17th century Spanish mission and Indian settlement created 200 years before Florida became a state. You can

Three kids, a line and some bait and lets see what's jumpin'.

observe their ongoing excavations, and in October a festival with colonial soldiers will be held. 2020 Mission Road. Tel: (904) 487 3711.

Southwest of the city is the **Tallahassee Museum of History and Natural Science**, a 52-acre natural habitat zoo, with red wolves, Florida panthers, alligators and other native wildlife. There is also an authentic 1880s farm, a plantation home, nature trails, and a delightful hands-on Discovery Center for kids. 3945 Museum Drive. Tel: (904) 576 1636.

Fifteen miles south of downtown is **Wakulla Springs**, one of the world's deepest freshwater springs, with glass-bottom boat cruises. Several 1930s Tarzan movies were filmed here, and the 1937 lodge has been restored to a popular hotel and conference center. 1 Spring Drive, Wakulla Springs. Tel: (904) 222 7279.

Recreation & Mother Nature

is blessed with 65 miles of bikeways, several "pars cours" exercise trails and 30 public tennis courts. Surrounding the city area are a number of beautiful parks, where you can hike, fish, camp, horseback ride, bike ride, hunt, and crab. Here are some you will enjoy:

• **Apalachicola National Forest** on US 319, 15 miles south, is one of the city's greatest natural resources, a 630,000-acre wilderness of towering pines for hiking, camping, picnicking and fishing. Tel: (904) 926 3561.

• **Falling Waters State Recreational Area** on 77A, 84 miles west, has a breathtaking 67-foot waterfall. Tel: (904) 638 6130.

• **Florida Caverns State Park** on State Route 12, 55 miles west, is on the Chipola River. Horseback ride on the trails or take a guided cave tour.

• **Saint Marks Historic Railroad Trail** on State Route 363, $1/_2$ a mile south, has a 16-mile paved trail next to an off-road bicycle trail. "Cyclelogical" bike rentals. Tel: (904) 922 6121.

• **Three Rivers State Recreation Area** on State Route 271, 45 miles west, has boat and canoe rentals, nature trails, camping and picnic areas. Tel: (904) 482 9006.

• **Torreya State Park** on State Route 12, 50 miles west, has 150 foot bluffs along the Apalachicola River and the **Gregory House Museum**, the pre-Civil War headquarters for a cotton plantation. Camping, picnicking and a seven mile hiking course. Tel: (904) 643 2674.

Special Events

If you are a football fan and are here in the fall, catch some great gridiron action at Florida State and Florida A&M games. For schedules and tickets call FSU. Tel: (904) 644 1830 or FAMU at Tel: (904) 599 3230. In September, the Native American Heritage Festival has native arts and crafts demonstrations

and traditional games featuring several Indian tribes. Tel: (904) 576 1636. In December, the Winter Festival and Celebration of Lights presents a re-enactment of North America's first Christmas and a downtown twilight parade. Tel (904) 222 7529. March and April bring

Bellevue, another "belle" maison.

Springtime Tallahassee, four weeks of parades, hot air balloons, stage performances and 250 vendors. Tel: (904) 224 1373. And in May at **Killearn Coun-** **try Club and Inn**, the richest LPGA TOUR golf tournament takes place, with a purse of $1.2 million. Tel: (904) 893 4653.

Everglades

Nothing anywhere else is like them: their vast glittering openess, wider than the enormous visible round of the horizon, the racing free saltiness and sweetness of their massive winds, under the dazzling blue heights of space...The miracle of the light pours over the green and brown expanse of sawgrass and of water, shining and slow-moving below; the grass and water that is the meaning and the central fact of the Everglades of Florida. It is a "river of grass."

The smallest Post Office in the world in Ochopee along the Tamiami Trail.

311

Poetic Landscape

This poetic description of Florida's Everglades was penned by Marjory Stoneman Douglas in her 1947 book, *The Everglades: River of Grass*.

What began as a geography book on one of America's rivers, became an impassioned

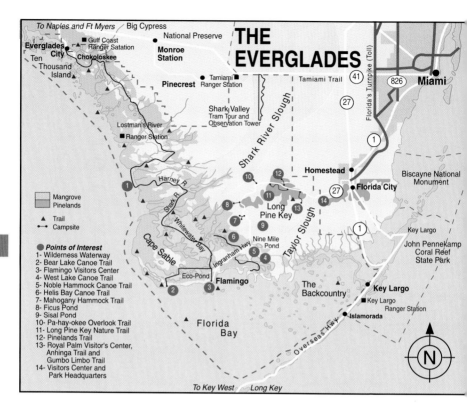

THE
THE EVERGLADES

To Naples and Ft Myers / Big Cypress
National Preserve
Gulf Coast Ranger Satation
Everglades City
Chokoloskee
Ten Thousand Island
Monroe Station
Pinecrest
Tamiami Ranger Station
Tamiami Trail
Shark Valley Tram Tour and Observation Tower
Lostman's River
Ranger Station
Homestead
Biscayne National Monument
Florida City
Long Pine Key
Nine Mile Pond
Key Largo
John Pennekamp Coral Reef State Park
Eco-Pond
Flamingo
The Backcountry
Key Largo
Key Largo Ranger Station
Islamorada
Florida Bay
Overseas Hwy
To Key West   Long Key

Mangrove
Pinelands
▲ Trail
•—• Campsite

● **Points of Interest**
1- Wilderness Waterway
2- Bear Lake Canoe Trail
3- Flamingo Visitors Center
4- West Lake Canoe Trail
5- Noble Hammock Canoe Trail
6- Helis Bay Canoe Trail
7- Mahogany Hammock Trail
8- Ficus Pond
9- Sisal Pond
10- Pa-hay-okee Overlook Trail
11- Long Pine Key Nature Trail
12- Pinelands Trail
13- Royal Palm Visitor's Center, Anhinga Trail and Gumbo Limbo Trail
14- Visitors Center and Park Headquarters

chronicle of the historic bloody skirmishes between Native Americans and European settlers in the Glades, and contemporary struggles of the wetland to survive.

River of Grass brought Stoneman Douglas international acclaim, and united her name forever with the Everglades. In 1970 she formed "Friends of the Everglades", a support group of concerned watchdogs whose members stand guard over the Everglades, preventing destruction by agricultural, real-estate and political interests.

Efforts to keep the Everglades intact go back to 1916, when the Florida Federation of Women's Clubs acquired the Royal Palm Hammock, to preserve its plants and royal palms. In the 1920s a campaign to establish an Everglades National Park was launched by Ernest F Coe, an ardent supporter who became known as the "Father of the Everglades National Park". Between 1934 and 1935, civilian conservation workers built trails and a shelter, and in 1947 President Harry S Truman finally dedicated the Everglades as a 1,400,000 acre National Park. In 1976, the United Nations designated the park a Biosphere Reserve and in 1979, designated it a World Heritage Site. Thanks to the dedication and foresight of people like Ernest Coe, Marjory Stoneman Douglas and thousands of ecologically-minded private citizens, the Everglades will hopefully live on forever

Spot some birds and wildlife along the Anhinga Trail.

for the wildlife, plants, and trees that call it home.

Exploring The Everglades

Most visitors come to the park from December to April because it is the dry season with generally clear weather and moderate temperatures. Trails are open for driving and hiking and abundant with wildlife. In contrast, the summer months are rainy with temperatures in the 80 to 90°F, and the park is rampant with mosquitoes and biting insects, so bear this in mind when planning your trip.

On arrival, you should first stop for an orientation at the Main Visitor Center,

which is 10 miles southwest of Homestead/Florida City on Route 9336. Tel : (305) 247 6211 or (305) 242 7700. Park rangers will provide you with maps, schedules, books, insect repellent, and show you an excellent 15 minute film on some of the wildlife you might spot.

From the Main Visitor Center you can drive 38 miles west and south along route 9336 towards the **Flamingo Visitor Center**, stopping to explore the many walking trails off this road. Here are some you will enjoy, all marked on the maps can get at the center. Trails marked by an asterisk (*) are accessible for the handicapped:

• **The Anhinga Trail***: A $^1/_2$ mile trail where you will see alligators, turtles, fish, marsh rabbits, and many birds,

Wildlife In Danger

The fierce glare of the predatory Osprey.

The fragile ecosystem of the Everglades National Park supports hundreds of species of birds and wildlife. It is fragile because the slightest variation in water levels can mean the loss of feeding habitat for birds, or the flooding of alligator nests. The current absence of a natural water flow through the park because of manmade canals throughout Florida is continuing to affect habitats, especially for nesting wading birds, whose population has decreased from 300,000 in the 1930s to 5,000 in the 1990s.

Birds

Great Egret: One of the most commonly seen birds, but almost hunted to extinction by late 19th and early 20th century plume hunters.

Snowy Egret: Stirs shallow water to attract fish with its yellow feet, this beautiful white bird favors salt or brackish water during the breeding season.

Roseate Spoonbill: During breeding their bodies turn pink, and when feeding, they swing their spatulate bills **Snail Kite**: Feeding almost exclusively on apple snails, there are fewer than

500 of these birds left in the United States.

Purple Gallinule: Striking with a yellow beak and green, blue, red plumage, uses its large feet to walk across aquatic plants looking for insects.

Wood Storks: Due to a continued loss of peripheral wetlands and the elimination of early dry season feeding grounds, this bird has gone from 12,000 nesting pairs in the 1930s to less than 1,200 in the 1990s. Referred to as the "barometer of the Everglades."

Great Blue Heron: The largest of the herons, usually seen hunting for fish in shallow waters. The solitary green-backed heron is more difficult to find along the water's edge.

Brown Pelican: Dives head first into the water after fish, using its huge throat pouch as a dip net to catch food.

Osprey: Frequently seen through out the marine sections of the park, the osprey is a common resident of the Ten Thousand Islands.

Southern Bald Eagle: Eagles have been nesting in the park since the mid-1800s. Now there are about 52 nesting pairs.

The American Coot: These white-billed birds were hunted extensively before becoming protected by the park.

Wildlife

Alligators: Once threatened with extinction, these "caretakers of the glades" have made an amazing recovery. They dig holes that provide water for other wildlife during the dry season.

Crocodiles: An endangered species, they are related to alligators but prefer salty or brackish water. There are only 200 in the Park, mostly living in a sanctuary in northeast Florida Bay.

Florida Panther: There are fewer than 50 of these tawny cats left in Florida, and less than 10 in the Park, due to man's encroachment on its habitat and food sources.

Opossum: Normally a nocturnal animal, but sometimes seen during the day in trees.

Raccoon: Known for its cunning and curiosity, raccoons favor the wetlands and brackish lagoons where they prey upon Loggerhead Turtle nests in early summer.

Florida White-tailed Deer: Living almost entirely in a wet environment, it feeds each evening on its favorite food, sawgrass.

Manatee: Florida's state marine mammal, the "sea cow" feeds on submerged plants near the water's edge. Are greatly endangered due to fatal injuries from boat propellers and shoreline development destroying its habitat.

Green Tree Frog: Living in freshwater or brackish water, the frog's breeding call may be heard from March through October.

Green Anole: Most often found in shrubs, trees and vines, it displays its throat-like a fan during courtship or when defending its territory.

Florida Atala: A threatened orange and black winged butterfly whose larvae feed on Florida coontie–a threatened plant.

Apple Snail: Burrows in the mud during the dry season and lays eggs on plants above water. An important food source for the snail kite and other birds.

These are just some of the birds and wildlife you may be lucky to see in the Everglades. If you would like to make sure this incredible Park is around for your grandchildren, get involved by contacting Friends Of The Everglades, 9331 NW 48th Dorel Terrace, Miami, Florida 33178, Tel: (305) 899 0195.

Get some hands-on experience at the Miccosukee Indian Village.

such as anhingas, herons, egrets, and purple gallinules.

• **The Gumbo Limbo Trail***: A half mile trail that winds through a hardwood hammock, a jungle-like grove of tropical trees and smaller plants. Growing here are royal palms, gumbo limbo trees, wild coffee and aerial gardens of ferns and orchids.

• **Long Pine Key**: A network of interconnecting trails, seven miles long, runing through a pine forest with 200 types of plants, including 30 that are found nowhere else on earth. Living here are whitetail deer, opossums, raccoons and the endangered Florida panther.

• **The Pineland Trail***: A half mile trail with shallow beds of limestone.

Touring The Everglades By Boat

Paddle your own canoe along the Bear Lake Canoe Trail.

Few moments in life are as exhilarating as gliding inside and through this "river of grass", as Marjory Stoneman Douglas called her beloved Everglades.

Twisting and turning from on board an airboat, you careen through tunnels of watery grass and grassy water that reflects whipped cream clouds and sapphire skies until it all blurs into a dizzying kaleidoscope of emerald, cobalt and ochre heaven. Red mangroves arch their roots like maternal claws to protect both the shoreline and the wild creatures living within. Bulbous-eyed baby' gators sunbathe serenely on mounds of mud, as their mothers hover nearby. A sweet pungence fills this vast Everglades universe, like some hypnotic erotic "eau de Earth".

Boats are the way of life here, the only way in unless you can walk on water. Airboats, canoes and power cruisers are the preferred modes of transportation.

Airboats are speedy, windy and noisy, buzzing along the river through sawgrass prairies, cypress hammocks and tunnels of mangrove jungle. You wonder if the noise will chase the animals away, but they seem used to it.

There is an interesting history to these strange looking boats.

A Historical Invention

Before WW I, Glenn Curtiss, a giant of American aviation, wintered in Miami. A speedster who once held the world's motorcycle speed record of 137 miles per hour, Curtiss loved hunting in Florida's backwoods. But as getting around in the Everglades was no easy matter, he designed a shallow draft motorboat, powered by an aircraft engine connected to a propeller mounted on the stern.

His airboat was called "Scooter", and could

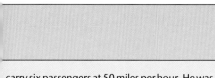

carry six passengers at 50 miles per hour. He was photographed in his airboat on March 5, 1920. By 1933, Everglades frog hunters realized Curtiss was onto something, and soon they built their own versions of what some called the "Whoosh-mobile." Today, thousands of airboats whoosh through the Everglades, giving tourists a close up look at the exotic plant and wildlife. You have not seen an alligator until you've been close enough to count his teeth!

Another Perspective Of The Everglades

Another perspective of the Everglades is from **Chokoloskee Bay**, where flat-bottom boats cruise along the shoreline. In the Bay you will see manatees surfacing for air, brown pelicans sunning on sand bars, snowy egrets, Roseate Spoonbills, ospreys, sea turtles, blue crabs and silvery tarpon fish leaping out of the water. It is a feast of nature and the show is never the same.

Some cruise boats give tours among the outer mangrove islands bordering the Gulf of Mexico, called The Ten Thousand Islands. You may have porpoises playing in the wake of your boat or spot American Bald Eagles nesting.

For Real Adventure

If you crave real adventure, try the **Wilderness Waterway**, a well-marked 99 mile inland water route running from Flamingo to Everglades City. The route takes six hours by outboard motor (boats over 18 feet long are not allowed because of narrow channels and overhanging foliage), or seven days by canoe. Campsites are available along the waterway and backcountry camping permits are required. This is only for those experienced in roughing it, not for you resort types. Whether you explore The Everglades for an hour or a week, this is where you will discover the "real" Florida. It is truly the Original Theme Park.

Write Everglades Area Chamber of Commerce, PO Box 130, Everglades City, Florida 33929, Tel: (813) 695 3941.

Leave the crocs to the experts at the Miccosukee Indian Village.

• **The Pa-hay-okee Overlook Trail**: A $^1/_2$ mile trail leading to an observation tower where you will see why the Everglades is called a "river of grass". There are many types of grass, Muhly grass, Everglades beardgrass, arrowhead and sawgrass. Along the trail keep an eye out for red-shouldered hawks, red-winged blackbirds, vultures, pygmy rattlesnakes, indigo and king snakes, and alligators.

• **The Mahogany Hammock Trail***: A half mile trail enters the cooler damp environment of a dark, jungle-like hardwood hammock. Rare paurotis palms and massive mahogany trees give shelter to Liguus tree snails, and golden orb weaver spiders.

• **The West Lake Trail***: A half mile trail

The untamed mangrove landscape of the Everglades.

winding through red, black, white and buttonwood mangrove trees along the edge of the lake. This area is home to fish, mullet, snapper, stone crabs, shrimp and spiny lobsters.

Other Visitor Centers

• **Flamingo Visitor Center**, 38 miles south from the Main Visitor Center has a ranger station and visitor center with exhibits on natural history. The Flamingo Lodge, Marina and Outpost Resort has motel and housekeeping cottage units, pool, restaurant, marina, sightseeing cruises, tram tours, charter fishing, and canoe, skiffs, motors, houseboats and bicycle rentals. Tel: (305) 253 2241.

• **Shark Valley**, north of the Main Visitor Center, on Route 41 Tamiami Trail has a visitor center, bookshop, nature trail, trams, and rental bikes. Tel: (305) 221 8776.

• **Everglades City Visitor Center** is north of Flamingo Visitor Center, off-Chokoloskee Causeway on Route 29. The center has a ranger station but the visitor center is intermittently staffed, so call before you go there. Tel: (813) 695 3311. You can take a 1 hour 45 minute boat tour of the 10,000 islands.

Safety Notes

Animals in the park are wild and roam freely. It is prohibited to feed them. Keep

An Antibellum Plantation in Cypress gardens.

a respectful distance from alligators: although they appear to be slow moving, they move with amazing speed and are carnivorous.

During the summer months, a trip to the park requires extra planning because of the abundant mosquito population. Do not roll down your windows when stopping along the trails to view wildlife. Walk on the paved areas instead of grassy ones. Do not get out of the car without applying non-aerosol insect repellent. Bring lots of your own repellent, or purchase some at the Visitors Centers and Flamingo Marina Store.

If you are going to be hiking, wear sturdy walking shoes or boots with socks. Lightweight long slacks are a good idea. Wear a hat to protect against sunburn and cover exposed areas of skin with sunblock. Be sure to carry bottles of water to prevent against dehydration.

If you observe these safety tips, your trip to the Everglades will be much more enjoyable.

Outside The Park

On Route 41, just west of the Shark Valley Information Center is a Miccosukee Indian Reservation where you can buy shirts, beads, wood carvings, woven baskets and other crafts.

Continuing west on Route 41 you will see **Joan's Kwik Stop Country Store,** a funky food and beverage store decorated with plastic soda bottles carved into alligators, snakes and butterflies, hundreds of postcards sent from fans around the world and delicious home-made sandwiches. This is a good place to get out of the sun and ask locals for what is going on. Tel: (813) 695 2682. A few miles further west in Ochopee, is the smallest Post Office building in the United States, a tiny one-room house where you can buy stamps and send picture postcards. Also in Ochopee is **Wooten's Alligator & Crocodile Farm and Snake Exhibit**. They also have airboat and swamp buggy rides. Tel: 1 800 282 2781.

South of the Everglades, 4 miles on State Road 29 in Chokoloskee is **Smallwood's Store** where you can browse back in time with all sorts of farm and country stuff. A National Register of Historic Places, established in 1906 as "the ole' Indian Trading Post in the 10,000 Islands." Tel: (813) 695 2989.

Big Cypress National Preserve

Adjoining the northwest section of Everglades National Park is **Big Cypress National Preserve**, a 712,000 acre preserve that provides a freshwater supply crucial to the Park's survival.

Two major highways cross the preserve, Alligator Alley (Interstate 75) and Tamiami Trail (US 41). With State Route 29 to the west, they enable you to explore the Big Cypress. The fascinating Loop Road (Route 94) from 40 Mile Bend to Monroe Station is paved for eight miles, with the graded dirt Turner River Road connecting Tamiami Trail and Alligator Alley.

The word "Big" refers to the swamp's vast 2,400 square miles. The preserve consists of sandy islands of slash pine, mixed hardwood hammock, wet prairies, dry prairies, marshes and estuarine mangrove forests. Airplants, both bromeliads and orchids perch on the cypress and hammock trees like strange bird nests. If lucky you may see the "calling cards" of Big Cyprus' residents: large paw marks of the Florida panther in the wet dirt, or cabbage palmetto that has been ripped apart by Black bears. Hunting, fishing and trapping of game animals is permitted in Big Cypress, but you must obtain a license from the Visitor Information Centers. At Preserve Headquarters, west of Ochopee on Satinwood Drive and Oasis Visitor Center, 55 miles east of Naples on US 41.

You may also bring in off-road vehicles such as swamp buggies, airboats and tracked vehicles, but obtain a permit from the National Park Service first. There is one privately-owned and five undeveloped vehicle accessible campgrounds in the preserve, all which border on the Tamiami Trail. Like the Everglades National Park, Big Cypress is abundant in wildlife: herons, egrets, wood stork, alligators, woodpeckers, wild turkey, deer, mink, bald eagle. Enjoying the Preserves' broad sweeps and limitless horizons is an incredible introduction to Mother Nature's beauty that you are not likely to ever forget.

W hen you arrive in Florida's Keys, you will know what international singing star Jimmy Buffet means when he croons, "changes in latitudes, changes in attitudes." A necklace of beautiful tropical islands dominated by emerald green lagoons, deep blue seas, rustling pines and olive green mangroves, The Keys are geographically connected to the Florida mainland, but spiritually and philosophically exist on a whole other planet.

Florida Keys

The fish are certainly biting in Key West.

Island Variety

The 113 mile chain is linked by 42 bridges and the Overseas Highway, a wide modern highway whose horizons stretch to the Atlantic Ocean on one side and The Gulf of Mexico on the other. Each key has its own unique

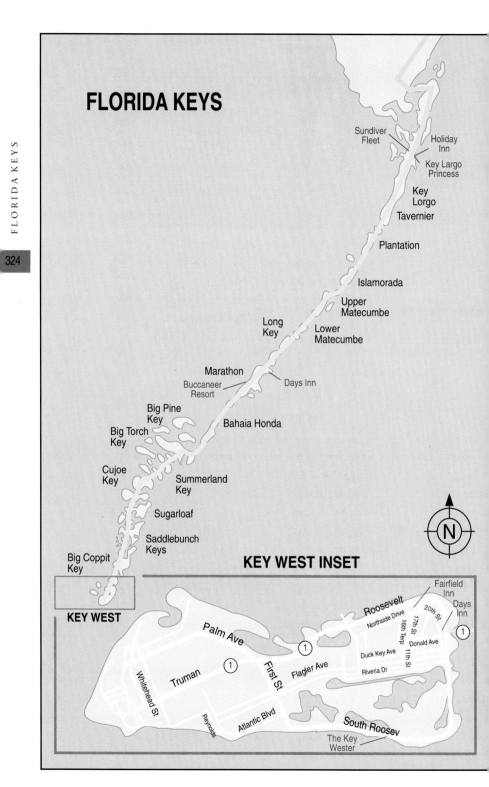

FLORIDA KEYS

Sundiver
Fleet

Holiday
Inn

Key Largo
Princess

**Key
Lorgo**

Tavernier

Plantation

Islamorada

Upper
Matecumbe

Long
Key

Lower
Matecumbe

Marathon

Days Inn

Buccaneer
Resort

Big Pine
Key

Bahaia Honda

Big Torch
Key

Cujoe
Key

Summerland
Key

Sugarloaf

Saddlebunch
Keys

Big Coppit
Key

N

KEY WEST INSET

KEY WEST

Fairfield
Inn

Days
Inn

Roosevelt

Northside Drive

17th St.

20th St.

16th Terp

Palm Ave

Duck Key Ave

Donald Ave

11th St

①

Truman

First St

Flagler Ave

Riveria Dr

①

Whitehead St

①

Reynolds

Atlantic Blvd

South Roosev

The Key
Wester

John Pennekamp Coral Reef State Park, the first underwater preserve in the US.

history, cuisine, festivals, fishing and local idiosyncrasies.

Key Largo is the largest island, home to **John Pennekamp Coral Reef State Park**, the first underwater preserve in the US. This is where Lauren Bacall, Humphrey Bogart and Edward G Robinson shot the legendary movie of the same name.

Islamorada is the centerpiece of a group of islands called the "purple isles", after the Spanish meaning of the word "morada" which refers to the heavy concentration of violet sea snails on the seashore here. Islands here are Plantation Key, Windley Key, Upper Matecumbe Key, Lower Matecumbe Key. Known as the "Sport Fishing Capital", Islamorada has internationally famous gamefish tournaments.

Long Key has a **State Park** where nature trails lead to tropical hammocks that are much like the Key's wilderness of a century ago.

Grass Key is the site of the **Dolphin Research Center**, one of several centers where you can swim and play with some very friendly flirtatious mammals.

Marathon has nine and 18 hole golf courses, as well as **Crane Point Hammock**, a 63 acre land tract that contains pre-Colombian and prehistoric Bahamian artifacts. The majority of Florida Keys natives, whose extensive use of the conch mollusk earned them the name "Conchs", trace their ancestry back to the island of Eleuthera in the Bahamas, a colony of British subjects

Fishing For Big Ones

The fish jumped three more times, and there was in each soaring leap a union of power and grace that arrested my heart and brought a tightness to my throat. For the next 15 minutes the marlin leaped and made long runs that made the reel hot as an iron; it greyhounded across the ocean in one direction, turned, and went off in the other; it pounded the seas with its head to dislodge the hook; it tailwalked, its tail whipping up a whirling mist like a waterspout before it flung itself on its side to run again.

Key West author Philip Caputo beautifully describes reeling in his record breaking 569 pound, 12 feet, 3 inch blue marlin, in his masterful story, *The Ahab Complex.*

With excitement like that out on the open seas, why are you reading this book? Get down to the Keys, book yourself out on a charter boat, and reel in your own record breaking Big Fish.

There are lots of options: fishing from shore off a bridge, renting a small boat and heading off to the bays and creeks, reef fishing, or taking a charter into the deep blue Gulf Stream waters. Fishing charters can be reserved at marinas in Key Largo, Islamorada, Marathon, Lower Keys and Key West, so take your pick as you drive on through.

South past Key Largo, Channels Two and Five (mile marker 72) begin a series of new bridges paralleled by old bridges which are perfect for wetting a line. No need for a boat here. If you would rather be floating, take a small boat out into the bays and creeks where you will find trout and snapper, especially if yo use live shrimp as bait.

Reef fishing from an anchored boat wit Chum ® as a draw will attract yellowtail snap per, bonito, grouper. Expect greetings fror barracuda and sharks as well. Offshore in th deep blue is where the Big Ones live: sailfish mahi, blackfin tuna, and if you are lucky, bi marlin, maybe a 200-pound yellowfin tuna c two. Shipwrecks up in the Gulf of Mexico offe good fishing too, for cobia and yellowtail snap per.

Marathon hosts several fishing tournament each year: the "Tarpon Wear Classic" in May the "Marathon Ladies Invitational" in early June and "Father's Day Dolphin Derby" in mid-June Anglers come from all over the world for thes tournaments. Talk about fish stories....

In Key West there's the *Texaco/Hemingwa Key West Classic,* the *Key West Fishing Tournc ment* (April 15-November 30), the *South Florid Metropolitan Fishing Tournament* and the *Ke West Marlin Tournament.*

Angler/journalist Michael Lewis writes weekly "Gone Fishing" column in Key West newspaper *Island Life,* and he is a friendl source to find out what fish is biting where. Yo can even call him for advice at Tel: (305) 29 9802.

To get in on the fishing fun, contact th Marathon Chamber of Commerce, 3330 Over seas Highway, Marathon 33050. Tel : 1 800 84 9580; or the Florida Keys Chamber of Com merce, 402 Wall Street, Key West, FL 3304(

seeking religious freedom. Learn more about this history at the Museum of Natural History of the Florida Keys, and the Florida Keys Children's Museum. Tel: (305) 743 9100.

Lower Keys are across the breathtakingly beautiful Seven Mile Bridge which shares its sheer sweep of paradise with white herons, Roseate Spoonbills, pelicans, sea gulls and ospreys.

Bahia Honda Key has a state par of the same name where you can camp picnic, fish for tarpon off the bridges, o tour the area by boat or canoe to se turtles, sea rays and dolphins.

Big Pine Key, with its dense pin woods and freshwater, is totally unlik the other Keys in geography, and hom to several hundred miniature deer a the **National Key Deer Refuge**. Withir

Ernest Hemingway purchased a pre-Civil War mansion here and lived in Key West for 10 years while writing some of his best known novels, *For Whom the Bell Tolls*, *A Farewell to Arms*, *The Snows of Kilimanjaro*, and *Death in the Afternoon*," amongst others.

So take your choice: Spend a week meandering along this gorgeous mostly undeveloped 113 mile stretch of Keys, stopping to fish, swim, dive, picnic and explore where your heart leads you; or head straight to Key West for a week that is as relaxing or stimulating as you want it to be.

Key West

America's southernmost point, where the land ends and meets the sea. Where locals celebrate the sunset each evening, and stage festivals for anything they find amusing. Where artists, writers, composers, and photographers come to create, daydream, party and live a freer life without suits, city highrises, or rigid societal rules. Leave your watches, ties, and appointment calendars behind, allow your creativity to be reborn, and who knows how it will change your life?

Touring Key West

Getting around this four mile long, two mile wide town is easy. There are the Old Town Trolley and Conch Trains, which wend their way through the

The one that did not get away.

Tel: 1 800 648 6269.

Michael Lewis signs off his excellent "Gone Fishing" column with the best advice we have heard in a long time: "Fishing is good for you. Do it!"

Need we say more?

the refuge you can take a privately guided canoe tour at **Watson's Hammock**, and visit the **Blue** Hole, an artificial lake where alligators, turtles, fish and wading birds live.

Key West, the most famous of the Keys, with quaint palm-lined streets, historic gingerbread mansions and an energetic community of creative artists, writers and entrepreneurs. In 1931,

A deep blue that you would never believe off Little Palm Island.

The Audubon House at 205 Whitehead Street, is a fine restoration
of a 19th century house.

neighborhoods as guides point out historic and interesting sights.

Rent a bike or moped to explore by yourself or pick up self guided walking tour maps from the Key West Welcome Center, 3840 N Roosevelt Boulevard. Tel: (305) 296 4444.

Key West Sights

Here are some of Key West's most interesting sights:

• **The Audubon House** at 20. Whitehead Street, is a fine restoration o

Hemingway Country

One of the 50 three-toed cats wandering around the Hemingway estate.

"...Conch town, where all was starched, well-shuttered, virtue, failure, grits, and boiled grunts, undernourishment, prejudice, righteousness, interbreeding and the comforts of religion; the open-doored, lighted Cuban bolito houses, shacks whose only romance was their names..."

Hemingway, *To Have and Have Not*

There is the Hemingway admired and adored: Author, Nobel Prize winner, bullfight aficionado, big game hunter, deep sea-fisherman, and world adventurer. Dapper handsome "Papa", who gave us *To Have and Have Not, A Farewell to Arms, Death in the Afternoon, The Snows of Kilimanjaro, For Whom the Bell Tolls,* and more.

Enigmatic "Papa"

Then there's the Hemingway that is difficult to understand, a man we do not know at all. The man who married four times, breaking the heart of each woman he left for another. A man who battled alcoholism, depression, debt and overeating who survived airplane crashes, a US citizen under FBI surveillance and the saddest most incomprehensible of all: a man who ended his life through suicide. It seems our heroes are all too human, they topple from the golden pedestals we place them on.

Ernest Hemingway made Key West his home from 1931 to 1961, living with his second wife Pauline and their two sons in a beautiful Spanish Colonial house on Whitehead Street. Entering the grounds, six of Hemingway's 50 three-toed cats come to rub your leg in a feline act of judgement. If you pass their muster, then the house is all yours to explore. A magnificent structure, with 14 foot ceilings, huge curved floor to ceiling windows, with splendid views of the luxurious exotic garden from every one. The rugs, tile, chandeliers and furniture are as the Hemingways left them, bought from their travels through Spain, Africa, France and Cuba.

In their bedroom, a yellow and red ceramic cat stands guard, a gift to Ernest from Pablo Picasso. Each morning before dawn, Hemingway crossed the catwalk outside his bedroom balcony over to his carriage house writing studio

The Ernest Hemingway House.

though the catwalk has long since fallen down,
141- year old Chinese Banyan still towers
rotectively over the sacred study.

Hemingway's work schedule began early
morning, and "if the words are coming hard, I
ften quit before noon", he told a reporter. The
st of the day and evening was for fishing,
vimming and socializing. His studio is gloomier
an you would think a writer could stand.
ookcases line the walls, stuffed antelope and
azelle heads staring glassy-eyed at the titles for
l eternity. His writing table is tiny – only 4 feet
ound – and the black typewriter seems almost
y-like. Only the chaise lounge might have
ffered comfort. Everything else is somber,
olorless, spartan.

No wonder Hemingway was eager to spend
ternoons with the blinding yellow sunshine,
zure skies and fighting sportfish. Outside in the
arden is the swimming pool that Pauline built,
the hope that her husband would be at home

more. He hated the $20,000 pool. Pressing a
penny into the wet patio cement he is said to
have snarled, "Here, take the last penny I've
got." The penny is still there.

Eccentric "Papa"

One night Hemingway dragged a urinal home
from Sloppy Joe's bar and put it in the garden
near the pool. To mask this embarrassment,
Pauline covered it with a 4-foot olive jar and
made it into a fountain. Today the urinal is a
communal water trough where his loyal cats
drink to his memory. Standing very quietly you
may hear those gifted fingers tapping out another Nobel Prize winner. Underneath the Chinese Banyan, 50 three-toed cats wait for Papa's
return. Ernest Hemingway Home & Museum,
907 Whitehead Street, Key West. FL 33040. Tel:
(305) 294 1575.

Pillage from the sea – gold from the Spanish galleon.

for 121 years. Climb the 88 steps to the observation platform for one of the best panoramic views in Florida.

• **Little White House Museum** at 111 Front Street, was where President Harry Truman spent 175 days of his 6 $\frac{1}{2}$ year presidency. Now meticulously restored to its 1940s appearance, the Museum provides a fascinating glimpse of the Truman era in Key West.

• **Mel Fisher Maritime Heritage Society Museum** at 200 Greene Street, displays gold, silver, jewels and artifacts from a number of shipwrecks, including the *Atocha*, the *Santa Margarita*, and the *Henrietta Marie*.

• **The Southernmost Point** at at Whitehead and South Streets, is a huge multicolored marker overlooking the Atlantic Ocean proudly proclaimin that the island lies only 90 miles fror Cuba. One of the most photographe spots in America, and a great spot t buy sea shells from the open air marke

Sunset at **Mallory Square** is wher locals, tourists, jugglers, fire eaters, ver dors, musicians and street actors gathe every evening to applaud the sunset. is the perfect way to end any day in Ke West.

Creativity At Work & Play

Key West is famous for unlocking th creative genius in many of the world renowned novelists, poets, artists, com posers and craftsmen.

A Scottish serenade – bagpiper on Mallory Square Bridge.

Painters like Henry Faulkner, Sal alinaro, Van Eno, John Crowley, Bob ranke, and painter/woodcarvers Mario anchez and Peter Suarez have made heir home here.

You will see artists at work all around ne island, and numerous galleries dis-play their smashing results in a variety of media: Haitian art, acrylics, sculp-ture, oils, pastels, watercolors, prints, ceramics, jewelry, stained glass, wall hangings, rugs and clocks.

Besides being an artists' haven, the allure of Key West has drawn great

Diving Floridas' Keys

Getting ready for a dip into a whole new world.

over a watery Garden of Eden fields of brown and purple se fans, orange fire coral, and whit brain coral were glorious back drops for schools of silver barjacks, 60-pound tige grouper, yellow and gree Queen angelfish, blue chrom and a graceful spotted eagle ray

I would have stayed all da except a very aggressive tw inch long Dusky Damselfis chased me back onto the boat. I was out of a anyway. There are so many dive sites through out Florida's Keys you would have to spen several months to see them all.

Moses felt like I imagined a wet innertube would feel. But then I had never hugged a 6-foot green moray eel before. Harry Welch, my handsome beach blonde dive master, held out some Bally-hoo bait fish which Moses just could not resist. Slithering out of his deep dark rock hole home he gulped that Ballyhoo in one swift bite. All I saw were his cold beady eyes, and teeth, acres of them.

But after his snack, Moses was a whole different animal, so to speak. He snuggled up close and gave Harry and me a good old-fashioned eel hug like we had been buddies forever. Was it the ballyhoo, or my Chanel #5?

There was more to see in the coral reef, and Harry was only too happy to show me around. Being a dive master, he prefers breathing un-derwater and all. A pair of bug-eyed tentacled squid passed by, a curious spiny lobster waved his antenna hello and soon we were floating out

A whole New World

One of the most famous is **John Pennekam Coral Reef State Park** and the **Key Larg National Marine Sanctuary**, both in Key Largo The park and sanctuary are 21 miles long, wit 500 species of fish and 55 varieties of coral. Yo can sail, snorkel or dive in the park to see th starfishes, sea cucumbers, shrimp, sand dollar barnacle and sponges.

There are also glass-bottomed boats tha tour **Molasses Reef** for those who do not war to get their feet wet. If you are a new snorkele or diver you may feel more comfortable divin

writers here for over 150 years. Tennes-see Williams, Wallace Stevens, James Leo Herlihy, Philip Caputo, James Merrill, Thomas McGuane, Elizabeth Bishop, Philip Burton, John Dos Passos, John Ciardi, Richard Wilbur, Alison Lurie, Robert Frost, Thornton Wilder, Hart Crane, Gore Vidal, Peter Taylor,

and of course, Ernest Hemingway are all Key West authors you will want to read. Pick up the excellent *Key Wes Reader: The Best of Key West's Writer 1830-1990*, which features many o these authors.

If you are a writer, garner som inspiration from Hemingway, who cre

n an enclosed lagoon, rather than out in the open ocean. **Key Largo Undersea Park** is sort of a giant aquarium with guided tours of marine plant and animal life. However there is an unusual aspect to this attraction. Also in the lagoon is an underwater hotel that accommodates six guests, a working undersea marine research center, marine archaeology experiments, and an underwater art studio.

Further south on Islamorada, you can dive in the Keys' oldest artificial reef to visit the **San Pedro**, a Spanish treasure ship that was wrecked in 1733, taking down 16,000 pesos of silver and crates of valuable Chinese porcelain. Although the San Pedro is empty of its long ago treasures, the vessel has become a haven for colorful living corals and bright tropical fish. To recreate the appearance of the wreck prior to its modern discovery, seven cannon reproductions have been lowered onto the ship.

South on Looe Key, the **National Marine Sanctuary** has many varieties of soft and hard corals and prolific marine life.

Down in Key West there is excellent diving, especially on the Marquesas, a circle of islands 22 miles west where large coral heads are beached in shallow water. This is where the famous 1622 Spanish treasure ships the *Atocha* and *Santa Margarita* were found. Some top drawer dive operations: Captain Slate's Atlantis Dive Center, Key Largo; Lady Cyana Diver, Islamorada; Jollymon Charter, Inc, Islamorada; The Diving Site, Marathon; Looe Key Dive Center, Ramrod Key; and Admiral Busby's, Key West.

If you come to Floridas' Keys, try not to forget to see all the beauty under the water as well as on top. And say hello to Moses for me.

ated the only sane work schedule: writing from 5am till noon, break for coffee and lunch, finish by 2 or 3pm, and spend the rest of the day and evening swimming, fishing and/or bar hopping. Think how happy you would be living like that!

The list of creative artists goes on:

The graceful dive of the dolphins at Hawks Cay.

Jimmy Buffet, the musical poet laureate of the Keys, with his nautical, sometimes naughty ballads. Shel Silverstein, successful songwriter, cartoonist and a masterful writer of children's books. James Kirkwood, awards and accolades for his work on *A Chorus Line*, and Broadway great Jerry Herman. All are familiar Key West faces.

Theater attractions galore: **The Tennessee Williams Fine Arts Center**, at 5901 Junior College Road present plays, concerts, performing arts, and dance. You can also tour the modern Bauhaus style theater by calling Tel: (305) 296 9081. The **Red Barn Theater** on Duval Street stages popular plays along with new works by local playwrights. There's also The **Waterfront Playhouse** in

Mallory Square, as well as street musicians, mimes and singers to bring out the music in your soul. Join in anytime, no one cares if you can carry a tune!

Special Events

In Key West, just living is excuse enough for a celebration or a party. Time your visit with some of these:

• *Old Island Days*: From mid-January to late March, celebrates the Bahamian heritage of Key West aristocrats, wreckers and shipbuilders. Events include Bahamas Village night, theater, food, sidewalk art show and a flower show. Tel: (305) 294 9501.

• *Key West Literary Seminar*: A week long event featuring renowned writers, publishers, agents and reviewers. Each year focusses on a different theme. An excellent networking experience for aspiring and professional writers. They also conduct a weekly "Writer's Walk" of Key West literary sites, Sundays at 10:30am. Tel: (305) 293 9291.

• *Hemingway Days*: Features a Writer's Workshop, Hemingway Conference, short story competition, a 5 kilometres run, arm wrestling, storytelling competition and the Hemingway Lookalike Contest. During the week of July 21, the anniversary of Papa's birth. Tel: (305) 294 4440.

• *Fantasy Fest*:Ten days of marvelous madness featuring street fairs, dress up balls, maskmaking workshops and lavish costume competitions capped by a Saturday night parade of floats an costumed dancers. Late October. Te (305) 296 1817.

Sports

Golfers, try your skills at Key West Reso Golf Course, a $6 million Rees Jone

Boats moored off Bight Marina.

designed 18-hole championship course. You will run into doglegs, water hazards, mangroves, and the lake behind hole #10 is a rare bird sanctuary. Tel: (305) 294 5232.

Boat lovers rejoice! In early to mid-November, Key West hosts the biggest collection of high performance ocean racing boats in the world. For a week, boats, drivers and crews race to determine the world offshore champion in four racing classes. Tel: (305) 296 8963.

Everybody has an opinion on sports: Samuel Johnson said "a fishing rod is a stick with a hook at one end and a fool at the other."

Mark Twain described golf as "a good walk, spoiled." And F. Scott Fitzgerald wryly admitted "I had to sink my yacht to make the guests go home."Florida is a 24 hour playground for sports lovers, as you'll soon find out. Entire guidebooks have been written just on the state's legendary golf courses, fishing tournaments, and yacht spots. Here's a brief list of where to find which Florida sport. Get out of that hotel room and into the sunshine and fresh air!

A bit of beach volleyball to chase the blues away.

Sports & Recreation

341

Air Boating Everglades

• **Everglades Private Airboat Tours**
1 mile past bridge on Hwy 29 Everglades City, FL
Tel: 1 800 2 8 2 9194

• **Florida Jet-Airboat Tours**
Located on Highway 29,

An air boat ride is the only way to enjoy the Everglades.

4 miles south of US Hwy 41
Everglades City, FL 33929
Tel: 1 800 282 9194
• Jungle Erv's Airboat Ride Boat Tours
Over bridge on left
Everglades City, FL 33929
Tel: 1 800 432 3367
• Swampland Private Airboat Tours
PO Box 619
Everglades City, FL 33929
Tel: (813) 695 2740
• Air Boat Guide Services
Everglades City, FL 33929
Tel: (813) 695 2716
• Rod & Gun Club
 (private airboat guide)
PO Box 190
Everglades City, FL 33929
Tel: (813) 695 2101

• Wooten's Swamp Boat Ride
(35 miles south of Naples)
US 41 (5 miles tour)
Ochopee, FL 33943
Tel: 1 800 282 2781
Haines City
• Pioneer Airboat Rides
US Highway 27, south of Haines City
Tel: (813) 439 5258
Key West
• Air Boat Key West
3501 North Roosevelt Blvd
Key West, FL
Tel: (305) 296 1043
Kissimmee
• Airboat Rentals
4266 West Vine Street
Kissimmee, FL 34741
Tel: (407) 847 3672

American football as enjoyed in a stadium in Saint Petersburg.

• **Toho Airboat Excursions**
Located at East Lake Fish Camp
3705 Big Bass Road
Kissimmee, FL 34744
Tel: (407) 348 2040

Baseball

Bradenton
• **Pittsburgh Pirates**
McKechnie Field
Ninth St W at 17th Ave W
Bradenton
Tel: (813) 747 3031
Clearwater
• **Philadelphia Phillies**
Jack Russell Stadium
800 Phillies Drive

Clearwater
Tel: (813) 441 8638
Dunedin
• **Toronto Blue Jays**
Dunedin Stadium
373 Douglas Ave
Dunedin
Tel: (813) 773 0429
Fort Lauderdale
• **Florida Marlins**
100 Northeast 3rd Ave
Fort Lauderdale
Tel: (305) 779 7070
Kissimmee
• **Houston Astros Spring Training**
Osceola County Stadium
Tel: (407) 933 2520
Lakeland
• **Detroit Tigers**

Joker Marchant Stadium
2301 Lakeland Hills Blvd
Lakeland
Tel: (813) 682 1401
Sarasota
• **Chicago White Sox**
Ed Smith Sports Complex
12th St and Tuttle Ave
Sarasota
Tel: (813) 953 3388
 St Petersburg
• **St Louis Cardinals**
Al Lang Stadium
180 2nd Ave SE
St Petersburg
Tel: (813) 822 3384
Tampa Bay (Plant City)
• **Cincinnati Reds**
Plant City Stadium
1900 S Park Road
Plant City
Tel: (813) 757 6712

Biking

Florida Bicycle Trails system is made up
of 11 loop trails covering a total of 1220
miles. The trails range from a one day,
30 mile circuit of southeast Florida to a
week long, 300 mile trek along the
backroads of the northeast region. The
trails were created by the Florida Department of Transportation, the Florida
Department of Natural Resources, the
Florida Bicycle Council and volunteer
bicycle cartographers. To receive Florida
Bicycle Trail maps, write the Department of Transportation, Map and Pub-

lication Sales, 605 Suwannee Street, MS
12, Tallahassee, Florida 32301.

Canoeing

Daytona Beach
• **Tomoka State Park**
4 miles north of State Road 40
Ormond Beach
Tel: (904) 676 4050
Everglades
• **North American Canoe Tours, Inc**
Everglades Outpost
Glades Haven RV Park
across from Everglades National Park
800 SE Copeland
Everglades City, FL
Tel: (813) 695 4666
• **Glades Haven Campground**
800 SE Copeland
Everglades City, FL 33929
Tel: (813) 695 2746
Located on water opposite Everglades
National Park.

Car Racing

Clearwater:
• **Sunshine Speedway**
4500 Ulmerton Road
Clearwater, FL 34620
Tel: (813) 573 4598
Daytona
• **Daytona Beach International
Speedway**
1801 Volusia Avenue
Daytona Beach 32114-1243

Be like the Indians and paddle your own canoe down the Wekiwa Springs.

Tel: (904) 254 6728

• **International Motor Sports Association**

Tampa

Tel: (813) 877 4672

• **International Drag Racing Hall of Fame**

Ocala

Tel: (904) 245 8661

• **Moroso Motorsports Park**

West Palm Beach

Tel: (407) 622 1400

Fishing

There are literally thousands of saltwater and freshwater fishing operations and facilities throughout the state. To learn more about fishing in the area where you'll be travelling, contact the Florida Game & Fish Commission, 620 South Meridian Street, Tallahassee, Florida 32399-1600 or call (904) 488 2975.

Everglades City

• **Rod & Gun Club**

PO Box 190

Everglades City, FL 33929

Tel: (813) 695 2101

• **Chokoloskee Island Park**

(4 miles south of Everglades City)

PO Box 430

Chokoloskee, FL 33925

Destination Walton Beach for a big catch.

Tel: (813) 595 2414
• **Outdoor Resorts**
Chokoloskee Island
The RV Resort & Marina Boat Rentals
Nationwide: 1 800 237 8247
In FL: 1 800 282 9028
Local: 1 813 695 2881
The Florida Keys
• **Gulf Lady**
Deep Sea Fishing
Bud & Mary S Marina
MM 79.8
Islamorada
Tel: 664 2461 or 664 2628
• **Robbie's**
MM 84.5 Holiday Isle
Islamorada
Tel: (305) 664 4196 or 664 8070
• **Sea Wolf Charters**

Captain Joe Hopp
Buccaneer Lodge
Marathon
Tel: (305) 743 4118 or 743 501
• **Captain Ron Ward**
MM 17
Sugarloaf Marina
Tel: (305) 872 0290
• **"Sea Boots"**
Captain Jim Sharpe
MM 245
PO Box 1203
Summerland Key, FL 33042
Tel: (305) 745 1530 or 1 800 238 1746
• **Tarpon Guaranteed and Deep Sea Fishing**
Captain Randy Rode
PO Box 235
Marathon, FL 33050
Tel: 1 800 345 1698
• **Amorous, Amorous AJ**
Slips #12, 18 Amberjack Pier
City Marina, Garrison Bight Boat
Tel: (305) 296 7674
• **Captain Bill Wickers Jr**
Dock #19 & 20
Tel: 1 800 299 9798
• **Amberjack Pier**
Tel: (305) 296 9798
• **City Marina**
Key West, FL 33040
• **Club Nautico**
MM 61
Tel: 1 800 432 2242
Marathon, FL
Tel: (305) 743 9000
• **Jarmada Boat Rentals**
Gilberts
MM108

PO Box 725

Key Largo, FL 33037

Tel: (305) 451 2628

• **Dolphin Marina Resort**

MM 28.5 Rt 4

Box 1038

Little Torch Key, FL 33042

• **Fish n' Fun Boat Rentals**

MM 53.5

Tel: (305) 743 2275

Key West

• **Charterboat Lucky Strike & Lucky Too**

Lands End Marina

Tel: 294 7988

• **City Marina**

Tel: 296 3751

• **Club Nautico**

Garrison Bight Marina

Tel: 294 2225; 1 800 338 7161

• **Can't Miss Party Fishing Yacht**

Tel: 296 3751

Marathon

• **Poseidon Harbour, Inc**

Mile Marker 63, Conch Key

Mailing Address: Rt 1, Box 521

Marathon, FL 33050

• **Captain Pip's Marina Boat Rentals**

1410 Overseas Hwy

Marathon, FL 33050

Tel: (305) 743 4403

• **Captain Hooks Marina and Blue Water Tackle Shop**

Marathon, Florida Keys

1183 Overseas Hwy

MM 53 at Vaca Cut Bridge

• **Looe Key Marine Sanctuary**

MM 27.5

PO Box 509 H

Tel: 1 800 942 5397

Ramrod Key, FL 33042

Tel: (305) 872 2215

Kissimmee/St Cloud:

Fish Camps:

• **Alligator Lakeside Inn Fish Camp**

6264 East Irlo Bronson Memorial Highway

St Cloud, FL 34771

Tel: (407) 892 3195

• **Big Toho Marina**

101 Lakeshore Boulevard

Kissimmee, FL 34741

Tel: 846 2124

• **Harbor Oaks Marina**

3605 Marsh Road

Kissimmee, FL 34741

Tel: (407) 846 1321

• **Lake Marian Paradise**

901 Arnold Road

Kenansville, FL 34739

Tel: (407) 436 1464; (407) 436 1021

• **Overstreet Landing**

4500 Joe Overstreet Road

Kenansville, FL 34739

Tel: (407) 436 1700

• **Red's Fish Camp**

4715 Kissimmee Park Road

St Cloud, FL 34772

Tel: (407) 892 8795

• **Richardson's Fish Camp**

1550 Scotty's Road

Kissimmee, FL 34744

Tel: (407) 846 6540

• **Lake Okeechobee**

750 square miles, the second largest freshwater lake in the United States.

Okeechobee Chamber of Commerce

Tel: (813) 763 6464

Fishing Guide Services:
- **Bass Challenger Guide Service**
PO Box 679155
Orlando, FL 32867-9155
Tel: (407) 273 8045
- **Bass Fishing Guide**
5280 Haywood Ruffin Road
St Cloud, FL 34771
Tel: (407) 892 7184
- **Big Toho Marina**
101 Lake Shore Boulevard
Kissimmee, FL 34741
Tel: (407) 846 2124
- **Buchanan's Bass Guide Service**
500 Mississippi Avenue
St Cloud, FL 34742
Tel: 407-957-4517
- **Evans Shiner King Guide Service**
P.O. Box 422707
Kissimmee, FL 34742-2707
Tel: (407) 348 2202; 846 0661
- **Florida Fishmaster's Pro Guides**
3325 13th Street
St Cloud, FL 34769
Tel: (407) 892 5962
- **Kissimmee Bait & Tackle**
18 South Bermuda Avenue
Kissimmee, FL 34741
Tel: (407) 933 2791
- **Main Bass Guide Service**
141 Florida Parkway
Kissimmee, FL 34743
Tel: (407) 348 2399
- **Osceola Fishin' Center**
4824 Wren Drive
St Cloud, FL 34769
Tel: 957 2781
Licenses can be purchased at fish camps, tackle shops, hardware stores, K-Mart and Wal-Mart stores. For additional information contact Florida Game and Freshwater Commission, (904) 488 4676.

Naples
Freshwater and saltwater licenses available at the Collier County Courthouse Tax Collector's Office (3301 Tamiami Trail E, Bldg C-1, Naples. Tel: 774 8176) and at some of the bait-and-tackle shops.
- **Club Nautico**
Boat Haven of Naples
1484 5th Ave S
Naples
Tel: 774 0100 or 1 800 448 6372
- **CS A Charters**
Naples
Tel: 649 99081
- **Old Marine Market Place**
1200 5th Ave S
Naples
Tel: 434 0441 or 598 1184
Dunedin:
- **Caladesi Island**
#1 Causeway Blvd
Dunedin, FL 34698
Tel: (813) 469 5942
- **Honeymoon Island**
#1 Causeway Blvd
Dunedin, FL 34698
Tel: (813) 469 5942
Fort DeSoto Park
- **Pinellas Bayway**
Off I-275 and 54th Ave South
or from St Pete Beach
Tel: (813) 866 2662
St Petersburg
- **The Pier**
St Petersburg
Tel: (813) 893 7437

Sport of Kings: Treasure Hunting

Sunday, September 4, 1622. A combined fleet of 28 ships left Havana Harbor for Spain carrying a huge cargo of silver, gold, pearls, indigo, tobacco, coral and other New World merchandise. Only one day into their journey, nine of the ships were hurled off course into the Florida Straits by a savage hurricane.

By dawn the next morning, 550 sailors and their valuable treasures were lost at sea, never to be heard from again.

Never that is until 1969, when an adventurer named Mel Fisher began his search for the lost galleons. In 1985, after years of searching the ocean floor, Fisher and his team recovered the "Atocha's" motherlode from nearly 370 years of exile.

One of the greatest archaeological and commercial discoveries in treasure salvaging history, the "Atocha" yielded artifacts worth $200 million. And there was more: they also recovered remains of the "Santa Margarita", and an English merchant slaver, the "Henrietta Marie."

To conserve and exhibit these historic artifacts, Fisher set up a non-profit maritime history organization in Key West, The Mel Fisher Maritime Heritage Society.

If you love gold, silver, emeralds, maritime weaponry, and navigational instruments, you'll enjoy touring the Museum. Some of the more interesting booty:

A "Bosun's" Pipe, a long thin whistle the "Atocha" Boatswain used to relay orders to the crew over the sound of stormy winds and waves.

An "Astrolab" used on board the "Atocha" to determine latitude, considered the most sophisticated navigational device of its day.

Bronze cannons from "Santa Margarita" cast from Cuban copper.

A 12 foot long, 65 ounce gold "Wedding Chain", worn at the altar by couples reciting their wedding vows.

A 7 emerald Colombian cross set engraved with St. Anthony, the Virgin and child.

Gold bars, clumps of 2500 silver coins, swords, daggers and all sorts of ancient treasure are beautifully displayed throughout the Museum. A film shows highlights of Fisher's exciting 1985 "Atocha" discovery.

If you're interested in helping Mel Fisher bring up more treasure, the Heritage Society is presently recovering artifacts from the "St. Johns", a 16th century Spanish discovery vessel off the Bahamas.

Over three hundred objects have already been raised, including a conquistador's helmet, and a rare rail gun.

Divers interested in being part of the archaeological diving team should write Mel Fisher Maritime Heritage Society, 200 Greene Street, Key West, FL 33040; Tel (305) 294 2633.

If you're not that adventurous, stop by the Museum anyway for a look at a truly spectacular "sport," salvaging ancient buried treasure.

• **Florida Deep Sea Fishing, Inc**
Dolphin Landings
4737 Gulf Blvd
St Petersburg Beach
• Tel: 360 2082
• **Florida Sportfishing Center**
13201 Gulf Blvd
Madeira Beach
Tel: 393 0407
Sarasota
• **Midnite Son Charter Service**

Marina Jack Plaza at US 41
Sarasota
Tel: 349 7677

• **2801 Kissimmee Bay Boulevard**
Kissimmee, FL 34744
Tel: (407) 348 4653

Golf

• **Grenelefe Golf Club & Resort**

Tee-off any of the greens in Palm Beach.

3200 State Road 546
Grenelefe
Tel: (813) 421 5050
• **Marriot's Orlando World Center**
1 World Center Drive
Orlando, FL 32821
Tel: (407) 239 5659
• **Overoaks Country Club**
3232 South Bermuda Ave
Kissimmee, FL 34741
Tel: (407) 847 3773
• **Poinciana Golf & Racquet Resort**
5000 East Cypress Parkway
Kissimmee, FL 34759
Tel: (407) 933 5300 (pro Shop)
or (407) 933 0700
Walt Disney World Resort Golf Courses
• **Lake Buena Vista Course**
(located at Lake Buena Vista Club)

2200 Club Drive
Lake Buena Vista
Orlando
Tel: (407) 828 3741
• **Executive Course**
(located at the Disney Inn)
1 Palm-Magnolia Drive
Lake Buena Vista, FL 32830
Orlando
Tel: (407) 824 2288
• **Magnolia Golf Course**
(located at The Disney Inn)
1 Palm-Magnolia Drive
Lake Buena Vista, FL 32830
Orlando
Tel: (407) 824 228
• **Palm Golf Course**
(located at The Disney Inn)
1 Palm-Magnolia Drive
Lake Buena Vista, FL 32830
Orlando
Tel: (407) 824 2288
Miami
• **Doral Resort**
4400 NW 87th Avenue
Miami
Tel: (305) 592 2000
Naples
• **Imperial Golf Club**
1808 Imperial Golf Club Boulevard
Naples
Tel: (813) 597 8165
Ocala
• **Country Club at Silver Springs Shores**
565 Silver Road, Ocala
Tel: (904) 687 2828
• **Golden Ocala Golf Club**
7300 US Highway 27 NW
Tel: (904) 629 6229.

Marion Oaks Golf and Country Club
620 SW 162nd St Rd
Tel: (904) 347 1271

Ocala Municipal Golf Club
130 NE Silver Springs Blvd
Tel: (904) 622 8681

Pine Oaks of Ocala
201 NW 21st St
Tel: (904) 622 8558

Ponte Vedra

Marriott at Sawgrass Resort
1000 TPC Boulevard
Ponte Vedra BEach
Tel: 800 457 GO

Ponte Vedra Club
200 Ponte Vedra Boulevard
Ponte Vedra Beach
Tel: (904) 285 6911

Sarasota

The Meadows
3101 Longmeadow Drive
Sarasota
Tel: (813) 378 5153

Tallahassee

Killearn Golf & Country Club
100 Tyron Circle
Tallahassee
Tel: (904) 893 2144

Venice

Plantation Golf & Country Club
500 Rockley Boulevard
Venice
Tel: (813) 493 2000

Greyhound Racing

Jacksonville

St Johns Greyhound Racing Park

Tel: (904) 646 0001

Miami

• Biscayne Greyhound
320 NW 115th Street
Miami Shores
Tel: (305) 754 3484

St Petersburg

• Derby Lane
10490 Gandy Blvd
St Petersburg, FL 33702
Tel: (813) 576 1361

Naples

• Fort Myers Greyhound Track
Bonita Beach Road and Old US 41
Bonita Springs, FL
Tel: 992 2411 or 334 6555

Tampa Bay

• Tampa Greyhound Track
Tel: (813) 932 4313
8300 Nebraska Avenue

Horse Racing

Hallandale

• Gulfstream Park
901 S Federal Highway
Hallandale

Hialeah

• Hialeah Park
102 East 21st Street
Hialeah

Kissimmee

• Pinciana Horse World
3705 Poinciana Boulevard
Kissimmee, FL 34758
Tel: (407) 847 4343

Miami

• Calder Race Course

Hire a boat and cut through Florida's coastal waters.

1001 NW 27th Avenue

Miami

Ocala

Classic Mile (Quarter Horse)

Pompano Beach

Pompano Park Harness Racing

800 SW Third Street

Pompano Beach

Tampa

Tampa Bay Downs

11225 Race Track Road

Oldsmar

Tel: (813) 855 4401

• **Florida Cowboys Association Rodeo**

Florida State Fairgrounds

Tel: (813) 627 7821

• **Five Star Pro Rodeo Series**

Florida State Fairgrounds

Tel: (813) 757 0846

Sailing/Boating

The Florida Sports Foundation has recently published an excellent "Florida Boating & Diving Guide" which you can order by writing them at 107 West Gaines Street, Tallahassee, Florida 32399-2000 or call (904) 488 8347. Here are a few sailing and boating spots to get you going:

Cape Canaveral on the Space Coast Two full service marinas; Cape Marina, a 105-slip marina, and Port Canaveral Marina, with 48 slips. Tel: (407) 783 8410 and (407) 783 5480

Coconut Grove

• **US Sailing Center**

2482 S Bayshore Drive

Tel: (305) 856 8412

Everglades City

• **Outdoor Resorts** - Chokoloskee Island

Tel: (800) 237 8247

• **Chokoloskee Island Park**

PO Box 430

Chokoloskee, FL 33925

Tel: (813) 695 2414

Fort Myers

• **Offshore Sailing School**

16731 McGregor Blvd.

Fort Myers

Tel: 1 800 221 4236

Key West

• **Sebago**

Key West Seaport

Duval & Front

Tel: (305) 294 5687

• **Windjammer Appledore**

Tel: (305) 296 9992

• **Club Nautico Boat Rentals**

Tel: 294 2225; 1 800 338 7161

• **Lucky Stripe/Too Charter Boats**

Tel: (305) 294 7988

Lands End Marina

• **Ocean Key House Suite Resort & Marina**

Tel: (305) 296 7701

• **Key West Boat Rentals**

Tel: (305) 292 7984

Charters

• **Trawler Yacht**

Land's End Marina

Tel: (305) 292 7984

• **Trilby's**

Land's End Marina

Equipped with scuba equipment – into a world of sea fans and hydroids.

Tel: (305) 293 9558

Key Largo

• **Witts End Snorkel & Sail Charter**

Coconuts-Marina Del Mar Docks

MM 100

PO Box 625

Key Largo, FL 33037

Tel: (305) 451 3354

• **John Pennekamp Coral Reef State Park**

Tel: (305) 451 1621

MM 102.5 US 1 Key Largo 33037

Marathon

• **Captain Pip's Marina Boat Rentals**

1410 Overseas Hwy

Marathon, FL 33050

Tel: (305) 743 4403

• **Poseideon Harbour, Inc**

Mile Mrker 63, Conch Key

Mailing Address: Rt 1, Box 521, Marathon, FL 33050

Tel: (305) 289 1525

• **Captain Hooks Marina and Blue Water Tackle Shop**

Marathon, Florida Keys

1183 Overseas Hwy - MM 53 at Vaca Cut Bridge

Tel: 743 2444

Snorkeling/Diving

Key Largo

• **Pennekamp Park in Key Largo**

Tel: 1 800 451 1113 or (305) 451 1113

• **Atlantis Captain Slate's Dive or Snorkel**

Pennekamp Park

Key Largo

Tel: 1 800 331 Dive or 451 3020

Witts End Charters

Snorkel & Sail

Marina Del Mar Docks

MM 100

PO Box 625

Key Largo, FL 33037

Tel: (305) 451 3354

John Pennekamp Coral Reef

State Park

MM102.5 US 1

Key Largo 33037

• **Reef Tix**

MM 103.5 Bayside

Key Largo, FL 33037

Tel: (305) 451 6309 or 1 800 637 2822

• **Key Largo Undersea Park**

Tel: 451 2353

• **Lady Cyana Divers**

MM 85.9

PO Box 1157

Islamorada, FL 33036

Tel: (305) 664 8717 or 1 800 221 8717

• **Jollymon Charter, Inc**

MM 83.5

at Chesapeake Resort

PO Box 909

Islamorada, FL 33036

Tel: (305) 664 4662 or 1 800 338 3395

• **The Diving Site**

MM 53.5

12399 Overseas Hwy

Marathon, FL 33050

Tel: (305) 289 1021 or 1 800 634 3935

• **Looe Key Dive Center**

MM 27.5

PO Box 509

Ramrod Key, FL 33042

Tel: (305) 872 2215 or 1 800 942 5397

• **Tavernier Dive Center**

MM 90.5 S Tavernier

Tel: (305) 852 4007 or 1 800 537 3253

• **Jarmada Boat Rentals**

Gilbert's

MM 108 PO Box 725

Key Largo, FL 33037

Tel: (305) 451 2628

• **Club Nautico**

MM 61

Marathon, FL

Tel: (305) 743 9000 or 1 800 432 2242

• **Fish n' Fun Boat Rentals**

The Boat House Marina

MM 53.5

Tel: (305) 743 2275

Marathon

• **Poseidon Harbour, Inc**

Mile Marker 63, Conch Key

Mailing Address: Rt 1, Box 521, Marathon, FL 33050

Tel: (305) 289 1525

Key West

• **Lost Reef Adventures**

Land's End Marina

Foot of Margaret Street

Key West

Tel: 296 9737 or 1 800 633 6833

• **Key West Diver Inc**

MM 4.5 US 1

Stock Island

Tel: 1 800 87DIVER or 294 7177

Soccer

Fort Lauderdale

• **Fort Lauderdale Strikers**

Duane Hanson, sculpture.

5620 Yankee Boulevard

Tel: (305) 776 1991

Miami

• **Miami Freedom**

1801 Coral Way

Tel: (305) 446 3136

Orlando

Hosted World Cup Soccer 1994

800 North Magnolia Avenue, 9th floor

Tel: (407) 246 0012

Tampa

• **Tampa Bay Rowdies**

2225 North Westshore Boulevard

Tel: (813) 877 7800

Swimming/Beaches

Contact the International Swimming

Sporting with Dolphins

At the Dolphin Research Center on Grassy Key
Delphi and Kiwi shriek and whistle in delight a
they inhale their morning fish. Energized now
from this high protein breakfast, these slee
powerful dolphins are ready to strut their stuf
slicing through the water at 20 miles per hou
Delphi spins and rolls like a giant slippery ciga
Kiwi smacks her lips in approval and counter
with back flips that would make a Chines
acrobat envious.

We applaud them. They applaud us. Of
who's having more fun?

It is clear they are delighted with our atter
tion, and we are delighted with theirs.

But now it's time for the ultimate swim
where two legged mammals get to play in th
water with two flippered ones.

If you've ever dreamed of swimming wit
dolphins, there are three Florida Keys facilitie
that are happy to introduce you to this ver
participatory sport.

The Dolphin Research Center is a not-for
profit teaching and research facility that treat
sick and wounded dolphins found in the area
They also accept dolphins from overcrowde
marine research centers, and dolphins whe
need to "retire" after years of jumping throug
hoops at aquarium shows.

One of their more unique programs is "Dol
phin/Child Special Education" where childre
with Down's syndrome, cancer, cerebral palsy
and head and spinal injuries swim with dolphin
as part of therapy. The children are able to gai
more confidence in themselves psychologically
as well as benefit from the physical interactio
with these gentle creatures.

At Dolphins Plus on Key Largo, your dolphir
swim includes an hour and a half pre-swim
seminar on dolphin general awareness. Afte

Hall of Fame, 1 Hall of Fame Drive, F
Lauderdale, to find out where the bes
Olympic size pools are.

Tel: (305) 462 6536

Canaveral

• **Playalinda Beach**

he swim, there's a question and answer session with center researchers.

The center also has in depth multiday programs featuring seminars on dolphin intelligence, anatomy and communication, and they make scuba/snorkel excursions to nearby reefs to study wild dolphins.

In Islamorada, there's another place you can swim with dolphins, a theme park called Theater of the Sea,built in 1946, which conducts no research but does compile information on dolphins that is sent to government researchers. Their facilities are also used for therapy by patients with spinal cord injuries from the University of Miami's teaching hospital.

Unlike Dolphin Research Center and Dolphins Plus, Theater of the Sea puts on theatrical marine shows featuring sea lions, sharks and of course, dolphins.

When you enter the water, the dolphin's home", you are their "entertainment", not the other way around. As their human "playtoy", you'll be nudged on different parts of your body as each dolphin decides which is his or her favorite shape.

Don't be surprised if you're presented with a bottle shaped nose for a scratch or kiss! It's all in fun.

Dolphins have many similarities to humans. Like us, they are susceptible to stress, and can develop ulcers. Extremely intelligent, they require a great deal of stimulation in order to avoid boredom. Who knows, maybe they even need vacations!

Actually, dolphins are most attracted to children because they consider kids to be less inhibited and more fun to be with. Who could argue that logic?

So act like a kid, and maybe Delphi and Kiwi

The ultimate watery high – skipping with a dolphin!

will choose you as their "toy du jour".

Advance reservations in writing are required. Contact each facility directly.

• *Dolphin Research Center*, Box 522875, Marathon Shores, 33052-2875, no calls please.

•**Dolphins Plus**, Box 2728, Key Largo, 33037, or call 305-451-1993. Theater of the Sea, Box 407, Islamorada 33036, or call 305-664-2431.

Happy swimming, give Delphi and Kiwi a kiss.

---

at eastern most end of SR 402

For more information stop by Canaveral National Seashore on the corner of US1 South and Julia Street in Titusville

Everglades

• **Fort DeSoto Park**

• **Pinellas Bayway**

Off I-275 and 54th Ave South

or from St Pete Beach

Tel: (813) 866 2262

Key West

• **Smathers, Higgs & South Beaches**

Hit a few balls at Hawks Bay

Naples
• **Barefoot Beach**
Bonita Beach Road
at the foot of SR 865
• **Lowdermilk Beach Park**
Marco Island
• **Tiger Tail Beach Park**
at the End of Hernando Drive
Marco Island.
Panama City
• **Panama City Beach, FL**
For further information call Tel: 1 800
PCBeach
• **Sanibel/Captiva Islands-Bowman Beach**
• **Sarasota Beaches-North Lido Beach, Siesta Key Beach**
St Petersburg Beaches
Best Swimming: Caladesi Island

Best Surfing : Redington Beach
Best Windsurfing : Bay side of Sand Key
north of the Belleair Causeway Bridge
Best Fishing: Indian Rocks Beach (sur
fishing for whiting)
Best Kids' : Indian Rocks Beach
Best Picnic: Fort DeSoto Park (ample park
ing, many shaded picnic tables)
Best Overall: Caladesi Island

Tennis

Contact the Florida Tennis Association
in North Miami Beach at Tel: (305) 652
2866 for a complete listing.
Here are just a few tennis centers:
Boca Raton
• **The Racquet Club of Boca Raton**
21618 St Andrews Boulevard
Tel: (407) 393 0333
Delray Beach
• **The International Tennis Center of
Delray Beach**
2350 Jaeger Road
Tel: (407) 278 1602
24 courts
Ft Lauderdale
• **Brian Piccolo Park**
9501 Sheridan Street
Cooper City (south of Ft Lauderdale)
12 lighted clay tennis courts
Tel: (305) 357 8100
• **Holiday Park Tennis Center**
18 clay courts, 4 asphalt courts
Fort Lauderdale
Tel: (305) 761 5378
Key Biscayne
• **International Tennis Center**

300 Crandon Boulevard
el: (305) 361 9725
3 tennis courts

issimmee
Buenaventura Lakes Country Club
01 Buenaventura Boulevard
.issimmee, FL 34743
el: (407) 348 2394
**Eve Ellis School of Tennis at Orange
.ake Country Club**
505 West Irlo Bronson Mem Hwy
.issimmee, FL 34746
el: 1 800 800 3768
H I Godwin Park
t Cloud Parks & Recreation Tennis
.ourts
)elaware & Wyoming & 3rd & 4th Streets
t Cloud, FL 34769
el: (407) 957 7243
O P Jounson Park
.th Street between Georgia & Louisiana
.venues
.t Cloud, FL 34769
el: (407) 957 7243
Oak Street Park
.ity of Kissimmee Parks & Recreation
.ennis Courts
.alm & Oak Streets
.issimmee, FL 34721
el: (407) 847 2388
Poinciana Golf & Racquet Resort
.00 East Cypress Parkway
.issimmee, FL 32758
.el: (407) 933 5300
**Walt Disney World Resort Tennis
.ourts**
.O Box 10,000, Lake Buena Vista, FL
.2830
Contemporary Racquet Club,

located at the Contemporary Resort,
World Drive, Orlando
Tel: (407) 824 357
• **Disney Inn Courts, located at The
Disney Inn,**
1 Palm-Magnolia Drive, Orlando
Tel: (407) 824 2288
• **Fort Wilderness Courts,**
located at the Fort Wilderness Resort
and Campgrounds, Orlando
Tel: (407) 824 2800
• **Grand Floridian Courts,**
located at the Grand Floridian Beach
Resort, Floridian Way, Orlando
Tel: (407) 824 3000
• **Lake Buena Vista Club,**
2200 Club Drive, Lake Buena Vista,
32830, Orlando
Tel: (407) 828 3741
• **Beach Club Courts,**
located at the Beach Club Resort,
Orlando:
Tel: (407) 934 1228
Naples
• **The Tennis Village**
4500 Bayshore Drive
Naples
Tel: 775 1400
• **4800 Airpoat Road**
Naples
Tel: 263 1900 or 1 800 292 6663
For information of where to find the
sport you're interested in, write or call
the Florida Sports Foundation, 107 West
Gaines Street, #342, Tallahassee, Florida
32399-2000. Tel: (904) 488 8347. The
Foundation is a not-for-profit organiza-
tion dedicated to the promotion and
protection of the Florida sports industry.

Nightlife: one of those mysterious terms that's more of a concept than an activity. What does a great evening out mean to you?

Slipping into a satin ballgown and rubbing elbows with "society" at a charity ball?

Easing into those tight white jeans topped with a sexy T shirt for a flirtatious night out at a hip biker's bar?

How about dinner and a wild wild west music show with the whole family?

If you're a wildlife lover, perhaps nightlife means watching thousands of newly hatched baby turtles making the most important run of their lives into a moonlit ocean.

For romantic lovers, nightlife can be strolling hand in hand along the

You will find more clowns per square foot in Florida than anywhere else.

Entertainment

361

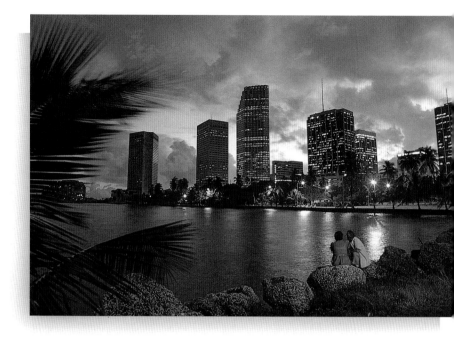

The sun goes down and the spandex gets drawn on in Miami.

beach under a starry sky. Or not going out at all.

Nightlife. Really it depends on your mood and your personality. Dancing serenely cheek to cheek, or bumping wildly hip to hip. Listening to Mozart or Madonna, sipping Martinis or chugging beers, cruising into a glittering neon city harbor, or relaxing at an outdoor cafe, ogling the p assing parade of pretty people.

Here's a mini-guide to some of Florida's nightlife possibilities. The setting is ideal. The fun is up to you.

Daytona Beach

- **Blackbeard's Backroom Comedy Club**: Lots of laughs, oyster happy hou 4-7 pm. 4200 S Atlantic Ave, Ponc Inlet. Tel: (904) 788 9644.
- **Aku Tiki's Lower Lounge:** Country western music featuring Tommy Brown & The Sugar Mill Express. Free danc lessons. 2225 S Atlantic Ave Tel: (904) 252 9631.
- **Seafair**: Karaoke singing for Madonn wannabes. 612 Seabreeze Boulevard Tel: (904) 252 1042.
- **Coliseum**: Dance club playing hous and high energy music. 176 N Beach Street. Tel: (904) 257 9982.
- **Hook's Landing**: Dance to live 50s 60s and 70s tunes. 2025 S Atlantic. Tel (904) 255 8371.
- **Razzles:** Huge dance floor, light shows six bars. Contest nightly. 611 Seabreez

Miami Arena

Got your ticket for the hot and heavy frenzied MC Hammer show? How about tickets to hear that gorgeous golden throated songbird, Whitney Houston?

Of course if you've already SEEN them, you could always get a ticket for The Harlem Globetrotters, Eric Clapton, Jimmy Buffet, Paul Simon, Frank Sinatra, Baryshinikov, Sesame Street Live, Disney on Ice, Gloria Estefan, Ringling Brothers Circus, or the World of Horses.

That's just a short list of the recent spectacular entertainment line up at Miami's Arena. Over 6 million fans have enjoyed the 16,627 seat Arena so far, at some 600 concerts, basketball games, hockey games, wrestling matches, and musical extravaganzas within the past 4 years.

The $53 million state of the art indoor facility has outstanding acoustics, large hanging video screens, and in the entire house there's not a bad seat, which incidentally are fully upholstered for maximum comfort. Landscaped plazas, painted surfaces and marble tile floors add to the pleasant ambiance.

Miami Arena is easy to find, just six blocks from the heart of downtown Miami, two blocks from Interstate 95, and 150 feet from the Metrorail commuter station. If you're touring around the Port of Miami, Bayside Marketplace, or downtown Miami, you can walk or take a 5 minute cab ride.

One of the best ways to get a sense of a city is to party with the locals. In Miami, energy levels get cranked way up when locals cheer on their beloved NBA team "MIAMI HEAT", and the University of Miami's HURRICANES. Check to see who's playing on the basketball court when you're in town. Whether you love country music, rap, rock 'n roll, blues, top 40s torch tunes; family shows, or the best in sports, Miami's Arena is an easy to find, easy to enjoy night on the town for the whole family. And a great way to meet local Miami fans.

Miami Arena, 701 Arena Boulevard, Miami. Events/Tickets: Tel: (305) 530 4400. Wheelchair accessible. Fast food concessions. Parking.

Boulevard. Tel: (904) 257 6236.

• **Dixie Queen Riverboat**: Dance party cruise with rock n' roll and country western music. Contests, hula hoops. Mainland side of Seabreeze Bridge. Tel: (904) 255 1997.

• **Oyster Pub**: Pool tables, video arcades, big screen TV. Happy hour 4-7. 555 Seabreeze. Tel: (904) 255 6348.

Fort Lauderdale

• **The Comic Strip Comedy Club**: A million laughs with top Los Angeles/New York comedians. Restaurant. 1432 N Federal Highway. Tel: (305) 565 8887.

• **Cafe 66**: A waterfront nightclub & bistro on the Intracoastal Waterway. Revolving rooftop bar. Pier 66 Resort & Marina.

• **Cheers**: Listen to Big Mama Blu & her Allstar Band. Cypress Ck. & Dixie Highway. Tel: (305) 771 6337.

• **Hoops**: Dance inside a boxing ring. 4000 Hollywood Boulevard in the Presidential Building. Tel: (305) 961 6677.

• **Do Da's American Country Saloon**: Ear pleasin' Country Western music and dance. Wear your cowboy boots. Free dance classes. 700 S State Route 7, Plantation. Tel: (305) 791 1477.

• **O'Hara's Pub**: Hot jazz with local and touring artists. 724 E Las Olas Boulevard. Tel: (305) 524 1764.

• **Crocco's**: Sports club/restaurant. Bas-

A juggler doing what he does best on Mallory Square Pier in Key West.

ketball, baseball batting cages, darts, billiards, large TV, music, dancing, many bars. 3339 N Federal Highway. Tel: (305) 566 2406.

• **Mai Kai**: Islanders Polynesian Revue. Rain forest setting. Cantonese/American food. 3599 N Federal Highway. Tel: (305) 563 3272.

Keys

• **Caribbean Club**: Where the famous movie "Key Largo" was filmed. Live band Thursday-Sunday. Jukebox. Mile Marker 105, Key Largo. Tel: (305) 451 9970.

• **Lorelei**: Indoor/outdoor cabana bar with live entertainment and sunset views. Mile Marker 82, Islamorada. Te (305) 664 4656.

• **Woody's-Entertainment** The Gon Show, Laser Karaoke, Radio broadcast: Family dining. Mile Marker 81.9 Islamorada. Tel: (305) 664 4335.

• **Brass Monkey**: Late night live enter tainment. Mile Marker 50, Key Colon Beach. Tel: (305) 743 4028.

• **Havana Docks Bar & Club**: Grea sunset views and live reggae music. Pie House Resort, Zero Duval Street. Ke West. Tel: (305) 296 4600.

• **Sloppy Joe's Bar**: A renowned water ing hole where Hemingway once dran a lot more than water. Rocking islan music, dance floor. 201 Duval Street Key West. Tel: (305) 294 5717.

• **Captain Hornblowers**: The island best jazz from Captain and hi hornblowing buddies. 300 Front Street Key West. Tel: (305) 294 1435.

• **Margaritaville**: Hot rock and blue acts until the wee hours. If you're lucky Jimmy Buffet may drop by. 500 Duva Street, Key West. Tel: (305) 292 1435.

Lakeland/Winter Haven Area

• Square Dance Clubs invite visiting Square Dancers to join in Tuesday-Thurs day and Saturday evenings in Lakeland Winter Haven and Mulberry. For loca tion and schedules call Cris Nissen Tel: (813) 665 9528.

• **Harborside Lounge**: Overlooking Lake Shipp. Live entertainment Thursday Sunday. 2435 7th Street, South East

There's a band around every corner in Busch Gardens, Adventure Island.

Winter Haven. Tel: (813) 293 7070.

Harriston's Lounge: Happy Hour 5-7 pm, complimentary hors d'oeuvres. Steak house. 230 Cypress Gardens Boulevard. Winter Haven. Tel: (813) 294 4300.

Jimmy D's Lounge: Top 40s, 50s, 60s. Live music Wednesday, Friday, Saturday. Karaoke. 4141 South Florida Ave, Lakeland. Tel: (813) 647 3000.

Norma Jean's Club: Karaoke. 50 beers. Howard Johnson's. 1300 3rd Street SW, Winter Haven. Tel: (813) 294 7321.

Rum Keg Pub: A quiet little lounge. Howard Johnson's. 1300 3rd Street SW, Winter Haven. Tel: (813) 294 7321.

Ski One Lounge: Dee Jay spins 50s and 60s music. Wednesday is Ladies Night at the Admiral's Inn. 5651 Cy-press Gardens Boulevard, Winter Haven. Tel: (813) 324 5950.

Miami Area

• **Improv at Coconut Grove**: America's original comedy showcase. Restaurant. Reservations required. Cocowalk, 3015 Grand Ave, Coconut Grove. Tel: (305) 441 8200.

• **Baja Beach Club**: Dance club with Top 40 music, dueling pianos, Sports cafe, billiards, game room. Happy hour with a 30 foot buffet. Cocowalk, 3015 Grand Ave, Coconut Grove. Tel: (305) 445 5499.

• **Facade Nightclub**: Dance to a 10 piece showband. Sound, light and video

Nightclubbing in Miami Beach.

show around a sunken dance floor. Six bars, two champagne rooms. Italian food. 3509 North East 163rd Street, North Miami Beach. Tel: (305) 948 6868.

• **Las Olas Del Malecon**: Dance to Latin music. Howard Johnson Oceanfront Resort Hotel. 6551 Collins Ave, Miami Beach. Tel: (305) 861 5222.

• **Luke's Miami Beach**: Plush, Art Deco style nightclub featuring Top 40 dance music, jazz. Four bars, three stages. Reggae music on Fridays. 1045 5th Street, South Miami Beach. Tel: (305) 531 0464.

• **Regine's**: Spectacular views from atop the Grand Bay Hotel. Very sophisticated. Grand Bay Hotel, 2669 S Bayshore Drive, Coconut Grove. Tel: (305) 858 9500.

• **Tobacco Road Bar**: One of South Florida's premiere blues showcases. Res-

taurant. 626 S Miami Ave, Brickell. Tel: (305) 374 1198.

• **Christine Lee's Gaslight Lounge**: Live music with dance floor. In the south dining room of Christine Lee's Restaurant. Thunderbird Resort Hotel. 18401 Collins Ave, Sunny Isles Beach. Tel: (305) 931 7700.

• **Club Tropigala at La Ronde**: Award winning floor shows, entertainers and 10 piece orchestra in an exotic Caribbean setting. Fontainebleau Hilton Resort and Spa. 4441 Collins Ave, Miami Beach. Tel: (305) 672 7469.

• **Jillian's Billiard Club and Cafe**: Brass furnishings, 30 pool tables, shuffleboard, ping pong, darts. Cafe menu. 12070 N Kendall Drive, Kendall. Tel: (305) 59 0070.

Orlando/Kissimmee Area

• **Arabian Nights Dinner Attraction**: 80 horses in a 25 act performance. course dinner. 6225 West Irlo Bronson Memorial Highway. Kissimmee. Tel (800) 553 6116.

• **Caruso's Palace**: Strolling musicians in an Italian Renaissance style restaurant. 8986 International Drive, Orlando Tel: (800) 776 3501.

• **Church Street Station**: Dixieland Jazz Country and Western music, rock and roll and Rosie O'Grady's saloon. Dining/shopping. 129 W Church Street Orlando. Tel: (407) 422 2434.

• **Fort Liberty Wild West Dinner Show** Cavalry soldiers, Comanche Indians

All-day entertainment at Disney's MGM Studio in Orlando.

Dance Hall Girls in a slapstick comedy. course Western meal. 5260 West rlo Bronson Memorial Highway, Kissimmee. Tel: (800) 347 8181.

Wolfman Jack's Rock 'N Roll Palace: he world's greatest 50s stars live on tage. Dining and dancing. 5770 West rlo Bronson Memorial Highway, Kissimmee. Tel: (407) 396 6499.

Mardi Gras: International revue recreates the West Indies, Moulin Rouge, European circus. 8445 International Drive, Orlando. Tel: (800) 347 8181.

Medieval Times Dinner and Tournament: 11th Century European style castle, knights on horseback, sword fighting and jousting. 4510 West Irlo Bronson Memorial Highway, Kissimmee. Tel: (800)-327 4024.

• **Walt Disney World Resort: Pleasure Island**: Six clubs, New Year's Eve Show, street celebrations for the whole family. Lake Buena Vista. Tel: (407) 934 7781.

Palm Beach County

• **Club Safari**: High energy nightclub with live animation. DJ nightly. Palm Beach Gardens Marriott. 8000 RCA Boulevard, Palm Beach Gardens. Tel: (407) 622 8888.

• **It's Comedy**: Professional comedy club with national comedians. 420 US Highway 1, North Palm Beach. Tel: (407) 845 5232.

• **That's Dancin'**: Ballroom dancing. 9091 N. Military Trail, Palm Beach Gardens. Tel: (407) 627 0804.

• **The Breakers**: Big Band dancing in a lavish historic hotel. Fine dining. Breakers Hotel, S County Road, Palm Beach. Tel: (407) 655 6611.

• **Brazilian Court**: Piano entertainment, cocktails, dinner. 301 Australian Ave, Palm Beach. Tel: (407) 655 7740.

• **The Colony Hotel**: Live music and dancing nightly. Resident psychic gives readings. 155 Hammon Ave, Palm Beach. Tel: (407) 655 5430.

• **Kicker's Dance Hall & Saloon**: Country music. 308 N Dixie Highway, Lantana. Tel: (407) 586 8854.

• **Phoenix**: Live rock n' roll. Fridays, Saturdays. 6 S Ocean Boulevard, Delray Beach. Tel: (407) 278 6082.

Panama City

• **Breakwater**: Country, Top 40, Rock 'n Roll. 6400 Front Beach Road. Tel: (904) 234 2114.

• **Circes Lounge**: Disco, show band,, dancing, Top 40. Marriott Hotel. 100 Delwood Road. Tel: (904) 234 0220.

• **Good Times Charlie's**: Show band, country, Top 40. 16422 Front Beach Road. Tel: (904) 234 0114.

• **Harpoon Harry's**: Show band, dancing, Top 40, rock 'n roll. 12627 Front Beach Road. Tel: (904) 234 6060.

• **Pineapple Willie's Lounge**: Disco, show band, dancing, top 40, rock 'n roll. 9900 Beach Boulevard. Tel: (904) 235 0928.

• **Rock 'N Roll Cafe & Lounge**:

Meet You On The Water

Take a bevy of hot bods, add sleek sexy power-boats, some ice cold brews, and what do you get?

Shooters, 1992's 10th busiest restaurant in the USA. Though that distinction was awarded by Restaurant Hospitality Magazine, you don't have to read the magazine to find out they're busy, just go there and join the happy crowds of shooters.

You're probably wondering what's a shooter anyway?

"A shooter," says Reg Moreau, one of the chain's three owners, "is a guy who spends a lot of money and maybe has a big car, or a fancy boat. He has a good time and goes out dancing every night."

Ok, Shooters does have some of those types, but there's also a hip mix of singles who don't spend a lot of money, and families who do spend it, but on their kids, instead of fancy cars. Everyone seems to get along just fine, enjoying the waterfront beauty, fresh air, live entertainment, music, and Shooters special events.

Owners Reg Moreau, Mel Burge, and Al Lahaye are big boat lovers, and back in 1980 decided to come up with a waterfront concept for casual drinking and dining, where you could pull up dockside in your boat. They opened their first Shooters in Ft Lauderdale in 1982 right on the Intracoastal Waterway, and soon the pleasure boats were docked at their pier several rows deep. Boaters would hop off in bathing suits or t-shirts and shorts and settle at Shooters for drinks and dinner. The concept was perfect, and it's worked ever since.

Shooters has taken off in a big way with restaurants opening in Ft. Lauderdale, North Miami Beach and Orlando. There's also a Shooters in Cleveland, Ohio, Buffalo, New York, and Providence, Rhode Island.

All the Shooters' "sun and funplexes", as they are fondly referred to, have 15,000 square feet, and 350 to 400 seats. Each has its own 300 foot dock area, swimming pool, sun deck, patio and indoor/outdoor bars. Sliding glass doors open to the water, so even when you're inside, you feel you're outside. What could be a better way to enjoy a night out?

The decor features lots of glass, wood, and

Cruise in the moonlight while you are in Florida.

brass paddle fans. In case anyone gets too rowdy, Mel Burge's vast collection of antique guns is prominently displayed near the entrance which tends to bring on instant sobriety! (That's a joke, folks.)

The Orlando Shooters has a dance floor, and all the other locations have a mixture of live entertainment, calypso bands, taped music, and overhead TV monitors broadcasting sporting events.

If you're looking to meet some new friends, it takes about 30 seconds at Shooters. Everyone is dressed in bare beach chic, glowing from the sun, checking out each other's tan lines.

It's real easy to see those tan lines at the "Hot Bod" bikini contest, which features cash prizes, trips or clothing for women who are blessed by nature or cosmetic surgery to have the hottest body in the teeniest bikini. It's all in good fun, so why not sign up?

If you're not that much of an exhibitionist, then stop in on Tuesday for the "Mexi-Night", when Shooters has Mariachi bands, Mexican beers and specials on margaritas and sangria.

On other nights Shooters stages stunts with boat races, jet skis and fireworks. And if you've ever worried about sharp dark fins sticking out of the ocean, you're sure to love "Get Even With Jaws" Night, when they serve shark.

The food menu is eclectic. Appetizers might be fettucine alfredo, escargot, peel n' eat shrimp. Entrees include filet mignon, roasted chicken, prime rib, scampi. There's also seafood, Oriental stir-fry, sandwiches and burgers. Kids get their own menu.

Tropical drinks sound like the beginning of a good party: Goom Bay Smash, Grape Quencher, Long Island Iced Tea, and the Hurricane. And you've got to have a Shooters signature shooter:

Fuzzy Navel, After 5, Alabama Slammer, or a B-52. If you want to know what's in the drinks, well you'll just have to go there and try one or two.

Shooters has become so popular, they even get love letters from Mayors and Congressmen who commend the restaurant as "a great asset to our city"... "drawing very large crowds, which benefits all surrounding businesses." How many nightspots do you know get letters like that?

But the real test of success are those sleek sexy boats tied up four and five deep by the docks, and the throngs of sunburned beach bods looking for good food, tropical drinks, and admiring glances.

At Shooters everyone gets their share.

3033 NE 32nd Avenue, Fort Lauderdale. Tel: (305) 566 2953. Also Orlando and North Miami Beach.

Shows, Top 40, rock 'n roll. 5518 Thomas Drive. Tel: (904) 233 1717.

• **Spinmaker**: Disco, show band, country, Top 40, rock n' roll. 8795 Thomas Drive. Tel: (904) 234 7882.

• **U Turn Sunburn Saloon**: Disco, show band, country, Top 40, rock 'n roll. 17283 Front Beach Road. Tel: (904) 233 6625.

Sarasota

• **Lido Beach Inn Lounge**: Ralph Shannon in the piano bar lounge. Wednesday-Sunday. 1234 Benjamin Franklin Drive. Tel: (813) 388 2171.

• **Poki Joes**: Excellent guitar and vocals by Bill & Danu, Fridays to Saturdays. Tel: (813) 922 5915.

• **Summerhouse Lounge**:Mike Moran, and his Dixieland Jazz Band, Sundays, Mondays; Pangaea Tuesday-Saturday. 6101 Midnight Pass Road. Tel: (813) 349 1100.

• **The Box Seat Sports Bar & Grill**: Sports entertainment, games, Karoake. 7111 S Tamiami Trail. Tel: (813) 747 6688.

• **Scoreboard Sports Pub**: Big screen TV, Families welcome. 7004 Cortez Road. Tel: (813) 792 6768.

• **Top of the Quay**: Dancing, Blues, Karaoke with cash prizes and gifts. Sarasota Quay. Tel: (813) 953 9444.

• **Club Bandstand**: High energy Top 40 dance club with the West coast's largest dance floor, light show. Sarasota Quay. Tel: (813) 951 2467.

• **Columbia's Patio**: Voted Sarasota's

Best Night Club and Omni, Best Dance Band. St Armands Circle. Tel: (813) 388 3987.

Tallahassee

• **Cafe' di Lorenzo**: Grand piano, weekend jazz and reggae. 1003 N Monroe Street. Tel: (904) 224 1783.

• **Club Park Ave**: Progressive nightclub with 2 dance floors, DJ, pool table. 115 E Park Ave. Tel: (904) 599 9143.

• **Clydes & Costello's**: Downtown pubs atmosphere, pool table. 210 S Adams Street. Tel: (904) 224 2173.

• **Dooley's Downunder/The Comedy Zone**: Live comedy on weekends Ramada Inn. 2900 N Monroe Street. Tel (904) 386 1027.

• **Diamond Jim's Lounge**: Rock 'n roll top 40, country. Silver Slipper Restaurant. 531 Scotty Lane. Tel: (904) 386 9366.

• **Halligan's Pub n Pool**: upscale billiard room, pub. 1700 Halstead Boulevard. Tel: (904) 668 7665.

• **Mr. Joe's Place Lounge**: Live bands 1355 Apalachee Parkway. Tel: (904) 877 3171.

• **Posey's Oyster Bar**: Country western dancing and fabulous fresh oysters South on Monroe Street, 18 miles from Tallahassee. Tel: (904) 925 6172.

Tampa

• **Cha Cha Coconuts** – Live entertain

ment, jazz, reggae, rock. 777 S Harbour Island, Tampa. Tel: (813) 223 3101.

Reflections: Sing along piano bar. Trade Winds , 5500 Gulf Boulevard, St Petersburg Beach. Tel: (813) 367 6461.

Brothers Lounge: Live jazz. 5401 W Kennedy Boulevard, Tampa. Tel: (813) 286 8882.

Columbia Restaurant: Spanish flamenco dance show Monday-Saturdays. Reservations required. 2117 E 7th Ave, Ybor City. Tel: (813) 248 4961

Clearwater

Surf Club: Dance to Top 40 on a multilevel dance floor Monday-Saturday. Holiday Inn Surfside, 400 Mandalay Ave, Clearwater Beach. Tel: (813) 461 3222.

Yucatan Liquor Stand: Dance to Top 40 rock'n roll and reggae. 4811 W Cypress, Tampa. Tel: (813) 289 8454.

FunKruz/SeaKruz: Evening/day cruises on ships with live bands, comedy, dancing, casinos. The Pier, St Petersburg, Tel: (800) 688 7529; John's Pass Marina, Madeira Beach, Tel: (800) 688 7529.

The Admiral Dinner Boat: Dinner,dancing, Tuesday-Saturday evenings. Clearwater Beach Marina, Clearwater Beach. Tel: (813) 462 2628.

Starlite Princess: A three deck 106 foot paddle wheel boat. Lunch, dinner dance and skyway cruises. Hamlin's Landing, Tampa. Tel: (800) 722 6645.

Captain Anderson Dinner Boat: Din-

Blow your blues away as the buskers entertain.

ner dance cruises with live band. 3400 Pasadena Ave South, St Petersburg. Tel: (813) 367 7804.

• **Coliseum Ballroom**: Big Band dancing in a 1924 ballroom where the movie "Cocoon" was filmed. Dances held Monday, Wednesday, Saturday. Sockhops once each month. 535 Fourth Ave North, St Petersburg. Tel: (813) 892 5202.

• **Florida Suncoast Dome**: Florida's first domed stadium hosts athletic events, concerts and other entertainment. One Stadium Drive, St Petersburg. Tel: (813) 825 3100.

• **Casablanca Cruises**: Fine dining, live entertainment, dancing, cruising scenic Anclote River. 697 Dodecanese Boulevard, Tarpon Springs. Tel: (813) 942 4452.

Whether you're buying a $10 T shirt or a $10,000 diamond necklace, Florida's diversity of merchandise is mind-boggling. Ease into an itsy bitsy bikini or splurge on a designer ballgown. Wear them both on your gleaming new yacht!

Pick up a state of the art TV set, or cart home a stuffed sailfish. Seashells, sea sails, sandals. Neon nail polish, neon surfboards, neon running shoes. Buy a beachfront vacation home, or take some Florida home to your old home: elegant antiques, whimsical rattan, one of a kind sculpture, or a poster of your favorite landscape. If you can not find what you want in Florida, it does not exist. Of course you can have fun shopping without spending money. Window shopping is great entertainment and it is FREE!

Here's a mini-guide to shopping throughout the state:

Shopping

373

■ ■ ■ ■ ■

Hats to shade you from the sun and provide a colourful souvenir.

Fort Lauderdale

From one of a kind boutiques along tree shaded Las Olas Boul-

View from a bubble lift at the Neiman Marcus in Bal Harbour.

evard, to the splendors of specialty shops in The Galleria; from American and Japanese avant garde fashions to the 50s and 60s Retro look, Fort Lauderdale will have something you'll like. Some popular shopping malls:

• **Broward Mall**: 135 specialty shops, 3 major department stores. 8000 W Broward Boulevard, Plantation. Tel: (305) 473 8100.

• **Coral Square**: 140 stores, 4 major dept. stores. 9469 W Atlantic Boulevard, Coral Springs. Tel: (305) 755 5550.

• **Fashion Mall at Plantation**: Outdoor ambiance with 100 stores; Macy's, Lord & Taylor's. 321 N University Drive, Plantation. Tel: (305) 370 1884.

• **The Galleria:** 150 shops; Saks Fifth Avenue, Burdines, Neiman Marcus,

Cartier. 2414 E Sunrise Boulevard, Fort Lauderdale. Tel: (305) 564 1015.

• **Sawgrass Mills**: 200 discount shops Spiegel Outlet, Ann Taylor Clearance, Eddie Bauer, Macy's Close out. 5 themed courtyards. Sunrise Boulevard and Flamingo Road, Sunrise. Tel: (305) 846 2350.

• **Antique Center of the South**: 75 dealers. 10 minutes south of beaches in Dania. Tel: (305) 925 6725.

• **East Las Olas Boulevard**: blocks of boutiques, art galleries restaurants. Bed & Bath Shop, The Store for Brides, Robt Drake.

• **Fort Lauderdale Swap Shop**: 2000 vendors in tents and outdoor stalls. 3291 W Sunrise Blvd, Fort Lauderdale. Tel: (305) 791 7927.

Jacksonville

With its dramatic skyline along the historic St Johns River, this city offers relaxed shopping in a number of attractive settings.

• **The Jacksonville Landing**: A festive indoor/outdoor waterfront marketplace with specialty shops and casual restaurants. Laura Ashley, Banana Republic, The Limited, B Dalton Bookstore. Independent Drive on the St Johns River. Tel: (904) 353 1188.

• **Riverwalk**: More than a mile long boardwalk with shops, dining and entertainment. Great view of city skyline. Southbank of the St Johns River. Tel: (904) 396 4900.

The exterior of the Bal Harbour Shopping Center.

• **San Marco District**: Antiques, gifts, clothing, bookshops, in a historic, quaint residential setting. Outdoor cafes. Southbank of downtown. Tel: (904) 353 9736.

The Keys

Although the dress here rarely goes beyond shorts and t shirts, there are lots of funky shops with sportswear, home accessories and of course, sea shells. In Key West you can find wonderful art, books, gifts and more sophisticated resort wear.

• **Anthony's**: The Keys' largest women's clothing store. Sportswear, swimwear, lingerie, accessories. Mile Marker 98.5, Key Largo. Tel: (305) 852 4515.

• **Shell World**: Tropical seashells, nautical jewelry, sharks' teeth, candy. Mile Marker 97.5, Key Largo. Tel: (305) 852 8245.

• **Artisan's Village**: Stained and sculptured glass, wood boxes, paintings, chimes by South Florida artists. Mile Marker 86.7, Islamorada. Tel: (305) 852 3084.

• **Duval Street**: Key West's main street, blocks of trendy sportswear, home furnishings, books, t-shirts, outdoor restaurants. Duval Street, Key West.

• **Greenpeace**: Cards, books, jewelry, posters, toys, sweats, gifts. Proceeds benefit Greenpeace International Organization. 719 Duval Street, Key West. Tel: (305) 296 4442.

• **Haitian Art Company**: Primitive and

Shells from Shell World – an unique souvenir.

modern Haitian paintings, sculptures in wood, steel, papier-mache. Tel: (305) 296 8932.

• **Key West Hand Print Fabrics**: Beautiful silk screened fabrics and sportswear. Accessories and home items. 201 Simonton Street, Key West. Tel: (800) 866 0333.

Miami

From classic tailored designs to hip streetwear, this international city with a Latin beat has an eclectic diversity.

Prices range from discount to very expensive, so shop around.

• **Aventura Mall**: 200 shops, Macy's, Lord & Taylor, JC Penney and Sears. 19501 Biscayne Boulevard. Tel: (305) 935 4222.

• **Bal Harbour Shops**: Specialty boutiques. Martha, FAO Schwarz, Gucci, Cartier, Fendi, Neiman Marcus, Saks Fifth Avenue. 9700 Collins Avenue, Bal Harbour. Tel: (305) 866 0311.

• **Bayside Marketplace**: Downtown waterfront marketplace with 150 shops, live performers and local art shows. 40 Biscayne Boulevard, Miami. Tel: (305) 577 3344.

• **Caribbean Marketplace**: Caribbean arts and crafts in a colorful setting. Tropical ice cream. 5925 NE 2nd Avenue, Little Haiti. Tel: (305) 758 8708.

• **Cocowalk**: A European village style center. The Gap, Limited Express. Comedy club, restaurants. 3015 Grand Ave.

Buy your string bikini in Florida

Coconut Grove. Tel: (305) 444 0777.

• **Mayfair Shops in the Grove**: European shopping plaza. Gifts, art, antiques, apparel for the whole family. 2911 Grand Avenue, Coconut Grove. Tel: (305) 448 1700.

• **Omni International Mall**: 125 stores. Burdines and JC Penney. Movie theaters, restaurants, carousel. 1601 Biscayne Boulevard. Downtown Miami. Tel: (305) 374 6664.

Naples

Some tourists love Naples shopping so much, they arrive with empty suitcases so they can fill them up with new wardrobes and decorative home accessories.

Gifts, apparel, furnishings, and art are top quality in this lovely Gulfside town.

• **Third Street South**: Cozy arcades and courtyards house 100 shops. Antiques, designer clothes, children's wear, jewelry, fine art. 1262 3rd Street South. Tel: (813) 649 6707.

• **Fifth Avenue**: Naples original downtown, with antiques, books, apparel, electronics, furniture, jewelry. South area of Naples on Fifth Avenue. Tel: (813) 262 4744.

• **Old Marine Market Place**: Rustic flair with cobbles, planked floors. Souvenirs, beach fashions, outdoor dining. At Tin City on Naples Bay. 1200 5th Avenue South. Tel: (813) 262 4200.

• **Dockside Boardwalk**: Yacht atmosphere, shops feature nautical gear, kites, gifts. Near Old Marine Market Place on Naples Bay. 1100 6th Avenue South. Tel: (813) 649 7730.

• **Hibiscus Center**: Shops include Kangaroo Klub, Miahcel's and Zazou Sport. 2950 9th Street North. Tel: (813) 262 2270.

• **The Pavilion Shopping Center**: Shops include China Pavilion, Pavilion Shoes, Young Once. Vanderbilt Beach Road. Tel: (813) 261 4455.

• **The Village on Venetian Bay**: Shops include Bayside, Jami's. Restaurants, Maxwell's on the Bay, Ben & Jerry's Ice Cream. 4200 Gulf Shore Boulevard. Tel: (813) 261 0030.

• **Waterside Shops at Pelican Bay**: Shops include Jacobsen's, Saks Fifth Ave, Talbots. Silver Spoon Restaurant. 801 Laurel Oak Drive. Tel: (813) 598 1605.

The Mayfair Shopping Mall in Coconut Grove.

Orlando/ Kissimmee

Driving along Highway 192 in Kissimmee, you'll pass literally thousands of discount stores selling t-shirts, sportswear, household accessories, luggage, electronics. Here are some other options.

• **Church Street Station**: Three-level Victorian style center with 40 shops. Lingerie, sportswear, jewelry. 129 West Church Street, Orlando. Tel: (407) 849 0904.

• **Florida Mall**: 160 shops. Sears, JC Penney, Maison Blanche. 8001 South Orange Blossom Trail, Orlando. Tel: (407) 851 6255.

• **Kissimmee Manufacturer's Mall**: Outlet Shopping Center. Nike, Manhattan, Hanes, Totes, London Fog, etc 2517 Old Vineland Road, Kissimmee. Tel: (407) 396 8900.

• **The Neighborhood Shops**: Turn of the century homes with gifts, children's boutique, country store. South of Highway 192 on Orange Blossom Trail/Main Street. Tel: (407) 846 4552.

• **Osceola Square Mall**: Enclosed shopping mall. Wal-Mart, Lane Bryant, 12 movie theaters. 3831 West Vine Street, Kissimmee. Tel: (407) 847 6941.

• **Flea World**: America's largest flea market. 1500 booths. Highway 17-92, Sanford. Tel: (407) 647 3976.

Palm Beach

Shopping here is a humbling experience unless you're living on the interest from your trust fund, or married to a major CEO. If you're a rock or movie star cruising town in your white limo that's also an appropriate calling card.

Basically you're going to want everything you see, so bring lots of credit cards. Worth Avenue is strictly for those of substantial financial worth, but Palm Beach County does have other shopping options for regular folks.

• **Worth Avenue**: Four fabulous blocks of expensive art, clothing, jewelry and everything exquisite. Cartier, Van Cleef & Arpels, Bottega Veneta, Gucci, Brooks Brothers, Calvin Klein, Chanel, dozens more of the world's most famous designers. Worth Avenue, Palm Beach

The infamous Ron-Jon's Surf Shop in Cocoa Beach.

Tel: (407) 659 6909.

• **Mizner Park**: Dozens of shops, six restaurants, 8 movies in Boca Raton village-in-the city style. Tel: (407) 362 - 0606.

• **Boynton Beach Mall**: 150 stores in a mall setting. Burdines, Macy's Mervyn's. On Congress Avenue between Boynton Beach Boulevard and Hypoluxo Road. Tel: (407) 736 7900.

• **The Gardens Mall**: A two story mall of 180 shops. Bloomingdale's Burdines, Macy's, Sears, Saks Fifth Avenue. PGA Boulevard in Palm Beach Gardens. Tel: (407) 622 2115.

• **Palm Beach Mall**: Skylights and fountains create a tropical ambiance. Burdines, Mervyn's, Lord& Taylor, JC Penney, Sears. Palm Beach Lakes Boul-evard, east of I095, West Palm Beach. Tel: (407) 683 9186.

• **Palm Beach Outlet Center**: Factory direct merchandise with discounts of 30-70 percent below retail. $^1/_2$ mile east of Florida's Turnpike, West Palm Beach. Tel: (407) 684 5700.

• **Town Center Mall of Boca Raton**: Elegant Spanish Colonial architecture and 6 anchor stores: Bloomingdale's Burdines, Mervyn's, Lord&Taylor, Saks Fifth Avenue, Sears. Tel: (407) 368 6000.

Pensacola

In this laid back historic city, the shopping is as relaxed as the warm southern hospitality.

Decisions, decisions, decisions at Saint Armand's Circle.

• **Antiques**: There are 37 shops known as "The Greater Pensacola Area Antique Dealers", located in Downtown and in the Historic Districts. The "Ninth Avenue Antique Mall" has 50 shops featuring jewelry, lamps, baskets, pottery, china, crystal, vintage clothing, American & European furniture. 380 N 9th Avenue. Tel: (904) 438 3961.

• **Quayside Art Gallery**: the largest co-op in the Southeast, a fine place to buy original oil, acrylic, pastel and watercolor paintings. Also soft sculpture, art furniture, jewelry, photography. Plaza Ferdinand, 15-17 E Zarragossa Street. Tel: (904) 438 2363.

• **Quayside Market**: A cozy marketplace on the waterfront, featuring furniture, lamps, jewelry, kitchen collectibles,

books, quilts, antiques. 712 S Palafox. Tel: (904) 433 9930.

Saint Petersburg

Just because there are miles of incredible beaches does not mean you have to stay on them forever.

St Petersburg also offers the visitor and resident alike some great shopping too.

• **Downtown**: Downtown St Petersburg shops offer fashions, gifts, art, jewelry and eyewear. Stroll along Beach Drive.

• Gas Plant Antique Arcade-One of Florida's largest antique malls. Over 70 dealers of fine furniture, sterling silver, cut glass, paintings etc 1246 Central Ave at 13th Street, St Pete. Tel: (813) 895 0368.

• **John's Pass Village & Boardwalk**: A quaint shopping district on the waterfront.

Art Galleries, boutiques, restaurants. Home of Johns Pass Seafood Festival in October. 12901 Gulf Boulevard East, Madeira Beach. Tel: (813) 393 2885.

• **Tyrone Square**: 150 shops. Burdine's, Dillard's, JC Penney, Sears. 66th St and 22nd Avenue N St Pete. Tel: (813) 345 0126.

Sarasota

International boutiques with fine Italian leather are next door to funky beach shops selling surfboards and Jimmy Buffet tapes.

With all of Sarasota's theater, opera, dance and art gallery openings, you've just got to splurge on something wonderful to wear! So grab your credit cards and shop til you drop.

• **Downtown**: Antiques, interior design showrooms, art galleries in a charming historic setting. On Palm Avenue off lower Main Street. The Art Dealers Association offers Gallery Walks in Spring and Fall. Tel: (813) 955 9495.

• **Avenue of the Flowers**: Ten specialty boutiques offering resort wear, gourmet cheese, and art in an intimate lush garden setting. Gulf of Mexico Drive, Longboat Key.

• **Gulf Gate Mall**: For bargain hunters. Marshall's, Hit or Miss, Terry Shulman's discount drugstore. South Tamiami Trail. 600 Gulf Gate Mall. Tel: (813) 921 5200.

• **Sarasota Quay**: Multi-level pink waterfront building with fountains, a piazza surrounded by elegant shops, restaurants, jazz bar, ice cream. On US 41 at 3rd Street. Tel: (813) 957 0192.

• **Sarasota Square Mall**: Largest mall in the area, with JC Penney, Sears, Maas Brothers, Parisian. 12 movie theaters. 8201 South Tamiami Trail. Tel: (813) 922 9600.

• **Siesta Village**: Antique shops, florists, jewelers, fashions, gifts, travel agencies near world famous beaches. Ocean Boulevard, Siesta Key.

• **Saint Armands Circle**: Elegant fashions, home accessories, souvenir shops in a gorgeous neighborhood setting of courtyards, patios and statues. St

Armands Key. Tel: (813) 388 1554.

Tampa

Those 13 soaring minarets on Henry Plant's Tampa Bay hotel, now the University of Tampa, and the sleek modern skyline, is proof that the city of Tampa knows all about style. The shopping is just as exciting.

• **Gulf Coast Factory Shops**: Caribbean village with 45 specialty shops offering 30-70 percent off retail. Carol Little, Donna Karan, Jones New York, Mikasa. I-75 at Exit 43, Tampa. Tel: (813) 723 1150.

• **Old Hyde Park Village**: A park setting with 60 shops. The Sharper Image, Williams, Sonoma, Talbots, Laura Ashley, Polo/Ralph Lauren. Live jazz concerts. Swann and Dakota Avenues, Tampa. Tel: (813) 251 3500.

• **The Shops on Harbour Island**: On Tampa Bay with 40 boutiques. Four waterfront restaurants. 777 S Harbour Island Boulevard, Tampa. Tel: (813) 223 9898.

• **West Shore Plaza**: Shopping center with Burdine's, Dillards, JC Penney, Lillie Rubin, The Limited. Westshore and Kennedy Boulevards, Tampa. Tel: (813) 286 0790.

• **Ybor Square**: Original cigar factories turned into boutiques selling funky clothing, art, books, gifts. National Register of Historic Places. South of 9th Avenue, between 13th and 14th Streets, Ybor City. Tel: (813) 247 4497.

C u i s i n e

Florida is paradise for food lovers. Fruits in every size, shape and color grow on fragrant trees throughout the state. An alphabet of vegetables flourish in fields and gardens. From the Atlantic Ocean to the east, and the Gulf of Mexico to the west, comes a fantastic variety of fresh fish and seafood. And Florida is one of the United States' top cattle producers as well, turning out delicious beef. On top of it all, the Sunshine State also produces sugar, honey, pecans, peanuts and honey.

Shelled delights – Florida oysters enjoyed in Key Biscayne.

What more could any chef or gourmand ask for?

Florida's recipes reflect the heritage and traditions of the many cultures who have made their home here. A dizzying variety of choices wait to be savored: Deep South, Cuban, Jewish, Greek, Afro-American, Spanish, Asian.

If you crave Southern style dishes-fried chicken, barbecued pork, hoecakes,

383

red beans and rice, pickled shrimp, smoked mullet, key lime pie- not to worry, there's plenty of it in Florida, especially in Tallahassee and Key West.

Spanish specialties more to your tastebuds? Chicken and yellow rice, seafood paella, cafe cubano, and flan de leche are most everywhere, especially Miami and Tampa.

How about latkes, stuffed cabbage, chopped chicken livers, and a fresh toasted bagel with cream cheese? Let your Jewish grandmother help you eat, eat, eat in Miami Beach. And remember calories are mind over matter: if you don't mind, they don't matter.

If you make it to Tarpon Springs, and we hope you will, Greek chefs are behind those irresistible aromas of shrimp in garlic, pan fried squid, pickled octopus and sweet flaky baklava.

And over in Tampa at Bern's Steak House, there's dozens of different cuts of steak along with 7,000 wine choices. That's right, 7,000, all neatly catalogued in a telephone size album.

If it is fresh seafood you love, well, you can eat it for breakfast, lunch and dinner in Florida. Broiled, boiled, baked, fried, steamed. Eggs and salmon in the morning; fresh grouper sandwich at noon; whole steamed lobster with a side of freshly shucked oysters at sunset on the beach.

The point is, you're not going to go hungry in Florida. Far from it. In fact, the only thing that will hold you back from eating night and day is the thought of having to put on your bathing suit.

But then you could throw caution to the winds and just wear a nice roomy cover up, right?

Following is a brief list of favorite recipes from some of Florida's best restaurants.

Sophie Kay's Top of Daytona

Sophie Kay's is known for spectacular ocean views and delicious food. Author of 12 cookbooks and host of a popular local TV show, "Cooking With Sophie", Sophie is there every night to oversee the kitchen and visit with her guests who come from all over Daytona and the world to sample her food.

2625 S Atlantic Ave, Daytona Beach Shores, FL 32018. Tel: (904) 767 5791.

• *Mushrooms Stuffed With Crabmeat*
Ingredients: 1 pound large fresh mushrooms; 2 tablespoons butter; $1/2$ cup finely sliced green onion tops; 1/3 cup minced green pepper; 6 ounce can crab meat, drained well, flaked; 2 tablespoons Marsala wine; 1/4 cup mayonnaise; 1 teaspoon Old Bay seasoning; 2 tablespoons butter, melted; Paprika; parsley sprigs for garnish.

Method: Remove mushroom stems; chop fine. Melt 2 tablespoons butter in large frying pan. Saute mushroom stems, green onion and green pepper until golden. Remove from heat. Cool slightly. Mix crabmeat with the Marsala wine in medium bowl; add green onion mixture, mayonnaise and Old Bay seasoning. Mix well. Spoon into mushroom

Kissimmee – cattle country and the best place to enjoy a Florida beef steak.

caps. Drizzle 2 tablespoons melted butter over filled mushrooms. Sprinkle tops with paprika. Bake in preheated 375° oven 20 minutes or until tender. Garnish with parsley. Makes 20.

The Dock At Crayton Cove

This lively outdoor restaurant is the perfect spot to watch birds, boats and beautiful people down at Naples dock. If you see a gorgeous guy on the premises that's owner Vin DePasquale, who moved to Naples because "I don't need to wear a three piece suit here." Deedee Brown, the Dock's Chef for 16 years, also loves Naples' casual life and offers this easy popular dish. Twelfth Avenue South at Eight Street, Naples, FL 33940. Tel: (813) 263 9940.

• *Conch Ceviche (Cold Conch Salad)*
Ingredients: 1 pound whole conch cut up in $1/_2$" cubes; 6 limes juiced; 4 ripe tomatoes; 1 cup chopped red onion; 1 cup chopped green onion; 1 cup chopped green pepper; 3 tablespoons Tabasco sauce; 1 teaspoon salt; 2 teaspoons black pepper; 2 cups V-8 or tomato juice.
Method: Marinate conch in lime juice 4 hours or overnight. Add remaining ingredients and chill. Serve with crackers.

JD's Southern Oaks

Far away from the madding crowds is one of Florida's most charming Bed and

Citrus World

Floridians are never short of Vitamin C in this citrus state.

Did you know that Florida grows more than 70 percent of all the oranges and almost 80% of the grapefruit produced in the United States today? Citrus is Florida's number one agricultural crop and contributes more than $8 billion a year to the state's economy.

Historians believe that Ponce de Leon and his men brought the first citrus to Florida during their explorations back in 1513. As they searched for the "Fountain of Youth", they dropped seeds from fruit that had made the journey across the ocean with them, and so began the first citrus farms. The earliest groves developed around the Saint Augustine and Tampa seaports. At the time, Central Florida was an unmapped wilderness. The orange came to Florida first, followed by the tangerine, lemons, limes and other varieties. In 1823, French Count Odet Phillippe planted the state's first grapefruit grove near Tampa. Because of his pioneering, Count Phillippe's name is enshrined in the Citrus Hall of Fame at the Citrus Research and Education Center in Lake Alfred.

Today, citrus is produced throughout the state. South of Daytona Beach to Palm Beach is the famous Indian River production area, which account for over 30 percent of all the citrus acreage in the state. Citrus has been commercially grown in this area for 150 years.

Along the southwestern coast of Florida, citrus production has increased tremendously during the past ten years. This area, known as the Gulf citrus growing region, has more than 110,000 acres of groves, with more planned.

The heart of the citrus industry is in the central part of Florida, where about 55% of the citrus is grown. This area has been producing citrus for 70-80 years. While freezes have hurt some of the groves, many new young trees have been planted and more are planned in the future. Most of Florida's fresh citrus packinghouses and processing plants are in the

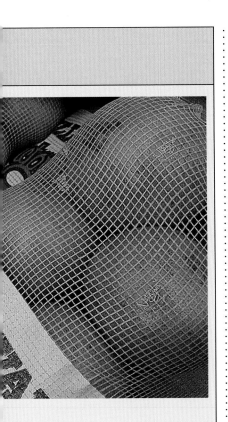

center of the state, and many welcome tours.
• **Bunkley's Grove,**(grove and packinghouse.) 3131 N Tropical Trail, Merritt Island. Tel: (407) 452 5348.
• **Golden Gem Growers, Inc,** (grove, packinghouse, processing plant.) 38851 State Road 19 North, Umatilla. Tel: (904) 669 2101.
• **Maxwell Grove Service, Inc,** (grove and packinghouse.) 607 E Pleasant Street, Avon Park. Tel: (813) 453 3938.
• *Mixon Fruit Farms, Inc,* (grove, packinghouse, processing plant.) 2712 26th Avenue East, Bradenton. Tel: (813) 748 5829.
• **Spyke's Grove.** (grove) 7250 Griffin Road, Davie. Tel: (305) 583 0426.
• **Walker Grove, Inc** (grove, gift fruit packing house) 580 State Road 559, Auburndale. Tel: (813) 967 1253.
• *Winter Haven Citrus Growers Association.* (grove, packinghouse) 351 Avenue K South West, Winter Haven. Tel: (813) 293 9679.
   Questions? Write or call the Florida Department of Citrus, Public Relations, PO Box 148, Lakeland, FL 33802. Tel: (813) 682 0171.

Breakfasts, a 1925 Southern Mansion that beckons you to enjoy peaceful walks along tree canopied lanes, and delicious home cooked food. Juanita and Dallas Abercrombie are gracious hosts who will show you what real Southern hospitality is all about. 3800 Country Club Road, Winter Haven, FL 33881. Tel: 1 800 771 6257.

• *Juanita's Sausage Quiche*
Ingredients: 1 pound sausage cooked and drained; 12 eggs slightly beaten; 2 cups grated sharp cheese; 1 can cream of mushroom soup.
Method: Mix all together and pour into a greased baking dish. Bake at 350° for 35 minutes or until center is firm.

Park Plaza Gardens

Superb continental cuisine served in an upscale indoor garden setting of trees and brick walkways, the Park Plaza Gardens restaurants consistently wins Central Florida Magazine's award for Best Restaurant of the Year. 307 Park Avenue South, Winter Park, FL 32789. Tel: 1 800 228 7220. Executive Chef Philippe Gehin presents his favorite:

• *Grilled Sea Scallops Key West*
Ingredients: 16 jumbo sea scallops; $^1/_2$ pound of fresh tricolor pasta; 16 lime segments; 4 tablespoons chopped chives; cracked black peppercorns; juice of 1 lime; $^1/_4$ cup champagne; 1 cup heavy cream; $^1/_4$ stick butter, chilled out in pats.
Method: Cook the pasta "al dente" in

Healthy eating in Florida.

boiling salted water with $1/4$ cup of oil. Rinse under cold water, set aside. Grease a small mold with butter, season the pasta with salt, pepper and soft butter. Pack the pasta in the mold, covering tightly with aluminum foil. Grill the scallops until tender. Finish cooking them in a double boiler. To make the sauce, in a pan combine lime juice and champagne, reduce to one third. Add the cream and reduce until cream is thickened. Add the butter pats one at time, swirling the pan to mix. Reheat the pasta and scallops in the double boiler. Pour the sauce onto each plate and top with pasta. Arrange scallops out lengthwise around the plate, sprinkle with chopped chives, black peppercorn and garnish each scallop with one

lime segment. Serves four.

Mykonos

Tarpon Springs is Florida's Greek fishing community, where divers bring up sea sponges for world export and chefs cook up tantalizing Mediterranean delights. 628 Dodecanese Boulevard, Tarpon Springs, FL 34689. Tel: (813) 934 4306. Chef Andy Salivaris offers this Greek favorite:

• **Garides Mykonos**

Ingredients: 1 pound raw shrimp, peeled; 1 whole Spanish onion; 2 tablespoons parsley; 1 cup celery; 4 scallions; 1 large whole tomato, peeled, chopped very fine; 2 tablespoons olive oil; 2 bay leaves; 1 teaspoon oregano; $1/2$ cup Greek white wine; $1/2$ pound American feta cheese. *Method*: Saute onions with celery in olive oil. Add parsley. When onions are brown, add scallions, tomato, bay leaves and oregano. Add Greek white wine and simmer 5 minutes. Add shrimp to vegetables and fry 2 minutes. Crumble and add Feta cheese. Serve over rice or eat as it is. Enjoy!

Five Star

This two year old Key West Cuban restaurant has been packing in locals and tourists who crave the spicy concoctions and home made flan and rice pudding cooked up by owner Ana Agiviar. There are only 9 tables among the plants, and

Up From The Deep: Florida's Fresh Seafood

Crustaceans transformed into edible sensations - a dish of Joe's stone crabs.

The Timucuan Indians were probably the first Floridians to perfect the preparation of the seafood treasures that lay just beyond the shore. Many of the Indian mounds being excavated today are made up of shells from the oysters, clams and mussels they consumed on a daily basis. And studies show they were heathy eaters, subsisting on a diet mostly made up of fish and vegetables. Here's a seafood lover's guide to some of what you'll see on Florida's menus:

Catfish: A staple of regional Southern cuisine, also known as "sharpie." Flesh is mild, sweet and moist, usually served baked or fried.

Conch: Although endangered in Florida, this mollusk is still available from the Bahamas and Cayman Islands. A delicate sweet flavor with a chewy texture. Often served in chowder or battered and fried as a fritter.

Cooter: A soft shelled turtle eaten shell and all. The meat is lean and similar in taste to veal. Usually served pan fried.

Grouper: Very popular, with its moist flaky texture. Usually grilled, sauteed with seasonings.

Mullet: Found only in Florida's warm Gulf of Mexico waters, this richly flavored fish is usually served Southern style , with hush puppies and grits.

Red Snapper: Like grouper with a moist flaky flavor. Usually broiled and fried.

Shrimp: Florida's are the biggest in the United States, with rock, royal red and golden brown as the most popular varieties. Rock are hard to peel, but have a rich meat. Royal red have sweet succulent meat; and golden brown are very sweet. All can be steamed, sauteed, broiled or boiled.

Stone Crab: Coral pink meat is usually served cold with melted butter or mayonnaise dipping sauce. Local law allows the taking of only one claw from male crabs, which are returned to the ocean to grow another. Don't miss this unique Florida taste treat!

Rick's for some cheap drinks.

neon guitar signs, so go early. 1100 Packer Street, Key West, FL 33041. Tel: (305) 296 0650

• **Cuban Roast Pork**

Ingredients: 3 pounds Boston butt pork; 1 tablespoon of: cumin, oregano, garlic, salt, sugar, olive oil, onion; 2 tablespoons soy sauce and $1/2$ cup water.

Method: Put soy sauce and water in bottom of large baking pan. Cover pork with spices and marinate overnight in refrigerator. Roast in oven at 358° for 4-5 hours until meat is tender. Serve with yellow saffron rice.

Fiddlestix

Ocala is known for thoroughbred race-horses, charming B&B's, crystal clear springs and excellent beef.

Owner Steve Christoff loves to visit with his guests and may challenge you to stimulating discussion of politics, so bone up on your general knowledge and better bring your newspaper in case a heated debate ensues! 1016 SE Third Avenue, Ocala. FL 32671. Tel: (904) 629 8000.

• **Blackened Prime Rib**

Ingredients: 15 pounds choice rib roast with ribs; $1/2$ cup Lea & Perrins Worcestershire sauce; 5 tablespoons salt; 4 tablespoons minced garlic; 3 tablespoons black pepper; 1 head of leaf lettuce; 2 cups of water; 5 celery stalks; 2 large white onions, diced; 2 tablespoons of each: paprika, cayenne pepper, garlic

Grab your garlic and visit Mario's Restaurant on a full moon night.

alt, horseradish.

Method: Baste the meat with the worcestershire sauce. Rub the salt, minced garlic and black pepper into the meat.

Cover the whole roast with leaf lettuce leaves. Place in pan on top of steam rack. Put the water in bottom of pan. Add the celery stalks and diced white onions.

Cook for $3\frac{1}{2}$ hours at 275°. Let sit at 145° for 1 hour. To blacken the sliced meat: bread the meat on both sides with the seasoning mixture of paprika, cayenne pepper, garlic salt and horseradish.

Sear meat for 15 seconds, serve hot. Best with baked potatoes, steamed vegetables, red wine and raspberry sherbet.

Cafe L'Europe

One of Palm Beach's most elegant restaurants, Cafe L'Europe consistently wins top awards for its food, service and atmosphere. The charming sophisticated setting features walnut wall panels, ceiling fans, pink banquettes, individual table lamps, and soft classical music. Service is attentive and courteous.

Proceeds from their Summer Specials are donated to the World Hunger Foundation. 150 Worth Avenue, Palm Beach. Tel: (407) 655 4020.

• *Champagne Poached Norwegian Salmon with Salmon Caviar and Wilted Spinach*
Ingredients: 1 pound filet skinned

salmon; 24 ounces leaf spinach, washed and dried; 2 cups champagne; 1 cup fish stock; 1 cup heavy cream; 3 ounces salmon caviar; 1 clove minced garlic; 1 clove nutmeg; 2 ounce minced shallot; 1 pinch saffron; 2 ounces butter (unsalted); 1 lemon; 12 sprigs fresh dill.

Method: Cut salmon into 4 ounce diamonds. In sauce pan lightly saute minced shallots, adding juice of lemon, fish stock and $1/2$ cup of champagne. Place Salmon in pan, cover with tight fitting lid.

Place in oven for 5 minutes. Saute garlic , add spinach until softened. Using a 2 inch circular ring mold, place spinach on plate. Remove salmon from oven, and reduce liquid. Add saffron, cream, reduce by half. Pass through fine strainer, add remaining butter. Whisk and season, spooning around spinanch. Spoon remaining champagne over warm salmon and place on top of spinach. Garnish with caviar and dill sprigs.

Bern's Steak House

Since 1956, Bern's Steak House has been serving up unforgettable steaks, fish, chicken, and desserts amidst a bizarre decor that one could only describe as 'early American bordello.' Locals and tourists are more than willing to stand in line for Bern's top quality prime USDA steaks, served by cut, thickness, weight and style. He has collected over 7,000 wines for you to choose from, and the dessert menu is so vast you couldn't get

through it in one lifetime. Owner Bern Laxer, a charming eccentric who dresses like a high school janitor, will personally escort you through his incredible state of the art kitchen, where the fish is so fresh they wait to be selected from Bern's 4 1200 gallon tanks. He also grows the restaurant's vegetables himself, designs his own dinnerware, and mills his own flour. If Bern can't find what he wants for his unusual restaurant, he invents it. A food orgy you'll never forget. 1208 South Howard Ave Tampa. FL 33606. Tel: (813) 251 2421.

• *Brazilian Snow*

Ingredients: 4 ounces fresh coffee beans roasted but unground; 1 pint vanilla ice cream; whipped cream and cherries.

Method: Using a small grain grinder grind the coffee as finely as possible Sprinkle a medium coating of the coffee, mixing ice cream carefully with the coffee. Scoop the coffee and ice cream 7-8 times. Top with a dollop of whipped cream. Garnish with a sprinkle of the ground coffee and a cherry. Serves 3-4, make as quickly as possible!

Raintree Restaurant

In the spirit of other adventurers, Raintree owners Tristan and Alex MacDonald left England in 1979 in a 45 foot yacht, navigating the open Atlantic for their final stop in St. Augustine. In 1980, they opened the beautiful Raintree and have received Golden Spoon and Silver Spoon awards ever since for their

naginative, delicious food. 102 San
Marco Avenue, St. Augustine. Tel: (904)
24 7211.

Chef Gaere MacDonald's Roasted Pe-
an Meringue

Ingredients: 8 egg whites; 1 pound confectioner's sugar, sifted; 2 tablespoons
cornstarch; 1 teaspoon red wine vin-
gar; $1/2$ pound roasted chopped pecan
nuts; fresh raspberries; 1 pint cream; 1
tablespoon sugar;1 teaspoon vanilla
xtract. Fresh mint sprigs.

Method: To make meringue, whip egg
whites at medium speed until creamy,
then at high speed until peaks are stiff
but not dry. Add sifted confectioner's
sugar, cornstarch, red wine vinegar,
using hand whip. Take care not to flat-
ten egg whites. Gently fold in roasted
pecan pieces. Split the meringue into 2
1x 8 inch pans, lined with lightly oiled
wax paper. Bake in 325° oven until light
brown with a crisp top. Allow to cool
unrefrigerated.

While meringues cool, prepare
chantilly cream", by whipping the
cream until stiff. Add the sugar, vanilla
xtract. Let set in the refrigerator a few
minutes. Layer the meringue with the
chantilly cream. Garnish top with fresh
raspberries and a fresh sprig of mint.

We could not leave you without the
recipe for a very popular Florida dessert,
Key Lime Pie.

Sophie Kay's Key Lime Pie

Ingredients: 2 envelopes unflavored gelatin; 1 cup sugar, divided in half portions; $1/4$ teaspoon salt, 4 eggs separated; $1/2$ cup lime juice, $1/4$ cup water,

Gutted and descaled fish when you buy from the waterfront.

1 teaspoon grated lime peel; 2 cups
whipped cream; 9 inch baked cooled OR
graham cracker pie shell; lime slices
and whipped cream to garnish.

Method: Combine gelatin, $1/2$ cup sugar
and salt in medium sauce pan. Beat egg
yolks, lime juice and water; stir into
gelatin mixture. Cook and stir until
mixture comes to a boil. Remove from
heat. Stir in lime peel. Chill until mixture mounds slightly when dropped from
a spoon. Beat egg whites until soft peaks
form. Gradually beat in remaining $1/2$
cup sugar until still peaks form. Fold egg
white mixture into gelatin mixture. Fold
in whipped cream. Chill until mixture
is almost firm. Put into prepared pie
shell. Garnish with lime slices and
whipped cream.

TRAVEL TIPS

ACCOMMODATION

Budget motel or deluxe resort? Cosy B&B or self-catering apartment? The choice of accommodation in Florida is enormous, varied and extraordinarily good value.

You can save money by visiting Florida out of season (April to December) when accommodation prices plummet by as much as half. The exception is the Panhandle and northern East Coast, the only bit of Florida to feel the cold in winter, where prices are lower in October to May. Here, for visitors from abroad, is a run-down on some of the accommodation options and facilities on offer. Florida accommodations are generally spacious with room for up to four people in some double rooms. There is often no charge for children under 18 sharing with their parents. Another popular option is self-catering accommodation. Rooms supplied with cooking facilities are known as 'efficiencies' and can be found in most budget or moderate hotels and motels. Self-catering apartments (condominiums or 'condos') are an excellent solution for families, though most have a minimum stay of three to seven days. Families should also look out for hotel resorts. A 'resort' in local terms does not mean a town. Instead it refers to the facilities provided by a hotel, motel or condo property, such as a range of different accommodation, sports facilities, games rooms, health club and a choice of dining. Many resorts now offer special children's programmes as well.

ARRIVAL

Most US airlines operate regular scheduled services to Florida from numerous destinations within the US and Canada. But since deregulation of the airways and the air traffic controllers' strike, routes and schedules have been slightly irregular. Visitors, are therefore advised to consult a travel agent before choosing a flight. A variety of discount fares and "package deals" which can significantly cut round-trip rates to and from Florida are also available. Generally, domestic carriers with regular commuter services to Miami International Airport are American, Pan Am, United, Continental, TWA, Delta, Northwest, Braniff, Piedmont and Western.

- **Tampa International Airport**: Is served by US Air, American, Continental, Delta, Pan Am, Northwest, Piedmont, TWA, Air Canada and United
- **Orlando International Airport**: Is served by Northwest, US Air, Continental, Delta, American, Pan Am, Ozark, TWA, Air Canada and United.
- **Fort Lauderdale-Hollywood:** Is served by Continental, United, TWA, Delta, Pan Am, Northwest, Ozark and Western.
- **Jacksonville:** Is served by Delta and Pan Am.
- **Miami International Airport:** Is served by many international airline companies including Air Panama, Cayman Airways, Lacasa, Iberia, Aeroperu, Lan Chile, Air France, British Airways, KLM-Royal Dutch Airlines, Air Jamaica, BWIA, Dominica, Mexico, Aerolines Argentinas and Air Canada. Air Canada, CP Air, Eastern Provincial, Nordair and Western offer connecting flights, usually through Montreal, to major destinations in Florida. Jacksonville features direct routes to Spain and from London, and Orlando features a direct service to Belgium.

The only direct scheduled flights from the UK are London to Miami and Orlando, though several airlines and tour operators offer direct charter flights and one-stop services from regional airports such as Manchester and Glasgow. There are one-stop flights from Dublin's Eire Airport as well as from Auckland's New Zealand Airport and flights that stop twice departing from Melbourne and Brisbane in Australia.

Florida is also a good jumping-off point for

direct flights to many exotic destinations including the islands of the Caribbean. Non-stop services to foreign destinations such as Mexico City, Acapulco, Rio de Janeiro, Buenos Aires, Paris and Amsterdam are sometimes offered.

Piedmont is the major intra-Florida carrier, although a number of smaller air commuter, charter and taxi lines serve outlying communities. Check with any travel bureau for the lastest details. In these times of competitive ticket pricing, some major carriers serve smaller cities at competitive fares.

In total Florida has 32 airports. Tampa International, opened in 1971 and renovated in 1982, has been rated the best airport in the United States by the Airline Passengers Association. However, the new Orlando Jetport looks set to overtake it.

Major Florida Airports
• Fort Lauderdale Tel: (305) 357 6100
• Jacksonville Tel: (904) 741 2000
• Key West Tel: (305) 296 5439
• Miami Tel: (305) 871 7090
• Orlando Tel: (407) 471 7400
• St Petersburg/Clearwater Tel: (813) 531 1451
• Tampa Tel: (813) 276 3400

Some hotels provide airport transfers, while car rental companies operate shuttle services to their parking lots. There are also local bus services and lots of taxis.

By Sea
• **Cruise Ship**: You can travel to or leave Florida on a cruise ship. You can also book one of many ships while in the state for cruises to a variety of exotic ports including South American and Caribbean ports.

There are seven major cruise ship ports in Florida, with Miami and Port Everglades being the leading ports in terms of volume. Minor ports include St Petersburg, Madeira Beach, Treasure Island and Port Manatee. You can choose from a variety of ship sizes, fares, ports of calls and destinations and period of sailing.

Once again check with a local travel or cruise agent or study the travel advertisments once you reach Florida and you will be able to find a cruise that best caters to your needs and schedules. All cruise ports offer free parking facilities for those who are driving their own car to their cruise departure point.

Although Florida offers year-round cruise

departures into either the Atlantic, Caribbean or Gulf of Mexico, there are also seasonal - warr weather - cruises. If you are short of time you ca also embark on a short trip or a dinner cruise o along the waterways and rivers.

• **Yacht**: You can cruise into any of Florida ports, on your own yacht. Most marinas offe slips and facilities for waterway transients. Th Intracostal Waterway parallels the east and wes coasts of the state. Write to the Department c Natural Resources, Crown Building, Tallahassee FL 32304 for a copy of Florida Boating.

By Rail
Amtrak offers slow, but leisurely, service to Florid. from America's Midwest, Northeast and South and connecting service from points west - t many Florida cities. Amtrak stations are locate at Jacksonville, Kissimmee, Lakeland, Ocala Orlando, Sanford, Sebring, Winter Haven, Win ter Park, Tampa, Delray Beach, Deerfield Beach Fort Lauderdale, Hollywood, Miami and Wes Palm Beach. Amtrak offers Auto Train ferry-type service from Lorton, Virginia (near Washington DC), to Sanford, near Orlando for passenger who want to take their car along. For information on all rail service to Florida, call Amtrak's toll free number: Tel: (800) 872 7245.

By Road
The Greyhound service at Tel: (800) 237 821 provides plies throughout the state of Florida Smaller operators which boast of Florida route include North Star Lines, Gulf Transportatio Co, ABC Coach Lines, Jefferson Lines, Inc, Or ange Belt Stages, Southeastern Stages, Bluebird Iowa Coaches, Inc, and Illini-Swallow Lines Inc

The Gray Line bus service also offers a variety of sightseeing tours within Florida, while Greyhound, Trailways and Gulf Coast Moto Lines have special travel services between Florida cities.

CAMPING

Camping is popular in Florida where there are privately run campgrounds in resorts and na tional and state parks which boast ideal camping facilities which range from elaborate to no-frills rustic. Many campgrounds offer on-site trailer and tent hire, but it is advisable to make reserva tions in advance.

The Florida Camping Directory lists some 200 sites around the state which list facilities and on-site amenities. For a copy of the directory ntact the Florida Campground Association, 538 N Plaza Drive, Tallahassee, FL 32308-364. Tel: (904) 656 8878. For information about mping in the state's parks, contact the Florida epartment of Natural Resources, Bureau of perational Services, Mail Station 535, 3900 ommonwealth Boulevard, Tallahassee, FL 2399. Tel: (904) 488 9872.

You can even hire a recreational vehicle V) from Cruise America, 5959 Blue Lagoon rive, Suite 250, Miami, FL 33126. Tel: (305) 52 9611 or (800) 327 7778 which provides cal motorhome rentals from several destina- ns within Florida. The service also includes rport transfers.

AR HIRE

ar hire firms like **Hertz**, **Avis**, **Budget** and **Na- onal** can be found in most Florida tourism nters, at international airports and even some naller airports. Shop around for the best rates nd features. Often, smaller local rental firms utside the airports offer less expensive, more exible rates than the large national companies. heck insurance coverage provisions before you re a car.

Most automobile rental agencies require ou to be at least 21 years old (sometimes 25), nd to hold a valid driver's license and a major edit card, before permitting you to drive off in ne of their cars. Some will take cash deposit, metimes as high as $500, in lieu of a credit ard. Foreign travelers may need to produce an ternational driver's license or a license from eir own country. Liability is not automatically cluded in the terms of your lease, so advertised tes usually do not include additional fees for surance. You should also check with your rline, bus or rail agent or travel agent for special ackage deals that provide rental cars at reduced tes.

Drivers must abide by Florida traffic laws. r a copy of *Florida Driver Information*, write to e following address: Division of Tourism, Di- ct Mail Section, 107 W Gaines St, Tallahassee, 32304.

HILDREN

orida's may be one of the few vacation getaways at cater to the entire family and especially nildren. Children are welcome in restaurants, nd many family-style eateries feature kid's por- ns. Many hotels in every price bracket frequenty fer free lodging for children up to 18 staying with their parents, so look out for bargains. Babies' and children's items such as baby foods and high sun protection factor sunblock are readily available. Larger theme parks provide a range of child services from changing rooms with all the requisite toiletries to prams. Name tags for kids are often available at park information of- fices so that lost children can be speedily reu- nited with their family if the authorities know who to contact.

Perhaps the greatest danger to young chil- dren is the sun. Children who are going to be exposed to the sunlight for any length of time should be liberally doused in high protection sunscreen. Hats and caps should be used for both younger and teenaged children.

CLIMATE

Florida's official nickname "The Sunshine State" reflects the economic importance of climate to its visitors and residents. Often called Florida's most important resource, the climate is usually pleas- ant and uniform. General climatic conditions range from a zone of transition between temper- ate and sub-tropical conditions in the extreme northern interior to the tropical climate found in the Florida Keys. The chief factors affecting the state's climate are latitude, proximity to the cur- rents of the Atlantic Ocean or the Gulf of Mexico and numerous inland lakes.

Summers throughout the state are long, warm and relatively humid. Winters although punctuated with periodic invasions of cool to occasionally cold air, are mild due to the south- erly latitude (24° 20' and 31°N) and relatively warm adjacent sea waters.

Coastal areas in all sections of Florida aver- age slightly warmer in winter and cooler in summer than inland points at the same latitude. The Gulf Stream, which flows around the western tip of Cuba through the Florida Straits and north- ward around the lower east coast, exerts a warm- ing influence to the southern east coast because of the prevailing easterly winds in that direction.

Frost: Although average minimum temperatures during the coolest months range from the middle 40s in the north to the middle 50s in the south, no place on the mainland is entirely safe from frost or freezing. With few exceptions, these cold waves seldom last more than two or three consecutive days. It is rare for temperatures to remain below freezing throughout the day any- where in the state. On the first night of a cold wave there usually is considerable wind which, because of the continual mixing of the air, prevents marked temperature differences between high and low ground. By the second night, winds usually have subsided and radiational cooling under clear skies accelerates the temperature drop after sundown.

Some winters, often several in succession, pass without widespread freezing in the southern areas. The most distressing winters to the agriculture industry are those with more than one severe cold wave, interspersed with periods of relative warmth. The later freezes almost always find vegetation in a tender stage of new growth.

Noteworthy cold spells of the 20th century were in January 1905, December 1906, December 1928, December 1934, January 1940, February 1947, the winter of 1957-58, December 1962, January 1977, January 1981, January 1982, Christmas 1983 and January 1985. It was the 1962 freeze that killed many tropical palms and Australian pines thoughout the central part of the state. The most severe freezes recoded in the state were those of 1894, 1895, 1899, 1983 and 1985. The lowest recorded Florida temperature was 2 degrees below zero at Tallahassee on Feb 13, 1899.

Humidity & Fog: Humidity is the degree of wetness or dryness of the air and is measured by a percentage ratio called "relative humidity." This is a ratio of the amount of moisture and temperature at a given spot to the maximum amount (99 percent) of moisture that could be contained by the same air at the same spot. The warmer the air becomes the more moisture it can hold. Therefore a person can feel stickier on a warm day with 80 percent humidity than on a cold day with same humidity.

The climate of Florida is humid. In land areas with greater temperature extremes enjoy slightly lower relative humidity, especially during hot weather. On the average, variations in relative humidity from one place to another are small.

Heavy fogs are usually confined to the night and early morning hours when the humidity range is about 85 to 95 percent. Fogs are more prevalent in the late fall, winter, and early spring months. They occur on the average about 35 to 40 days per year over the extreme northern portion; 25 to 30 days per year in the central portion; and less than 10 days per year in the extreme southern areas. These fogs usually dissi-

pate soon after sunrise. Heavy daytime fog seldom observed in the state.

Temperature: In winter, Southern Florida is or of the warmest places on the United State mainland. Summers generally are hot througho the state, although sea breezes tend to modify th climate along the coastal areas. Even thoug Southern Florida is 400 miles closer to the tropi than Nothern Florida, it has fewer hot days eac summer because of the sea breezes. Summe heat is tempered in all areas by frequent afternoo or early evening thunderstorms. These shower which occur on the average of about half of th summer days, are accompanied frequently by rapid 10 to 20° drop in temperature, resulting comfortable weather for the remainder of the da

Because most of the large scale wind pa terns affecting Florida have passed over wate surfaces, hot drying winds seldom occur.

The highest recorded temperature was 10€ at Monticello on June 29, 1931.

Rainfall: An estimated 148 billion gallons of ra falls upon Florida daily. Because of the State relatively flat terrain, much of the rainwater filte through porous 7,000 lakes (of 10 acres surfac area or more) in Florida. The Floridan Aquife which underlies most of the State, supplie groundwater to all but the southernmost an westernmost sections of Florida. It feeds mo than 100 large springs that add more than billion gallons of water daily to runoff. Seventee of these springs are of the first magnitude, eac contributing flows in excess of 65 million gallor per day.

The state's rainfall is varied both in annu amount and in seasonal distribution. Individu rainfall measuring stations have annual average from about 50 to 65 inches. In the Florida Key annual averages are only about 40 inches. Th main areas of high annual rainfall are in th extreme northerwestern counties and at the south eastern end of the peninsula. Many localitie have received more than 100 inches in a caler dar year. In contrast, most localities received le than 40 inches in a calendar year.

In the summer "rainy season" there is clos to a 50-50 chance some rain will fall on a give day. During the remainder of the year, the chance are much less, some rain being likely on one c two days per week. The seasonal distributio changes somewhat from north to south. In th northwestern areas or Panhandle, there are tw vet periods: late winter or early spring, and again during summer, and one pronounced low point, October-November. A secondary low point occurs in April and May. On the peninsula, the most striking features of the seasonal distribution are the dominance of summer rainfall (generally more than half the average annual total falls in the four-month period June through September) and the rather abrupt start and end of the summer rainy season."

Most localities have at some time experienced two-hours rainfalls in excess of three inches, and 24 hour amounts of near or greater than 10 inches.

Thunderstorms: Florida is the thunderstorm capital of the nation. A study by the National Oceanic and Atmospheric Administration shows Fort Myers averages 100 days with lightning annually, the Tampa Bay area, 90 and Miami, 76. The so-called "lightning belt" in Florida is an area from between Orlando and Tampa south along the west coast to Fort Myers and east to Lake Okeechobee.

Few of the state's thunderstorms last more than two hours and are attributed to hot, wet air close to the ground combined with an unstable atmosphere. A lightning bolt lasts just a thousandth of a second, but packs around 30,000 degrees Fahrenheit in a one-inch channel that can deliver a shock in the 6,000-10,000 amp range.

Snow: Snowfall in Florida is rare. The greatest recorded snowfalls in Florida occured on the same date, February 13, in 1899 and 1958. In 1899, four inches were measured at Lake Butler in Union County, and one-half inch at Bartow in Polk County. In 1958, most of Florida west of the Swannee River received two to three inches of snow while areas east of the river and north of about latitude 30 degrees measured one to two inches. Three inches measured at Tallahassee in February 1958 is the greatest ever recorded there since records began in 1886.

It is doubtful, however, that Florida ever experienced as wide-ranging a snowfall as occurred in the winter of 1977. Recorded as the most consistently cold January on record, the first month of that year saw the appearance of snow all the way from Georgia border into Miami. Traces were measured in Broward and Dade counties, in Palm Beach for the first time. A half inch was measured in the Tampa Bay area, and an inch in Saint Augustine and parts of Volusia County. Snow and sleet fell on three different days during that month in 1977 in Jacksonville. And in Fort Myers, recordkeepers recorded snowflakes during that spell for only the forth time in its history. Pensacola also measured an inch, and Orlando reported snow on two consecutive days.

Drought: Drought is a prolonged period of below normal or expected precipitation. The annual cycle of temperature and rainfall leads to seasonal droughts in many areas of the state. Drought conditions in South Florida occur every year that winter rainfall is even slightly below normal. In North Florida, a seasonal drought occurs most often in fall and spring.

A study of several regions of the state from 1980 to 1982, when compared against a 30-year mean (1951-1980), revealed a decline in rainfall for the Penascola, Tallahassee, Jacksonville and Lake Okeechobee areas. By contrast, that same study revealed a rise in rainfall for the Fort Myers and West Palm Beach areas.

The most severe lack of rainfall was recorded for the Pensacola area during the years 1889-1894, when three consecutive years recorded less than 45 inches of rainfall.

Earthquakes: Florida is relatively free of earthquakes, thanks to the limestone base that supports the land and tends to act as a shock absorber for any subterranean shifting that might occur.

The University of Florida is the state's only seismographic recording station affliated with the national network that monitors earthquake activity.

Tornadoes: April, May and June are considered peak periods for tornadoes. Florida, with 20 twisters a year, ranks eighth in the nation's annual numbers of tornadoes. Fortunately, many of Florida's tornadoes are the weaker, waterspout-type of storm. The more severe tornadoes, associated with a squall-line, occur mainly in Florida's Panhandle during February and March.

Tornadoes can surpass hurricanes in deadly force. The counterclockwise, upward movement of air within the twister causes rapid expansion, cooling and condensation, which contribute to the formation of the dark clouds of the tornado funnel. A tornado is seen most often in muggy, oppressive weather when large thunderstorms are apparent. Rain, hail and flashes of lightning may precede the storm. Inside the funnel, air pressure is so low it can cause structures to explode. Destructive paths of tornadoes average about a quarter mile wide and 16 miles long, although many in Florida are shorter. Tornadoes travel from southwest to northeast.

Over water, a tornado takes the form of a waterspout. It is safe boating practice to stay away from any thunderstorm cell, especially any so-called "anvil-shaped" clouds whose level bases can form the deadly swirling winds.

If a tornado is spotted, move away from it. Persons in open country should seek a depression and hide inside it. In a house, residents are advised to open windows to help balance the air pressure and then move to a secure location such as a bathroom or another room centrally situated within the house.

If tornado conditions are present, weather forecasters will issue warnings or watches on emergency broadcasting stations. A "tornado watch" means tornadoes and severe thunderstorms are possible in the area; a "tornado warning" means a tornado has been detected in the area.

Hurricanes Florida and other Gulf and Atlantic coastal states lie in the general path of tropical hurricanes. Most of these vicious storms spawn in the Carribbean Sea or in an area east of the Lesser Antilles in the Atlantic Ocean.

Florida's vulnerability varies with the progress of the hurricane season. August and early September tropical storms normally approach the state from the east or southeast, but as the season progresses into late September and October, the region of maximum hurricane activity (concerning Florida) shifts to the western Caribbean. Most storms that move into Florida approach from the south or southwest, entering the Keys, the Miami area or along the west coast.

Caused by wind rushing toward a low-pressure area, hurricanes take the form of huge doughnuts. In the northern hemisphere, high winds revolve counterclockwise around a calm center or "eye". The movement is clockwise in the southern hemisphere.

The lowest sea level pressure ever recorded in an Atlantic storm was 26.13 inches measured inside Hurricane Gilbert on Sept. 13, 1988. I t was the most intense storm ever measured in the western hemisphere. Its winds gusted at rimes 218 mph. Gilbert's destuctive path took it across Jamaica, the Cayman Islands and the Yucatan Peninsula, making final landfall on the norhern Mexican coast.

The second lowest barometric reading, 26.35 inches, occurred at Long Key in the Florida Keys on Sept. 2, 1935. This occurred during the infamous "Labor Day Hurricane" when maximum winds were not recorded because wind measuring equipment was blown down before the peak of the storm was reached. Engineer calculated that winds of 200 to 250 mph would have been required to account for some of the damage caused.

Ranging from 60 to 1,000 miles in diameter a hurricane is defined by winds of more than 74 mph, accompanied by heavy rains, extremely large waves and dangerously high tides. Immediately outside the eye, winds may surge as high a 125 to 150 mph or more, blowing rain in horizontal sheets. The storm, itself, has forward movement and can travel very slowly or at speeds of more than 60 mph.

Once a hurricane is formed, it poses a triple threat to people and property in its path. Wind waves and rain are its three most destructive forces. Any one of these forces is capable of causing severe damage.

Hurricane rains often come as a blessing to parched lands, but they may also come too fast and cause wholesale flooding and destruction The average hurricane will drop some six inches of water over a given area. The extremes of this average range from practically no rain to down pours measured in feet.

After an average of eight to ten days of blowing, the normal hurricane dies by either running too far from the tropical latitudes of its birth, or by advancing over land. Uneven land masses hinder the free flow of winds and fail to offer the supply of moisture the storm needs to keep going. Many hurricanes lose their punch while still at sea and hit land classified only a tropical storms (winds under 74 mph).

Winds: Prevailing winds over the southern peninsula are southeast and east. Over the remainder of the state, wind directions are influenced locally by convectional forces inland and the "land and sea breeze" effect near the coast Consequently, prevailing directions are somewhat erratic but, in general, follow a pattern of northerly in winter and southerly in summer Martch and April average the windinest months High local winds of short duration occur occasionally with thunderstorms in summer and with old fronts moving across the state in other seasons. Average annual wind speed in Florida is 8.6 mph.

CRIME & SAFETY

The following safety tips are offered to help you and your family have a safe and enjoyable vacation in Florida. Please take the same precautions on your Floridian vacation as you would at home.

• Invest in travelers' checks. Secure your checks and other valuables – jewelry, cash, cameras and travel documents in your hotel safe. Only take the essential valuables you will need when traveling.

• Always lock your vehicle. Lock valuables in the trunk or glove compartment so that they are out of sight.

• Park under a street light whenever possible. Make sure that the doors are locked. Avoid suspicious characterers in parking lots.

• If you are unsure about the safety of an area, seek advice from the front desk staff of your hotel, motel or campground.

• Teach your children to find the proper authorities should they wander away from you. Police officers and security guards are familiar to most children.

• Always lock your front and patio doors while you are in your hotel rooms and when you leave. Ask for identification from anyone unfamiliar who comes to your door.

• If an emergency arises, seek the nearest telephone and dial 911. Someone will be able to assist you in securing an ambulance, law enforcement agent and/or the fire department.

CUSTOMS

Customs declarations must be filled in by all travelers arriving from outside the US Fresh foods, agricultural products, items from Cuba, Kampuchea, North Korea and Vietnam, obscene material, lottery tickets, chocolates, liqueurs and pre-Columbian art will be confiscated on arrival. Illegal drug smuggling is subject to harsh penalties. There is no limit on currency brought into the US, but amounts exceeding US$5,000 (or their foreign equivalent) must be declared.

Visitors who are over 18 years of age are given the following duty free allowance: 200 cigarettes and 100 cigars (not Cuban). Visitors of 21 years and over are allowed an additional one liter of alcohol for personal consumption.

DISABLED TRAVELLERS

Facilities for the disabled are widespread in the US, and Florida is no exception. Public buildings are required to have some form of access for the wheelchair-bound, and many public buses are now supplied with wheelchair lifts. Local telephone directories list disabled support groups such as deaf service centres which can provide 'interpreters' who 'speak' American Sign Language, and information on TDDs (Telecommunication Devices for the Deaf) - telephones whereby deaf travelers can send and receive messages. The visually impaired, traveling with guide dogs, will find it relatively easy to take their dogs into attractions.

Most attractions accept disabled visitors, though viewing may be somewhat restricted and access to certain rides impossible or forbidden for safety reasons. Generally, efforts are made to provide tips, assistance and wheelchairs for disabled visitors. Walt Disney World offers a useful Guidebook for Disabled Visitors, and transport services with motorised platforms between its hotels and the parks.

Specially equipped hotel rooms are also available and should be booked well in advance. Avis, Hertz and National car rentals have a limited number of hand-controlled cars available. Again, early reservations are a must.

Useful Addresses: Information about individual and group tours for disabled travellers is available from *The Society for the Advancement of Travel for the Handicapped*, 26 Court Street (Penthouse), Brooklyn NY 11242. (Tel: (781) 858 5483). For a brochure and further details about services for disabled visitors to Florida, contact the *Bureau of Domestic Tourism*, Collins Building (Room 526), 107 Gains Street, Tallahassee, FL 32399-2000.

Immigration laws covering the entry qualifications for mentally handicapped travellers to the US should be checked out in advance with a travel agent or directly with the US Embassy before departure.

DRINKING

The sale and consumption of alcohol in bars, restaurants, stores and other public places is restricted to adults aged 21 and over. It is also illegal to drink have an opened can or bottle of an alcoholic beverage in a car.

DRIVING

Renting a car in Florida is cheaper than anywhere

else in the US. Car rental companies are located throughout the state, with concessions at major airports and some hotels. Car rental companies operating in Florida include:

Alamo Tel: (305) 522 0000/(800) 327 9633
Avis Tel: (305) 635 7777/(800) 331 1212
Budget Tel: (407) 423 4141/(800) 525 0700
Dollar Tel: (813) 289 4912/(800) 421 6868
Hertz Tel: (407) 275 6430/(800) 654 3131
National Tel: (305) 638 5900/(800) 328 4567
Thrifty Tel: (305) 871 2277/(800) 376 2277
Value Tel: (305) 429 8300/(800) 327 2501

The minimum age limit for a driver's licence in Florida is 16; the minimum car rental limit is 21, though many companies impose the limit at 25. Arranging car rental in advance can prevent the latter restriction from ruining a holiday. Additions to the basic rental charge include CDW (Collision Damage Waiver), which covers damage to the vehicle, and a small state tax; both of these are charged on a daily basis, full insurance is also available.

Credit cards are the preferred method of payment, otherwise a large cash deposit will be required. Major airlines and tour companies offer a wide range of good value fly-drive packages which conveniently tie up all these details in advance.

In general, foreign nationals can drive and hire a car in the US for a period of up to one year with a valid full driver's licence from their country of origin, provided they have held it for one year. Before setting off in an unfamiliar rented car, check all the systems. Power steering is common even in the lowest range cars; be aware of central locking; and beware of automatic seatbelts which pinion unsuspecting drivers and front seat passengers to their seats as the doors shut.

Fuel Gas (petrol) is cheap. It is sold by the US gallon (3.8 litres), and rental cars generally run on unleaded gas available in three grades. At many self-service gas stations it is necessary to pay first (or leave a credit card with the cashier) to release the pump.

Rules and Regulations
• Driving is on the right
• Speed limits on interstate roads and highways are set at 55mph, with some exceptions where the limit is raised to 65mph. In built-up areas limit vary between 20 and 40 mph.
• In Florida it is legal to turn right on a red light unless posted otherwise. The car must come to a complete half before turning. In built-up area avoid the right-hand lane unless intending to turn right.
• Parking can be a problem. Look for designated metered parking places or find a car park. Illegally parked vehicles are ticketed and/or towed away with remarkable alacrity.

ELECTRICITY

The electrical current: in the US is 110 volts AC most sockets are designed for two-pronged plugs. Most European visitors will need an adaptor for their electrical appliances; these can be purchased from some electrical goods stores, or ask at the front desk of large tourist hotels.

EMERGENCIES

Dial: 911
Emergency help is eaily summoned in the US by the use of this single number. An operator or despatcher will connect calls to the appropriate emergency service including the police and fire departments, ambulance and medical services. To ensure the emergency services arrive as quickly as possible give accurate directions including the street name and nearest cross-section together with any further details to assist them.

On interstate highways, call boxes have been installed every quarter to half mile. These boxes allow callers to alert police, ambulance and mechanical services without dialing 911.

ETIQUETTE

In general Floridians are so laid back and welcoming it is difficult to image how to offend them. Certainly the dress code for restaurants and social gatherings is informal to a degree, but this does not apply on the beach. Topless sunbathing for women is actually illegal, though allowances are made for bare-breasted visitors on certain sections of the beach in more risqué resort areas such as Miami. Do not try this around the hotel swimming pool, or on a family beach in the Panhandle.

Check out local reaction with a discreet enquiry at the hotel. Smokers in Florida will find the atmosphere a lot more friendly than in health crazed California.

Some restaurants, particularly of the family variety, will provide both smoking areas for addicts of the weed and non-smoking areas. Movie theaters, public transport, elevators and many public buildings are smoke-free zones.

HEALTH

There is no national health system to provide medical cover for foreign citizens visiting the US, and private health care is exorbitantly expensive. Therefore, it is vital for foreign travellers to arrange health insurance before they leave home. Travel agents and tour companies can provide information and arrange a policy. Keep all insurance documents in a safe place.

For minor ailments, pharmacies (drug stores) are plentiful and usually open between 09.00 hrs and 21.00hrs; most larger towns and cities have walk-in medical and dental clinics listed in the telephone directory.

Sunburn is a common complaint, and a chronic case of it is agony. If you are set on getting a suntan, do so gradually. Begin with a sunscreen, containing PABA and marked with its numerical level of safeguard, and work up to less protective tanning lotions. The glare from Florida's azure seas and white sands increases the sun's intensity. Don't neglect to apply sunscreen on overcast days; the sun's ultra-violet rays still penetrate the cloud cover and the shade can lull you into staying outside too long. Just remember the following points:

- Use plenty of sunscreen.
- Wear a hat.
- Restrict the time you spend in the sun, at least on the first few days.
- Drink plenty (not alcohol, which is dehydrating).

Insects: Include a variety of pests.

Bibinoid Flies: Known as love bugs fly in couples into your hair, face or car's windshield.

They do not bite, as they are too busy mating. But they can cause trouble during their May and September appearances in various parts of the state. In moist or wooded hammock areas, black clouds of love bugs occasionally hang over interstates and highways, slowing down traffic as they clog radiators and splatter windshields.

Mosquitoes: Florida is even more infamous for its swarms of mosquitoes. Most big cities have effective mosquito control programes that have effectively curtailed the pest's activities. But pack a bottle of army-issue insect repellent when venturing into backwoods areas like the Everglades is indispensable.

Fire Ants: Tread carefully when outdoors, particularly when barefoot. Grassy fields are prime locations for mounds of fire ants. These tiny red ants inflict a painful, burning sting and leave a reddish weal that turns into a chickenpox-like blister. The blister can become infected if scratched. Some persons are allergic to the sting of a fire ant, and can suffer chest constriction, wheezing, nausea or dizziness that requires prompt medical attention.

Visitors new to tropical or subtropical regions may be startled during their first confrontation with the local cockroach. Often called palmetto bugs, they grow to a large size. They eat book bindings, clothing, paper, garbage, but steer clear of people. Pest control services and regular house cleaning will aid in control, but rarely eradicate roaches.

Sand Flies: Appropriately called "no-see-ums' by the locals, are another pest to sunset beachgoers. They gnaw at your legs as you sink your toes into the sand. Insect repellent can help.

Red Tide: This forms of "sea sickness" is caused by a microscopic organism called gymnodinium brevis (or "Jim Brevis"), always present in Gulf Coast waters in small quantities. It becomes deadly to fish and other marine life when its numbers multipy suddenly, for reasons still unknown to scientists. The coastal waters turn a brownish red color and thousands of dead fish wash ashore. After a few hours in the hot sun, they make beaches unbearable with their foul odor.

HITCHHIKING

Hitchhiking is not advised and may prove to be hazardous in Florida. Legally, hitchhiking is forbidden on toll roads and interstates, and throughout the Florida Keys.

Picking up hitchhiking strangers is also potentially dangerous. If you choose to drive, you should also learn what areas of cities to avoid before starting out. Miami's Liberty City has most notoriously been the scene of criminal incidents involving motorists unfamiliar with the city. Ask questions of your rental clerk at the airport when you arrive or check with tourism offices before taking a drive.

LOST PROPERTY

For lost property in hotels, check with the front desk or hotel security. Cab companies and public transport telephone numbers are listed in local telephone directories. Lost or stolen travellers' cheques and credit cards should be reported to the issuing company immediately (keep a list of the numbers) and to the police. The police should also be informed of lost travel documents, and it is advisable to obtain a police report about valuable items for insurance.

MAPS

Car rental companies are a good source of basic maps, but for extensive touring it is a good idea to pick up large scale Rand McNally motoring maps from a bookstore. (If lost in a city, a helpful rule of thumb is to remember avenues run north-south, and streets east-west.)

Chambers of Commerce produce local maps, details of walking tours, bicycle routes and other points of interest; while state and national parks issue maps of scenic drives, hiking and interpretive trails on admission. The Florida Division of Tourism will provide state maps on application to the Department of Commerce, Division of Tourism, 107 W Gaines Street, Tallahassee, FL 32399-2000 (Tel: (904) 487 1462), or at their offices abroad.

MEDIA

Newspapers: Most Florida communities produce weekly bulletins, while the main cities all have their own daily newspapers such as the Miami Herald, Orlando Sentinel, Tampa Tribune and Jacksonville's Florida Times-Union. There are more than 125 weeklies; including the Spanish language El Imparcial and El Noticiero. The Miami Herald also has a Spanish language section.

The national daily USA Today is widely available from self-service news bins in every town; the New York Times and Wall Street Journal can be found at news stands. A small selection of foreign newspapers may be available in tourist areas.

MONEY MATTERS

Visitors to Florida may encounter problems exchanging foreign currency; the use of American dollar traveler's checks is advised. Foreign currency is extremely difficult to exchange throughout the US.

US travelers' cheques and major credit cards (American Express, Carte Balanche, Diners Club, Mastercard Visa) can be used for most transactions from buying gas to paying restaurant bills. An increasing number of statewide banking corporations and community banks in Florida, including the Barnett, Southeast and Sun Bank

chains, offer foreign exchange services, but this practice is not universal. Banks generally close on Saturday afternoons and Sundays. The increase in the number of foreign visitors has led some department store chains to offer foreign currency exchange services. For non-US visitors here is a run-down on the currency.

The dollar is divided into 100 cents. Dollar bills are all green ($1, 5, 10, 20, 50, 100) so look carefully before spending; coins are half a dollar (50 cents), a quarter (25 cents), a dime (10 cents), a nickel (5 cents),and one cent. Local taxes, which vary throughout the state, are levied on a range of items including clothes, books, sightseeing attractions, restaurant meals and accommodation. The tax may not appear on the price tag.

NATIONAL HOLIDAYS

New Year's Day 1 January
Martin Luther King's Birthday 15 January
President's Day February (third Monday)
Good Friday
Memorial Day May (last Monday)
Independence Day 4 July
Labor Day September (first Monday)
Veterans' Day 11 November
Thanksgiving November (fourth Thursday)
Christmas Day 25 December

OPENING HOURS

Banks: Monday to Thursday
9 am-3 pm, Friday
9 am-5 pm
Drugstores: daily 9am-9pm
some are open 24 hours.
Offices: Monday to Friday 8 am or 9 am-5 pm or 6 pm.
Shops: Supermarkets, Monday to Saturday
8 am-9 pm, Sunday
8 am-7 pm; some are open 24 hours; downtown, Monday to Friday
10 am-6 pm, Saturday
10 am-1 pm or 6 pm; malls,
Monday to Saturday 10 am-9 pm,
Sunday 10 am-6 pm.

ORGANISED TOURS

With Florida's many miles of coastline and proximity to offshore islands, the most obvious opportunity for touring is taking a cruise. These range from two-hour cruises to week-long (or longer) trips to Bermuda, the Bahamas, and beyond.

Many of these longer trips depart from

Miami, but shorter excursions - one-day, half-day, or evening cruises - depart from many places in the state. A few of the shorter trips offer casino gambling on board. For information about local cruises, contact the Visitors and Convention Bureau where you are staying.

PLACES OF WORSHIP
Most communities have churches of several denominations. Contact the local Chamber of Commerce.

POLICE
Law enforcement in the US is divided into three main jurisdictions: City Police within the urban areas; the Sheriff outside the city limits; and the Highway Patrol, who handle traffic accidents and offences beyond the city limits. Other agencies also deal with specific areas of law enforcement such as drugs and major criminal investigations

In an emergency dial 911 for all services. Non-emergency police numbers are listed in local telephone directories.

POST OFFICE
Post office hours vary, but in most places are 09.00 to 16.30 or 17.00hrs on weekdays. Some are open on Saturday mornings. Postage stamps may be purchased at hotels and drugstores as well as post offices. Keep small change for stamp machines. US Mail boxes are blue bins on legs on the sidewalk.

POSTAL SERVICES
Post office hours vary in central, big-city branches and smaller cities and towns. Hotel or motel personnel will answer questions about post office hours nearest you. If you do not know where you will be staying in any particular town, you can receive mail simply by having it addressed to your name, care of General Delivery at the main post office in that town. But you must pick up such mail personally. Check with postal officials about current charges and the variety of mail delivery service available.

PUBLIC TRANSPORT
The most popular method of transport on the ground is, without doubt, the car (see Driving). For more economical, though less convenient travel options, check out Greyhound/Trailways' extensive bus network which con-

nects some 148 Florida destinations. Skeleton Amtrak rail services call at Miami, Jacksonville, Orlando, Tallahassee, Tampa and 19 other stops. Amtrak, 60 NE Massachusetts Avenue, Washington, DC 2002 (Tel: (202) 906 2002/(800) USA RAIL). Lines Inc, PO Box 660362, Dallas, TX 75266-0362 (Tel: (214) 419 3905/(800) 531 5332.

Taxi cabs can be picked up at airports, bus and rail stations or from major hotels. They tend not to cruise the streets looking for fares.

SENIOR CITIZENS
Many hotels, resorts, restaurants and attractions offer seniors discounts or special rates. Be sure to ask if no information is on display.

SPORTS AND RECREATION
Regional visitors' information bureaux can provide a wealth of information about sporting and recreational opportunities in their areas. For the statewide picture, contact:
• *Diving*
Department of Commerce
Division of Tourism Office of Sports Promotion
Collins Building (Suite 510E)
Tallahassee
FL 32399-2000
Tel: (904) 488 8347

• *Fishing and Hunting*
Game and Freshwater Commission
620 S Meridian Street
Tallahassee
FL 32399-1600
Tel: (904) 488 1860

• *Golf*
Florida State Gold Association
PO Box 21177
Sarasota, FL 33585
Tel: (813) 921 5695

• *Polo*
Palm Beach Polo and Country Club,
13198 Forest Hill Boulevard
West Palm Beach, FL 33414
Tel: (407) 798 7000

• *State Parks*
Department of Natural Resources
Office of Communications
3900 Commonwealth Boulevard
Tallahassee, FL 32399-3000
Tel: (904) 488 9872

• *Tennis*
Florida Tennis Association
801 NE 167th Street (Suite 301)
North Miami Beach, FL 33162
Tel: (305) 652 2866

STUDENT AND YOUTH TRAVEL

There are ten youth hostels in Florida, one each in Miami Beach, Daytona Beach, Saint Augustine and Panama City, and two each in Fort Lauderdale, Orlando and St Petersburg. For complete information on these facilities and their requirements, contact the Florida American Youth Hostel, PO Box 533097, Orlando, FL, 32853-3097. Tel: (407) 649 8761.

TELEGRAMS AND TELEX

Western Union and International Telephone and Telegraph (ITT) will take telegram and telex messages by phone. You can check the local phone directory or you can call local information .

TELEPHONE

Public telephones are located in hotel lobbies, drugstores, restaurants, garages, roadside kiosks, convenience stores and other locations through out the state. The cost of making a local call is 25 cents at all pay telephones throughout the state. Long distance call rates decrease after 5 pm, decrease further after 11 pm, and are lower on weekends and holidays.

Florida's telephone system is divided between half a dozen companies. Overseas visitors should note that some of these do not route overseas calls: AT&T and ITT do.

The simplest solution is to call overseas collect via the operator (dial 0), who can also place telephone credit card calls (overseas credit cards are valid). To dial direct from a coin box (dial 011 + country code + area code + telephone number) bring at least $6-worth of quarters, dimes and nickels. This is an appalling juggling operation. Calling from a hotel room will cost more, but it can be worth the time and energy saved.

Codes: Florida is divided into four area codes: north Florida, 904; west central, 813; east central, 407; extreme south, 305. To call within the area code dial 1+telephone number; to call outside the area code dial 1+area code+number. All 800 (toll free) numbers must be prefixed with 1, ie 1+800+telephone number. To call home from anywhere in Florida, you will need first to dial 011 to get the international operator.

Then dial the access code for the country 44 for the UK, 353 for Eire, 61 for Australia, 64 for New Zealand.

TELEVISION AND RADIO

All major Florida cities have stations affiliated with major national networks, local stations and a vast offering of cable television hookups. Local newspapers provide daily and weekly information about television and radio programs.

Among the main stations are CNN for continuous news reports, and ESPN for sports. Radio stations abound with a wide range of formats such as hard or soft rock, easy listening and country-and-western, broken up by news, weather bulletins and commercials.

TIME

Florida has two time zones. Most of the state operates on Eastern Standard Time (GMT -5), while the Panhandle region west of the Apalachicola River keeps Central Standard Time (GMT-6) which is an hour earlier than the rest of the state. All clocks go forward one hour for Daylight Saving begins in May and ends in October.

TIPPING

Service personnel expect tips in Florida. Tipping is at least 15% of the bill, except in extreme cases. A higher tip is expected for exceptional services. Tipping is expected by valet parking in a hotel. Some establishments will include a tip on the bill if the party is large.

The standard tip for a restaurant bill or taxi ride is 15 per cent; 10-20 per cent for barbers and hairdresses; 50 cents per bag for the bellman. Generally, tipping is not required in cafeterias where you serve yourself, unless your tray is carried to your table for you. It is not necessary to tip chambermaids unless you stay several days. Florida hotels generally do not add a service charge to cover gratuities.

TOURIST INFORMATION

Most towns throughout Florida boast at least a Chamber of Commerce, while other cites offer Convention and Visitors Bureaus which will satisfy all travel related enquiries. For basic information before you arrive in Florida you can contact the Florida Division of Tourism, USTTA (US ravel & Tourism Administration) or any of the main regional offices listed in the Directory.

RESTAURANTS

Florida offers a wide variety of foods that can be eaten in the setting of your choice.

These include sandwiches, succulent steaks, juicy fruit, fresh seafood all enjoyed in a variety of restaurants from plush five-star eating to outdoor cafes. Although the basic ingredients are the same they are cooked in a vast variety of styles such as; Bahamian and Creole cooking in the Keys; Cuban cuisine in Miami and Tampa, French and Greek styles, nouvelle cuisine New American-style, spicy Cajun food, and down home country cooking with a distinctive Southern flavour.

Dining out in Florida is a casual affair. Even top restaurants which prefer gentlemen in jackets do not expect ties. Families are welcome just about everywhere, with special children's portions a regular feature on most menus, and money-saving 'early bird' specials (usually served between 17.00 and 19.00hrs) especially popular.

VISA REGULATION

Holders of full valid passports can fill a visa waiver form issued by travel agents or at your airline check-in. This form is to be handed to US immigration control on arrival. Irish and Australian nationals still need a non-immigrant visitor's visa. Forms are available from travel agents to be completed and sent to the nearest US embassy or consulate together with a full passport. Leave sufficient time for the documentation to be completed before departure.

For foreign visitors to Florida, a passport, a passport-size photograph, a visitor's visa, evidence that you intend to leave the US after your visit is over, and (depending upon your country of origin) an international vaccination certificate will help smooth your entry into the US and Florida at government customs booths. Canadian citizens, and British subjects residing in Canada and Bermuda, are normally exempted from these requirements when arriving from countries in the Western Hemisphere.

Citizens of Mexico bearing Form 1-136 and coming from Canada or Mexico are normally exempted from passport and visa requirements. UK and New Zealand residents with return or onward flight tickets on a business or holiday trip lasting less than 90 days no longer require a visa.

Obtain your visa by mail, by personal application or via your travel agent at the US Embassy or American consulate nearest your home. Evidence of intent to leave the United States may be furnished in the form of a return ticket .

Vaccination certificate requirements vary, but proof of immunization against smallpox or cholera may be necessary.

DIRECTORY

AIRLINES

Aer Lingus-Irish Airlines
Tel: 1-800-223-6537

Aerolineas Argentinas
Tel: 1-800-327-0276

Aeromexico
Tel: 1-800-237-6639

Air Canada
Tel: 1-800-422-6232

Air Jamaica
Tel: 1-800-523-5585

Alitalia Airlines
Tel: 1-800-223-5730

American Airlines
Tel: 1-800-443-7300

British Airways
Tel: 1-800-247-9297

Delta Air Lines
Tel: 1-800-638-7333

Eastern Airlines
Tel: 1-800-327-8376

Iberia Air Lines of Spain
Tel: 1-800-221-9741

Japan Air Lines
Tel: 1-800-525-3663

KLM-Royal Dutch Airlines
Tel: 1-800-556-7777

Lan-Chile Airlines
Tel: 1-800-255-5526

Northwest Orient
Tel: 1-800-447-4747

Pan Am
Tel: 1-800-221-1111

Piedmont Airlines
Tel: 1-800-251-5720

Sabena Belgian
Tel: 1-800-645-3790

Scandinavian Airlines
Tel: 1-800-221-2350

Swissair
Tel: 1-800-221-04750

TAP Air Portugal
Tel: 1-800-221-7370

Trans World Airlines
Tel: 1-800-221-2000

US Air
Tel: 1-800-428-4322

United Airlines
Tel: 1-800-521-4041

Varig Brazilian Airlines
Tel: 1-800-468-2744

Viasa Venezuelan International
Tel: 1-800-432-9070

Wardair Canada 1975 Ltd

Tel: 1-800-282-4751

ACCOMMODATION
MIAMI
Expensive
Cavalier
1320 Ocean Drive
Miami Beach
Tel: (305)534 2135/
    (800) 338 9076
Art Deco district gem (see also
Art Deco Hotels *under Moder
ate).

Doral Ocean Beach Resort
4833 Collins Avenue
Miami Beach
Tel: (305) 532 3600/
    (800) FOR-ATAN
420-room beachfront spread
with watersports, fitness centre
restaurants and free transport to
sister resorts.

**Doral Saturnia International Spa
Doral Resort and Country
Club**
400 NW 87th Avenue
Tel: (305) 592 2000
Superb complex with 550 room
and suites, golf, tennis, Olympic
pool, restaurants, nightclub
child care.

**Fontainebleu Hilton Resort and
Spa**
4441 Collins Avenue
Miami Beach
Tel: (305) 538 2000/
    (800) 548 8886

Monster jewel in Miami's crown. ,226 rooms and suites on 20 acres of oceanfront; tennis, watersports, 6 restaurants, nightclubs. .

Mayfair House
3000 Florida Avenue
Coconut Grove
Tel: (305) 441 0000/
      (800) 341 0809
78 individual suites with private balconies around an exclusive shopping mall; rooftop pool, bar, restaurant and nightclub.

Sheraton River House
(Miami Airport)
3900 NW 21st Street
Tel: (305) 871 3800/
      (800) 325 3535
408 rooms/suites; vast facilities from restaurant and nightclub to tennis, pool, and saunas.

Sonesta Beach Hotel
350 Ocean Drive, Key Biscayne
Tel: (305) 361 2021/
      (800) 343 7170
278 rooms and suites in luxurious beachfront resort; tennis, watersports, free children's entertainment programme.

Moderate
Airport Regency
1000 NW LeJeune Road
Tel: (305) 441 1600/
      (800) 432 1192
175 rooms; tropical decor; facilities include pool, restaurant, nightclub.

Cardozo
Carlyle
Leslie
(Art Deco Hotels)
1320 Ocean Drive
Miami Beach
Tel: (305) 534 2135/
      (800) 338 9076
Three archetypal Deco hotels, restored and furnished in period style. Ocean views, complimen-

tary breakfast, terrace cafe.

Bay Harbor Inn
9660 E Bay Harbor Drive
Bay Harbor Islands/Miami Beach
Tel: (305) 8684141
36 attractive rooms/suites in waterfront location; pool, good restaurants, breakfast.

Best Western Miami Airport
1550 NW Le Jeune Road
Tel: (305)871 2345/
      (800) 528 1234
207 rooms/suites. Good facilities include pool, child care nursery, restaurant.

Deauville Hotel and Tennis Club
6701 Collins Avenue
Miami Beach
Tel: (305) 865 8511/
      (800) 327 6656
560 rooms/suites in recently renovated oceanfront complex; pool, tennis, watersports, restaurants nightclub, child care nursery.

Hampton Inn
2500 Brickell Avenue
Tel: (305) 854 2070/
      (800) HAMPTON
69 rooms by entrance to Key Biscayne; pool, breakfast, child care. Good for sightseei ng.

Hotel Place St Michael
162 Alcazar Avenue
Coral Gables
Tel: (305) 444 1666/
      (800) 247 8526
Charming 30-room hotel on the expensive side of moderate. Ceiling fans, antiques, award-winning restaurant.

Ocean on the Palm
9449 Collins Avenue
Miami Beach
Tel: (305)865 3551/
      (800) 327 6644
170 rooms/suites near Bal Harbor; pool, fitness, restaurant.

Park Central
640 Ocean Drive
Miami Beach
Tel: (305)538 1611
76 rooms in Art Deco classic; restaurant, complimentary breakfast, child care.

Budget
Budgetel Inn
3501 NW LeJeune Road
Tel: (305) 871 1777/
      (800) 528 1234
Modern motel near airport; 150 rooms and suites in efficiencies; pool, breakfast, airport transport.

Days Inn - Miami Airport
3401 LeJeune Road
Tel: (305) 871 4221/
      (800) 325 2525
155 rooms; pool, restaurant, airport transport.

Golden Sands Hotel
6901 Collins Avenue
Miami Beach
Tel: (305) 866 8734/
      (800)932 0333
102 rooms/efficiencies on ocean; pool, restaurant, close to shopping, dining.

Howard Johnson Port of Miami
1100 Biscayne Boulevard
Tel: (305)358 3080
115 rooms in central Downtown location; pool, restaurant.

Inn on the Bay
1819 79th Street Causeway
Tel: (305)865 7100/
      (800) 351 2131
120 rooms in friendly, family B&B hotel with marina between Miami Beach and mainland; pool.

Miami Beach Youth Hostel
1438 Washington Avenue
Miami Beach
Tel: (305)534 2988
Beach bargain, 80 rooms in the Art Deco district.

Seabrook Resort Hotel & Apartments
9401 Collins Avenue
Miami Beach
Tel: (305) 866 5446
90 rooms/efficiencies by beach; pool, restaurant, close to shops.

KEYS & EVERGLADES
Expensive
Banyan Resort
3444 N Roosevelt Boulevard
Key West
Tel: (305) 296 7593/
      (800) 624 2401
38 suites/efficiencies in 8 buildings, including 4 Victorian houses; downtown location; gorgeous gardens, pools, bar, breakfast.

Cheeca Lodge
MM 82.5
Islamorada
Tel: (305) 664 4651/
      (800) 327 2888
203 units in famous resort complex with gold, tennis, fishing, watersports, fine dining, and children's activities.

Curry Mansion Inn
512 Caroline Street
Key West
Tel: (305) 294 5349
15 enchanting rooms in historic house and modern annexe off Duval. Home-cooked breakfasts; tiny pool, but use of facilities at **Pier House**.

Pier House
1 Duval Street
Key West
Tel: (305) 294 9541/
      (800) 432 3414
Rambling, relaxing, 101-room hotel; beach area, pool, convivial bars, five restaurants and terrace cafe.

Sheraton Key Largo Resort
MM 97
Key Largo

Tel: (305) 852 5553/
      (800) 826 1006
200 attractive rooms and suites on private bayside beach. Boat trips, fishing, watersports, pools, tennis, three restaurants, children's activities.

Moderate
Chesapeake Motel
MM 83.5
Islamorada
Tel: (305) 664 4662/
      (800) 338 3395
65 rooms/efficiencies; beach, freshwater pool, tropical gardens and boat dock.

Flamingo Lodge
Everglades National Park
Tel: (305) 253 2241
102 modern rooms and cottages; facilities include pool, camper's store, marina, restaurant.

Kingsail Resort Motel
MM 50.5
Marathon
Tel: (305) 743 5246/
      (800) 423 7474
43 rooms/efficiencies; pool, boat ramp, dive/fishing charters.

Largo Lodge Motel
MM 101.5
Key Largo
Tel: (305) 451 0424/
      (800) IN THE SUN
Six efficiencies seet in a tropical garden; airconditioning, screened porches.

Marina del Mar Resort and Marina
MM100
Key Largo
Tel: (305) 451 042/
      (800) 253 3483
130 well-equipped rooms, suites and villas in bayside resort and oceanside marina. Dive packages, dining and dancing.

Ragged Edge Resort

MM 86.5
Treasure Harbor Drive
Islamorada
Tel: (305) 852 5389
10 rooms/efficiencies with tropical decor on ocean; pool, marina, fishing pier.

South Beach Oceanfront Motel
508 South Street
Key West
Tel: (305) 296 5611/
      (800) 354 4455
49 pleasant rooms at the southern end of Duval. Pier, small public beach, use of facilities at **Southernmost Motel**.

Southernmost Motel
1319 Duval Street
Key West
Tel: (305) 296 6577/
      (800)354 4455
127 rooms in tropical setting. Daytime snacks and drinks from poolside tiki bar; close to restaurants and nightlife.

Sugarloaf Loadge
MM 17
Sugarloaf Key
Tel: (305) 745 3211
55 rooms in 120-acre island complex; pool, mini-golf, tennis, pet dolphin show.

Budget
Econo Lodge Resort
MM 3
Key West
Tel: (305) 294 5511/
      (800)KEY WEST
43-room motel; off-season bargains (but expensive in the season); pool, tennis, family restaurant.

Gilbert's Resort
MM 107.9
Key Largo
Tel: (305) 451 1133
36 units by marina; pool, restaurant.

Grandma Newton's Bed & Breakfast
40 NW 5th Avenue
Florida City
Tel: (305) 247 4413
Five comfortable rooms; enormous breakfasts. Close to Everglades National Park.

Harbor Lights Motel
MM 85
Islamorada
Tel: (305) 664 3611/
      (800) 327 7070
Budget corner of Holiday Isle Resort, 33 rooms/efficiencies on ocean; good facilities.

Island Bay Resort
MM 92.5
Tavernier
Tel: (305) 852 4087
Eight small guesthouse/efficiencies in friendly complex; dive boat and dock.

Key West Hostel
718 South Street
Key West
Tel: (305) 296 5719
International youth hostel; central.

CENTRAL
Expensive
Buena Vista Palace
Lake Buena Vista
Tel: (407) 827 2727
1,028 deluxe rooms; pool, fitness, golf, tennis, restaurants, transport to WDW.

Grand Cypress
60 Grand Cypress Boulevard
Orlando
Tel: (407) 239 4600
750-room resort with tennis, golf, equestrian and fitness centres, nature reserve.

The Peabody
9801 International Drive
Orlando
Tel: (407) 352 4000

891 luxurious rooms; fine restaurants, pool, tennis, fitness.

WDW Disney Inn
Grand Floridian Beach Resort
Polynesian Resort (Magic Kingdom)
Dolphin
Caribbean Beach Resort
Swan, Yacht and Beach Club Resorts (Epcot)
Central Reservations
Box 10100
Lake Buena Vista
FL 32830
Tel: (407) 934 7639/
      (800) 647 7900).
Spacious family rooms, excellent facilities, transport to parks.

Moderate
Cabot Lodge Bed and Breakfast
3726 SW 40th Boulevard
Gainesville
Tel: (904) 375 2400/
      (800) 331 8215
208 comfortable modern rooms off interstate 75; pool, complimentary breakfast.

Chalet Suzanne
off US27
Lake Wales
Tel: (813) 676 6011
30 rooms in cute and quirky country inn on lake. Good restaurant.

Homewood Suites
3100 Parkway Boulevard
Kissimmee
Tel: (407) 396 2229
112 attractive suites (sleep 4) with efficiencies close to WDW; pool, fitness centre, shop, breakfast.

Radisson Inn Maingate
7501 W Irlo Bronson Highway
Kissimmee
Tel: (407) 396 1400
580 pleasant rooms 1 mile from WDW; pool, tennis, health club, family restaurant.

Ramada Resort Maingate East at the Parkway
2900 Parkway
Kissimmee
Tel: (407) 396 7000/
      (800) 225 3939
716 spacious rooms; pool, spa, tennis, deli, restaurant.

Residence Inn by Marriott
4001 SW 13th Street
Gainesville
Tel: (904) 371 2101/
      (800) 331 3131
80 suites with efficiencies and complimentary breakfast; central location; swimming pool.

Residence Inn by Marriott-on Lake Cecile
4786 W Irlo Bronson Memorial Highway
Kissimmee
Tel: (407) 396 2056/
      (800) 648 7408
160 roomy efficiency suites on lakeside close to WDW; pool, tennis, watersports, breakfast, grocery service.

Seven Sisters
820 SE Fort King Street
Ocala
Tel: (904) 867 1170
B & B in lovely Queen Anne house; five antique-filled rooms.

Port Orleans
Dixie landings
(WDW Caribbean Beach Resort)
Central Reservations
Box 10100
Lake Buena Vista
FL 32830
Tel: (407) 934 7639
Caribbean/Deep South themed resort hotels; great Disney facilities at moderate prices.

Budget
Comfort Inn
Lake Buena Vista
Tel: (407) 239 7300
604 rooms close to WDW; pool,

restaurant

Condo Care Vacation Rentals Inc.
250 N Orange Avenue/Suite 820
Orlando
FL 32801
Tel: (800) 633 9474
2-3 bedroom fully-equipped villas (sleep 6-8) close to Orlando area sights.

CRS - Orlando Budget Hotels Reservation Service
300 Wilshire Boulevard/Suite 225
Orlando
FL 32730
Tel: (800) 548 3311.

Econo Lodge Maingate Hawaiian Resort
4311 W Irlo Bronson Memorial Highway
Kissimmee
Tel: (407) 396 7100/
(800) 826 0778
173 rooms with tropical theme; close to WDW; pool.

Howard Johnson Downtown
304 W Colonial Drive
Orlando
Tel: (407) 843 8700/
(800) 826 1365
273 rooms in chain motel with personal touch; swimming pool, good family restaurant.

Langford Resort Hotel
300 E New England Avenue
Winter Park
Tel: (407) 644 3400
214 very pleasant rooms just north of Orlando; pool, golf, health club, restaurant, Bargain.

Larson's Lodge
2009 W Vine Street
Kissimmee
Tel: (407) 846 2713/
(800) 624 5905
212 pretty rooms/suites 10 minutes from WDW; pools, tennis,

family restaurant, playground; also 128-room.

Larson's Lodge - Maingate
6075 W Irlo Bronson Memorial Highway
Kissimmee
Tel: (407) 396 6100/
(800) 327 9074
With similar facilities.

Orlando International Youth Hostel
227 N Eola Drive
Orlando
Tel: (407) 843 8888
Shared/single rooms in downtown location; kitchen, pool.

WDW Fort Wilderness Resort and Campground
Central Reservations/Box 10100
Lake Buena Vista
FL 32830
Tel: (407) 934 7639
407 fully-equipped trailers (sleep 4-6). Woodland setting; great facilities.

GOLD COAST
Expensive
Boca Raton Resort & Club
501 E Camino Real
Boca Raton
Tel: (407) 395 3000
963 deluxe rooms in superb Mizner/modern creation; golf, pools, tennis, restaurants.

Breakers
1 S Country Road
Palm Beach
Tel: (407) 655 6611
Fabulous 528-room historic landmark on the ocean; golf, tennis, fine dining.

Colony Hotel
155 Hammon Avenue
Palm Beach
Tel: (407) 655 5430
94 classy rooms between beach and Worth Avenue; pool, fitness, restaurant.

Marriott's Harbor Beach Resor
3030 Holiday Drive
Ft Lauderdale
Tel: (305) 525 40000
660 chic rooms on the beach attractive setting and excellen facilities.

Palm Beach Polo and Country Club
13198 Forest Hill Boulevard
West Palm Beach
Tel: (407) 798 7000
Golf and tennis packages with villa accommodation; superb facilities set in 2,200-acre estate; fine dining.

Moderate
Best Western Sea Spray Inn
123 Ocean Avenue
West Palm Beach
Tel: (407) 844 0233
50 rooms/efficiencies on beach pool, tennis, restaurants, etc.

Hollywood Beach Resort Hotel
101 N Ocean Drive
Hollywood
Tel: (305) 921 0990/
(800) 331 6103
360 rooms/studios with Deco touches; pool, tennis, fitness, restaurants, shopping, child care

Howard Johnson Oceanside
930 US1
Juno Beach
Tel: (407) 626 1531
108 rooms/suites (some efficiencies) near beach; pool, restaurant.

Inn at Boca Teeca
5800 NW Second Avenue
Boca Raton
Tel: (407) 994 0400
47 rooms (1 mile from beach); pool, tennis, gold, fitness.

Largo Mar Resort & Club
1700 S Ocean Lane
Ft Lauderdale
Tel: (305) 523 6511/

(800) 366 5246
80 rooms/suites in attractive
eachfront complex; pools, ten-
is, mini-golf, restaurant and
ntertainment.

**'alm Beach Hawaiian Ocean
Inn**
550 S Ocean Boulevard
outh Palm Beach
el: (407) 582 5631
8 rooms/suites on beach; at-
ractive South Seas decor, pool,
aw bar, restaurant.

'elican Beach Resort
000 N Atlantic Boulevard
t Lauderdale
el: (305) 568 9431
8 good value rooms/
fficiencies on beach.

Riverside Hotel
20 E Las Olas Boulevard
t Lauderdale
el: (305) 467 0671
17 spacious rooms in attrac-
ive old hotel; central location;
ool, restaurant.

Sailfish Marina
8 Lake Drive
Palm Beach Shores
el: (407) 844 1724
4 rooms two blocks from beach;
ool, sportfishing charters, shut-
le.

Sun Castle Resort
380 S Ocean Boulevard
Pompano Beach
Tel: (305) 941 7700
105 rooms/efficiencies in landscaped grounds; pool, tennis,
golf, dining. Families welcome.

Budget
**Admiral's Court Apartment Mo-
tel and Marina**
21 Hendricks Isle
Ft Lauderdale
Tel: (305) 462 5072/
     (800) 248 6669
37 rooms/efficiencies in villa by

canal; privte dock, gardens,
close beaches/Las Olas.

**Bayshore Waterfront Apart-
ments**
341 N Birch Road
Ft Lauderdale
Tel: (305) 463 2821
38 units on waterway (1 mile to
beach); efficiencies; quiet.

**Howard Johnson Oceans Edge
Resort**
700 N Atlantic Boulevard
Ft Lauderdale
Tel: (305) 563 2451
144 rooms; pool, restaurant,
beach frontage.

Island Queen Motel
2634 West Way
Singer Island
Tel: (407) 848 4448
80 rooms by ocean, lake or pool;
tennis, shuttle to town/airport.
Ocean Lodge, 570 Ocean Drive,
Juno Beach (tel: (407) 626 1528).
32 rooms on beach; pool.

Riviera Palms Motel
3960 N Ocean Boulevard
Delray Beach
Tel: (407) 276 3032
17 rooms/efficiencies 100ft from
beach; pool.

Sea Chateau Motel
555 N Birch Road
Ft Lauderdale
Tel: (305) 566 8331
16 pretty rooms/efficienices 200
yards from beach; pool, coffee
and pastries.

Villas-by-the-Sea
4456 El Mar Drive
Lauderdale-by-the-Sea
Tel: (305) 772 3550/
     (800) 247 8963
148 smart rooms/efficiencies in
landscaped grounds by beach;
pool, tennis, barbecue grills, airport shuttle.

EAST COAST
Expensive
Amelia Island Plantation
3000 First Coast Highway
Amelia Island
Tel: (904)261 6161/
     (800) 873 6878
Superb resort set in 1,000-acre
nature preserve; beach, pools,
tennis, golf, fishisng, riding, fine
dining.

Cocoa Beach Hilton
1550 N Atlantic Avenue
Cocoa Beach
Tel: (407) 799 0003
300 rooms by the ocean; swimming pool, tennis, restaurants,
nightclub, children's activities,
babysitting.

Daytona Beach Marriott
100 N Atlantic Avenue
Daytona
Tel: (904) 254 8200
405 rooms on oceanfront; prime
location; pools, fitness, children's facilities, restaurants.

Omni Hotel
245 Water Street
Jacksonville
Tel: (904) 355 6664/
     (800) THE OMNI
354 classy rooms/suites around
luxuriant atrium; pool, health
club, excellent restaurant.

Moderate
Anastasia Inn
A1A at Pope Road
Anastasia Island
Tel: (904) 471 2575
142 rooms in St Augustine's
beach annexe; pool, restaurant.

Conch House Marina Resort
57 Comares Avenue
Anastasia Island
Tel: (904)829 8646
21 rooms/efficiencies with tropical flavour; pool, bayside beach,
restaurant.

Crossway Inn

3901 N Atlantic Avenue
Cocoa Beach
Tel: (407) 783 2221
144 rooms/50 suites (some efficiencies) in beachfront resort; pool, playground, restaurant.

Days Inn
1920 Seaway Drive
Ft Pierce
Tel: (407) 461 8737/
   (800) 447 4732
40 rooms/efficiencies near beach; pool, fishing.

1890 Inn
83 Cedar Street
St Augustine
Tel: (904) 826 0287
Friendly B&B; 3 chintzy rooms in town centre.

House on Cherry Street
1844 Cherry Street
Jacksonville
Tel: (904) 384 1999
4-room B&B in beautiful old house down leafy Riverside lane.

Hutchinson Inn Seaside Resort
9750 S Ocean Drive
Jensen Beach
Ft Pierce
Tel: (407) 229 2000
21 units on ocean; pool, tennis, friendly free barbecue for guests Saturday nights.

Perry's Ocean Edge
2209 S Atlantic Avenue
Daytona
Tel: (904) 255 0581
204 rooms/efficiencies on beach; family orientated; pool, breakfast.

Sea Turtle Inn
1 Ocean Boulevard
Jacksonville Beach
Tel: (904) 249 7402
200 rooms by the ocean; pool, restaurant, lounge, airport shuttle.

Seaside Inn
1998 S Fletcher Avenue
Fernandina Beach
Tel: (904) 261 0954
10 rooms in delightful restored inn by the beach; restaurant.

Sun Viking Lodge
2411 S Atlantic Avenue
Daytona Beach Shores
Tel: (904) 252 6252/
   (800) 874 4469
91 rooms and efficiencies in friendly family resort; activity programme, beachfront, pools, waterslide, spa, cafe.

Budget
Bayfront Inn
138 Avenida Menendez
St Augustine
Tel: (904) 824 1681
39 Spanish-style unit around pool; convenient for historic quarter.

Best Western Aku Tiki
2225 S Atlantic Avenue
Daytona
Tel: (904) 252 9631
132 rooms/efficiencies on oceanfront; pool, restaurant.

Days Inn Oceanfront
5600 N Atlantic Avenue
ocoa Beach
Tel: (407) 783 7621
120 rooms in family-style motel; pool, 24-hour restaurant.

Eastwinds Motel
1505 S First Street
Jacksonville Beach
Tel: (904) 249 3858
25 cheerful rooms/efficiencies; pool.

Harbour Light Inn
1160 Seaway Drive
Ft Pierce
Tel: (407) 468 3555/
   (800) 433 0004
34 units with balconies on inlet; pool, barbecue, fishing.

Mainsail Motel
281 S Atlantic Avenue
Ormond Beach
Tel: (904) 677 2131/
   (800) 843 5142
50 nautical-style rooms on beach (north of Daytona); pools, restaurant, family resort.

Marine Terrace Apartments
306 S Ocean Drive
Ft Pierce
Tel: (407) 461 8909
Spick-and-span efficienices on beach; family owned; fishing.

Villas de Marin
142 Avenida Menendez
St Augustine
Tel: (904) 829 1725
16 tasteful efficiencies with views with restored bayfron building.

WEST COAST
Expensive
Don Cesar
3400 Gulf Boulevard
St Petersburg Beach
Tel: (813) 360 1881
226 rooms/51 suites in fabulous pink palace on beach; pool, watersports, children's programme.

Edgewater Beach Hotel
1901 Gulf Shore Boulevard
Naples
Tel: (813) 262 6511/
   (800) 282 3766
124 attractive suites with kitchenette and balcony; friendly atmosphere; beach, pool, fitness, chic dining room.

Innisbrook Resort
US19, Tarpon Springs
Tel: (813) 937 3124/
   (800) 456 2000
1,200 rooms/suites in 1,000-acre woodland setting; golf and tennis packages, children's programme, fine dining, nightclub.
Saddlebrook Golf & Tennis Re-

sort
00 Saddlebrook Way
Wesley Chapel
Tel: (813) 973 1111/
(800) 222 2222
700 rooms/suites in countryside
5 miles north of Tampa; Palmer-
designed golf course, tennis, fitness, award-winning dining.
Good value packages.

South Seas Plantation
Capitva Island
Tel: (813) 472 5111/
(800) 282 3402
556 deluxe rooms/suites in fam-
ily/sporting resort; beach, pools,
golf, tennis, watersports, boat
trips, dining choice.

**Wyndham Harbour Island Ho-
tel**
725 S Harbour Island Boulevard
Tampa
Tel: (813) 229 5000/
(800) 822 4200
300 spacious rooms/suites with
views in central Downtown location; pool, health club, restaurants, shopping.

Moderate
Beach Castle
5310 Gulf of Mexico Drive
Longboat Key
Sarasota
Tel: (813) 383 2639
19 lovely apartments with gulf/
bay views (1-week minimum
stay); gardens, swimming pool,
dock, canoes.

Breckenridge Resort Hotel
5700 Gulf Boulevard
St Petersburg Beach
Tel: (813) 360 1833
200 fine rooms/efficiencies on
beach; pool, tennis, watersports,
restaurant.

Days Inn Marina Beach Resort
6800 S 34th Street
St Petersburg
Tel: (813) 867 1151

212 rooms/efficiencies on bay;
pools, tennis, sailing school, fishing, restaurant.

Half Moon Beach Club
2050 Ben Franklin Drive
Lido Key
Sarasota
Tel: (813) 388 3694/
(800) 358 3245
85 spacious rooms/efficiencies
around pool and courtyard;
beach frontage, restaurant, easy
drive from sights.

Hilton
17120 Gulf Boulevard
North Redington Beach
Tel: (813) 391 4000
124 airy rooms on ocean; pool,
watersports, fishing, restaurant.

Holiday Inn Busch Gardens
2701 E Fowler Avenue
Tampa
Tel: (813) 971 4710
399 rooms; pool, fitness centre,
restaurant.

Outrigger Beach Resort
6200 Estero Boulevard
Ft Myers Beach
Tel: (813) 463 3131/
(800) 226 3131
144 rooms/efficiencies on Gulf;
pool, tiki bar, coffee shop.

**Pink Shell Beach and Bay Re-
sort**
275 Estero Boulevard
Ft Myers Beach
Tel: (813) 463 6181/
(800) 237 5786
180 rooms/condos/cottages in
landscaped surrounds; family
style, with pool, tennis,
watersports, fishing.

Radisson Bay Harbor Inn
7700 Courtney Campbell Causeway
Tampa
Tel: (813) 281 8900/
(800) 333 3333

257 rooms on beach; pool, fitness centre, restaurant, child
care.

Safari Resort Inn
4139E Busch Boulevard
Tampa
Tel: (813) 988 9191
100 rooms in Serengeti trim close
to Busch Gardens; pool, restaurant, entertainment lounge.

Sailport Resort
2506 Rocky Point Drive
Tampa
Tel: (813) 281 9599/
(800) 255 9599
237 full-equipped efficiencies
with waterfront balconies; pool,
breakfast. Value for families.

Tradewinds
5500 Gulf Boulevard
St Petersburg Beach
Tel: (813) 367 6461
95 (moderate to expensive)
rooms/efficiencies in excellent
resort; pools, tennis, sailing, children's activities.

Vanderbilt Beach Motel
9225 N Gulf Shore Drive
Naples
Tel: (813) 597 3144
66 rooms/efficiencies on shore;
pool, tennis, fishing pier.

Budget
Bay Winds Resort Motel
7345 Bay Street
St Petersburg Beach
Tel: (813) 267 2721
24 rooms/suites on oceanfront;
pool, windsurfer rental, boat
charters, restaurant.

Beach House
4960 Estero Boulevard
Ft Myers Beach
Tel: (813) 992 2644
14 rooms/apartments in delightful house amid condos.

Beach View Cottages

3306 W Gulf Drive
Sanibel Island
Tel: (813) 472 1202
Efficiencies in relaxed family-style complex right on beach.

Best Western Golden Host
4675 N Tamiami Trail
Sarasota
Tel: (813) 355 5741
80 rooms in landscaped grounds; pool, close to restaurant.

Buccaneer Resort Motel
10800 Gulf Boulevard
Treasure Island
Tel: (813) 367 1908/
(800) 826 2120
62 rooms/efficiencies on beach; pool.

Comfort Inn
9800 Bonita Beach Road
Bonita Springs
Tel: (813) 992 5001/
(800) 221 2222
69 pleasant modern rooms/efficiencies around pool.

Days Inn
2520 N 50th Street
Tampa
Tel: (813) 247 3300/
(800) 433 8033
200 rooms in central location; pool, restaurant.

Diplomat Resort
3155 Gulf of Mexico Drive
Longboat Key
Sarasota
Tel: (813) 383 3791
50 spacious units in beachfront apartment complex (2-day minimum stay); pool.

Expressway Inns
3688 and 3693 Gandy Boulevard (US92)
Tampa
Tel: (813) 837 1921/
(813) 837 1971
Pleasant motels with pool.

Fairways Motel
103 Palm River Boulevard
Naples
Tel: (813) 597 8181
32 fine rooms around pool courtyard; quiet and close to golf.

PANHANDLE
Expensive
Edgewater Beach Resort
11212 Front Beach Road
Panama City Beach
Tel: (904) 235 4044/
(800) 874 8686
464 deluxe units/villas by beach or golf course in good central location; pools, tennis, watersports.

Governor's Inn
209 S Adams Street
Tallahassee
Tel: (904) 681 6855/
(800) 342 7717
40 luxurious rooms/suites in central historic district; VIP treatment, elegant, dining room, breakfast, airport shuttle.

Marriott's Bay Point Resort
100 Delwood Beach Road
Panama City Beach
Tel: (904) 234 3307/
(800) 874 7105
400 elegant rooms/suites/villas; beach, woods, golf, tennis, watersports, children's activities.

New World Inn
600 S Palafox Street
Pensacola
Tel: (904) 432 4111
16 deluxe rooms/suites each reflecting a famous historic US personality and featuring antique furnishings; excellent restaurant; airport shuttle.

Sandestin
5500 US98
Destin
Tel: (904) 277 0800
500 rooms/efficiencies in complex spanning barrier island from bay to seashore; pools, golf, tennis, fitness, fine dining.

Moderate
Cabot Lodge West
2735 N Monroe Street
Tallahassee
Tel: (904) 386 8880/
(800) 223 1964
160 comfortable B&B rooms, pool, restaurant near by.

Carousel Beach Resort
571 Santa Rosa Boulevard
Ft Walton Beach
Tel: (904) 243 7658/
(800) 523 0208
105 rooms/efficiencies on Gulf; pool, fishing, bar, close to shops.

Conquistador
874 Venus Court
Ft Walton Beach
Tel: (904) 244 6155/
(800) 824 7112
87 apartments/efficiencies on dunes; pool, close to shopping.

Dunes
333 Ft Pickens Road
Pensacola Beach
Tel: (904) 932 3536
140 rooms in friendly, family-orientated complex beside beach; pool.

Gibson Inn
Market Street
Apalachicola
Tel: (904) 653 2191
30 rooms in fine restored building; dining.

Holiday Inn
165 Ft Pickens Road
Pensacola Beach
Tel: (904) 932 5361/
(800) 465 4329
150 rooms on Gulf; pool, tennis, watersports, dining, airport shuttle, child care.

Killeran Country Club & Inn
100 Tyron Circle

Tallahassee
Tel: (904) 893 2186/
(800) 476 4101
40 units in relaxing woodland
setting; pool, city's finest golf
course, tennis, fitness fine din-
ng.

Mark II Beach Resort
15285 Front Beach Road (U98)
Panama City Beach
Tel: (904) 234 8845/
(800) 874 7170
202 spacious rooms/efficiencies
on beach; pools, watersports,
tennis, restaurant, close to attractions.

Rendezvous Inn Resort
17281 Front Beach Road (US98)
Panama City Beach
Tel: (904) 234 8841/
(800) 874 6617
72 efficiencies in lively
beachside complex; pool, tennis, restaurant.

St George Inn
St George Island
Apalachicola
Tel: (904) 670 2903
8 rooms in lively wood-frame
house close to beach, nature
reserve.

Wakulla Springs Lodge
1 Springs Drive (SR26)
Wakulla Springs (15 miles south
of Tallahassee)
27 rooms in Spanish-style inn in
State Park; home-cooked meals
in large dining room, dusk and
dawn animal-spotting.

Budget
Days Inn
710 N Palafox Street
Pensacola
Tel: (904) 438 4922/
(800) 325 2525
157 rooms/efficiencies near historic district; pool, coffee shop,
airport shuttle.

Driftwood Beach Club
683 Nautilus Court
Ft Walton Beach
Tel: (904) 243 1716/
(800) 336 3630
28 rooms/efficiencies on beach;
pool, close to shopping, restaurants, watersports.

Flamingo Motel
15525 Front Beach Road (US98)
Panama City Beach
Tel: (904) 234 2232/
(800) 828 0400
67 pleasant efficiencies around
tropical garden on beach; family atmosphere; pool.

Georgian Terrace
14415 Front Beach Road (US98)
Panama City Beach
Tel: (904) 234 3322
30 wood-panelled, cosy
efficiencies on beach; pool.

Holiday Inn Parkway
1302 Apalachee Parkway
Tallahassee
Tel: (904) 877 3141/
(800) HOLIDAY
167 units around pool; fitness,
family restaurant.

Hospitality Inn
6900 Pensacola Boulevard
Pensacola
Tel: (904) 477 2333/
(800) 821 2073
126 efficiencies; swimming
pool, breakfast.

Leeside Inn & Marina
1350 US98 Ft Walton Beach
Tel: (904) 243 7359/
(800) 824 2747
109 rooms/efficiencies adjoining National Seashore; pool,
watersports, fishing, restaurant.

Sandpiper Inn
23 Via de Luna
Pensacola Beach
Tel: (904) 932 2516
32 compact, attractive units

close to beach; pool.

Sportman's Lodge
SR65 (north of US98)
Eastpoint
Aplachiocola
Tel: (904) 670 8423
22 rooms/efficiencies by se-
cluded bayside marina; fishing.

Tallahassee Motor Lodge
1630 N Monroe Street
Tallahassee
Tel: (904) 224 6183
92 spacious rooms close to
Downtown and shopping; pool.

Tomahawk Landing
SR 87 12 miles north of Miltin
Tel: (904) 623 6197
Fully equipped woodland cab-
ins for visitors to Blackwater
River.

RESTAURANTS
MIAMI
Expensive
Chef Allen's
19088 NE 29th Avenue
North Miami Beach
Tel: (305)935 2900
New American 'spa cuisine' at
its tilillating best; elegant
Decoesque furnishings.

Dominique's
Alexander Hotel
5225 Collins Avenue
Miami Beach
Tel: (305) 865 6500
Sumptuous surroundings, dra-
matic presentation, classic/ex-
otic menu, outdoor arrea.

Grand Cafe
Grand Bay Hotel
2669 S Bayshore Drive
Cocont Grove
Tel: (305) 858 9600
Elegant dining room, award-win-
ning international cuisine, sea-
food specialities, al fresco.

Le Pavillon

Hotel Inter-Continental
100 Chopin Plaza
Miami
Tel: (305) 577 1000
Distinguished continental cuisine, innovative specials, harpist for musical accompaniment.

Mark's Place
2286 NE 123rd Street
North Miami
Tel: (305) 893 6888
Pretty setting with plenty of greenery; inspired New American menu, fresh fish, warm salads.

Mayfair Grill
Mayfair House Hotel
3000 Florida Avenue
Coconut Grove
Tel: (305)441 0000
Intimate, low lit dining room; well-constructed, appealing New American cuisine.

St Michel
Hotel Place St Michel
162 Alcazar Avenue
Coral Gables
Tel: (305)444 1666
Enchanting Old World dining room; deliciously tempting French/American cuisine.

Moderate
Casa Juancho
2436 SW 8th Street
Little Havana
Tel: (305) 642 2542
Authentic Spanish cuisine in rustic surrounds; entertainment nightly.

Chart House
51 Chart House Drive
Coconut Grove
Tel: (305)856 9741
Nautical decor, waterfront location; seafood, steaks and salad bar.

Crawdaddy's
1 Washington Avenue

Miami Beach
Tel: (305) 673 1708
Fun spot stuffed with Victoriana; bay views; large and eclectic menu.

Firehouse Four
1000 S Miami Avenue
Miami
Tel: (305) 379 1923
Renovated 1923 fire station; broad menu, entertainment, outdoor seating area.

Giovanni's
801 S Bayshore Drive
Miami
Tel: (305)673 0365
Seafood institution; informal atmosphere; expect queues. (Closed June to early October.)

Las Tapas
Bayside Marketplace
401 Biscayne Boulevard
Miami
Tel: (305) 372 2737
Spanish decor, paella a specialty, outdoor seating area.

Monty's Bayshore
2550 S Bayshore Drive
Coconut Grove
Tel: (305) 858 1431
Steaks, seafood, snacks; raw bar, restaurant and entertainment.
Ruty Pelican
3201 Rickenbacker Causeway
Key Biscayne
Tel: (305) 361 3818
Panoramic views from the rustic bayside dining room; fresh seafood specialities, steaks.

Senor Frog's
3008 Grand Avenue
Coconut Grove
Tel: (305)448 0999
Copious Mexican food; mariachi band.

Stefano's
24 Crandon Boulevard
Key Biscayne

Tel: (305) 361 7007
Fresh pasta, seafood and northern Italian specialities; dancing in nightclub.

Trattoria Pampered Chef
3145 Commodore Plaza
Coconut Grove
Tel: (305) 567 0104
Convivial candle-lit spot serving creative pasta dishes.

Two Dragons
Sonesta Beach Resort
350 Ocean Drive
Key Biscayne
Tel: (305) 361 2021
Cantonese, Mandarine and Szechuan cuisine in pretty Oriental surroundings.

Victor's Cafe
2340 SW 32nd Avenue
Coral Gables
Tel: (305) 445 1313
Traditional Cuban cuisine served in elegant, Old Havana colonial style.

Zanzibar Cafe
3468 Main Highway
Coconut Grove
Tel: (305) 444 0244
Trendy sidewalk cafe on the main drag; soups, salad, fresh fish.

Budget
Benihana
1665 NE 79th Street
North Bay Village
Tel: (305) 866 2786
Sushi and American favourites with a special Japanese twist.

Big Fish
55 SW Miami Avenue Road
Miami
Tel: (305) 372 3725
Small menu, fresh fish; outdoors and informal.

Bijan's Fort Dallas Restaurant & Raw Bar

4 SE 4th Street
Miami
Tel: (305) 381 7778
Seafood by the Miami River;
weekend entertainment.

Cafe Tu Tu Tango
CocoWalk
3015 Grand Avenue
Coconut Grove
Tel: (305) 448 6942
Pizza, chicken wings, steak;
outdoor seating, early bird specials.

Chichuahua Charlie's
1580 Washington Avenue
Miami Beach
Tel: (305) 531 9082
Friendly Mexican joint; award-winning fajitas.

Granny Feelgood's
190 SE First Avenue
Miami
Tel: (305) 358 6233
Terrific vegetarian menu with some chicken dishes.

La Carreta
3632 SW 8th Street
Little Havana
Tel: (305) 446 4915
Cuban specials served in casual, family atmosphere.

News Cafe
800-804 Ocean Drive
Miami Beach
Tel: (305) 538 6397
Hip cafe-society hang-out on the Beach: great brunches.

Waldorf Cafe
Waldorf Towers Hotel
860 Ocean Drive
Miami Beach
Tel: (305) 531 4612
People-watching a speciality; hamburgers, pizza, pasta and salads in the Art Deco district.

Wolfie's
2038 Collins Avenue
Miami Beach

Tel: (305) 538 6626
Landmark Jewish deli-restaurant with mile-high bagels.

KEYS & EVERGLADES
Expensive
Atlantic's Edge
Cheeca Lodge Resort
MM 82.5
Islamorada
Tel: (305) 664 4651
Elegant semi-circular dining room on the ocean with award-winning cuisine and fine wines.

Louie's Backyard
700 Waddell Avenue
Key West
Tel: (305) 294 1061
Intriguing and innovative menu with local specialities featuring a Spanish-Caribbean twist; eclectic art works on the walls; chic diners.

Marker 88
MM 88
Plantation Key
Tel: (305) 852 9315
Spectacular sunset views accompany adventurous seafood dishes, steaks (including alligator) and wonderful salads.

Pier Hose
1 Duval Street
Key West
Tel: (305) 296 4600
Bayside setting for gourmet New American cuisine. Local seafood with fruits and baby vegetables or plain grilled; non-fish choices; perfect Key lime pie.

Snook's Bayside
MM 100
Key Largo
Tel: (9305) 451 3070
Fine dining on Florida Bay; this local favourite offers a chance to dress up a bit. Mainly seafood.

Moderate

Bagatelle
115 Duval Street
Key West
Tel: (305) 296 6609
Historic 'conch' architecture and interesting Caribbean specials on the main drag.

Buttery
1208 Simonton Street
Key West
Tel: (305) 294 0717
Innovative New American cuisine in a collection of attractively quirky dining rooms.

Coconuts Lounge
Marina del Mar Resort
MM 100
Key Largo
Tel: (305) 451 4107
Steaks, seafood and dancing nightly on the waterfront.

Fish House Restaurant & Seafood Market
MM 102.4
Key Largo
Tel: (305) 451 HOOK
Home-made conch specialities and a singing waiter.

Flamingo Lodge
Everglades National Park
Flamingo
Tel: (305) 253 2241
Closed May-October. Steak, ribs, seafood; overlooks Florida Bay.

Green Turtle Inn
MM 81.5
Islamorada
Tel: (305) 664 9031
Local favourite since 1947. Great home-baking (Key lime pie) and chowders. Often busy.

Pepe's
806 Caroline Street
Key West
Tel: (305) 294 7192
Little pine-clad diner with garden. Big breakfasts, daily specials, barbecues.

Rod & Gun Club
200 Riverside Drive
Everglades City
Tel: (813) 695 2101
Old hunting and fishing lodge
by the water. Dine on veranda
from small but well-prepared
menu.

Whale Harbor Inn
MM 84
Islamorada
Tel: (305) 664 4959
Staggering all-you-can-eat buffet, raw bar, grill, nightly entertainment.

Budget
A&B Lobster House
700 Front Street
Key West
Tel: (305) 294 2535
Local seafood institution overlooking the harbour marinas.

Baiamonte's
1223 White Street
Key West
Tel: (305) 296 2200
Popular budget spot; seafood and Italian specials, submarine sandwiches.

Coral Grill
MM 83.5
Islamorada
Tel: (305) 664 4803
Restaurant dining downstairs and generous buffet upstairs; good for families.

Ganim's Country Kitchen
MM 99.6
Key Largo
Tel: (305) 451 2895
Home-cooking, monster subs, lunchtime specials.

Half Shell Raw Bar
Land's End Village
Key West
Tel: (305) 294 7496
Oysters, fish sandwiches and specials; overlooking the docks.

Herbie's
MM 50.5
Marathon
Tel: (305) 743 6373
Informal, friendly budget find; great spicy chowder.

Mac's Bar-B-Q
MM 101.5
Key Largo
Tel: (305) 451 9954
Hickory-smoked chicken and ribs, steaks, fresh seafood and Key lime pie.

Mrs Mac's Kitchen
MM 99.9
Key Largo
Tel: (305) 451 3722
International beer-obilia galore; home-cooked specials such as meatloaf and chili.

Shuckers Raw Bar & Grill
1415 15th Street
Marathon
Tel: (305) 743 8686
Nautical decor to match fishy menu; great value fish baskets.

Turtle Kraals
Land's End Village
Key West
Tel: (305) 294 2640
Noisy, popular dockside bar-restaurant; turtles for viewing only.

Woody's Italian Gardens Pizza
MM 82
Key Largo
Tel: (305) 664 4335
Pizza, pasta and subs for filling up the family.

CENTRAL
Expensive
Chalet Suzanne
off US 27
Lake Wales
Tel: (813) 676 6011
Charming, eccentric country inn with tempting small menu of chef's specials.

Chefs de France
Epcot Center
Walt Disney World
Tel: (407) 824 4000
Classic French menu devised by three of France's top chefs Verge, Bocuse and Lenotre. Elegant surroundings in the French pavilion; a real treat.

Dux
Peabody Hotel
9801 International Drive
Orlando
Tel: (407) 352 4000
Sumptuous gourmet restaurant with innovative menu; fine cellar.

Empress Room
Empress Lilly
Walt Disney World Village
Buena Vista
Tel: (407) 828 3900
Plush Victorian dining room on permanently moored riverboat; very popular (make reservations well in advance).

Maison et Jardin
430 S Wymore Road
Altamonte Springs
Tel: (407) 862 4410
Romantic French restaurant in lovely surroundings; revered by Orlando's gourment connoisseurs.

Moderate
Bubble Room
1351 S Orlando Avenue
Maitland
Tel: (407) 628 3331
Kitsch treasure trove with emphasis on fun and monumental portion control.

Cheyenne Saloon
Church Street Station
129 W Church Street
Orlando
Tel: (407) 422 2434
Generous barbecue platters in Wild West setting.

Clewiston Inn
108 Royal Palm Avenue
Clewiston
Tel: (813) 983 8151
Fine old Southern-style dining
room in historic innn; local specials.

Gary's Duck Inn
3974 S Orang Blossom Trail
Orlando
Tel: (407) 843 0270
Nautical decor and seafood
menu, which includes fresh
snapper and crab.

Fiddler's
University Center Hotel
1535 SW Archer Road
Gainesville
Tel: (904) 371 3333
Fine continental cuisine, great
rooftop views.

Fort Liberty
5260 US 192 East
Kissimmee
Tel: (407) 351 5151
Themed four-course dinner with
Wild West show and trading
post.

Ming Court
9188 International Drive
Orlando
Tel: (407) 351 9988
Chinese food in attractive Ori-
ental surroundings; dancing.

Mitsukoshi
Epcot Center
Walt Disney World
Tel: (407) 824 4000
Watch the preparations and sam-
ple traditional Japanese cuisine.

Outback
Buena Vista Palace Hotel
1900 Buena Vista Drive
Buena Vista
Tel: (407) 827 3430
Luxuriant greenery, waiters in
nifty bush suits; grilled steaks
and seafood.

Royal Orleans
8445 International Drive
Orlando
Tel: (407) 352 8200
Superb Cajun cuisine; Louisiana blue crabs and crawfish
flown in daily.

Yearling Cross Creek
CR 325, Cross Creek
Tel: (904) 466 3033
Cracker cooking as recorded by
literary type Marjorie Kinnan
Rawlings.

Budget
Cattle Range
6129 Old Winter Garden Road
Orlando
Tel: (407) 298 7334
Vast steaks sizzled over orange
wood in cowboy-style tourist-
free zone.

**Commander Ragtime's Midway
Grill**
Church Street Station
129 W Church Street
Orlando
Tel: (407) 422 2434
Hamburgers, fast food snacks
and video games; popular with
the young.

Garden Cafe
Bok Tower Gardens
Lake Wales
Tel: (813) 676 1408
Soups, sandwiches and snacks
from terrace-cafe set in ravish-
ing gardens.

Hard Rock Cafe
Universal Studios
5401 Kirkman Road
Orlando
Tel: (407) 363 ROLL
Hamburgers, barbecue and sal-
ads in guitar-shaped diner.

Johnny's Pizza Palace
4908 Lake Underhill Road
Orlando
Tel: (407) 277 3452

Pizzas of every description, pasta
and sandwiches.

Numero Uno
2499 S Orange Avenue
Orlando
Tel: (407) 841 3840
Hearty Cuban specialities such
as pork and beans in busy,
friendly dining room.

Ponderosa Steak House
7598 W Irlo Bronson Memorial
Highway
Kissimmee
Tel: (407) 396 7721
Family restaurant, breakfast buf-
fet, salad bar.

TGI Friday's
6426 Carrier Drive
Orlando
Tel: (407) 345 8822
Popular and lively; big menu;
happy hour.

Wheeler's Goody Cafe
13 S Monroe Avenue
Arcadia
Tel: (813) 494 3909
Cracker country cooking; steaks,
pies, cold drinks and sandwiches.

GOLD COAST
Expensive
Brazilian Court Diing Room
301 Australian Avenue
Palm Beach
Tel: (407) 655 7740
Gorgeous 1920s dining room
opening on to fountain court;
superlative light, elegant cuisine.

Burt & Jack's
Berth 23
Port Everglades
Ft Lauderdale
Tel: (305) 522 2878
Elegant Spanish villa on the
waterfront with impressive
American menu. (Co-owned by
the local actor.)

Cafe L'Europe
150 Worth Avenue
Palm Beach
Tel: (407) 655 4020
Stylish European dining room serving superb French dishes with finesse.

Cafe Max
2601 E Atlantic Boulevard
Pompano Beach
Tel: (305) 782 0606
American cooking meets the classics to delicious effect; fresh seafood specialities; Art Deco styling.

Casa Vecchia
209 N Birch Road
Ft Lauderdale
Tel: (305) 463 7575
Lovely 1930s villa on the water; Mediterranean cuisine from France, Spain, Turkey and North Africa.

Down Under
3000 E Oakland Park Boulevard
Ft Lauderdale
Tel: (305) 563 4123
Elegant waterfront bistro; jazz piano accompanies diverse American-French menu.

Moderate
15th Street Fisheries
1900 SE 15th Street
Ft Lauderdale
Tel: (305) 763 2777
Award-winning seafood specialities with waterfront views.

By Word of Mouth
3200 NE 12th Avenue
Ft Lauderdale
Tel: (305) 564 3663
Ingenious New American cuisine in cosy, small restaurant.

Chuck & Harold's
207 Royal Poinciana Way
Palm Beach
Tel: (407) 659 1440
Tropical decor, tiles and beams

frame varied Californian menu.

Harpoon Louie's
1065 A1A (at US1)
Jupiter
Tel: (407) 744 1300
Casual waterfront eatery; innovative menu with surf and turf combinations.

Il Giardino
609 E Las Olas Boulevard
Ft Lauderdale
Tel: (305) 763 3733
Northern Italian specialities; chic modern decor and garden.

Paesano
1301 E Las Olas Boulevard
Ft Lauderdale
Tel: (305) 467 3266
Elegant presentation; specialities include charcoal grilled seafood.

Riverview
1741 E Riverview Road
Deerfield Beach
Tel: (305) 428 3463
Old Florida seafood house on the Intracoastal Waterway; prime beef too.

Taboo
221 Worth Avenue
Palm Beach
Tel: (407) 835 3500
Diverse and tempting menu; generous starters make a light meal; busy bar.

This Is It Pub
424 24th Street
West Palm Beach
Tel: (407) 833 4997
Rack of lamb or seafood, pasta or bouillabaisse in pubby ambience.

Budget
Banana Boat
739 E Ocean Avenue
Boynton Beach
Tel: (407) 732 9400

Casual waterfront spot; mostly seafood, dockside bar, entertainment.

Bimini Boatyard
1555 SE 17th Street
Ft Lauderdale
Tel: (305) 525 7400
Informal waterfront cafe with diverse California-style menu.

Cafe L'Express
150 Worth Avenue
Palm Beach
Tel: (407) 833 2117
Pasta, seafood and take-out deli delights on balcony of Esplanade.

Cielito Lindo
4480 N Federal Highway
Pompano Beach
Tel: (305) 941 8226
Tex-Mex cuisine in South of the Border setting; margaritas.

Docksiders
908 N Ocean Drive
Hollywood
Tel: (305) 922 2265
Family dining on the Intracoastal Waterway; open air terrace.

Hortz Bar-B-Q-Shanty
4261 Griffin Road
Ft Lauderdale
Tel: (305) 581 9085
Great barbecue and Cajun home-cooking in friendly atmosphere.

John G's
10 S Ocean Boulevard
Lake Worth
Tel: (407) 585 9860
Busy, informal and on the beach; burgers, omelettes, pasta and sandwiches.

Lester's Diner
250 SR 84
Ft Lauderdale
Tel: (305) 525 5641
Local institution with 24-hour

breakfast service (lunch/dinner).

Tom's Place
1198N Dixie Highway
Boca Raton
Tel: (407) 368 3502
Lip-smackin' barbecued ribs and chicken; home-cooking favoured by NFL giants.

Tony Roma's
2215 Palm Beach Lakes Boulevard
West Palm Beach
Tel: (407) 689 1703
Family-dining chain; burgers, ribs and other fillers.

EAST COAST
Expensive
Mango Tree
118 N Atlantic Avenue
Cocoa Beach
Tel: (407) 799 0513
Elegant tropical decor, garden aviary; delicious light, fresh American cuisine.

Raintree
102 San Marco Avenue
St Augustine
Tel: (904) 824 7211
Beautifully restored old house; seasonal menu with plenty of seafood, marvellous puddings.

Sterling's Flamingo Cafe
3351 St Johns Avenue
Jacksonville
Tel: (904) 387 0700
Romantic and elegant small restaurant serving gourmet; New American cuisine in Riverside area.

Moderate
Columbia
98 St George Street
St Augustine
Tel: (904) 824 3341
Paella and other Spanish specialities in the historic district.

Crustaceans
2321 Beach Boulevard

Jacksonville Beach
Tel: (904) 241 8238
Seafod menu and live music on summer weekends.

Gatsby's
520 W Cocoa Beach Causeway
Cocoa Beach
Tel: (407) 783 2389
Dining and entertainment complex with choice of eateries.

Grenamyer's
4000 St Johns Avenue
Jacksonville
Tel: (904) 387 38880
Fun, popular jazz cafe with eceletic menu in Riverside district.

Jad's
Palmetto Walk Village
Fernandina Beach
Tel: (904) 277 2350
Pretty, relaxing setting; tempting seasonal menu with local seafood.

Kay's Coach House
734 Main Street
Daytona Beach
Tel: (904) 253 1944
Long menu of ribs, steaks and seafood. Families welcome; cocktails.

Mangrove Matties
1640 Seaway Drive
Ft Pierce
Tel: (407) 466 1044
Great waterfront views, broad menu and sumptuous Sunday brunch.

Ocean Grill
1050 Sexton Plaza (Beachland Boulevard)
Vero Beach
Tel: (407) 231 5409
Candlelit local favourite; fish, steaks, ocean view.

Ragtime
207 Atlantic Boulevard
Atlantic Beach

Tel: (904) 241 7877
Young, fun and New Orleans jazzy; Creole and Cajun specialities.

Sliders
Seaside Inn
1998 S Fletcher Street
Fernandina Beach
Tel: (904) 261 0954
Rustic beach hang-out which offers mainly seafood menu

Topaz Cafe
1224 S A1A
Flagler Beach
Tel: (904) 439 3275
A real find serving fresh, home-cooked and inventive New American cuisine.

Budget
Checker's Cafe
Broadway & A1A
Daytona Beach
Tel: (904) 252 3626
Burgers, sandwiches and inner specials in family-friendly cafe.

Chimes
12 Avenida Menendez
St Augustine
Tel: (904) 829 8141
Good value home-cooking in the centre of town.

Crawdaddy's
1643 Prudential Drive
Jacksonville
Tel: (904) 396 3546
Casual riverfront seafood and Cajun spot; dancing.

Homestead
1712 Beach Boulevard
Jacksonville Beach
Tel: (904) 249 5240
Generous country cooking and homey atmosphere.

Kountry Kitche
1115N Courtenay Parkway
Meritt Island
Tel: (407) 459 3457

Generous home-cooked spread; near Kennedy Space Center.

Norris's Famous Place for Ribs
3080 N US1
Ft Pierce
Tel: (407) 464 4000
Local family-style favourite; groaning platters of barbecue goodies.

Ocean Pier
A1A at Main Street
Daytona Beach
Tel: (904) 238 1212
Fast food with a view right in the heart of things.

Panama Hattie's
A1A (opposite the Pier)
St Augustine Beach
Tel: (904) 471 2255
Lively youth favourite; broad snacky menu; open-air bar.

Santa Maria
135 Avenida Menendez
St Augustine
Tel: (904) 829 6578
Seafood, steaks and chicken in family-run landmark by the marina.

TC's Top Dog
425 N Atlantic Avenue
Daytona Beach
Tel: (904) 257 7766
Hot dog heaven; also chilli, cheese or coleslaw on a bun. Kids' choice.

WEST COAST
Expensive
Bern's Steak House
1208 S Howard Avenue
Tampa
Tel: (813) 251 2421
Clubby decor, exemplary service, aged prime steaks accompanied by taste-sensation organic vegetables.

Black Swan
13707 N 58th Street

Clearwater
Tel: (813) 535 SWAN
Perfect for romantic evening; varied and innovative cuisine with classic base, stunning desserts.

Cafe L'Europe
431 St Armand's Circle
Sarasota
Tel: (813) 388 4415
Fashionably elegant, arty setting; delicate French nouvelle cuisine seafood, veal and beef dishes.

Chef's Garden
1300 Third Street,
Naples
Tel: (813) 262 5500
Culinary landmark in delightful surroundings; creative seasonal cuisine; also moderately-priced bistro, Truffles.

Moderate
Bubble Room
Captiva Road
Captiva
Tel: (813) 472 5353
Wacky 1940s kitsch decor; monster platters of home-cooking and killer desseerts.

Columbia
21st Street at Broadway
Ybor City
Tel: (813) 248 4961
Landmark Spanish restaurant; rustic decor and traditional menu.

Joe Di's
3260W Hillsborough Avenue
Tampa
Tel: (813) 876 666
Smart, romantic and renowned for creative pasta and fresh seafood.

Kapok Tree
923 McMullen-Booth Road
Clearwater
Tel: (813) 726 0504).
Take a camera to this al fresco

mirage; luxuriant greenery, simple food.

Lobster Pot
17814 Gulf Boulevard
Redington Shores
Tel: (813) 391 8592
Local favourite renowned for its seafood; also prime steaks.

Louis Pappas' Riverside
10 W Dodecanese Boulevard
Tarpon Springs
Tel: (813) 937 5101
Busy tourist sport; great Greek food.

McCully's Rooftop
Hickory Boulevard
Bonita Springs
Tel: (813) 463 7010
Lovely waterfront views; steaks, seafood and entertainmnet.

Prawnbroker
6535 McGregor Boulevard
Fort Myers
Tel: (813) 489 2226
Long-time local favourite; mainly fish menu, steak and poultry.

Ristorante Bellini's
1549 Main Street
Sarasota
Tel: (813) 365 7380
Robust Italian cuisine and extensive wine list.

Riverwalk Fish & Ale House
1200 S Fifth Avenue
Naples
Tel: (813) 263 2734
Informal dockside dining in the Old Marine Marketplace.

Rosario's Italian
1930 E 7th Avenue
Ybor City
Tel: (813) 247 6764
Old World Italian cuisine; pasta, chicken, seafood and steaks.

Sunset Cafe

537 Douglas Avenue
Dunedin
Tel: (813) 736 3973
Small, welcoming cafe with terrific pasta and seasonal specialities.

Veranda
2122 Second Street
Fort Myers
Tel: (813) 332 2065
Historic buildings with garden court; innovative regional Southern menu.

Wine Cellar
17307 N Gulf Boulevard
Redington Beach
Tel: (813) 393 3491
Warm atmosphere, plus award-winning American and Mittel-European menu.

Budget
Algiers Seafood Market
1473 Periwinkle Way
Sanibel
Tremendous range of seafood cooked to order; home-baking, ice creams.

Big Apple Bistro
4000 Central Avenue
St Petersburg
Tel: (813) 327 5784
All American cuisine from Detroit B-B-Q to Creole shrimp.

Cactus Club
1601 Snow Avenue
Tampa
Tel: (813) 251 4089
Lively and fun; Southwestern cuisine, huge desserts.

Captain's Table
Dock Street
Cedar Key
Tel: (904) 543 5441
Great dockside position; seafood specialities.

Doe-Al's Southern Cookin'
85 Corey Avenue

St Petersburg Beach
Tel: (813) 360 8026
Family-style home cooking (XXX-large portion control).

Frascati's Italian
1258 N Airport Road
Naples
Tel: (813) 262 6511
Convenient restaurant-deli for museums; good sandwiches.

Roger's Real Pit Bar-B-Que
12150 Seminole Boulevard
Largo
Tel: (813) 586 2629
Baby back ribs, franks and beans plus wonderful salad bar.

Silver Ring Cafe
1831 E 7th Avenue
Ybor City
Tel: (813) 248 2549
Cuban sandwich emporium since 1947.

Walt's Fish Market
560 N Washington Boulevard
Sarasota
Tel: (813) 365 1735
Terrific choice of fish dinners, plus Raw Oyster Bar.

Wildflower
5218 Ocean Boulevard
Siesta Key
Sarasota
Tel: (813) 349 1758
Exotic vegetarian and fish dishes in friendly cafe.

PANHANDLE
Expensive
Andrew's Second Act
102 W Jefferson Street
Tallahassee
Tel: (904) 222 2759
Political district favourite serving small, elegant New American menu in a Frenchified setting.

Fiddler's Green
Marriott's Bay Point Resort

100 Delwood Road
Panama City Beach
Tel: (904) 234 0220
Refined gourmet dining in deluxe resort overlooking lagoon.

Jamie's
424 E Zaragoza Street
Pensacola
Tel: (904) 434 2911
Lovely historic home transformed into gourmet candlelit restaurant; delicate, classic cuisine.

Moderate
Boar's Head
17290 Front Beach Road
Panama City Beach
Tel: (904) 234 6628
Woodsy interior; generous prime rib and seafood platters.

Chez Pierre
115 N Adams Street
Tallahassee
Tel: (904) 222 0936
Attractive French cafe with broad menu, light lunches, patisseries.

Flamingo Cafe
414 E US98
Destin
Tel: (904) 837 0961
Chic black, white and pink decor, harbour views; veal and fish specialities.

Gibson Inn
Market Street
Apalachicola
Tel: (904) 653 2191
Historic inn serving varied menu of classic dishes; semi-formal.

Harbour House
3001-A W 10th Street
Panama City
Tel: (904) 785 9053
Waterfront family dining; great value lunch buffet.

Melting Pot

1832 N Monroe Street
Tallahassee
Tel: (904) 386 7440
Cheese, meat seafood and dessert foundues for a cosy evening.

Michael's
600 S Palafox Street
Pensacola
Tel: (904) 434 7736
Pretty dining rooms in downtown historic district; fresh, innovative cuisine.

Oaks Restaurant
US98
Panacea 20 miles outh of Tallahassee
Tel: (904) 984 5370
Popular out-of-town dining spot; seafood Southern style.

Perri's
300 Elgin Parkway
Forth Walton
Tel: (904) 862 4421
Popular Italian restaurant with broad menu and plenty of pasta favourites.

Scotto's
300 S Alcaniz Street
Pensacola
Tel: (904) 434 1932
Friendly family-run Italian restaurant in fine old house.

The Wharf
4141 Apalachee Parkway
Tallahassee
Tel: (904) 656 2332
The state capital's top seafood spot.

Budget
Andrew's Cafe
228 S Adams Street
Tallahassee
Tel: (904) 222 3444
New York-style deli and grill with outdoor seating in restored district.

Barnacle Bill's

1830 N Monroe Street
Tallahassee
Tel: (904) 385 8734
Pasta and poultry in addition to seafood; kids eat free on Sundays.

Billy's Oyster Bar I
3000 Thomas Drive
Panama City Beach
Tel: (904) 235 2349
Oysters every which way, lobster, crawfish, crab and shrimp.

Cajun Inn
477 Beckrich Drive
Panama City Beach
Tel: (904) 235 9987
Generous platters of Southern specials such as spicy jambalaya.

Captain Dave's
3796 Old Highway 98
Destin
Tel: (904) 837 2627
Family-style seafood spot overlooking the Gulf; dancing and entertainment.

Cap'n Jim's
905 E Gregory Street
Tallahassee
Tel: (904) 433 3526
Family-run fish restaurant on the bay; house specialities recommended.

Food Glorious Food
106E College Avenue
Tallahassee
Tel: (904) 222 5232
Modern American open-air cafe, great pastries.

The Hut
US98 Apalachicola
Tel: (904) 653 9410
Rustic seafood and steak joint; popular bar.

Liollio's
14 Miracle Strip Parkway
Ft Walton Beach
Tel: (904) 243 5011

Greek seafood, steaks and huge salads; families welcome.

McGuire's Irish Pub
600 E Gregory Street
Pensacola
Tel: (904) 433 6789
Ribs, burgers, sandwiches, seafood and rollicking good times.

Mr P's Sandwich Shop
221 E Zaragoza Street
Tallahassee
Tel: (904) 433 0294
Homey historic district soup, salad, sandwich and cool drink stop.

Spring Creek Restaurant
US365 Spring Creek
Tel: (904) 926 3751
Unpretentious seasonal seafood dishes in bayside fishing village.

CHAMBERS OF COMMERCE
This list also includes addresses of convention and visitors bureaus.

Alachua Chamber of Commerce
PO Box 387
Alachua
FL 32615
Tel: (904) 462-3333

Alachua County Tourist Development Council
PO Drawer CC
Gainesville
FL 32602
Tel: (904) 374-5210

Amelia Island Chamber of Commerce
PO Box 472
Fernandina Beach
FL 32034
Tel: (904) 261-3248

Anna Maria Island Chamber of Commerce
503 Manatee Ave

Suite A
Holmes Beach
FL 34217
Tel: (813) 778-1541

Apalachicola Bay Chamber of Commerce
28 Market St
Apalachiocola
FL 32320
Tel: (904) 653-9419

Apopka Area Chamber of Commerce
80E Main St
Apopka
FL 32703
Tel: (407) 886-1441

Auburndale Chamber of Commerce
111 E ParkSt
Auburndale
FL 33823
Tel: (813) 967-3400

Avon Park Chamber of Commerce
PO Box 1330
Avon Park
FL 33825
Tel: (813) 453-3350

Baker County Chamber of Commerce
20 East Macclenny Ave
Macclenny
FL 32063
Tel: (904) 259-6433

Bartow Chamber of Commerce
PO Box 956
Bartow
FL 33830
Tel: (813) 533-7125

Bay County Chamber of Commerce
PO Box 1850
Panama City
FL 32402
Tel: (904) 785-5206

Belleview-South Marion Chamber of Commerce
5301 SE Abshier Boulevard
Belleview
FL 32620
Tel: (904) 245-2178

Belle Glade Chamber of Commerce
540 S Main St
Belle Glade
FL 33430
Tel: (407) 996-2745

Bonita Springs Chambere of Commerce
PO Box 1240
Bonita Springs
FL 33959
Tel: (813) 992-2943

Brandon Chamber of Commerce
408 W Brandon Boulevard
Brandon
FL 33511
Tel: (813) 689-1221

Brevard County Tourist Development Council
2235 North Courtenay Parkway
Merritt Island
FL 32953
Tel: (407) 453-2211

Calhoun County Chamber of Commerce
314 East Central Ave
Blountstown
FL 32424
Tel: (904) 674-4519

Cedar Key Area Chamber of Commerce
Second St
Cedar Key
FL 32625
Tel: (904) 543-5600

Chamber of Commerce of South Brevard
1005 E Strawbridge Ave
Melbourne
FL 32901
Tel: (407) 724-5400

Chamber of Commerce of the Palm Beaches
5012 North Flagler Drive
West Palm Beach
FL 33401
Tel: (407) 833-3711

Chamber of SW Florida
PO Box CC
Fort Myers
FL 33902
Tel: (813) 334-1133

Chamber of SW Florida-Cape Coral
2051 Cape Coral Parkway
Cape Coral
FL 33904
Tel: (813) 542-3721

Charlotte County Chamber of Commerce
2702 Tamiami Trail
Port Charlotte
FL 33952
Tel: (813) 627-2222

Citrus County Chamber of Commerce
208 West Main St
Inverness
FL 32650
Tel: (904) 726-2801

Citrus County Commission and Tourist Development Council
110 North Apopka St
Inverness
FL 32650
Tel: (904) 726-8500

Clay County Chamber of Commerce
PO Box 1441
Orange Park
FL 32607-1441
Tel: (904) 264-2651

Clermont Area Chamber of Commerce
PO Box 417
Clermont
FL 32711
Tel: (904) 394-4191

Clewiston Chamber of Commerce
PO Box 275
Clewiston
FL 33440
Tel: (813) 983-7979

Cocoa Beach Area Chamber of Commerce
400 Fortenberry Road
Merrit Island
FL 32952
Tel: (407) 459-2200

Coconut Grove Chamber of Commerce
2820 McFarlane Road
Coconut Grove
Fl 33133
Tel: (305) 444-7270

Columbia County Chamber of Commerce
PO Box 566
Lake City
FL 32056
Tel: (904) 752-3690

Coral Sprigns Chamber of Commerce
7305 W Sample Road
#110
Coral Springs
FL 33065
Tel: (305) 752-4242

Crestview Area Chamber of Commerce
502 S Main St
Crestview
FL 32536
Tel: (904) 682-3212

Crystal River Chamber of Commerce
402 East Meridian Ave
Dade City
FL 33525
Tel: (904) 567-3769

Dania Chamber of Commerce
PO Box 838
Dania
FL 33004

Tel: (305) 927-3377

Davie-Cooper City Chamber of Commerce
4185 Southwest 64 Ave
Davie
FL 33314
Tel: (305) 581-0790

Daytona Beach Shores Chamber of Commerce
3048
South Atlantic Ave
Daytona Beach
FL 32018-6102
Tel: (904) 761-7163

DeBary Area Chamber of Commerce
PO Box One
DeBary
FL 32713
Tel: (407) 668-4614

DeLand Area Chamber of Commerce
PO Box 629
DeLand
FL 32721-0629
Tel: (904) 734-4331

Deltona Area Chamber of Commerce
PO Box 5152
Deltona
FL 32728l
Tel: (407) 574-5522

DeSoto County Chamber of Commerce
PO Box 149
Arcadia
FL 33821
Tel: (813) 494-4033

Destin Chambere of Commerce
PO Box Eight
Destin
FL 32541
Tel: (904) 837-6241

Destination Daytonal
PO Box 2775
Daytona Beach

FL 32014
Tel: (904) 255-0981

Dunnellon Area Chamber of Commerce
PO Box 868
Dunnellon
FL 32630
Tel: (904) 489-2320

East Orange Chamber of Commerce
PO Box 677027
Union Park Branch
Orlando
FL 32867-7027
Tel: (407) 277-5951

Englewood Area Chamber of Commerce
601 South Indiana Ave
Englewood
FL 34223
Tel: (813) 474-5511

Eustis Chamber of Commerce
PO Box 1210
Eustis
FL 32727-1210
Tel: (904) 357-3434

Everglades Area Chamber of Commerce
PO Box 130
Everglades City
FL 33929
Tel: (813) 695-3941

Flagler County Chamber of Commerce
Star Route 18-N
Bunnell
FL 32010
Tel: (904) 437-0106

Fort Meade Chamber of Commerce
PO Box 91
Fort Meade
FL 33841
Tel: (813) 285-8253

Fort Myers Beach Chamber of Commerce

PO Box 6109
Fort Myer
FL 33932
Tel: (813) 463-6451

Frostproof Chamber of Commerce
PO Box 968
Frostproof
FL 33843
Tel: (813) 635-9112

Gadsden County Chamber of Commerce
PO Box 389
Quincy
FL 32351
Tel: (904) 627-9231

Gainesville Area Chamber of Commerce Inc
PO Box 1187
Gainesville
FL 32602
Tel: (904) 372-4305

Gilchrist County Chamber of Commerce
PO Box 186
Trenton
FL 32693
Tel: (904) 463-6327

Glades County Chamber of Commerce
PO Box 490
Moore Haven
FL 33471
Tel: (813) 946-0440

Greater Boca Raton Chamber of Commerce
1800 North Dixie Hwy
Boca Raton
FL 33432
Tel: (407) 395-4433.

Greater Boynton Chamber of Commerce
639 E Ocean Ave
#108 Boynton Beach
FL 33435
Tel: (407) 732-9501

Greater Clearwater Chamber of Commerce
PO Box 2457
Clearwater
FL 33517
Tel: (813) 461-0011

Greater Deerfield Beach Chamber of Commerce
1601 East Hillsboro Boulevard
Deerfield Beach
FL 33441
Tel: (305) 427-1050

Greater Delray Beach Chamber of Commerce
64 Southeast Fifth Ave
Delray Beach
FL 33483
Tel: (407) 278-0424

Greater Dunedin Chamber of Commerce
434 Main St
Dunedin
FL 34698
Tel: (813) 736-5066

Greater Ford Lauderdale Chamber of Commerce
PO Box 14516
Fort Lauderdale
FL 33302
Tel: (305) 462-6000

Greater Ford Lauderdale Convention & Visitors Bureau
500 East Broward Blvd
#104 Fort Lauderdale
FL 33394
Tel: (305) 765-4466.

Greater Ford Walton Beach Chamber of Commerce
PO Drawer 640
Fort Walton Beach
FL 32549
Tel: (904) 244-8191

Greater Gulf Breeze Chamber of Commerce
913 Gulf Breeze Pkwy
Suite 17
Gulf Breeze

FL 32561
Tel: (904) 932-7888

Greater Hollywood Chamber of Commerce
PO Box 2345
Hollywood
FL 33022
Tel: (305) 920-3330

Greater Homestead-Florida City Chamber of Commerce
650 US Highway One
Homestead
FL 33030
Tel: (305) 247-2332

Greater Key West Chamber of Commerce
402 Wall St
Key West
FL 33040
Tel: (305) 294-2587

Greater LaBelle Chamber of Commerce
PO Box 456
LaBelle
FL 33935
Tel: (813)675-0125

Greater Lake Placid Chamber of Commerce
PO Box 187
Lake Placid
FL 33852
Tel: (813) 465-4331

Greater Lake Worth Chamber of Commerce
1702 Lake Worth Road
Lake Worth
FL 33460
Tel: (407) 582-4401

Greater Largo Chamber of Commerce
395 First Ave
SW Largo
FL 34640
Tel: (813) 584-2321

Greater Miami Convention & Visitors Bureau

4770 Biscayne Blvd
Miami 33137
Tel: (305) 573-4300

Greater Mulberry Chamber of Commerce
PO Box 254
Mulberry
FL 33860
Tel: (813) 425-1215

Greater Orange City Area Chamber of Commerce
520 N Volusia Ave
Orange City
FL 32763
Tel: (904) 775-2793

Greater Orlando Chamber of Commerce
PO Box 1234
Orlando
FL 32802
Tel: (407) 425-1234

Greater Palm Harbor Area Chamber of Commerce
1000 US 19 North
Suite 300
Palm Harbor
FL 34684
Tel: (813) 785-5205

Greater Pine Island Chamber of Commerce
PO Box 525
Matlacha
FL 33909
Tel: (813) 283-0888

Greater Pinellas Park Chamber of Commerce
5851 Park Boulevard
Pinellas Park
FL 34665
Tel: (813) 544-4777

Greater Plant City Chamber of Commerce
PO Drawer CC
Plant City
FL 33566
Tel: (813) 754-3707

Greater Riverview Chamber of Commerce
PO Box 18
Riverview
FL 33569
Tel: (813) 677-26074

Greater Sanford Chamber of Commerce
PO Drawer CC
Sanford
FL 32772-0868
Tel: (407) 322-2212

Greater Sebring Chamber of Commerce
309 South Circle
Sebring
FL 33870
Tel: (813) 385-8448

Greater Seminole Area Chamber of Commerce
PO Box 3337
Seminole
FL 34642
Tel: (813) 392-3245

Greater Seminole County Chamber of Commerce
PO Box 784
Altamonte Springs
FL 32715-0784
Tel: (407) 834-4404

Greater Tampa Chamber of Commerce
PO Box 420
Tampa
FL 33601
Tel: (813) 228-7777

Greater Tarpon Springs Chamber of Commerce
210 S Pinellas Ave
#120 Tarpon Springs
FL 34689
Tel: (813) 937-6109

Groveland/Mascotte Chamber of Commerce
PO Box 115
Groveland
FL 32736

Tel: (904) 429-3678

Gulf Beaches Chamber of Commerce
PO Box 273
Indian Rocks Beach
FL 34635
Tel: (813) 595-4575

Haines City Chamber of Commerce
PO Box 986
Haines City
FL 33844
Tel: (813) 422-3751

Halifax Area Chamber of Commerce
PO Box 2775
Daytona Beach
FL 32015
Tel: (904) 255-0981

Hamilton County Chamber of Commerce
PO Drawer P
Jasper
FL 32052
Tel: (904) 792-1200

Hardee County Chamber of Commerce
PO Box 683
Wauchula
FL 33873
Tel: (813) 773-6967

Hawthorne Area Chamber of Commerce
101 East Fort Dade Ave
Brooksville
FL 34601
Tel: (904) 796-2420

High Springs Chamber of Commerce
PO Box 863
High Springs
FL 32643
Tel: (904) 454-3120

Hobe Sound Chamber of Commerce
PO Box 1507

Hobe Sound
FL 33455
Tel: (407) 546-4724

Holly Hill Chamber of Commerce
PO Box 615
Holly Hill
FL 32017
Tel: (904) 255-7311

Holmes County Chamber of Commerce
PO Box 1977
Bonifay
FL 32425
Tel: (904) 547-4682

Homosassa Springs Area Chamber of Commerce
PO Box 1098
Homosassa Springs
FL 32647
Tel: (904) 628-2666

Immokalee Chamber of Commerce
907 Roberts Ave
Immokalee
FL 33934
Tel: (813) 657-3237

Jackson County Chamber of Commerce
PO Box 130
Marianna
FL 32446
Tel: (904) 482-8061

Jacksonville and its Beaches Convention & Visitors Bureau
Six E Bay St
Suite 200
Jacksonville
FL 32202
Tel: (904) 353-0736

Jacksonville Chamber of Commerce
Three Independent Drive
Jacksonville
FL 32201
Tel: (904) 353-0300

Jensen Beach Chamber of Commerce
1910 NE
Jensen Beach Boulevard
Jensen Beach
FL 34957
Tel: (407) 334-3444

Kissimmee-Osceola County Chamber of Commerce
320 East Monument Ave
Kissimmee
FL 32741
Tel: (407) 847-3174

Kissimmee/St Cloud Convention & Visitors Bureau
PO Box 2007
Kissimmee
FL 32742-2007
Tel: (407) 847-5000

Lake Alfred Chamber of Commerce
PO Box 956
Lake Alfred
FL 33850
Tel: (813) 956-1334

Lake City-Columbia County Chamber of Commerce
15 East Orange St
PO Box 566
Lake City
FL 32056-0566
Tel: (904) 752-3690

Lake County Tourist Development Council
315 West Main St
Tavares
FL 32778
Tel: (904) 343-9850

Lake Wales Area Chamber of Commerce
340 West Central Ave
Lake Wales
FL 33859-0191
Tel: (813) 676-3445

Lakeland Area Chamber of Commerce
PO Box 98

Lake O'Lakes
FL 34639
Tel: (813) 949-1582

Lee County Visitor & Convention Bureau
2180 W First St
Fort Myers
FL 33901
Tel: (813) 335-2631

Leesburg Area Chamber of Commerce
PO Box 269
Leesburg
FL 32749
Tel: (904) 787-2131

Lehigh Acres Chamber of Commerce Inc
PO Box 757
Lehigh Acres
FL 33970-0757
Tel: (813) 369-3322

Liberty County Chamber of Commerce
PO Box 523
Bristol
FL 32321
Tel: (904) 643-2359

Longboat Key Chamber of Commerce
510 Bay Isles Road
Longboat Key
FL 34228
Tel: (813) 383-2466

Longwood-Winter Springs Area Chamber of Commerce
PO Box 520963
Longwood
FL 32752-0963
Tel: (407) 831-9991

Madeira Beach Chamber of Commerce
501 150 Ave
Madeira Beach
FL 33708
Tel: (813) 391-7373

Madison County Chamber of

Commerce
105 North Range
Madison
FL 32340
Tel: (904) 973-2788

**Maitland-South Seminole
Chamber of Commerce**
110 North Maitland Ave
Maitland
FL 32751
Tel: (407) 644-0741

Manatee Chamber of Commerce
222 Tenth St
West Bradenton
FL 34205
Tel: (813) 748-3411

**Manatee County Convention &
Visitors Bureau**
PO Box 788
Brandenton
FL 34206-0788
Tel: (813) 746-5985

**Marco Island Area Chamber of
Commerce**
PO Box 913
Marco Island
FL 33969
Tel: (813) 394-7549

**Mayo-Lafayette Chamber of
Commerce**
PO Box 416
Mayo
FL 32066
Tel: (904) 294-2705

Monroe County Tourist Development Council
PO Box 866
Key West
FL 33041
Tel: (305) 296-2228

**Monticello-Jefferson County
Chamber of Commerce**
420 West Washington St
Monticello
FL 32344
Tel: (904) 997-5552

Mount Dora Chamber of Commerce
1700 North Tamiami Trail
Naples
FL 33940
Tel: (813) 262-6141

**Navarre Beach Chamber of
Commerce**
PO Box 5336
Navarre
FL 32569-5336
Tel: (904) 939-3267

**New Smyrna Beach-Edgewater-
Oak Hill Chamber of Commerce**
PO Box 129
New Smyrna Beach
FL 32070
Tel: (904) 428-2449

**Newberry Area Chamber of
Commerce**
PO Box 1004
Newberry
FL 32669
Tel: (904) 472-4121

**North Fort Myers Chamber of
Commerce**
PO Box 271629
Tampa
FL 33688
Tel: (813) 960-9344

**Ocala-Marion County Chamber
of Commerce**
PO Box 1210
Ocala
FL 32678
Tel: (904) 629-8051

**Okeechobee County Chamber
of Commerce**
55 South Parrot Ave
Okeechobee
FL 34972
Tel: (813) 763-6464

Oldsmar Chamber of Commerce
PO Box 521
Oldsmar

FL 34677
Tel: (813) 855-4233

Orlando/Orange County Convention & Visitors Bureau
7680 Republic Drive
Suite 200
Orlando
FL 32819
Tel: (407) 345-8882

**Ormond Beach Chamber of
Commerce**
PO Box 874
Ormond Beach
FL 32074
Tel: (904) 677-3454

**Palm Bay Area Chamber of
Commerce**
4100 Dixie Highway
NE Palm Bay
FL 32905
Tel: (407) 723-0801

**Palm Beach County Convention
& Visitors Bureau**
1555 Palm Beach Lakes Blvd
#204 West Palm Beach
FL 33401
Tel: (407) 471-3995

Palm City Chamber of Commerce
PO Box 530
Palm City
FL 33490
Tel: (407) 286-8121

**Panama City Beach Convention
& Visitors Bureau**
PO Box 9473
Panama City Beach
FL 32407
Tel: (904) 234-6575

Pensacola Chamber of Commerce
PO Box 550
Pensacola
FL 32593
Tel: (904) 438-4081

Pensacola Convention & Visi-

tors Information Center
401 East Gregory St
Pensacola
FL 32501
Tel: (904) 434-1234

Perry-Taylor County Chamber
of Commerce
PO Box 892
Perry
FL 32347
Tel: (904) 584-5366

Pinellas County Tourist Development Council
4625 East Bay Drive
Suite 109A
Clearwater
FL 34624
Tel: (813) 530-6452

Poet St Lucie Chamber of Commerce
626 SE Port St Lucie Boulevard
Port St Lucie
FL 33452
Tel: (407) 335-4422

Polk County Tourism Development Council
PO Box 1909
Bartow
FL 33830
Tel: (813) 533-1161

Ponce De Leon Area Chamber
of Commerce
3431 Ridgewood Ave
Port Orange
FL 32019
Tel: (904) 761-1601

Port St Joe-Gulf County Chamber of Commerce
PO Box 964
Port St Joe
FL 32456
Tel: (904) 227-1223

Putnam County Chamber of
Commerce
PO Box 550
Palatka
FL 32078
Tel: (904) 328-1503

Safety Harbor Chamber of Commerce
200 Main St
Safety Harbor
FL 34695
Tel: (813) 726-2890

Sanibel-Captival Island Chamber of Commerce
PO Box 166
Sanibel
FL 33957
Tel: (813) 472-3232

Santa Rosa County Chamber of
Commerce
501 Stewart St
SW Milton
FL 32570
Tel: (904) 623-2339

Sarasota Convention & Visitors
Bureau
655 North Tamiami Trail
Sarasota
FL 34236
Tel: (813) 957-1877

Sarasota County Chamber of
Commerce
PO Box 308
Sarasota
FL 34230
Tel: (813) 955-8187

Sebastian River Area Chamber
of Commerce
PO Box 780385
Sebastian
FL 332978-0385
Tel: (407) 589-5969

Siesta Key Chamber of Commerce
5263 Ocean Blvd, Sarasota
FL 34242
Tel: (813) 349-3800

South Hillsborough County
Chamber of Commerce
315 South Tamiami Trail
Ruskin
FL 33570

Tel: (813) 645-3808

St Augustine-St Johns Chamber
of Commerce
PO Drawer O
St Augustine
FL 32085
Tel: (904) 829-5681

St Cloud Area Chamber of Commerce
2200 Virginia Ave, Fort Pierce
FL 34982
Tel: (407) 461-2700

St Petersburg Area Chamber of
Commerce
6990 Gulf Boulevard
St Petersburg
FL 33706
Tel: (813) 360-6957

Starke-Bradford County Chamber of Commerce
1650 South Kanner Highway
Stuart
FL 33494
Tel: (407) 287-1088

Sumter County Chamber of
Commerce
PO Box 550, Bushnell
FL 33513
Tel: (904) 793-3099

Sun City Center Chamber of
Commerce
1651 Sun City Center Plaza
Sun City
FL 33570
Tel: (813) 634-5111

Suwanne County Chamber of
Commerce
PO Box C, Live Oak
FL 32060
Tel: (904) 362-3071

Tallahassee Convention & Visitors Bureau
PO Box 1639
Tallahassee
FL 32302
Tel: (904) 224-8116

Tampa/Hillsborough Convention & Visitors Association
100 South Ashley Drive
Suite 850
Tampa
FL 33602
Tel: (813) 223-1111

Tavares Chamber of Commerce
PO Box 697, Tavares
FL 32778
Tel: (904) 343-2531

The Jacksonville Chamber of Commerce, Beaches Development Department
413 Pablo Aven
Jacksonville Beach
FL 32250
Tel: (904) 249-3868

Titusville Chamber of Comerce
2000 South Washington Ave
Titusville
FL 327800
Tel: (407) 267-3036

Treasure Island Chamber of Commerce
152-108 Ave
Treasure Island
FL 33706
Tel: (813) 367-4529

Umatilla Chamber of Commerce
257 North Tamiami Trail
Venice
FL 34285
Tel: (813) 488-2236

Vero Beach-Indian River County Chamber of Commerce
1216 21 St, Vero Beach
FL 32960
Tel: (407) 567-3491

Walton County Chamber of Commerce
Chautauqua Building
Circle Drive
Defuniak Springs
FL 32422
Tel: (904) 267-3511

Washington County Chamber of Commerce
PO Box 457, Chipley
FL 32428
Tel: (904) 636-4157

West Hernando Chamber of Commerce
2563 Commercial Way
Spring Hill
FL 34606
Tel: (904) 683-3700

West Nassau Chamber of Commerce
PO Box 98, Callahan
FL 32011
Tel: (904) 879-1441

West Orange Chamber of Commerce
PO Box 522, Winter Garden
FL 32787
Tel: (407) 656-1304

West Pasco Chamber of Commerce
407 West Main St
New Port Richey
FL 34652
Tel: (813) 842-7651

West Pasco Chamber of Commerce
Hudson Office
13740 Old Dixie Highway
Hudson
FL 34667
Tel: (813) 868-9395

West Tampa Chamber of Commerce
3005 West Columbus Drive
Tampa
FL 33607
Tel: (813) 879-2866

Winter Haven Area Chamber of Commerce
PO Drawer 1420
Winter Haven
FL 33882-1420
Tel: (813) 293-2138

Winter Park Chamber of Commerce
PO Box 280, Winter Park
FL 32790
Tel: (407) 644-8281

Ybor City Chamber of Commerce
PO Box 5055, Tampa
FL 33675-5055
Tel: (813) 248-3712

Zephryhills Chamber of Commerce
691 Fifth Ave, Zephyrhills
FL 34248
Tel: (813) 782-1913

DAILY NEWSPAPERS

Boca Raton News
33 SE Third St
FL 33432

Bradenton Herald
102 Manatee Ave W
FL 33505

Brooksville Sun-Journal
703 Lamar Ave
FL 34601

Cape Coral Daily Breeze
PO Box 846
FL 33904

Charlotte Harbor Sun
23170 Harborview Road
FL 33980

Clearwater Sun
301 S Myrtle Ave
FL 33515

Daytona Beach News-Journal
901
6th St
FL 32014

Deland Sun News
111 S Alabama
FL 32724

Deland News-Sentinel
101 N New River Dr

't Lauderdale
FL 33302

Delray Beach News
34 SE 2nd Ave
FL 33432

Deltona Voulusian
PO Box 5339
FL 32728

Ft Lauderdale News
101 N New River Dr
FL 33302-2297

Ft Myers News-Press
2442 Anderson Ave
FL 33901-3987

Ft Pierce News-Tribune
PO Box 69
FL 33454

Ft Walton Beach Playground
Daily News
PO Box 2949
FL 32548

Gainesville Sun
Drawer A
FL 32602

Hollywood Sun-Tattler
2600 N 29th Ave
FL 33022

Homestead South Dade News
Leader
PO Box 339
FL 33090

Inverness Citrus County Chroni-
cle
130 Heights Ave
FL 32652

Jacksonville Florida Times Un-
ion
One Riverside Ave
FL 32201

Key West Citizen
PO Box 1800
FL 33040

Lake City Reporter
PO Box 1709
FL 32056

Lakeland Ledger
PO Box 408
FL 33802

Lake Wales Highlander
PO Box 872
FL 33853

Leesburg Commercial
Drawer 7
FL 32749-0600

Marianna Jackson County
Floridian
PO Box 520
FL 32446

Melbourne Florida Today
PO Box 363000
FL 32936

Miami Herald
One Herald Plaza
FL 33132-1693

Naples Daily News
1075 Central Ave
FL 33940

New Smyrna Beach News &
Observer
Drawer B
FL 32069

Ocala Star-Banner
PO Box 490
FL 32678-0490

Orange Park Clay Today
PO Box 1209
FL 32067-1209

Orlando Sentinel
633 N Orange Ave
FL 32801-1349

Palatka Daily News
PO Box 777
FL 32078-0777

Palm Beach Daily News
265 Royal Poinciana Way
FL 33480

Panama City News-Herald
PO Box 1940
FL 32402-1940

Pensacola News-Journal
PO Box 12710
FL 32574

Punta Gorda Charlotte Herald-
News
114 W Olympia Ave
FL 33951-1808

Sanford Herald
300 N French Ave
FL 32771

Sarasota Heerlad-Tribune
PO Box 1719
FL 33578-1719

St Augustine Record
Drawer 1630
FL 32085

St Petersburg Times
PO Box 1121
FL 33731

Stuart News
PO Box 9009
FL 34995.

Tallahassee Democrat
PO Box 990
Tallahassee
FL 32302-0990.

Tampa Tribune
PO Box 191
FL 33601-0191.

Vero Beach Press-Journal
PO Box 1268
FL 32961-1268.

West Palm Beach Post
Drawer T
FL 33402.

PHOTO CREDITS

Antiques of the Orient : 12, 14/15, 18/19
Randa Bishop : front endpaper, 6/7, 8, viii (bottom), xii, xiii (top), xiii (bottom), xv, 30, 68 (top), 68 (bottom),76, 90, 92, 99, 101, 102, 149, 222, 262, 263, 297, 362, 372, 379, 386/387, 389, 390, 394
Clive Briffett : 62 (top), 62 (bottom), 63 (bottom), 71 (top)
Emerald Coast TDC : 93, 166, 346
Florida Department of Commerce, Division of Tourism : xvi, 3 (top), 3 (bottom), 4, x (top), x (bottom), xi (top), 40, 42, 43, 72, 112, 120, 182, 185, 224, 225, 260/261, 343, 345, 388
Michele & Tom Grimm : backcover bottom, ix (top), xi (bottom), xiv (top), 16, 20, 22, 23, 24, 28, 32/33, 35, 36, 45, 56, 58, 60, 61 (top), 61 (bottom), 66, 69, 70, 79, 81 (top), 81 (bottom), 85, 87, 134, 143, 156, 157, 158, 162, 174, 188, 189, 194, 214, 227, 234, 236, 243, 249, 250, 252, 254, 255, 258, 265, 266, 269, 272, 274/275, 286, 289, 290, 292, 295, 314, 318/319, 322, 325, 330/331, 332, 333, 338/339, 382, 385
Jacksonville TDC : 276, 279, 280/281, 282, 285
Palm Beach County CVB : 2, 340, 350
Carl & Ann Purcell : backcover top left, backcover top right, back endpaper, viii (top), ix (bottom), 41, 44, 48/49, 50, 52/53, 54, 74, 82, 89, 98, 104, 106, 114/115, 129,133, 137, 138, 140, 142, 152, 155, 160, 163, 164, 168, 169, 170/171, 172, 177, 178, 180/181, 186/187, 192, 193, 196/197, 198, 200, 201, 202, 204, 206, 208, 210, 213, 215 (top), 215 (bottom), 216, 217, 218/219, 220, 223, 226, 228/229, 230, 233, 237, 238, 241, 242, 245, 246, 310, 313, 315, 316, 317, 320, 327, 328/329, 331, 334, 335, 336, 337, 342, 354, 356, 357, 358, 360, 364, 365, 366, 367, 369, 371, 374, 375, 376, 377, 378, 391
St Augustine TDC : 111, 271
Morten Strange : 63 (top), 64
Tallahassee Public Relations : 11, 71 (bottom), 116, 298, 301, 302, 303, 304, 305, 306, 307, 308/309
The Stock Market/Zviki Eshet : front cover
Bobbe Wolfe: 5, 38, 380, 393
Paul Zach : xiv (bottom), 118, 122, 190, 203, 352

INDEX

A

A Walk Through Time, 123
A&M University, 96, 99
Adventureland, 168
aerobatics, 123
African-Americans, 25, 33, 93, 96, 98, 99, 105, 110, 111, 124
agriculture, 41, 43, 82
air boating, 341
air fairs, 157, 159
Air Force Missile Center, 101
airlines, domestic, 41
Ais, 19
Alabama, 22, 293
Alachua, 141
Alaska, 54
Alexander Spring, 60
Alhambra Dinner Theater, 144, 284
Alligator Alley reservations, 100
Alligator Farms, 70
alligator wrestling, 70, 100, 161
Alligatorland Safari Zoo, 159
Alligators, 1, 55, 62, 66, 83, 86, 161, 170, 173, 181, 255, 259, 290, 302, 307, 313, 315, 317, 319, 320, 327
Alvin Ailey American Dance Theater, 136
Amelia Island, 117, 121, 123, 126, 133, 284
American colonists, 22
amusement parks, 291
Anastasia Island, 273
Anastasia State Recreation Area, 273
Andrews Bay, 291
Anheuser-Busch, 163
Anheuser Busch Brewery, 281

Anhinga Trail, 313
Annual Chili Cook-Off, 124, 131
Annual Destin Seafood Festival, 128
Annual Fall Festival, 132
Annual Florida Seafood Festival, 131
Annual Florida State Air Fair, 132
Annual Possum Festival And Parade, 125
Annual Southwest Florida Fair, 124
antiques, 155, 189, 191, 193, 209, 236, 277, 374, 380, 381, 377
Apalachee Indian, 305, 306
Apalachee, 19
Apalachicola National Forest, 60, 131, 307
Apalachicola River, 24, 79, 308
Apollo Beach, 254
Appalachian Mountains, 79
aquifiers, 54
Arabian Nights, 146
Arboleya, Carlos J, 94
archaeological diving, 349
architecture, 136, 169, 211, 214, 215, 242, 294, 379
Arizona, 100
Arkansas, 24
arm wrestling, 124
Armstrong, Louis, 98
Art & Culture, 135-151
Art Deco, 139, 211, 366
art galleries, 209, 380
Art Museum at Florida International University, 144
Art Nouveau, 136

art, 118, 120, 123, 126, 128, 132, 135, 139, 143, 199, 204, 211, 241, 305, 308, 327, 334, 335, 338, 377
Arts and Crafts Village, 115
Arts Festival, 100
Asian Adventure, 146
Asian cuisine, 383
Askew, Governor Reubin, 99
Asolo Center for the Performing Arts, 138, 204
Asolo Theater Company, 138, 147, 204
Assumption Ukrainian Catholic Church, 107
Astronaut Hall of Fame, 47
Astronauts Memorial, 256
Atlantic Beach, 280, 281
Atlantic Coast Line Railroad Station, 39, 189
Atlantic Coast, 16, 67
Atlantic Coastal Plain, 53, 54
Atlantic Ocean, 2, 55, 57, 82, 323, 383
Atlantis, 213
Atocha, 6
Audubon Island, 291
Audubon, John James, 331
Augustine's 423rd Founding Anniversary, 126
auto racing, 246, 247
aviation, 46, 123
Aviles de, Pedro Menendez, 3, 21, 106, 108, 117, 123, 267

B

Bahamas, 33, 225, 262, 325, 338
Bahama Channel, 88

Bahamians, 89
Bahia Cabana Beach Resort, 235
Bahia Honda Key, 326
Bahia Mar Resort & Yachting Center, 235
Bahia Mar Yachting Center, 234
Baker, Ted, 46
ballet, 9, 204
Ballet Flamenco La Rosa, 145
Ballet Florida, 139, 206, 249
balloon rides, 159
ballroom dancing, 367
Banana River, 264
banks, 47
Baptists, 111
Barefoot Beach, 358
Barnacle, 89
Barnacles State Historic Site, 89
Barrier Island, 176
bars, 5, 364, 366
Baryshinikov, Mikhail, 135
baseball, 47, 103, 177, 246, 247, 343, 364
Baseball Breakfast, 115
Baseball City, 10, 153, 156
basket weaving, 18
basketball, 157, 162, 246, 363, 364
Bass Museum, 144, 215
BASS Pro-Am Fishing Tournament, 118
Battle of Natural Bridge, 25
Bausch And Lomb Tennis Championship, 121
Bay Bluffs, 297
Bay Pines, 190
Bay View Park, 297
beachcombing, 207
beaches, 8, 9, 11, 26, 54, 75, 77, 113, 161, 173, 174, 177, 179, 183, 190, 195, 199, 202, 207, 226, 231, 237, 251, 253, 254, 273, 277, 284, 287, 289, 290, 291, 293, 296, 356, 358, 381
beach fashions, 377
Beach Fishing Classic, 126
bed and breakfasts, 387
Benjamin, Judah P, 84
Bethune, Mary Mcleod, 29, 96, 97
Bethune-Cookman College, 29, 96

big band dancing, 368, 371
Big Cypress National Preserve, 53, 61, 66, 100
Big Lagoon State Recreation Area, 75, 76, 296, 297
Big Pine Key, 131, 326
biking, 307, 308
Bimini, 17
biotechnology, 42
bird sanctuaries, 176, 203, 339
birding books, 65
birding, 8, 55, 62, 65, 68, 73, 78, 177, 192, 195, 254, 293, 303, 314
Biscayne Bay, 89, 225
Biscayne Greyhound, 351
Bishop, Elizabeth, 336
black bears, 11, 65, 66, 83, 176, 302
Black Heritage Month, 99
Black Heritage Trail, 99
Black Point Wildlife Drive, 254
Blackwater River State Forest, 60
Blackwater River State Park, 76
Blackwater River, 76
Blue Angels Air Show, 124
Blue Hole, 327
Blue Springs State Park, 255
Blueberry Festival, 124
Board of Regents, 99
boating, 54, 60, 75, 76, 77, 78, 79, 83, 84, 86, 88, 137, 175, 177, 185, 202, 263, 264, 288, 289, 296, 308, 316, 342, 339, 347, 353, 369
bobcats, 11, 66, 83
Boca Expo, 125
Boca Festival Days, 125
Boca Raton, 125, 241, 247, 358
    Mission Bay Aquatic Training Center, 247
    Museum of Art, 248
    Symphonic Pops, 249
Boender, Ronald, 235
Bogart, Humphrey, 325
Boggy Bayou Mullet Festival, 128
Bok Tower Botanical Gardens, 136
Bok Tower Gardens, 10, 155
Bolshoi Ballet, 136
Bonaparte, Napoleon, 95
Bonaventure Golf Course, 236

Bonaventure Racquet Club, 236
Bone Valley Fossil Society's Fossil Fair, 130
Bonita Springs, 131
Bonnie Lass beauty pageant, 115
Book of Mormon, 111
Bowlegs, Chief Billy, 100
Bowman's Beach, 180
Boyd Hill Nature Trail, 190
Boynton Beach, 247
Boynton Beach Mall, 379
Bradenton, 343
Brahman beef cattle, 72
Brancusi, 139
Brandon Balloon Festival, 117, 128
Braque, 139
Brazil, 48, 146
Brighton, 100
Bristol, 80
Brussels, 48
bubbas, 102
Buffet, Jimmy, 6, 323, 337, 364, 381
bug demos, 160
buggy races, 174
bungee jumping, 162
Burton, Philip, 336

C
Ca'd'Zan, 201
cabana bar, 364
Cabbage Key, 181
Caladesi Island, 83, 191
Calder Race Course, 351
California, 46, 49
Calle Ocho, 127, 213, 219, 220, 226
Calle Ocho Festival, 121
Calloway, Cab, 98
Calusa, 19
calypso bands, 369
Camp Blanding, 27
Camp Gordon Johnston, 27
Campbell, Sir Malcolm, 260
camping, 60, 61, 75, 76, 77, 78, 79, 83, 84, 86, 88, 155, 156, 190, 254, 281, 290, 296, 307, 308, 317, 326
Canada, 16, 48
Canaveral National Seashore, 256, 259
Cane Grinding Harvest Festival, Live Oak, 132

canoeing , 76, 84, 88, 123, 155, 157, 174, 176, 181, 190, 247, 253, 254, 306, 308, 317, 319, 326, 327, 344
Cape Canaveral, 18, 19, 43, 256
Cape Kennedy, 101
Cape Sable, 19
Capone's Dance, 146
Captiva Island, 9, 29, 124, 132
Caputo, Philip, 326, 336
Carnival Miami Ocho, 121
car racing, 344
Caribbean, 20, 47, 93, 234, 376
Carnaval Miami/Calle Ocho, 127, 226
Carriage Tours, 270
Cary State Forest, 61
Casey Key, 202
casino, 263, 371
Caspersen, 202
Castillo de San Marcos, 4, 106, 267, 272
Castro, Fidel, 47, 92, 94, 127, 219, 226
Catholicism, 105, 106, 107
cattle, 72, 73, 83, 157, 383
Caverns State Park, 308
Cedar Key, 11, 55, 56, 194
  City Marina, 195
  National Wildlife Refuge, 195
  Sidewalk Arts Festival, 195
  State Museum, 195
  U Turn Sunburn Saloon, 11
ceilidh, 115
Central Florida, 152-171
Centerville, 304
Central Florida, 9
Charles, Ray, 29, 35, 140
Charlotte County Christmas Parade, 133
charter boat rental, 353
charter fishing, 319
Che-cho-ter, 23
Chekika State Recreation Area, 86
Chekika, chief, 86
Cheyney, John, 188
Chicago White Sox, 344
Chicago, 84
Children's Museum of Boca, 248
Children's Museum of Tampa, 97
Children's Science Explorium, 248

Chiles, Governor Lawton, 37, 94, 299
Chipley, 77
Chipola River, 308
Choctawhatchee River, 77
Choctaws, 303
Chokoloskee Bay, 317
choral society, 297
Christmas, 117
Church of Jesus Christ of Latter-day Saints, 111
Church of Scientology, 109
Church Street Station, 161, 378
Ciardi, John, 336
Cincinnati Reds, 193, 344
Citrus Bowl And Parade, 118
citrus fruit industry, 25, 29, 103, 386
Citrus plants & tours, 387
Citrus Research and Education Center, 386
Citrus World, 386
Civil War, 98, 101, 117, 273, 304, 308, 331
Clark, Dr Eugenie, 205
Clearwater, 9, 103, 109, 137, 190, 191, 343, 344, 371
  Fort Harrison Hotel, 109
Cleveland Heights Golf & Country Club, 156
climate, 46, 49, 57, 183
coastline, 54
Cocoa, 137, 255, 259, 262
  Porcher House, 137, 259
  Village Playhouse, 259
Coconut Grove, 89, 94, 120, 124, 213, 217, 291, 353
  Arts Festival, 211
  Playhouse, 139, 141, 145, 217
  Vizcaya Museum and Gardens, 216
Coe, Ernest F, 312
Cole, Nat King, 98
Collier-Seminole State Park, 84
Colombia, 48, 93, 227
colonialism, 17
Columbus Day Weekend seafood festival, 275
Columbus, Christopher, 126
Comanche Indians, 159, 366
comedy, 363, 365, 366, 367, 370, 371
communications, 28, 41, 42, 43
concerts, 125, 130, 204, 363,

371
Conch Trains, 327
Conchs, 102, 325
Constitutional Convention, 33
construction, 41
continental cuisine, 387, 391
Continental Shelf, 16
Coolidge, President, 29
copper mining, 19
Coquina, 202, 273
Coral Gables, 213, 217, 219
  Biltmore Hotel, 218
coral reefs, 16, 88, 181, 191, 202, 263, 336, 337, 355
Corcoris, John, 188
Corkscrew Swamp Sanctuary, 65
Cornett, Leanza, 167
Cortez Fishing Festival, 119
Cortez, 119, 202
Cosmic Electronic Music Man, 259
cotton, 25, 26, 81
Country Club at Silver Springs Shores, 350
Cove Marina, 234
cowboys, 73, 153, 156, 363
Coyote, 66
Crackers, 92, 102
crafts, 119, 121, 123, 237
Crane Point Hammock, 325
Crane, Hart, 336
cranes, 71
creek tribes, 303
crocodiles, 67, 315
crop growing, 18
croquet, 246, 247
Cross Creek, 29, 141
Crowley, John, 335
cruising, 225, 246, 248, 253, 262, 270, 279, 296, 371
Cuba, 19, 20, 22, 44, 46, 97, 108, 127
Cuban cuisine, 119, 253, 383
Cuban Revolution, 44
Cuban theater, 127
Cuban-Americans, 107
Cubans, 47, 92, 93, 219
cuisine, 122, 124, 169, 192, 367, 369, 382-393
culture, 51, 199, 211, 241, 284, 304
Curtiss, Glenn, 316
cycling, 190, 207, 243, 263,

296, 297, 319, 344
Cypress Slough Preserve, 177
Cypress Strands, 55

D

Dade County, 57, 88, 93, 99
Dade County, Black Archives, 99
Dade Massacre, 24
Dali, Salvadore, 9, 185
dance, 119, 120, 138, 139, 145, 147, 148, 159, 199, 225, 226, 249, 337, 362, 363, 364, 365, 366, 367, 368, 370, 371, 381
Daytona, 10, 39, 60, 261, 344
Bandshell Concerts, 142
Beach Motor Speedway Corporation, 261
Beach Spring Speedway Spectacular, 261
Beach, 27, 29, 46, 95, 96, 98, 120, 142, 251, 253, 260, 261, 344, 362, 386
Camel Motorcycle Week, 261
Dolphin Beach club, 4
International Speedway, 10, 253, 261
Mermaid Beach Hotel, 4
Museum of Arts & Sciences, 95
Museum of Arts and Sciences and Planetarium, 142
Museums of Arts and Sciences, 253
Ormond Memorial Art Museum & Gardens, 142
Playhouse, 142
racetrack, 4
Raceway, 260
Seaside Music Theater, 142
deep sea cruises, 179
deep sea fishing, 289
deep South cuisine, 383
Deerfield, 132
Deering, James, 217
defense technology, 42
Deland, 101
DeLeon Springs State Park, 253
Delray Affair, 121
Delray Beach, 92, 121, 247, 358
DeLuna Treasure Hunt, 116
DeLuna, Don Tristan, 116
Democratic Leadership Council, 37
Democratic party, 24
Destin Cup Sailing Race, 126
Destin, 126, 128
Detroit Tigers, 343
Dickinson, Jonathan, 19
Ding Darling NWR, 65
dining, 165, 207, 225, 263, 296, 366, 368, 371
Dios de, Nombre, 126
disco, 368, 370
Disney World, 115
Great Movie Ride, 169
Indiana Jones Stunt Spectacular, 169
Liberty Square, 168
MGM Studios, 10, 28, 46, 163, 169
Mickey's Hollywood Theater, 168
Muppet Vision 3D, 169
Tomorrowland, 168
Typhoon Lagoon, 163
diving, 181, 188, 191, 205, 225, 235, 289, 327, 336, 354, 355
Dixie Queen Riverboat, 252
Dixieland jazz, 161, 253, 366, 370
dog racing, 246, 247
Dolphin Research Center, 6, 325, 356
dolphin, 1, 6, 8, 9, 162, 169, 179, 191, 205, 216, 234, 235, 289, 291, 356
Doral Resort, 350
Dos Passos, John, 336
Douglas, Marjorie Stoneman, 29, 94, 139, 311, 312, 316
Dow, Kenneth Worcester, 94
Drake, Sir Francis, 21
driving, 313
Dry Tortugas islands, 65
Dunedin, 83, 103, 115, 190, 343, 348
Dupont All American Tennis Championship, 126
DuVal, Williams, 33

E

Eagles, 71
East Coast, 250-265
East Coast Railroad, 39, 98
East Gulf Coastal Plain, 53
Eastern Airlines, 46
Eatonville, 98, 140
Eau Gallie Causeway, 264
economy, 10, 28, 38-49
Eden State Gardens, 76
Edison Festival of Light, 118
Edison Museum, 179
Edison, Thomas, 9, 118, 138, 178, 179
Edward Ball Nature Walk, 297
Eglin Air Force Base, 296
El Lectore, 44
Ellenton, 84
Emerald Coast, 126
Emerald Dunes, 246
Emerson, Ralph Waldo, 95
Entertainment, 360-371
Englewood, 126, 202
English colonialism, 22, 32, 116
Eno, Van, 335
environmentalism, 94, 176, 205
EPCOT Center, 10, 28, 163, 169
Epcot, Future World, 169
Escambia Bay, 297
Estefan, Gloria, 97
Estero, 84, 86
estuaries, 55
ethnic groups, 92
Everglades, 7, 8, 24, 53, 55, 61, 63, 84, 86, 94, 100, 139, 176, 310-320, 313, 344, 357
City, 119, 317, 353
Club, 242
Gumbo Limbo Trail, 315
National Park, 10, 62, 64, 65, 67, 234, 314
Seafood Festival, 119
Shark Valley Information Center, 320
Swallowtail Kite, 64
executive course, 350
executive government, 34

F

facilities, 290
facilities for the handicapped, 313
Fairchild Tropical Garden, 219
Falling Waters Sink Waterfall, 77
Falling Waters State Recreation Area, 77, 308
family beaches, 280
Fantasy Fest, 130, 338
Fantasyland, 168

arm, 153, 174, 307
Faulkner, Henry, 335
Fauna, 53, 75, 176, 177, 197, 253, 255, 264, 281, 283, 302, 307, 313, 315, 317, 319
Feast of Flowers, 17, 55
Feast of Saint Augustine, 106
feature film industry, 46
Ferdinand V, King, 17
Fernandina Beach, 123 , 128, 248
Fernandina Christmas Parade, 117
Fernandina Shrimp Festival, 123
Festival, 112-133
Festival de Mayo, 127
Festival of New Plays, 206
Festival of the States, 115
Festivals, 226, 277, 284, 303, 307, 325, 327
Fiesta of Five Flags, 116
Fifteen Annual Harvest, 131
Finance, 47
Firestone, George, 29, 141
Firestone, Harvey, 138, 179
First Presbyterian Church, 304
First Seminole War, 23
Fisher Island, 216
Fisher, Mel, 6, 349
Fishing Guide Services, 347
Fishing, 8, 11, 25, 54, 60, 61, 75, 76, 77, 78, 79, 82, 83, 84, 86, 88, 125, 155, 156, 157, 174, 177, 179, 189, 190, 194, 195, 202, 207, 209, 225, 231, 234, 246, 247, 248, 252, 254, 259, 262, 263, 264, 275, 280, 281, 284, 288, 290, 293, 294, 296, 306, 307
Fisk University, 29
Fitzgerald, Scott F, 209, 341
Fitzgerald, Ella, 98
Flagler, Henry Morrison, 4, 25, 29, 39, 40, 98, 239, 244, 270, 272, 284
Flagler Museum, 248
Flamenco, 127, 219, 226, 371
Flamingo City, 62, 317
Flamingo Visitor Center, 313, 319
Flatwoods, 59
Flatwoods, 86
Flea markets, 237
Flora, 53, 79, 259, 287, 315

Flora and Fauna, 58-73
Florida Aquarium, 197
Florida Bay, 62, 67
Florida City, 57
Florida Community College, 284
Florida Cowboys Association Rodeo, 353
Florida Department of Commerce Welcome Center, 35
Florida East Coast Railway, 29
Florida Folk Festival, 81
Florida Game and Fresh Water Fish Commission, 65
Florida International Airshow, 123
Florida Keys, 6, 56, 66, 88, 322-339, 326, 346, 364, 375
Artisan's Village, 375
Duval Street, 375
John Pennekamp Coral Reef State Park, 88, 325, 336
Mallory Square, 334
Mel Fisher Maritime Heritage Society Museum, 334, 349
Museum of Natural History of the Florida Keys, 326
Old Town Trolley, 301, 327
Red Barn Theater, 144, 337
Tennessee Williams Fine Arts Center, 337
Watson's Hammock, 327
Florida Legislature, 24, 33
Florida Marlins, 343
Florida panther, 61, 94, 302, 315
Florida Philharmonic Orchestra, 145, 148, 197, 249
Florida royal palm, 84
Florida Spaceport Authority, 43
Florida Stallion Station, 167
Florida State Fair, 117, 120, 122
Florida State Opera, 299
Florida State University, 148, 299, 303
Florida Strawberry Festival, 122
Florida Studio Theater, 144, 147, 206
Florida Symphonic Band, 147, 204
Florida Trail Association Fall Meeting, 131
Florida Uplands, 53
Florida West Coast Symphony,

147, 204
fly fishing, 288
food processing, 45
football, 117, 118, 119, 162, 194, 299, 308
Ford, Henry, 9, 138, 179
Fort Lauderdale, 117
Fort Caroline, 21, 55, 108, 277, 279
Fort Castillo de San Marcos, 22
Fort Christmas Museum, 146
Fort Clinch State Park, 117
Fort DeSoto Park, 65, 348, 357
Fort George, 82
Fort George Island, 26
Fort King, 23
Fort King Waterway, 170
Fort Lauderdale, 4, 99, 102, 103, 111, 133, 139, 142, 230-237, 343, 355, 358, 363, 368, 373, 374
Antique Center of the South, 374
Best Western Marina Inn & Yacht Harbor, 235
Blockbuster Bowl Reception, 117
Broward Art Guild, 143
Broward Center for the Performing Arts, 139, 143
Broward Mall, 374
Children's Theater, 143
Commercial Boulevard, 133, 233
Contemporary theater, 143
Coral Square, 374
East Las Olas Boulevard, 374
Fashion Mall at Plantation, 374
Galleria, 374
Grand Palms golf course, 236
Las Olas Boulevard, 236, 373
Marina Bay & Resort, 236
Museum of Archaeology, 143
Museum of Art, 139, 142
Museum of Discovery and Science, 143
Panama City Beach, 126, 287, 288, 289, 290, 291, 293, 358
Panama City nightspots, 368
Parker Playhouse, 143
Saks Fifth Avenue, 5
Swap Shop, 237, 374
Fort Liberty Ropers, 146

Fort Myers, 9, 20, 103, 118, 131, 132, 173, 177, 178, 179, 353
  Beach Swing Bridge Festival, 132
  Greyhound Track, 351
  Lee County Sports Complex, 177
  Nature Center and Planetarium, 177
  Sand Sculpture Competition, 131
Fort Pickens, 296, 297
Fort Pierce, 119, 124, 125
Fort Walton, 57
Foster, Stephen, 55, 81
Founding Anniverary of Saint Augustine, 117
fountain of youth, 17, 20, 105, 386
Fourth of July celebration, 81
Franke, Bob, 335
Franks Farm, 167
Fraser, Malcolm, 142
Freddick Bratcher and Company, 145
Freeport, 262
French, 21
Freshwater Marsh, 55
Friends of the Everglades, 29
frigatebirds, 63
Frontierland, 168
Frost, Robert, 336
fruit fly, 26

G

Gainesville, 18, 49, 81, 101
galleries, 248
Gallery of Spaceflight, 256
Gamble Mansion, 84
Gamble Plantation State Historic Site, 84
Gamble, Major John, 84
gambling, 222, 225
gamefish tournaments, 325
gardens, 9, 153, 155, 201, 235, 267, 299
Gaspar, José, 122, 192
Gasparilla Day, 192
Gasparilla Distance Classic, 122
Gasparilla Fiesta Of Tampa Bay, 119
Gasparilla Island, 202
Gator Lake, 290

Gatorland, 10, 70, 161
General Assembly, 24
geography, 17, 51
Geography and Climate, 50-57
George III, King, 32
George Island Chili Cook–Off, 121
Georgia, 22, 23, 56, 79
Germany, 48
Getty, William Henry, 261
Gibbs, Jonathan C, 98
Gibraltar, 33
glassbottom boats, 291, 307
Glendi, 113
Glover, Danny, 100
go-karting, 159, 253, 291
Gold Coast Railroad Museum, 130
gold coaster, 101
gold, 17, 19, 20
golf, 3, 8, 42, 47, 122, 155, 156, 157, 167, 173, 177, 183, 195, 207, 209, 222, 231, 235, 236, 241, 246, 275, 277, 280, 325, 341, 349, 350, 351
golf tournament, 309
Gong, Lue Gim, 29
Good Chance Farm, 167
Goofy, 168
Goombay, 211
gopher tortoises, 67
gospel music, 121
Goulds, 132
Gourgues de, Dominique, 21
government, 10, 30-37
Great Depression, 40
Grass Key, 325
Grayton Beach State Rcreation Area, 77
Great Depression, 26
Great Explorations Museum, 9, 185
Great Explorations Museum Reptile Zoo, 191
Great White Heron National Wildlife Refuge, 71
Great White Heron, 71
Greek cuisine, 119, 189, 383, 384, 388
Greek culture, 119
Greek Orthodox Church, 109, 110
Greeks, 102, 103, 272
Greeks of Tarpon Springs, 92

Greenpeace, 375
Gregory House, 80, 308
Grenelefe Golf Club & Resort, 349
greyhound racing, 194, 351
Guavaween Extravaganza, 130
Gulf Coast Factory Shops, 381
Gulf Coast, 16, 22, 54, 83, 103, 289
Gulf fishing, 288
Gulf Islands National Seashore, 11, 75, 293, 296
Gulf of Mexico, 2, 51, 53, 55, 56, 57, 62, 77, 78, 118, 124, 125, 128, 130, 175, 179, 190, 194, 202, 205, 207, 287, 290, 296, 323, 326, 383
Gulf Stream, 20, 57, 88, 247
Gulf World, 291

H

Haines City, 342
Haitian art, 335
Haitian Art Company, 375
Halifax River, 252
Hallandale, 351
Halloween, 130
hammock, 55, 62, 64, 84, 86, 89
handicapped, 290
handicrafts, 139
Hanson, Duane, 142
Harney, Lt Col William, 86
Hathaway Bridge, 289
Haunted House, 130
Havana, 22, 32
Havana Harbor, 349
Health services, 45, 48, 97
Heath Jr, Ralph T, 192
Hemingway, Country, 332
Hemingway, Days Festival, 116, 124, 338
Hemingway, Ernest, 6, 29, 35, 124, 141, 327, 333, 336, 364
Hemingway, Home and Museum, 331, 332, 333
Henrietta Marie, 349
Herlihy, James Leo, 336
Hermon, Jerry, 337
herons, 71
Herrmann's Lipizzan Ranch, 203
Hialeah, Park, 351
Hialeah, Race Track, 220

Hialeah, 351
Highland Games, 103, 115, 190
Viking, 60, 77, 78, 79, 80, 86,
131, 155, 156, 190, 254, 275,
306, 307, 308, 313, 320
Hillsboro Inlet, 234
Hillsborough Bay, 122
Hispanic Art, 144, 215
Hispanic community, 226
Hispanic cuisine, 219
Hispanic culture, 121, 126, 227
Hispanic Heritage Festival, 126
Hispanic Theater Festival, 127
Hispanics, 93
historical tours, 270
History, 12-29
History and Research Founda-
tion of South Florida, 99
Hitichiti language, 100
Hobe Sound, 19
hockey, 194, 363
Holiday, Billie, 98
Hollandale, Gulfstream Park,
351
Holocene era, 16
Homestead, 57, 62, 65
Homosassa Springs, 83
Honeymoon Island State Rec-
reation Area, 83
Hoover, President, 29
horse breeding, 167
horse racing, 10, 351
horseback riding, 61, 80, 157,
203, 246, 247, 307, 308
Hound and Hare race, 117
Houseman, Jacob, 88
Houston Astros Spring Train-
ing, 343
Hubbard, Ron L, 109
Hubert Humphrey Bridge, 259
hunting, 18, 60, 61, 66, 67, 246,
255, 307
Huntington Golf Club, 167
Hurricane Andrew, 57
Hurricane Cleo, 57
Hurricane Donna, 56
Hurricane Elena, 57
Hurricane Eloise, 57
hurricanes, 56
Hurston, Zora Neale, 29, 140

I

Ice Age, 52, 53
ice shows, 162

immigrants, 27, 91, 103, 105,
106, 227
Indian Aborigines, 18
Indian Key Fill, 88
Indian Key State Historic Site,
86
Indian natives, 17
Indian River, 19, 71, 254, 264,
386
Indians, 21, 31
industry, 10, 27
information technology, 42
Inness Jr, George, 110
Internal Improvement Act, 24
International Music and Crafts
Festival, 100
International Trade Bill, 48
international trade, 42, 48
Intracoastal Waterway, 123,
133, 231, 233, 243, 363, 368
Introduction, 1-11
Islamorada, 325, 326
Islamorada Seafood Festival,
118
Island Oktoberfest, 131

J

Jackson, Andrew, 23
Jackson, Michael, 135
Jacksonville, 3, 10, 18, 21, 25,
26, 55, 60, 80, 98, 99, 101,
103, 125, 128, 135, 136, 143,
276-285, 351, 374
Alexander Brest Museum, 281
Alexander Brest Planetarium,
278
American Lighthouse Mu-
seum, 280
Art Museum, 136, 144, 281
Beach Pier, 280
Cummer Gallery of Art, 143,
281
Dames Point Bridge, 279
Friendship Fountain, 278
Jazz Festival, 279
Kathryn Abbey Hanna State
Park, 281
Kingfish Tournament, 125
Landing, 277, 374
Metropolitan Park, 279, 284
Museum of Science and His-
tory, 144
Museum of Science and His-
tory, 278

Navy Memorial, 278
River City Playhouse, 284
Riverwalk, 278, 374
Shakespeare at the Met, 279
Symphony Orchestra, 135,
144, 284
Zoological Park, 10, 281, 283
jai alai, 194, 246, 247
Jamestown, 21
Jannus, Tony, 46
Japan, 48, 92
Jazz Club of Sarasota, 147
jazz, 135, 174, 284, 363, 364,
366, 370, 371, 381
Jeep Safari, 170
jetskiing, 179, 190, 202, 231,
252, 369
jewelry, 378, 380
Jewish cuisine, 383
Jewish culture, 221
Jews, 92, 101, 105, 109, 221
JN Ding Darling Wildlife Ref-
uge, 181
John F Kennedy Space Center,
10
John's Pass Village & Boardwalk,
380
John's Pass Seafood Festival, 380
Johns River City Band, 284
Johnson Beach, 296
Johnson, James Weldon, 278
Johnson, Philip, 144
Judaism, 107
Judd, James, 139, 249
judicial government, 36
July Fourth Celebration, 125
jungle cruise, 170
jungle trails, 201
Juniper Spring, 60
Juno Beach, 67
Jupiter, 67, 241, 247
Dinner Theater, 249
Dunes, 246

K

Kansas City Royals, 10
karaoke, 362, 364, 365, 370
kayaking, 123
Kennedy Space Center, 47, 65,
137, 254, 256, 257, 262
Rocket Garden, 256
Vehicle Assembly Building,
256
Key West, Audubon House, 330

Key Biscayne, 213, 216, 226, 358
Key Biscayne Golf Course, 222
Key Deer, 6, 66
Key Largo, 325, 326, 354, 356
National Marine Sanctuary, 336
Undersea Park, 337
Key West, 6, 25, 40, 44, 46, 62, 65, 88, 101, 102, 116, 124, 130, 141, 144, 244, 326, 327, 330, 332, 335, 342, 347, 349, 353, 355, 357, 375, 384, 388
Aquarium, 331
Conchs, 89, 92
East Martello Museum and Gallery, 331
Hand Print Fabrics, 376
Lighthouse Museum, 331
Literary Seminar, 338
Little White House Museum, 334
Resort Golf Course, 338
Waterfront Playhouse, 144, 337
Welcome Center, 330
Killearn Country Club and Inn, 309
Killearn Golf & Country Club, 351
killer whales, 162, 216
King Henry's Feast, 146
King Orange Jamboree Parade, 117, 133
Kingsley Plantation State Historic Site, 26, 27, 81, 82, 282
Kingsley, Ann Madegigne Jai, 27
Kirkwood, James, 337
Kissimmee, 10, 72, 73, 119, 121, 132, 153, 157, 159, 342, 343, 351, 359, 366, 378
Bluegrass Festival, 121
Convention & Visitor's Bureau, 73
Double C Bar Ranch, 72
Flea World, 378
Florida Mall, 378
Flying Tigers Warbird Air Museum, 159
Manufacturer's Mall, 378
Saint Cloud, 114, 117, 347
Tupperware "Awareness Center", 159

World Cup Soccer Championship, 157
Klutho, Henry J, 34
Knott, Luella, 304
Korea, 48
Koreshan State Historic Site, 84
Koreshanity, 84, 86
kosher food, 107

L
Labelle, 120
Ladies Professional Golfers Associations, 47
Lake Alfred, 386
Lake Arbuckle State Forest, 61
Lake Buena Vista Course, 350
Lake City, 130
Lake Jackson Indians, 306
Lake Jackson Mounds State Archaeological Site, 306
Lake Kissimmee State Park, 83, 156
Lake Maitland, 165
Lake Manatee State Recreation Area, 86
Lake Okeechobee, 54, 56, 62, 65, 100, 247
Lake Okefenokee, 52
Lake Osceola, 165
Lake Park, 247
Lake Rosalie, 83
Lake Seminole Park, 190
Lake Tiger, 83
Lake Tohopekaliga, 159
Lake Virginia, 165
Lake Wales Pioneer Day, 83, 128, 153, 155
Lake Wimico, 24
Lake Woodruff National Wildlife Refuge, 253
Lake Worth, 243, 244, 247
Lakeland, 9, 46, 123, 136, 153, 156, 343, 364, 365
Lands End Marina, 353
Langley Field, 47
language, 92
Lantan, 247
Late Tertiary period, 16
Latin America, 47
Latin cuisine, 227
Latin dance & music, 127, 226, 366
Latin Orange Festival, 127
Laver, Bern, 95

lawn bowling, 103
Lee, Spike, 100
Leesburg, 118
Legislative government, 35
Leon de, Juan Ponce, 2, 17, 19, 20, 55, 59, 77, 105, 386
Levy, Moses Elias, 101
Liberty City, 99
Lido Beach, 202
Lido Key, 207
Light Up Lauderdale, 117
Light Up Orlando, 132
Lincoln, Abraham, 24, 33
Lindberg, Anne, 179
Little Havana, 93, 107, 121, 127, 219, 226, 227
Live Oak Stud, 167
Lockloosa Lake, 80
Lombardi, John, 49
Lone Cabbage Fish Camp, 259
Long Key, 325
Long Pine Key, 315
Longboat Key, 207
Longboat Key Art Center, 207
Longwood, 131
Lopez, Tony, 127
Lost River Voyage, 161
Lowdermilk Beach Park, 358
Lower Keys, 326
Lower Keys Food Fest And Craft, 123
Lower Matecumbe Key, 325
Lowry Park Zoo, 10, 196, 197
Loxahatchee National Wildlife Refuge (NWR), 65, 248
Luna, de Tristan, 21, 294
Lurie, Alison, 336
Lyons, Ernest, 102

M
Mabry, Captain Dale, 46, 47
Macclenny, 80
MacDonald, John D, 140
Maclay, Alfred B, 78, 306
Maclay, Louise, 78
Madeira Beach, 130, 190
Magnolia Golf Course, 350
Mahogany Hammock Trail, 317
Main Street, 168
Major League Alumni baseball game, 115
Mama Guava Stumble Parade, 130
Manasota Beach, 202

Manatee Public Beach, 202
manatees, 9, 19, 52, 66, 83, 84, 169, 176, 195, 196, 255, 317
mangroves, 55, 60, 62, 88, 176, 202, 225, 316
manufacturing, 41
Marathon, 125, 195, 325, 326, 347, 354, 355
March Medival Fair, 121
Marco Island, 128, 176, 358
Mardi Gras, 146
Maria Sanchez Creek, 106
marina, 185, 225, 247, 278, 319, 347
marine life, 216
Marineland, 82
Marinelife Center of Juno Beach, 248
Marion Oaks Golf and Country Club, 167, 350
Marjorie Kinnan Rawlings State Historic Site, 80
Marriot's Orlando World Center, 350
Marriot's Sawgrass, 275, 351
Martin, Lieutenant Commander, 46
Marx Brothers, 26
Matanzas Bay, 273
Matanzas River, 82
Matisse, 139
Max Hoeck Creek Wildlife Drive, 254
Mayo, 128
Mayport ferry, 283
Mayport Naval Air Station, 284
McCrary Jr, Jesse, 98
McGregor Boulevard, 179
McGuane, Thomas, 336
McQueen, John, 82
medieval, 147, 159, 203
Meek, Carrie, 96
Melbourne, 137, 255, 263, 264
   Black Box Experimental Theater, 137
   Brevard Art Center and Museum, 264
   Brevard Community College Campus, 259
   Brevard Museum, 259
   Brevard Turtle Preservation Society, 264
   Greyhound, 263
   Maxwell C King Center for the

Performing Arts, 137
Mennonite Community, 110
Mennonites, 105
Mercedes I, 234
Meridian, 109, 304
Merrill, James, 336
Merritt Island National Wildlife Refuge, 65, 137, 254, 255, 256, 259, 264
Methodists, 111
Metro-Dade Art in Public Places, 139
Metromover, 213
MetroRail, 213
Mexico, 20, 93, 227
Miami, 40, 41, 46, 53, 56, 57, 62, 65, 89, 93, 94, 99, 100, 101, 103, 107, 111, 119, 126, 127, 130, 131, 133, 135, 144, 211, 220, 222, 225, 244, 351, 356, 376, 384
   Actors' Playhouse, 145, 229
   American Police Hall of Fame, 220
   Antonio Maceo Park, 127
   Area Stage, 215
   Area State Company, 145
   Arena, 363
   Around The World Fair, 119
   Art Deco District, 10, 214
   Art Deco Weekend Festival, 118
   Aventura Mall, 376
   Bahamas Goombay Festival, 124
   Bal Harbour Shops, 376
   Ballet, 139, 145, 215, 229, 249
   Bayside Marketplace, 211, 213, 220, 363, 376
   Bayside, 226
   Beach, 6, 10, 27, 65, 92, 101, 107, 118, 139, 214, 215, 221, 384
   book fair, 135
   Center for the Fine Arts, 144
   Cocowalk, 376
   Colony Hotel, 214
   Colony Theater, 215
   Confederate Garrison Weekend, 128
   Cuban Memorial Boulevard, 127
   Cuban Memorial Plaza, 226

   Cuban Museum of Arts & Culture, 144
   Dade Boulevard, 109
   Design Preservation League's Art Deco Welcome, 214
   Dome of Contemplation, 221
   Domino Park, 219, 220, 226
   downtown, 213, 363
   Film Festival, 211
   Florida Shakespeare Theater, 145
   Garden of Meditation, 221
   Grand Bay Hotel, 366
   Greater Miami Broadway Series, 145
   Greater Miami Opera, 139, 145, 229
   Greater Miami, 93
   Holocaust Memorial, 101, 107, 109, 221
   International Hispanic Theater Festival, 227
   Jackie Gleason Theater, 215, 229
   José Marti Park, 127
   Lake Nature Park, 190
   Lincoln Theater, 215
   M Ensemble Company, 145
   Mayfair Shops in the Grove, 377
   MetroZoo, 222
   Minorca Playhouse, 145
   Momentum Dance Company, 145
   Museum of Science and Space Transit Planetarium, 216
   National Hurricane Center, 57
   nightspots, 365
   North Miami Center of Contemporary Art, 144
   Ochlockonee River, 79
   Omni International Mall, 377
   Orange Bowl Festival, 117
   Orange Bowl Festival, 133
   Orange Bowl, 117, 121
   Parrot Jungle and Gardens, 222
   Rickenbacker Causeway, 213
   River, 220, 226
   Seaquarium, 216
   Sound Machine, 97
   South Beach, 107
   South Florida Art Center, 215
   Southern Ballet Theater, 136, 145

tropical jungles, 26
Youth Museum, 144
Micanopy, Chief, 97, 123
Miccosukee Indians, 7, 61, 91,
Miccosukee Indian Village, 100,
304, 320
Mickey Mouse, 10, 168
Mickey's Starland, 168
Milburn, Frank Pierce, 34
Miller, Robert, 191
Milton, 76
mini-golf, 291
miniature golf courses, 159
mining, 41
Mink, 66
Minorcans, 92
missionaries, 21,106
Mississippi, 20, 23, 293
Mississippi River, 25
Mizner, Addison, 139, 242, 243
mockingbird, 10
modern architecture, 139
Molasses Reef, 336
Monkey Jungle, 222
Monroe, President, 33
Moreno Cottage, 294
Mormons, 105
Morrow, 179
Morse Gallery of Art, 136, 146,
165
Moseley, William D, 24, 34
Mosquito Lagoon, 254
Mote, William R, 205
motels, 259
motor racing, 120, 175, 253,
261
motorboating, 88
Mount Art Festival, 120
Mount Dora, 120
movies, 28,169, 197, 199, 214,
256, 263, 271
Moyne le, Jacques, 31
Mulberry, 130, 153, 156
Munroe, Commodore Ralph, 89
Murat, Catherine, 303
museum, 142, 143, 144, 146,
147,155,183,185,192,199,
213, 241, 248, 277,
Music Festival of Florida, 207
music, 9, 139, 144, 145, 147,
148,159,177,199,204,211,
226,249,270, 363,364,365,
366,368

N

Naples, 8, 10, 84, 138, 139,
173,176,348,351,358,359,
377, 385
City Dock, 175
Collier Automotive Museum,
175
Collier County Museum, 139
Conservancy, Natural Science
Museum, 176
Dockside Boardwalk, 377
Fifth Avenue, 176, 377
Fishing Pier, 174
Frannie's Teddy Bear Museum,
175
Hibiscus Center, 377
Imperial Golf Club, 350
Old Marine Market Place, 377
Pavilion Shopping Center, 377
Philharmonic Center for the
Arts, 138, 177
Third Street South, 175, 377
Waterside Shops at Pelican Bay,
377
Marine Research Center, 9
Narvaez de, Panfilo, 19, 20, 79,
93
NAS Nature Trail, 297
NASA, 28, 47, 255
NASA Art Gallery, 256
Nassau, 262
National Airlines, 46
**National Association for the
Advancement of Colored Peo-
ple**, 29
national bird, 64
**National Commission to Pre-
vent Infant Mortality**, 37
**National Council of Negro
Women**, 29
**National Key Deer Wildlife Ref-
uge**, 66, 326
National landmark nature park,
170
National Marine Sanctuary, 337
**Native American Heritage Fes-
tival**, 303, 308
native Indians, 20
natural habitats, 65
nature study, 83, 86
nature trail, 76, 77,83,84,202,
275, 290, 306, 307, 313
nautical gear, 377
Naval Live Oaks National Park,

297
Navarre, 293
neighborhood shops, 378
Neptune Beach, 280, 281
New England intellectuals, 89
New River, 233
New Smyrna, 92
New World Symphony,139,
145, 215, 229
New York, 41, 44, 46
New York Yankees, 194
Nicaraguans, 93, 227
Niceville, 128
Nierenberg, Roger, 135, 144
nightclub, 207, 227, 365, 367,
370
nightlife, 197, 226, 361, 362
Nokomis Beach, 202
North Carolina, 23
North Florida, 286-297
North Florida Air Show, 130
North Key Largo, 67
North Lido Beach, 202
North Miami Beach, 368
North Palm Beach, 247
Northwest Florida Ballet, 136
Not Just A Seafood Festival, 123

O

O'Keefe, Georgia, 138
Ocala, 10,18,23,101,124,153,
167, 353, 390
Classic Mile (Quarter Horse),
353
Golden Ocala Golf Club, 350
Golf Club, 167
Municipal Golf Club, 351
National Forest, 60
Ocean Drive, 139
Southeastern Livestock Pavil-
ion, 124
Stud Farm, 167
Oglethorpe, James, 22
Okavango Village Petting Zoo,
283
Okefenokee Swamp, 56, 66
Oklahoma, 100
Old Bainbridge, 306
Old Island Days, 338
**Olustee Battlefield State His-
toric Site**, 80
**Homosassa Springs State Wild-
life**, 83
opera, 9, 199, 204, 206, 249,

Opossums, 66
orange blossom, 10
Orange Lake, 80
Orlando, 10, 41, 46, 70, 99, 111, 118, 132, 136, 146, 153,159, 356, 368, 378
  Arena, 162
  Cartoon Museum, 146
  Central Florida Railroad Museum, 146
  Cornell Fine Arts Museum, 146
  Museum of Art, 136, 146, 162
  nightspots, 366
  Orange County Convention and Visitor's Bureau, 163
  Orange County Historical Museum, 146
  Rosie O'Grady's Good Time Emporium, 161
  Science Center, 146
  Shooters, 369
  Sleuth's Mystery, 147
Ortiz, Juan, 20
Osceola, 23, 24
  Center for the Arts,146
  County Stadium, 159
  County, 73
  National Forest, 60
  Square Mall, 378
Osprey, 71
Overoaks Country Club, 350
Overtown, 98
owls, 72

P
Pa-hay-okee Overlook Trail, 317
paddleboats, 253
paella vallenciana, 9
Pahokee, 248
Palafox Historic District, 294
Palm Beach, 10, 40, 56, 101, 103, 121, 139, 238-249, 270, 378, 386
Ann Norton Sculpture Gardens, 248
  Breakers Hotel, 4, 10, 40
  Butterfly World, 5, 235
  Caldwell Theater Company, 249
  Gardens Mall, 379
  Mizner Park, 379
  Morikami Museum of Japanese Culture, 248

Moroso Motorsports Park, 247
Norton Gallery of Art,139, 248
Okeeheelee Park, 247
Opera, 249
Outlet Center, 379
Philharmonic Orchestra of Florida, 139
Raymond F Kravis Center for the Performing Arts, 249
Royal Palm Polo Sports Club, 247
Royal Poinciana Hotel, 239, 244
Royal Poinciana Playhouse, 249
Seven Mile bridge, 121, 326
South Florida Fair, 118
South Florida Science Museum, 248
The Breakers, 244
Town Center Mall of Boca Raton, 379
Worth Avenue, 242, 243, 378
Palm Beach Polo & Country Club, 247
Palm Golf Course, 350
Palm-Aire, 236
Palma Sola Causeway, 202
Palmer, Arnold, 8
Pan American Airlines, 46
Panama City Beach, Jellybeans Skate Park, 291
Panama City, 11, 57, 61, 136, 287, 289, 358
Panhandle region, 53
Panama City, Miracle Strip Amusement Park, 291
panthers, 11
parasailing, 179, 190, 247, 296
Parrish, Maxfield, 165
Pavarotti, Luciano, 135
Paynes Prairie State Preserve,123
Daytona Beach, The Dolphin Beach Club, 4
Peacock, Charles, 89
Pelican Island, 71
Pelican Man, 9, 96
pelican, 63, 68, 96, 173, 174, 195, 251,291, 292, 293
Pennekamp, John Coral Reef State Park, 10
Pensacola, 11, 17, 21, 22, 25, 33, 34, 57, 60, 76, 77, 96,99,

116, 117, 126, 136, 293, 379
Bay, 21
Beach, 116, 124,131, 293
Dorr House, 296
First City Dance, 297
Jazz Fest, 136
Museum of Art, 297
Museum of Industry, 296
Museums of Commerce, 296
National Museum of Naval Aviation, 11, 136, 296
Naval Air Station, 46, 294
North Hill Preservation District, 294
Old Pensacola, 294
Opera, 297
Palm Beach Gardens, 367
Palm Beach Jai Alai Fronton, 247
Palm Beach Kennel Club, 247
Palm Beach Mall, 379
Palm Beach nightspots, 367
Palm Beach Polo Equestrian Club, 247
Palm Beach Seafood Festival,119
Quayside Art Gallery, 380
Quayside Market, 380
Quietwater Boardwalk, 293
Saenger Theater, 297
Saint Michael's Cemetery, 294
Saint Michael's Creole Benevolent Association Meet, 294
San Carlos Hotel, 294
Seafood Festival, 126
Symphony Orchestra, 136
Symphony, 297
TT Wentworth Jr, Florida State Museum, 296
Vaudeville Saenger Theater, 294
Village, 296
People, 91-103
Perdido Key, 293
Beach, 296
State Recreation Area, 77
Performing Arts, 142, 337
PGA National Golf Club, 246
PGA, 47
Pheil, Mayor, 46
Philadelphia Phillies, 343
Philip King, 21
Phillippe, Count Odet, 103,386

piano bar, 368, 370, 371
Picasso, Pablo, 136, 139, 332
picnicking, 60, 75, 76, 77, 79, 82, 86, 88, 175, 189, 195, 202, 273, 281, 290, 296, 308, 326, 327, 358
Pinciana Horse World, 351
Pine Island Seafood Festival, 121
Pine Log State Forest, 61
Pine Oaks of Ocala Golf Course, 167
Pineland Trail, 315
Pinellas Bayway, 357
Pinellas Park, 190
Pinellas Suncoast, 183, 190
Pioneer Days, 126, 128
pioneers, 131, 304
Pirate's Island Adventure Golf, 159
Pirates, 122
Pittsburgh Pirates, 343
Plant City, 114, 115, 120
Plant, Henry, 9, 39, 192, 193, 381
Plantation Golf & Country Club, 351
Plantation Key, 325
Plantations, 22, 25, 26
Plate Fleets, 20
Playalinda Beach, 254, 356
Players of Sarasota, 147
Pleasure Island, 163
Pleistocene era, 16
Plymouth, 21
Poinciana Golf & Racquet Resort, 350
Polk County, 153
Polk Museum of Art, 136
Polk, President James, 100
polo, 120, 174, 241, 246, 247
Pompano Beach Seafood Festival, 123
Pompano Beach, 19, 123, 236, 353
Pompano Park Harness Racing, 353
Ponce De Leon Springs State Recreation Area, 77, 78
Ponce De Leon Inlet Lighthouse, 252
Ponte Vedra Beach, 3
Ponte Vedra Club, 351
Ponte Vedra, 351
population, 10, 23, 24, 26, 27,

40, 42, 91, 92, 99
Port Canaveral, 121, 262, 263
Port Everglades, 133, 233, 234
Port Everglades, Fish City Marina, 234
Port Panama City harbour, 291
Port Saint Joe, 78
Port Saint Lucie, 125
Port Saint Lucie, Jaycees Bed Race, 125
possum, 125
pottery, 18, 79
Powell, William, 23
power boating, 264
pubs, 370
Puerto Ricans, 93, 227
Punta Gorda, 123, 133

R

rafting, 123, 125, 159
railroads, 24, 25, 39, 44, 101, 244
Rambler, 244
Ramses II: The Pharaoh and His Time, 136
rap, 363
raptors, 63
Rauschenberg Overseas Cultural Exchange, 29
Rauschenberg, Robert, 29, 35, 141
Rawling, Marjorie Kinnan, 29, 80, 141
real estate, 26, 41, 43, 312
Red Stick tribe, 23
Redington, 191, 358
reef fishing, 326
reggae music, 364, 370, 371
reggae, 370, 371
religion, 10, 104-111
Rene de, Goulaine de Laudonniere, 21
Renoir, 139
Republican party, 24
Research at the Center for Research in Electro-optics, 45
restaurant, 365, 368, 380
retail trade, 41, 47
retirees, 92, 103
retirement industry, 43
Ribault, Jean, 21, 31, 55
Richmond, 39
Rickenbacker, Captain Eddie, 46
Rickenbacker, Eddie, 216

riding, 60
Ringling Brothers and Barnum & Bailey Circus, 201, 207
Ringling Circus Galleries, 201
Ringling Museum of Art, 9, 10, 121, 138, 142, 147, 199, 203
Ringling, John, 138, 141, 209
Ringling, Mable, 138, 201
Robinson, Edward G, 325
Rockefeller, John D, 40, 239, 244
Rockefellers, 40
rodeos, 120, 157, 162
Rolex 24 motor race, 261
roller skating, 162, 185, 291
Rolling Hills Resort and Country Club, 236
Rolling Stones, 135
Ron Jon Surf Shop, 262
Rookery Bay, 176
Roosevelt, 44
Roosevelt, President, 29
Rubens, 138
Dunedin Railroad Historical Museum, 103

S

sailing, 133, 181, 190, 252, 264, 319, 353
Saint Armands Circle, 381
Saint Augustine, 3, 10, 17, 19, 21, 22, 25, 33, 34, 39, 55, 96, 98, 106, 108, 117, 266-275
Amphitheater, 275
Bridge of Lions, 271
City Yacht Pier, 271
Folk Festival, 275
Lightner Museum, 10, 136, 270, 272
Marie Selby Botanical Gardens, 201
Mission of Nombre De Dios, 117
Mote Marine Aquarium, 203, 205
Mote Marine Laboratory, 205
Museum of Botany, 203
New Playmakers, 197
Old Saint Augustine, 304
oldest house, 4, 272
Oldest Wooden Schoolhouse, 4, 272, 273
oldest store, 4, 272, 273
Payne Mansion, 203

Ponce de Leon hotel, 244
Prince Murat House, 95
Saint Photios National Greek
  Orthodox Shrine and C, 272
Sixth Annual Maritime Festive,
  128
Visitor Information and Pre-
  view Center, 269
Saint George Island, 121
Saint John's County, 275
Saint John's River, 3, 55, 21, 24,
  26, 27, 106, 108, 143, 259,
  277, 278, 279, 283, 374
Saint Johns County, stadium,
  275
Saint Johns Greyhound Racing
  Park, 351
Saint Joseph, 24
  Bay, 78
  Peninsula State Park, 78
Saint Louis Cardinals, 344
Saint Lucie River, 19
Saint Marks, 24
  Historic Railroad Trail, 308
  River, 79
Saint Pete Beach, 190
Saint Petersburg, 9, 10, 27, 46,
  57, 65, 99, 111, 115, 138,
  344, 351
  Beaches, 358
  Brooker Creek Park, 190
  Indian Rocks Beach, 190
  Pier, 185
  Salvador Dali Museum,
    10, 138, 185
  Skyway bridge, 183
  Tyrone Square, 380
  Veterans Memorial Park, 190
Saint Petersburg & Tampa, 182-
  197
Salinaro, Sal, 335
San Felasco Hammock State
  Preserve, 80, 81
San Luis Archaeological and
  Historic Site, 136, 304, 305,
  306
San Luis, 305
San Marco District, 279, 374
San Marcos De Apalache State
  Historic Site, 79
San Pedro, 337
San Sebastian, 106
Sand Key, 358
Sanibel and Captiva Islands, 9,

173, 179, 180, 181
Sanibel/Captiva Islands-Bow-
  man Beach, 358
Santa Margarita, 349
Santa Maria de la Consolacion,
  17
Santa Rosa Island, 293
Santiago, 17
Sarasota, 9, 10, 19, 96, 110,
  121, 124, 125, 138, 140, 147,
  198-209, 344, 349, 351, 380
  AE Edwards Theater, 204
  Avenue of the Flowers, 381
  Ballet of Florida, 147
  Bay, 201, 204, 205
  Beaches-North Lido Beach,
    Siesta Key Beach, 358
  City Island, 96
  Cross And Sword, 124
  Ed Smith Stadium, 209
  French Film Festival, 147, 207
  Golden Apple Dinner Theater,
    147
  Gulf Gate Mall, 381
  Jazz Festival, 206
  Jungle Gardens, 201
  Music Festival, 124
  nightspots, 370
  North Jetty Park, 202
  Opera Association, 147
  Opera, 204, 207
  Quay, 381
  Saint Andrews State Recrea-
    tion Area, 290
  Saint Armands Key, 207, 209
  South Lido Park, 202
  Square Mall, 381
  Stickney Point Bridge, 207
  Theater Works, Inc, 147
  Van Wezel Performing Arts
    Hall, 147, 204, 206
savannas, 60, 73
Sawgrass Lake Park, 190
Sawgrass Mills, 237, 374
Sawgrass Recreation Marina,
  234
scientologists, 105
scorpions, 160
Scots, 102, 103
Scottish Dunfermline Opera
  House, 204
scrublands, 60
scuba diving, 88, 190, 202, 209,
  234, 248, 264, 357

sculpture, 142, 215, 237, 264,
  264, 281, 335, 380
sea turtles, 67
Sea World, 157, 162
Seafest '89, 128
seafood, 128, 191, 194, 195,
  291, 296, 370, 383, 384, 389
Seaside, 126, 130
Sebastian Inlet State Recreation
  Area, 264
Sebastian Inlet, 264
Sebastian, 71
Second Seminole Indian War,
  23, 86, 88, 98, 146
Seminole Wars, 273
Seminoles football team, 303
Seminoles Indians, 22 23, 24,
  61, 86, 88, 92, 96, 97, 100,
  108, 123, 190, 303
Senate, 34, 36, 97, 304
Seven Mile Bridge Run, 121
Seven Years' War, 22
Seville District, 294
Sewell, John, 98
Seymour, General Truman A,
  80
Shakespeare, 279
sharks, 169, 205
Shell Island, 289, 291
Shell World, 375
shelling, 83, 180, 202, 289
Shields, Dale, 96
Shipwreck Island Water Park,
  291
shipwreck/treasure museum,
  197
shipwrecks, 326, 337
shooters, 368
shopping, 9, 48, 51, 139, 157,
  161, 165, 175, 177, 209, 217,
  231, 237, 241, 243, 278, 279,
  293, 305, 373-381
shuffleboard, 103, 366
Siesta Key, 207
Siesta Key Beach, 202, 207
Siesta Village, 381
sightseeing trains, 269
Silver Bluff, 53
Silver River, 170
Silver Springs, 10, 160, 161,
  167, 170
Silver Springs Rodeo, 114
Silver Spurs Arena, 114, 159
Silver Spurs Quadrille, 120

Silver Spurs Rodeo, 73, 119
Silverstein, Shel, 337
Sixth Annual Taste Fair Of Bonita Springs, 131
Sixth Annual Taste Of The Town, 131
skydiving, 195, 225
Skyview Golf & Country Club, 156
slavery, 24, 25, 26, 27, 33, 92, 97, 282
Smathers, Higgs & South Beaches, 357
Smith, Joseph, 111
Snakes, 67
snorkeling, 78, 88, 181, 190, 190, 291, 336, 354, 357
soccer, 177, 355
Society of Four Arts, 243, 248
softball, 177
Sombrero Beach, 125
Soto de, Hernando, 19, 20
South Carolina, 21
South Seas Plantation Marina, 181
South Walton, 126
Southwest Florida, 172-181
Southern Florida, 210-229
Southernmost Point, 334
spa workouts, 241
Space Coast Science Center, 255, 264
Space Coast, US American Waterski Association Nationals & US Op, 126
space exploration, 47
Space Fest, 258
space technology, 43
Spaceport USA, 137, 256, 257
Spanish architecture, 217, 243
Spanish colonialism, 21, 22, 32,
Spanish colonists, 20
Spanish cuisine, 383, 384
Spanish culture, 119
Spanish Missionaries, 108
Spanish Quarter, 272
Spanish, 21
Spanish-American War, 101
Spanish colonialism, 116, 124, 271
Speed Weeks, 120
sponge displays, 191
sponge diving demonstrations, 188

Sponge, 103, 109, 188, 189, 190
sports, 47, 51, 116
Sports & Recreation, 340-359
square dancing, 364
Star Tours, 169
state constitution, 33
State Parks & State Historic Centers, 74-89
State Senate, 35, 141
State Song, 10
steak houses, 384, 392
Stephen Foster Folk Festival, 81, 123
Stephens, Wallace, 336
storks, 63
Stotesbury, Mrs Edward, 242
Stowe, Harriet Beecher, 278
Strawberry Festival, 114, 115, 120
Strawberry Queen contest, 121
streamline architecture, 139
Studio M, 141
Suarez, Mario & Peter, 335
Sun 'N Fun Eaa Fly In, 123
Suncoast Seabird Sanctuary, 65, 192
Sunshine Key, 123
Sunshine Skyway Bridge, 65
surf fishing, 77
surfing, 190, 252, 264, 358
Surfside International Fiesta, 125
Surfside, 125
Swamp Cabbage Festival, 120
swamp, 174
Swanee River, 56, 81
swimming, 60, 75, 77, 78, 83, 86, 88, 103, 175, 264, 288, 289, 290, 306, 327, 337, 358

T
Talamato Indians, 108
Tallahassee, 10, 11, 19, 23, 24, 25, 33, 34, 35, 37, 78, 98, 99, 103, 108, 125, 132, 136, 148, 298-309, 351, 384
Adams Street Commons, 303
Artists Hall of Fame, 35
Bellevue Plantation House, 303
Bethlehem Missionary Church, 303
Big Bend Farm, 302

Capitol Building, 33
Civic Ballet, 299
Civic Center, 148
Concord Schoolhouse, 303
Film Festival, 100, 147
Florida Museum of History, 305
Florida Supreme Court, 303
House of Representatives, 34, 36, 141, 304
Knott House, 303
Little Theater, 148
Lyric Theater, 99
Maclay State Gardens, 78, 306
Monticello Opera House, 148
Museum of Florida History, 11, 136, 301, 304
Museum of History & Natural Science, 302
Museum of History and Natural Science, 10, 11, 307
New Capitol building, 35, 301
nightspots, 370
Nucleus Entertainment Group: Florida Hysterical Society, 148
Old Capitol, 34, 136, 301, 304, 305
Old City Cemetery, 304
Park Avenue Historical District, 303
Posey's Oyster Bar, 11
Silver-Haired Legislature, 103
State Folk Culture Center, 81
Supreme Court, 36, 99, 304
Symphony Orchestra, 148, 299
The 1841 Union Bank, 304
The Discovery Center, 303
Union Bank, 305
Vietnam Veteran's Memorial, 301
Tamiami Trail, 7, 100
Tampa, 9, 10, 20, 25, 39, 44, 46, 61, 95, 99, 101, 103, 115, 119, 120, 123, 128, 130, 353, 356, 381, 384, 386
American Stage, 148
Ballet, 148
Bay Downs, 194, 353
Bay Hotel, 9, 39
Bay Lightning, 194
Bay Opera, 148
Bay Performing Arts Center,

137, 148, 197
Bay, 19, 185, 351
Busch Gardens, 9
cigars, 44, 101, 192, 193
Columbia Restaurant, 9, 193
Convention Center, 122
Derby Lane, 194, 351
Five Star Pro Rodeo Series, 353
Franklin Square Mall, 124
Greyhound Track, 351
Hall Of Fame Bowl, 119
Henry B Plant Museum, 193
Mahaffey Theater, 148
Manatee and Aquatic Center, 196
Museum of African-American Art, 197
Museum of Art, 197
Museum of Fine Arts, 137, 185
Museum of Science & Industry, 197
Music Dome Amphitheater, 197
nightspots, 370
Old Hyde Park Village, 381
Oratorio Society, 197
Players, 148, 197
Ruth Eckerd Hall, 137, 148
Spanish Lyric Theater, 197
Stadium, 194
Taste Of The Bay, 123
Theater, 197
West Shore Plaza, 381
Tarpon Springs, 19, 103, 110, 123, 188, 189, 190, 384
Anderson Park, 189, 190
City Hall, 189
Epiphany Celebration, 113
Fred Howard Park, 189
Saint Michael's Shrine, 189
Saint Nicholas Cathedral, 103
Saint Nicholas Greek Orthodox Church, 110, 113
Suncoast Offshore Grand Prix, 125
tarpon, 1
Taylor, Peter, 336
technological industries, 42
Teed, Cyrus Reed, 84, 86
telecommunications, 45
television industry, 46
Teneroc State Reserve, 156
Tennessee, Williams, 141
Tennessee Williams Fine Arts

Center, 144
tennis, 118, 121, 133, 183, 195, 207, 209, 231, 236, 241, 246, 247, 275, 277, 280, 358, 359
Tennis Professionals Association, 47
Tenth Annual John's Pass Seafood Festival And Art, 130
Tequesta, 19, 247
Texas, 100
Thanksgiving, 117, 132
The Atlantic Ocean, 51
The Conservancy, 10, **175**
Theater of the Sea, 357
theater, 9, 121, 139, 141, 143, 144, 147, 148, 177, 199, 204, 226, 249, 338, 377, 381
Theater Jacksonville, 144, 279, 284
theme park, 10, 11, 41, 159, 161, 163, 169, 357
Thomas, Michael Tilson, 139
Thornton, Wilder, 336
Three Kings Day Parade, 127
Three Rivers State Recreation Area, 308
Tiffany, Louis Comfort, 136, 146, 165, 270, 272
Tiger Tail Beach Park, 358
Tillis, Mel, 248
Timucuan Ecological and Historic Preserve, 282
Timucuan Indians, 18, 389
Tin Can Tourists, 40
Titusville, 10, 18, 47, 255, 258, 259
Tocobaga, 18
Torah, 107
Toronto Blue Jays, 343
Toronto, 48
Torreya State Park, 79, 80, 308
tourism, 29, 39, 41, 43, 48, 98
tourist trade, 25
Tournament Players Club, 47
Toussaint, Eddy, 206
tram rides, 219
tram tours, 319
Transportation Pavilion, 303
treasure hunting, 349
treasure island, 190
Triester, Kenneth, 109, 221
trolley tour, 213
Tropical Park, 119, 131
Tropicool Music Fest, 174

Truman, President Harry, 29, 312, 334
Tsalickis, Steve, 189
Turtle Beach, 202
Turtle Mound, 254
Tuthill, Bill, 260
Tuttle, Julia, 91, 226

U
Universal Studios, 10, 28, 46, 157, 163, 164, 165
Universalist Church, 110
University of Central Florida, 45
University of Florida, 45, 49
University of Miami, 45, 97
University of Michigan, 96
University of South Florida, 43
University of Tampa, 192, 193
University of West Florida, 297
Upper Matecumbe Key, 325
US Space Camp of Florida, 255, 258
Useppa Island, 181
USPA Rolex Gold Cup, 120

V
Valentino, Rudolph, 209
Valiant Air Command Museum, 258
Van Dyck, 138
Vanderbilts, 40
Vandercar, Lewis, 264
Venezuela, 48
Venice Municipal Beach, 202
Venice, 202, 207, 351
Via Mizner, 243
Victorian Seaside Christmas, 133
Vidal, Gore, 336
Vietnamese, 92
Village on Venetian Bay, 377
Villella, Edward, 139
Virginia, 21, 23, 39, 47
volleyball, 116, 125, 202, 273
voodoo rituals, 107

W
wade fishing, 288
Wakulla River, 78, 79
Wakulla Springs State Park, 78
Wakulla Springs Lodge Conference Center, 78
walking, 82, 270, 307

Wall Street crash, 26
Walt Disney World, 10, 28, 41, 73, 157, 163, 168
War Between the States, 25, 33, 84
Washington Oaks State Gardens, 82
Washington, 33, 107
water fun, 159, 163
water parks, 159, 291
water sports, 177, 179, 241, 247
water springs, 53
water taxi, 231, 233, 277
waterbirds, 63, 65
waterfowl, 78
waterskiing, 10, 123, 155, 157, 190, 226, 247, 275
Wausau, 125
weather, 57
Weismueller, Johnny, 219
West Indian Manatees, 66
West Lake Trail, 317
West Natural Wildlife Refuge, 71
West Palm Beach Municipal Stadium, 247
West Palm Beach, 118, 119, 120, 123, 247
West, Mae, 209
wetlands, 54, 55, 62, 86
White Springs, 123
Whitehall, 244
Wiesel, Eli, 109, 101
Wilbur, Richard, 336
wild west music show, 361
Wilderness Waterway, 317
Wildlife Rescue and Sanctuary Park, 296
Williams, Tennessee, 35, 336
Windley Key, 325
Windover, 18
window shopping, 373
windsurfing, 190, 247, 275, 288, 358
Winter Festival and Celebration of Lights, 132, 308
Winter Haven, 9, 10, 153, 155
Winter Haven, Chain 'O Lakes Complex, 156
Winter Haven, Cypress Gardens, 9, 10, 155
Winter Haven, Museum of Fishing, 155

Winter Park, 153, 163, 164, 165
Winterfest Boat Parade, 133
Winterfest, 117
Winter Haven nightspots, 364, 365
Wira Christmas In July, 125
Withlachoochee River, 60, 61
Witten, Albert, 46
Women's International Tennis Association, 47
wood stork, 64
world showcase, 169
World War II, 27, 40, 46, 101, 109
wrecks, 234
wrestling matches, 363
Wright, Frank Lloyd, 136, 146, 165, 204

Y

yachts, 9, 42, 231, 233, 246, 296, 341
Yankees, 92, 102
Ybor City, 9, 10, 25, 44, 119, 122, 130, 138, 192, 193
State Museum, 193
Fiesta Day, 122
Ybor Square, 44, 192, 381
Ybor, Don Vicente Martinez, 44, 192
Ye Olde Madrigal Christmas Feaste, 132
Yulee, David Levy, 101

Z

Zoo, 277, 296, 291
Zora Neale Hurston Festival, 141